Economics of
Industrial Structure

Selected Readings

Edited by Basil S. Yamey

Penguin Education

Penguin Education
A Division of Penguin Books Ltd,
Harmondsworth, Middlesex, England
Penguin Books Inc, 7110 Ambassador Road
Baltimore, Md 21207, USA
Penguin Books Australia Ltd,
Ringwood, Victoria, Australia

First published 1973
This selection copyright © Basil S. Yamey, 1973
Introduction and notes copyright © Basil S. Yamey, 1973
Copyright acknowledgement for items in this volume
will be found on page 357

Made and printed in Great Britain by
Richard Clay (The Chaucer Press) Ltd, Bungay, Suffolk
Set in Monotype Times New Roman

0140808736

300700

Contents

Introduction

Industries and trades differ from one another in many structural character-istics as well as in the economic achievements of the firms in them. Econo-mists have long been interested in the reasons for such differences as well as in the connection, if any, between particular structural characteristics and features of economic performance such as levels of product and factor prices, frequency of price changes, levels of profits and their stability over time, and technical progress.

The papers selected for this volume of Readings relate in the main to attempts to 'explain' various structural features; that is, they seek to identify factors and influences which are operative in shaping the structure of different industries and trades, and the circumstances in which (and sometimes the motives for which) changes in particular structural features occur. The emphasis is primarily on the 'explanation' of differences among industries rather than on detailed examination of individual industries or trades. This bias in the selection can be justified on the ground that students of industrial structure are more interested in developing a general analytical approach, including the checking of hypotheses against obser-vations, than in mastering the technological and economic complexities of a few selected industries. This is not to say, of course, that for the economist concerned with policy decisions (whether within a firm or industry or with-in government) the detailed knowledge of his industry is not essential. But his understanding of the details is likely to be improved if he can view his firm or industry in the setting of a more general framework. Again, it is not intended to imply that the detailed study of the evolution and present organization of a particular industry or branch of trade cannot be fruitful in suggesting new general hypotheses or in providing pointers to possible new lines of enquiry of wider application.

The papers which offer approaches to the explanation of industrial structure necessarily relate to major influences and moulding circum-stances, and do not purport to encompass *all* the factors and environ-mental constraints which may be operative in a particular case. Thus the papers refer to such considerations as extent of market, rate of change of the extent of market, characteristics of demand and variability of demand, market risks and uncertainty more generally, technological conditions and opportunities, and organizational limitations and possibilities. Motivation also enters the picture, whether the motive be that of achieving the profits of monopoly or the profits of improved efficiency, or whether it be the search for the fruits of the quiet life or response to the lure of large but chancy profits.

The twenty-five papers in this volume are grouped for convenience into five sections representing the major structural features distinguished in much of the literature on industrial structure, namely, size of firms, entry conditions, concentration, vertical integration and diversification.

Two of the five features, vertical integration and diversification, are features of firms rather than of industries: they refer to the extent of the participation of a firm in more than one industry. However, their inclusion is plainly sensible. It is arguable, for example, that the involvement of firms, especially of large firms, in several industries may affect structural features such as entry conditions or concentration in some or all of them. Moreover, an industry consists of the firms in it; and its economic performance depends upon their individual performance, which in turn may be conditioned by the extent of their diversification or vertical integration. What is more, in some cases patterns of vertical integration and diversification (including the pattern of low diversification, i.e. of a high degree of specialization by firms, both vertically and laterally) may be rather similar for all or most of the firms in the particular industry in which they are principally involved; while in other cases there may be a variety of structural 'solutions' reached by the various firms in it. Decisions as to the nature and extent of vertical integration and diversification are among the key strategic decisions taken by decision-makers in firms, as are those relating to total size and to rate of growth. These decisions do not figure prominently, if at all, in the conventional theories of the firm, in which the entrepreneur is limited to a single product. Moreover, such are the simplifications introduced into these theories that the entrepreneur generally is little more than a

... creature that moves
In predestinate grooves.
He is not even a bus; he's a tram.

The omission of strategic decisions from the scope of theoretical formulations is not necessarily a defect from the point of view of the uses to which the theories are put. But the omission has meant that the body of knowledge and analysis about these decisions has had to find a home in the more applied branch of economics known variously by such names as the economics of industry, the structure of industry, or industrial organization.

Reference to major strategic decisions taken by entrepreneurs raises the question of the 'determinateness' of the structure of industry, not only, but perhaps more especially, when it is recognized that entrepreneurs (or entrepreneurial groups) are not equally efficient and may differ in their preferences. The language used by cautious writers in this field of enquiry is guarded; and the claims that are made – or should properly be made – are modest. It is not generally asserted that one can accurately predict the structure of an industry from a detailed knowledge of past and present factor prices, conditions of technology and market conditions. It is generally accepted, for instance, that in the typical industry there is no single unique optimum size of firm such that the existence of smaller or larger firms can be ruled out as long-term impossibilities. Thus the number of firms in the same industry in the same circumstances could conceivably fall within quite a wide range, as could the size-distribution of firms and degree of concentration in that industry. Again, the conditions of entry into an industry cannot simply or solely be expressed in terms of the nature and severity of the prevailing 'objective' barriers to entry. Entry conditions are not independent of what is done by the established firms or what is contemplated by potential entrants. Decisions whether or not to enter an industry depend, at least in part, upon the business policies and strategies (including those involving vertical integration) adopted by the leading established firms, and upon the expectations about these matters entertained by the potential entrants. And what the established firms may be thought likely to do in the event of a new entry might depend materially upon the status of the potential entrant – is it a diversifying giant, a supplier- or customer-firm engaging in a vertical integration move, or a brand new firm without name or record?

It is thus incumbent on writers on the economics of the structure of industry not to pretend that their analyses of formative pressures and constraints can encompass all the 'determinants' affecting a particular case. The papers included in this volume have not been chosen as if, collectively, they provide the explanation of the specific details of structure of every or any branch of industry or trade. Moreover, it is inevitable that it must appear as if, in particular, the impact of the individual businessman is wholly left out of account – as if, that is, we have *Hamlet* without the Prince, the bath-water without the baby. The omission of studies of particular entrepreneurs and their impact is not, of course, intended to suggest that individual entrepreneurs have not brought about major changes in the structure (and performance) of their industries, and that some of these changes have not persisted for lengthy periods. It would be difficult, however, to fit into the analysis of industrial structure the particular activities and influences of each William Lever or John D. Rockefeller. Any attempt to do so would cause more to be lost than gained in the ability of the resulting analysis to provide guidance. insight or illumination: by attempting to explain too much one might easily end up by explaining too little or nothing at all. An attempt to make an analytical treatment more comprehensive to allow it to accommodate more specific detail might easily deteriorate into a mere cataloguing.

The student of the economics of industrial structure should read studies of the lives and activities of leading entrepreneurs – those of the less successful could also be interesting and instructive, but they rarely find their chroniclers. Wilson (1954, 1968), Barker (1960), and Coleman (1969) are three among several book-length studies of great intrinsic interest and relevance.

However, just as there is danger in trying to write history without referring to big names and big deeds, so there is danger in trying to write history only in terms of big names. The same notion can be applied to the study of industrial structure: industrial structure cannot be explained helpfully in terms of the presence or absence of great entrepreneurs. Broad similarities in the structure of the same industry in different advanced economies suggest that similar pressures and constraints leave their mark, however different the individual entrepreneurs may be who are subjected to them in different economies. Indeed, major inter-country differences in the structure of the same industry or trade are often explicable in terms of some specific government action, including the effects of taxation, rather than in terms of the differential impacts of the entrepreneurs involved. Thus the absence of vertical integration between the manufacture and the retailing of beer in the United States reflects a specific prohibition. The high degree of vertical integration by firms between and within the coal and iron industries in Germany before 1939 is usually explained in part in terms of the impact of sales taxation. And, in all countries, nationalization statutes define and strait-jacket the structure of the affected industries.

The interplay between entrepreneur and environment is complex and fascinating. In the study of the structure of industry the economist, at any rate, has addressed himself primarily to the constraining and moulding influence of the economic environment, although it is in some contexts seen also as an environment which itself can be moulded and one which not only constrains but offers opportunities to the resourceful or the fortunate.

A few of the papers refer specifically to the relation between industrial structure and economic performance. The planned revised edition of the late Alex Hunter's *Monopoly and Competition* will include a few more of such studies. However, inclusion in the present volume of a larger number of empirical studies of the relation between structural features and various aspects of economic performance would have been misconceived. Detailed studies of particular industries or trades are necessarily lengthy if they are to be informative and to present the supporting evidence for the analysis and the conclusions reached in them. This is evident, for example, in the length of reports on individual industries or trades made by official bodies, or of such studies as Markham (1952), Bauer (1954), and Maxcy and Silberston (1959). Again, journal articles presenting the results of statistical studies of a sample of industries or firms quite naturally tend to take up much space in setting out essential details of the sample of firms or industry included, the specification of the various variables deployed in the analysis, the sources of data, and the methods of statistical analysis used.

The list of references on pages 355–6 is intended as a guide to those who wish to pursue this branch of the subject more fully. Most of the papers refer to yet other, earlier, publications. Weiss (1971) and Yamey (1972) are surveys of work published up to about the middle of 1970, with detailed lists of references.

Several of the papers included in this volume could equally well have been assigned to two (or more) of the five sub-divisions into which the Readings are grouped. Many of the articles, listed in Further Reading, on the relation between industrial structure and economic performance, also cover more than one structural feature. The following may therefore be of some guidance. It shows relevant Readings in this volume and relevant structure-performance studies listed in Further Reading (pp. 355–6), for each of the five structural features.

Size of firm

Readings 1–4, 13, 25, this volume; and Adams (1970), Brozen (1971); Comanor (1969); Hall and Weiss (1967); Imel and Helmberger (1971); Mansfield (1963); Scherer (1965); Shepherd (1972); Weiss (1971).

Entry

Readings 5–8, 10–14, 17, 18, 22, 24, this volume; and Comanor (1969); Shepherd (1972); Telser (1972).

Concentration

Readings 3, 9–15, 23, this volume; and Allen (1969); Brozen (1971); Collins and Preston (1969); Comanor (1969); Comanor and Wilson (1967); Hall and Weiss (1967); Imel and Helmberger (1971); Kilpatrick (1968); Mansfield (1963; 1969); Scherer (1965; 1967; 1969); Schwartzman (1959); Shepherd (1972); Telser (1972); Weiss (1966a and b; 1971); Yamey (1972).

Vertical integration

Readings 16–21, this volume.

Diversification

Readings 12, 22–25, this volume; and Imel and Helmberger (1971); Reid (1971); Scherer (1965); Weston and Mansinghka (1971).

References

BARKER, T. C. (1960), *Pilkington Brothers and the Glass Industry*, Allen & Unwin.
BAUER, P. T. (1954), *West African Trade*, Cambridge University Press.
COLEMAN, D. C. (1969), *Courtaulds*, Oxford University Press.
MARKHAM, J. W. (1952), *Competition in the Rayon Industry*, Harvard University Press.
MAXCY, G. and SILBERTSON, A. (1959), *The Motor Industry*, Allen & Unwin.
WILSON, C. (1954, 1968), *The History of Unilever*, Cassell.

Part One
Size of Firms

The importance of economies of scale in plant and equipment is examined and illustrated in Haldi and Whitcomb (Reading 1). Williamson (Reading 2) and Schwartzman (Reading 3) explore sources of diseconomies of scale at the level of the firm (not the plant). The stress is on uncertainty. Williamson elaborates upon the connection between uncertainty and 'control loss' in large-scale organizations. Schwartzman, by developing an ingenious indicator of market uncertainty, tests the hypothesis that firm size and market uncertainty are inversely related. Marcus (Reading 4) examines the relationship between size of firm and profitability in a large number of industrial classifications and finds no evidence that large firms are invariably or even often more profitable than smaller firms in the same industry.

1 John Haldi and David Whitcomb

Economies of Scale in Industrial Plants

John Haldi and David Whitcomb, 'Economies of scale in industrial plants',
Journal of Political Economy, vol. 75, 1967, pp. 373–85.

This paper presents evidence derived from engineering data on economies
of scale in manufacturing and processing plants. The evidence presented
here relates solely to production cost. Costs associated with factors such as
marketing, general overhead, transportation, dispersal of market, and raw
materials are excluded from this study. The chief purpose underlying this
research was to provide some empirical justification for investigations into
the nature and extent of investment barriers created by economies of scale
in less developed countries.[1] In light of this purpose, certain dynamic
phenomena (such as learning curves) that have a scale effect will also be
discussed briefly.

Our main conclusion is that in many basic industries, such as petroleum
refining, primary metals, and electric power, economies of scale are found
up to very large plant sizes (often the largest built or contemplated). These
economies occur mostly in the initial investment cost and in operating
labor cost, with no significant economies observed in raw material cost.
Scale economies can also result from learning curve effects, spreading of
set-up costs, and certain stochastic processes associated with inventories.
With some reservations, we feel that these general results based on data
from Western countries can also be applied to less developed countries,
where limited demand and the resulting inability to realize potential economies of scale can present a barrier to investment.

Evidence that there are economies of scale in plant production cost is not
inconsistent with the observation that in the United States most industries
have at least several plants, often differing in size. This is explained both by
historical development and by the other elements of total cost which we
have excluded. Average transportation cost rises with the output of a single
plant, since average distance to market rises, *ceteris paribus*. Furthermore,
product differentiation may place an ultimate demand constraint on
expansion, with market diseconomies appearing as that constraint is
approached.

1. The implication of economies of scale for industrialization strategies is the subject
of two similar models by Chenery (1959) and Haldi (1960).

1 Economies of scale in static cost curves

The traditional long-run envelope cost curve assumes that all considerations like technology and price structure are fixed. Although the envelope curve is easily defined, its actual shape is difficult to determine even under the best conditions because it reflects only a small portion of the cost schedules of many plants of different sizes.

Sources and scope of the data

In determining short-run cost curves for entire plants, one can use either engineering studies or historical accounting data. We prefer engineering studies.

Data from accounting records. It is difficult to obtain actual data on the construction and operating costs of industrial plants because these data are usually closely held. If actual cost records were available, we still could not necessarily derive reliable estimates of economies of scale.[2] Even with complete historical cost data on any particular industry, one would have a major problem identifying cost changes due to differences in scale from those cost changes caused by other variables. Observed cost variation between two plants in an industry can result not only from differences in size but also from:

1. Unstable demand, so that existing capacity is used differently.
2. Non-homogeneous output.
3. Age differences, with the newer plant embodying technological improvements unrelated to scale and unavailable to the older plant.
4. Different locations, with the cost of preparing the construction site having little relationship to scale.
5. Other factors, such as different technology induced by differences in relative factor prices.

Besides the statistical identification problems inherent in the use of historical cost records, Friedman (1955) has noted that another serious conceptual problem may also arise with accounting data. If a firm has made a mistake and is either larger or smaller than the optimal size, the loss from that mistake will have become capitalized either by accounting practice or by changes in the ownership of the firm. Thus there is good reason to expect that accounting data may not yield reliable estimates of scale economies. In fact, in a perfect capital market, an estimating process based on market valuation of equity would always yield constant returns.

2. For a rather thorough treatment of the shortcomings of actual cost records, see Smith (1955).

Engineering studies. Engineers' cost estimates are especially useful to a study on economies of scale because they embody assumptions consistent with those underlying the envelope curve. That is, an engineering study generally varies capacity while keeping constant relative factor prices, supply conditions, product homogeneity, location, and so forth. Engineering studies do admit changes in technique but only within the limits of the technology available at a given time and optimal for each plant size. Such adjustments are, of course, not only admissible but are assumed in the construction of the envelope curve.

Engineering studies can, on the other hand, be rather unreliable. Sometimes engineers forecast cost rather accurately, and sometimes they err considerably. But it is the slope and not the height of the envelope curve that reflects economies of scale. Because those unforeseen factors that cause engineering estimates to err can shift the entire curve without seriously affecting the slope, engineering studies may successfully reflect the extent of economies of scale even when they are wrong about the absolute level of costs. Sometimes the usefulness of engineering studies is also limited by the fact that they estimate costs for only a few plant sizes in a relatively narrow capacity range. The range of sizes covered can often be much smaller than an economist would like. Fortunately, though, our data generally covered a wide range of sizes.

The bulk of our evidence on economies of scale as revealed through static cost curves is derived from the engineering literature. The information is mostly from the 1950s and 1960s and comes entirely from North American and European sources. The data are limited chiefly to manufacturing plants in certain industries, and omitted are other components of total 'system' cost, such as transportation and selling costs. We have thus adopted a sort of input–output approach to analyse manufacturing value added as a separate, distinguishable sector of the economy.[3] To isolate technological economies of scale in the manufacturing portion of total product cost, we have assumed that:

1. All labor and raw material inputs are available in unlimited quantities at constant prices.
2. Cost estimates for larger plants do not reflect demand conditions for output which might limit plant size.

Under these assumptions, production costs do not reflect any increasing or decreasing returns in other sectors of the economy; for example, any quantity discounts, or diseconomies in the gathering together of inputs or

3. For applications of such input–output type models, see Chenery (1959) and Haldi (1960).

dispersion of outputs, are assumed to be reflected in the production functions of other sectors.[4] To make inferences about total system cost one must, of course, aggregate over all relevant sectors.

To isolate better the various sources of scale economies within a single plant, we collected data on

1. The cost of individual units of industrial equipment.
2. The initial investment in plant and equipment.
3. Operating costs (namely, labor, raw materials, and utilities).

These three groups of data are discussed below.

Cost of basic industrial equipment

Equipment cost constitutes a major portion of the total investment in new plants. In this section we therefore present data on scale economies in numerous items of basic industrial equipment, along with a brief rationale for these observed economies. An outstanding virtue of equipment cost data is the almost total lack of problems caused by non-homogeneous product mixes, construction specially designed for expansion to avoid future bottlenecks, and so forth, which are so troublesome when dealing with complete plant data.

Technological scale economies. For many items of equipment and machinery, an increase in capacity and output does not require a proportionate increase in material and labor. This arises from two phenomena:

1. Indivisibilities of machinery and individual workers, which have been discussed at length in the literature.
2. A family of geometric relationships which relate the material required for the building of equipment to the equipment's capacity.[5] The amount of material required for containers (tanks, furnaces, kettles, pipes, and so on) depends principally on the surface area, whereas capacity depends on the volume inclosed. Thus for a pipe of a given length, for example, circumference will be the chief determinant of material requirements, whereas capacity depends on the cross-sectional area of the pipe.

4. These other sectors remain to be studied. For example, quantity discounts received by a firm may reflect production economies in other firms, marketing economies, reaction by sellers to uncertain demand conditions, or excessive bargaining power possessed by a buyer in an imperfect market. In a competitive market, economies of scale in the production of larger equipment sizes are passed on to buyers of the equipment via the price mechanism.

5. These and other technological relationships are discussed at some length by Chenery (1949). Note also that labor cost often varies with the amount of material being worked, rather than with capacity. Thus, these geometric relationships often save labor as well as material cost.

We can express all these geometric relationships by a generalized exponential function of the form

$$C = aX^b,$$ 1

where C represents cost, X output capacity, and a is a constant; the exponent b may be called the 'scale coefficient'. A value of $b < 1$ implies increasing returns to scale, $b = 1$ shows constant returns and $b > 1$ implies decreasing returns.[6] Geometric relationships apply to many basic industrial processes. An exponential function therefore provides an appropriate basis for fitting a least-squares line to cost-capacity data, and all data reported on in this paper have been fitted to equation 1.

Empirical results. Table 1 summarizes estimates of the scale coefficient for a large assortment of common industrial equipment. In most instances, the exponential or linear log function fits the data well throughout the observed range of capacities.[7]

Most of the underlying cost-size observations came from catalogues of industrial equipment. The bulk of these raw data was collected by industrial cost estimators and published in engineering journals.[8] A small amount of raw data was collected by the present authors, and in several instances we had to estimate the scale coefficient from the data given by other authors. Most of the equipment items are used in the chemical and other process industries; the choice of items was probably dictated by the

6. For a numerical example, consider two spherical containers. The above relationship can be expressed mathematically, letting r = radius, as

$$\frac{\text{surface area of } 1(= 4\,r_1^2)}{\text{surface area of } 2(= 4\,r_2^2)} = \frac{(\text{volume of } 1)^b}{(\text{volume of } 2)} = \frac{(\tfrac{4}{3}\,r_1^3)^b}{(\tfrac{4}{3}\,r_2^3)}$$

from which it can be derived that the exponent b equals 2.

7. Of the 687 estimates of the scale coefficient, 188 indicated some deviation from equation 1. In 87 per cent of these 188 cases, the equipment tended toward smaller scale economies in the larger size ranges. However, not all of the studies applied goodness-of-fit measures, and some reported deviations may not have been statistically significant. In a significant study by Bauman (1962), ninety-two of his 173 estimates (that is, 53 per cent) showed some curvilinearity in logs. Seventy-two of these showed smaller scale economies in the larger size ranges. Of these seventy-two, though, only ten ever reached constant returns at their largest sizes, and only three reached decreasing returns. Thus it is fair to say that our data support the conclusion that there are increasing returns in equipment up to and including the largest sizes built.

8. These sources are given in the bibliography to Table 4 of an Appendix which is available upon request from the authors and which gives more detail on the tables here. Whenever one of our sources gave data that also appeared in another source, we dropped the redundant estimate. Thus, to the best of our knowledge, the estimates of the scale coefficient here and in the other tables in this paper are independent. Also, we dropped any items of equipment for which the physical capacity measure did not relate directly to economic capacity.

Table 1 Summary distribution of economies of scale in basic industrial equipment

Value of the scale coefficient, b^a	Installed plant equipment^b		Other equipment^c		Total	
	No. of estimates of b	Percentage	No. of estimates of b	Percentage	No. of estimates of b	Percentage
	1	2	3	4	5	6
Under 0·30	22	3·3	5	20·0	27	3·9
0·30– 0·39	44	6·6	3	12·0	47	6·8
0·40– 0·49	96	14·5	6	24·0	102	14·9
0·50– 0·59	143	21·6	0	0	143	20·8
0·60– 0·69	142	21·5	5	20·0	147	21·4
0·70– 0·79	90	13·7	2	8·0	92	13·4
0·80– 0·89	60	9·0	0	0	60	8·7
0·90– 0·99	29	4·4	1	4·0	30	4·4
1·00– 1·09	18	2·7	2	8·0	20	2·9
Over 1·10	18	2·7	1	4·0	19	2·8
Totals	662	100·0	25	100·0	687	100·0

^{a} Estimate of b in $C = aX^b$.
^{b} Much of the equipment in this column directly embodies the technological relationships discussed in the text. Included here are containers, pipes, reaction vessels, kilns, and so forth.
^{c} This category includes equipment like construction and mining machinery.
Source: Table 4 of an Appendix available from the authors upon request.

various interests of the cost analysts. Frequently, an estimated installation cost was added to the basic equipment price. In these particular observations, the basic equipment price is not subject to estimation error, but the installation cost is. The articles from which these estimates are taken generally do not give enough information to permit us to apply standard statistical tests. To allow for sampling error, therefore, let us arbitrarily classify scale coefficients where b is between 0·90 and 1·10 as not significantly different from 1·0. With this adjustment, out of a total of 687 scale coefficients, 618 (90·0 per cent) show increasing returns, and 50 (7·3 per cent) show constant returns. Only 19 (2·8 per cent) observed scale coefficients reflect decreasing returns, which is not surprising. We should expect to observe few values of b greater than 1·0 because, when decreasing returns set in, large units usually are not built, and prices for these sizes are simply not available. Instead, multiple units are used (multiple pot lines in alumina reduction plants, for example).[9]

Possible bias. The scale coefficients summarized in Table 1 were derived from quoted market prices. If all sizes of a particular type of equipment were sold in perfectly competitive markets, prices would everywhere reflect true social cost. However, entry is generally easier for manufacturers of small equipment items, so there are usually more producers of an item of small equipment, and both the market and the profit rate for small items of equipment are at least as competitive as the market and the profit rate for large equipment. Hence our estimated scale coefficients may slightly overestimate social costs for the larger units, thereby understating the 'real' economies of scale.

For broad long-range planning, it would be desirable to know something about attainable social cost as well as actual cost under existing conditions. To evaluate our data under such a requirement, we would have to know the extent to which potential economies of scale are realized in the manufacture of various sizes of equipment. Unfortunately, available information did not allow us to make quantitative estimates of potential cost reduction from unexploited economies of scale. But we note that as a rule many small units of equipment are manufactured for each large unit produced. For example, many more small electric motors are made than large ones. Thus, manufacturers of smaller equipment probably come closer to achieving maximum potential economies of scale (and reflecting them in equipment prices)

9. Multiple units may not always be feasible, and some plants may, therefore, use equipment that seems to provide decreasing returns because on an over-all basis it is economic. Stamping presses offer a possible example. Since two 50,000-ton presses cannot perform certain tasks that a 100,000-ton press can, this larger press may be purchased even if it costs more than twice what two 50,000-ton presses would cost.

than do manufacturers of larger equipment.[10] Hence, any unexploited economies of scale in equipment manufacturing probably lie more with larger equipment, with resulting understatement of the potential scale economies in manufacturing and processing plant investment.

Construction cost of plants and process areas

Inferences from equipment cost data. Although Table 1 shows increasing returns for most equipment, it does not immediately follow that the investment cost of entire plants will exhibit a similar pattern. Nevertheless, the data encourage such an inference, and its basis is examined briefly here.

Engineers can design larger plants by

1. Expanding all equipment uniformly.
2. Breaking design bottlenecks.
3. Changing technique.
4. Using multiple units.

The first three methods generally lead to some economies of scale in total construction cost.

1. *Expand all equipment uniformly.* Let the installed cost of equipment be given by

$$C_i = a_i X_i^{b_i}. \qquad 2$$

where the terms are defined as in equation **1**. Then total equipment cost, C^*, is equal to the sum of the equipment cost,

$$C^* = \sum a_i X_i^{b_i}. \qquad 3$$

If all b_i are less than one, cost will not increase proportionately with capacity.[11]

2. *Break bottlenecks.* When bottlenecks are caused by indivisibilities in the size of some equipment, parts of the plant may possess unutilized capacity. In this case, we need enlarge only certain critical areas to increase total capacity. When it is possible to expand design capacity by breaking bottlenecks, any scale economy in the equipment or processes expanded will result in even larger economies for the whole plant. Even if the expanded

10. Unexploited scale economies probably arise from spreading of set-up costs, described in detail in part 2. When a job-lot manufacturer doubles the number of units to be produced, his unit-set-up cost should decrease, and *ceteris paribus*, he will be closer to achieving maximum potential economies of scale than a manufacturer producing half that number of units.

11. Note that $\log \sum X_i$ is not equal to $\sum \log X_i$. As capacity increases, therefore, those items of equipment with the greatest increasing returns (the smallest b_i) decline as a percentage of the total cost. If capacity could increase without bound, the rate of increase of C^* would asymptotically approach the largest b_i.

units exhibit diseconomies, the total plant may still achieve increasing returns until all major bottlenecks have been overcome. The economic literature frequently describes this situation as one in which economies of scale exist up to 'the point of the least common denominator'.

3. *Change technique*. When engineers change technique, they intend to accomplish the same end result by a different method (for example, pure capital substitution or capital-labor substitution). Since engineers can always duplicate smaller units of equipment and smaller plants, they will use different techniques in large plants only when these techniques are more economical. Thus when different techniques are observed in the design of of larger plants they will generally reflect economies of scale.

4. *Use multiple units*. Multiple units are normally used when equipment scale economies have been exhausted. Barring economies in peripheral equipment, expansion by this method alone should not be expected to give further plant economies of scale.

We know of no methods for directly estimating scale economies in plant investment cost by aggregating equipment data. However, this discussion of how engineers design larger plants helps show the relevance of the equipment cost data to our basic purpose: exploring the nature and extent of plant economies of scale. Cost-capacity figures for equipment are not subject to statistical confounding problems, and the scale coefficients are usually derived from actual price quotations rather than from engineers' estimates. For these reasons they tend to be the most accurate data available, and they considerably increase our confidence in the scale coefficients given in Table 2 for the investment cost of entire plants.

Data on actual plant costs. The engineering studies presented here usually represent a set of hypothetical plants, each producing the same product with the same technology available (although optimum technique may vary), and differing only in size. A few of the estimates are not for hypothetical plants but come instead from carefully selected historical data on actual plants.[12] Table 2 summarizes estimates of the scale coefficient for 221 long-run cost curves.[13] All estimates of plant cost and many of the scale coefficients were calculated by cost engineers and were reported in the journal articles given in the bibliography to the Appendix noted above. When only cost-capacity figures were available, scale coefficients were computed by the present authors. As with the equipment data, redundant estimates were eliminated. Building, equipment, and installation labor

12. See note *a* to Table 6 in the Appendix available from the authors.
13. The linear logarithmic form of the exponential function in equation 1 was used. In eleven out of the 221 observations, however, a curvilinear log function would have been more appropriate. For six of these eleven cases, an average slope was used in Table 2. For further details, see note *d* to Table 6 in the Appendix, see note 12.

make up the investment costs. Site preparation costs are sometimes included, but always on the basis of a 'standard site'. Interest on funds expended before the plant begins operating is not included. For these reasons, economies of scale may be overstated slightly, since larger plants may have longer gestation periods.

Virtually all of the plants reported on here produce fairly homogeneous standardized products (where non-homogeneous products are made, a standard product mix was used for all sizes). However, the 'industries' in Table 2 are not strictly homogeneous (we found a number of different scale coefficients for each industry), and industry-wide generalizations are limited. For the aluminium industry, where larger plants use multiple production units (pot lines), the scale coefficients are high, with seven of fifteen estimates at or above the 0·90 level (approximately constant returns). This result coincides with the *a priori* reasoning given above. Among various types of plants in the industry – bauxite, alumina, ingots, and extrusions – there seemed to be no uniformly consistent pattern. Another standardized product is sulfuric acid, but it is made by several processes. Table 2 contains eleven scale factors for sulfuric acid, and, despite the variety of processes, all scale coefficients fall within a narrower range than that exhibited by many other products with multiple estimates. This was also true for acetylene and hydrogen, but not for oxygen (all classed under 'gases').

Sample size and goodness-of-fit information were often unavailable for many of the original estimates because they were presented in summary form. However, the size range covered was usually available. The ratio of the largest to the smallest capacity varies from 1·33 to 1500, but most ratios fall between 4 and 20.[14] Because we know so little about most of the original estimates and what errors they may embody, we were not able to apply standard tests of statistical significance to the estimated scale coefficients. In the absence of better confidence limits, we again arbitrarily classify estimates of b between 0·90 and 1·10 as not significantly different from 1·0. By this criterion, 186 of 221 estimates of the scale coefficient show increasing returns, twenty-six show constant returns, and only nine show decreasing returns. The median scale coefficient is 0·73. On this basis, we conclude that economies of scale in production cost are significant and widespread for the types of plants surveyed here.

Operating cost

We defined operating cost as in-plant production cost less taxes and payments to capital (including depreciation). We relied exclusively on engi-

14. Extrapolation of the scale coefficient beyond the highest observed capacity would be dangerous. However, the highest observations were usually large by standards of industrial countries.

Table 2 Summary distribution of economies of scale in plant investment costs[a]
(number of estimates of scale coefficient b in $C = aX^b$)

Industry	Value of the scale coefficient, b									Totals
	Under 0·40	0·40– 0·49	0·50– 0·59	0·60– 0·69	0·70– 0·79	0·80– 0·89	0·90– 0·99	1·00– 1·09	1·10 and up	
	1	2	3	4	5	6	7	8	9	10
Cement				1	1			1		3
Chemicals, excluding petroleum										
Fertilizer				2	3				1	6
Gases	4	3	6	9	15	4	1	1	2	45
Industrial chemicals		2	3	10	11	9	6	1		42
Plastics					1		2			3
Rubber				2	1	2	1		2	8
Miscellaneous chemicals	3			2	1		1	1		8
Desalination					4	1		1		6
Electric power		1	7	1	2	2	2			15
Petroleum refining and by-products		5	6	15	15	13	2		1	57
Aluminium				2	3	3	4	1	2	15
Pulp and paper					2	3	1			6
Shipping				1						1
Miscellaneous	2	1			2				1	6
Totals	9	12	22	45	61	37	20	6	9	221
Percentage	4·1	5·4	10·0	20·4	27·6	16·7	9·0	2·7	4·1	100·0

[a] Number of individual plant studies classified by industry and by extent of scale economies.
Source: Table 6 of an Appendix available from the authors upon request.

neering estimates of operating cost. As with equipment and plant investment costs, we eliminated non-independent estimates. Multiple estimates
appear in the same 'industry' because industries are not homogeneous and
because there are often several processes for making the same product. The
results, given in Table 3, show clearly that many plants exhibit substantial
economies of scale in total operating costs.

In an independent study, Isard and Schooler (1955) derived thirty-five
estimates of scale coefficients for operating labor cost in the petrochemical
industry. These are shown in column 4 of Table 3. They differ considerably
from our seventeen labor scale coefficients for several industries, shown in
column 3 of Table 3. Their scale coefficients were mostly smaller than the
ten we were able to obtain for the petrochemical industry. Possible explanations may be that:

1. The petrochemical industry is not very homogeneous, and the types of
   plants surveyed vary from one study to the other; or
2. Most of our observations are for process units – plants within a petrochemical complex – whereas their estimates were for complete plants.

Many of the studies summarized in Table 3 did not break operating cost
into individual components; for example, operating labor, supervision,
raw material, and so on. Cost data that were available are summarized in
Table 7 of the Appendix, and following is a brief summary of what these
data show.

1. *Raw materials.* There appear to be no great scale economies attainable
in the consumption of primary raw materials.

2. *Utilities.* Unit costs for utilities sometimes decline slightly with size increases because larger furnaces, motors, and other such equipment units
perform more efficiently than smaller ones.

3. *Labor.* What data we could obtain showed that large economies of scale
in labor costs are possible for process-type plants. Labor's chief function in
process plants is to watch gauges, adjust valves, and perform maintenance
tasks. Consequently, large increases in capacity often require few extra
workers.[15]

4. *Supervision and management.* The data indicate substantial economies of
scale in supervisory and management costs, about on the order of economies of scale for operating labor.[16] We found no direct evidence for the
familiar proposition that diseconomies of scale arise through exhaustion of

15. For a discussion of how labor costs may fit a hyperbolic curve, see Bruni (1964).
16. An interesting theoretical analysis of the direct cost of supervision and management is given by Beckmann (1960).

managerial capability as plant scale increases. This source of diseconomies is usually thought to operate indirectly, however, and most estimates would not be expected to measure it.

5. *Maintenance.* The evidence in Table 7 of the Appendix indicates substantial economies of scale in maintenance costs. These arise from several sources:

(a) Some repair and janitorial costs have a geometric cost-capacity relationship similar to construction costs.

(b) There are indivisibilities in some labor costs for equipment repair.

(c) Costs of spare parts inventories often exhibit stochastic scale economies (discussed in section 2).

A few engineering studies on industries other than the ones considered here are available; their results generally coincide with ours. For example,

Table 3 **Summary distribution of economies of scale in plant operating costs**

Value of the scale coefficient, b*	Total operating cost		Labor cost only			
	No. of estimates	Percentage	Our results: no. of estimates	Isard and Schooler† no. of estimates	Total no. of estimates	Percentage
	1	2	3	4	5	6
Under 0·40	4	12·5	8	29	37	71·2
0·40– 0·49	1	3·1	1	4	5	9·6
0·50– 0·59	5	15·6	6	2	8	15·4
0·60– 0·69	3	9·4	1	0	1	1·9
0·70– 0·79	10	31·3	1	0	1	1·9
0·80– 0·89	9	28·1	0	0	0	0
0·90– 0·99	0	0	0	0	0	0
1·00– 1·09	0	0	0	0	0	0
1·10 and up	0	0	0	0	0	0
Totals	32	100·0	17	35	52	100·0

* Estimates of b in $C = aX^b$.

† Isard and Schooler (1955).

Source: Table 7 of an Appendix available from the authors upon request.

Chenery (1957) studied scale economies in the metalworking industry by applying linear programming techniques to data on metalworking processes developed by the RAND Corporation. He found that significant economies can be realized by substituting capital for labor as the desired output of an item increases. Along the same lines, Bain (1956) found significant economies of scale in auto production, also due in part to the big manufacturers' substitution of capital for labor.

Manufacturing and processing cost: conclusions

Determining the optimum plant size for a particular supply–demand situation requires more information than is outlined here. However, the data obtained in this study support the opinion of engineers who feel that unit processing and manufacturing costs decline as plants increase in size, up to very large plant sizes. More specifically:

1. We can generally expect initial investment cost (and, therefore, the amortization portion of total cost) in most types of plants and equipment to exhibit economies of scale up to the largest plants observed in industrial countries. In the more capital-intensive industries, savings in capital cost are an important source of scale economies.

2. In process plants, operating expenses for labor, supervision, and maintenance also show significant economies of scale.

3. Consumption of utility services shows slight economies of scale, and consumption of raw materials generally shows none.

2 Dynamic and stochastic sources of increasing returns

The envelope curve shows only how cost varies with changes in plant size and the average rate of output. Larger firms may also derive cost advantages from certain dynamic and stochastic processes. Like the more traditional economies of scale, these also give rise to some of the external economies so widely discussed in the development literature.[17]

Manufacturing progress functions and set-up costs. Within limits, workers become more efficient as they repeat the same task. For this reason, the length of production run can be an important factor in scale economies. Manufacturing progress functions, frequently called 'labor learning curves', introduce the length of production run as an explicit variable and depict growth in worker efficiency with repetition.[18]

Cost reduction from learning curves has consequences similar to those of other scale economies. Firms with the largest share of a given market can, in the absence of diseconomies elsewhere, achieve longer production runs than smaller firms. Verdoorn (1960), in assessing the importance of this source of increasing returns, estimates that between the United States and Europe, differences in production run length may affect costs more than differences in plant sizes. This source of cost reduction is probably somewhat more important in assembly-line or job-order type plants than in continuous-process plants like oil refineries.

17. See Scitovsky (1954) for a good discussion of external economies.
18. The extent to which 'learning' can reduce cost has been studied by Asher (1956), Hirsch (1956), and Alchian (1963) and has been treated in a broader economic setting by Arrow (1962).

Longer production runs can cause other and even more obvious econo-mies. Job-order shops must frequently incur a substantial set-up cost for each production run; the more units to which these costs can be allocated, the smaller will be the set-up cost per unit. Further, longer production runs often make it possible to reduce cost significantly by automating produc-tion and substituting capital for labor. As with other economies of scale, market size determines whether the potential economies from long pro-duction runs are in fact realizable.[19]

Stochastic increasing returns. The traditional theory of the firm does not consider ordinary day-to-day uncertainty from random variations in a firm's operations. But in many commonplace situations, random variations may be a factor in reducing costs in large plants. We might call the cause of such reductions 'stochastic economies of scale'. There are many stochastic models that cover differing sets of circumstances and that reflect prevailing cost-size relationships. Although describing such a model in detail is be-yond the scope of this discussion, we can outline the principle behind it.

Plants always keep spare parts on hand to take care of possible machin-ery breakdowns. Let one such part be a 'widget', and assume X widgets are in regular operation throughout the plant. Assume further that one widget failure is independent of other such failures. By constructing a model that embodies: (1) the probability function describing widget failures (2) the time necessary to replenish the inventory of widgets, (3) the cost of down-time, and other pertinent factors, we can determine the optimum inventory of spare widgets. If the number of widgets in regular operation increases as the plant grows (through duplication of machinery), the opti-mum inventory of spares per unit of capacity will decrease. This is because the variance of the number of expected breakdowns does not increase pro-portionately to increases in the number of widgets used (due to the law of large numbers).[20]

In conclusion, we point out that a great deal of additional empirical re-

19. Countries or regions with small internal markets and with little access to export markets will have a distinct disadvantage in manufacturing products requiring sub-stantial set-up costs (of course, as an economy grows, these disadvantages diminish). Since set-up costs represent social as well as private cost, less developed countries should take these costs into account in deciding which industries to encourage.

20. In the economic-lot-size problem, with known uniform demand plus known order costs and holding costs, the familiar 'square root rule' determines the optimum order size plus the average inventory. In this elementary but widely applied model, total inventory cost (exclusive of purchase cost) varies with the square root of demand. In terms of the exponential equation 1 used throughout section 1, this implies a scale factor (b) of 0·50. Increasing stochastic returns can also apply to the size of the labor force needed to repair periodic breakdowns. Large textile mills, for example, are said to require proportionately less standby labor than smaller mills.

search needs to be done in order to develop a broader base of understanding about economies of scale. We need to know more about economies in transportation relative to volume carried and diseconomies relative to length of haul; about economies in marketing, finance, and administration of multiplant firms; and about the effect of technological change on efficient scale.

References

ALCHIAN, A. (1963), 'Reliability of progress curves in airframe production', *Econometrica*, vol. 31, pp. 679–93.

ARROW, K. J. (1962), 'The economic implications of learning by doing', *Rev. econ. Stud.*, vol. 29, pp. 155–73.

ASHER, H. (1956), *Cost Quantity Relationships in the Airframe Industry*, no. R.291, Rand.

BAIN, J. S. (1956), *Barriers to New Competition*, Harvard University Press.

BAUMAN, H. (1962), 'Up-to-date equipment costs', *Indust. engin. Chemistry*, vol. 54, pp. 49–60.

BECKMANN, M. J. (1960), 'Some aspects of returns to scale in business administration', *Q.J. Econ.*, vol. 74, pp. 464–71.

BRUNI, L. (1964), 'Internal economies of scale with a given technique', *J. indust. Econ.*, vol. 12, pp. 175–90.

CHENERY, H. B. (1949), 'Engineering bases of economic analysis', Ph.D. dissertation, Harvard University.

CHENERY, H. B. (1957), 'Capital labor substitution in metal-working processes', (memorandum no. C.3 of the Stanford Project for Quantitative Research in Economic Development.) mimeo, Department of Economics, Stanford University.

CHENERY, H. B. (1959), 'The interdependence of investment decisions', in M. Abramovitz (ed.), *The Allocation of Economic Resources*, Stanford University Press.

FRIEDMAN, M. (1955), 'Comment' on Caleb Smith, 'A survey of the empirical evidence on economies of scale', in *Business Concentration and Price Policy*, Princeton University Press, pp. 230–38.

HALDI, J. (1960), 'Economies of scale in economic development', Ph.D. dissertation, Stanford University.

HIRSCH, W. (1956), 'Firm progress ratios', *Econometrica*, vol. 24, pp. 136–43.

ISARD, W., and SCHOOLER, E. W. (1955), *Location Factors in the Petrochemical Industry*, (PB. 111640), US Department of Commerce.

SCITOVSKY, T. (1954), 'Two concepts of external economies', *J. pol. Econ.*, vol. 62, pp. 143–51.

SMITH, C. (1955), 'A survey of the empirical evidence on economies of scale', *Business Concentration and Price Policy*, Princeton University Press.

VERDOORN, P. J. (1960), 'Debate' in E. A. G. Robinson (ed.), *Economic Consequences of the Size of Nations*, St. Martins Press.

2 Oliver E. Williamson

Hierarchical Control and Optimum Firm Size

Oliver E. Williamson, 'Hierarchical control and optimum firm size', *Journal of Political Economy*, vol. 75, 1967, pp. 123–138. Two Appendices ('Test of the wage model', and 'A digression on dynamics') are omitted.

There is a great deal of evidence that almost all organizational structures tend to produce false images in the decision-maker, and that the larger and more authoritarian the organization, the better the chance that its top decision-makers will be operating in purely imaginary worlds. This perhaps is the most fundamental reason for supposing that there are ultimately diminishing returns to scale.[1]

Although we are quite in agreement with Professor Boulding's judgement that problems of transmitting accurate images across successive levels in a hierarchical organization are fundamentally responsible for diminishing returns to scale, there is less than unanimity on this issue. Indeed, it has long been disputed whether or in what ways the management factor is responsible for a limitation to firm size. Although descriptive treatments of this question have been numerous, these have generally been too imprecise to permit testable implications to be derived. The present analysis attempts a partial remedy for this condition by embedding in a formal model the control-loss features of hierarchical organization that have recently been advanced in the bureaucratic-theory literature. The background to this discussion of control loss as a limitation to firm size is reviewed in section 1. A simple model possessing basic control-loss attributes is developed and its properties derived in section 2. In section 3, we extend and elaborate the model, developing additional implications and indicating some of the problems to expect in empirical testing. The conclusions are given in section 4.

1 Background to the analysis

That the question of the optimum size firm presented a serious dilemma for the theory of the firm was noted by Knight in 1933. Thus, he observed:

The relation between efficiency and size is one of the most serious problems of theory, being in contrast with the relation for a plant, largely a matter of personality and historical accident rather than of intelligible general principles. But this

1. Kenneth E. Boulding in Richard T. Ely Lecture, 78th Annual Meeting of the American Economic Association.

question is peculiarly vital because the possibility of monopoly gain offers a powerful incentive to *continuous and unlimited* expansion of the firm, which force must be offset by some equally powerful one making for decreased efficiency (in the production of money income) with growth in size, if even boundary competition is to exist (Knight, 1965, p. xxiii).

Within a year, Robinson (1934, 1962) proposed what we believe to be a substantially correct answer, namely, that problems of coordination imposed a static limitation to firm size; and Coase in his classic 1937 article on 'The nature of the firm' generally supports this position (1952, pp. 340–41). Kaldor (1934), however, argued that problems of coordination vanished under truly static conditions, and hence only declining product-demand curves or rising factor-supply curves could be responsible for a static limitation to firm size. Only in the context of firm dynamics did coordination problems, in his view, constitute a genuine limitation to firm size. But as Robinson was quick to point out, Kaldor's argument rested on his peculiar specification of the static condition as one in which the control problem is defined to be absent. This approach to the economics of the firm he found quite uninstructive for, as he pungently noted, 'In Mr Kaldor's long period we shall not only be dead but in Nirvana, and the economics of Nirvana ... is surely the most fruitless of sciences' (Robinson, 1934, p. 250).

The argument remained there[2] until Ross (1952–3, p. 148), in a sweeping attack on the economic treatments of this question, took the position that this whole literature bordered on the irrelevant for its failure to incorporate 'certain aspects of the theory of organization and management'. Recasting the problem in what he regarded as suitable organizational terms, he concluded that 'by appropriate measures of decentralization and control the firm may expand without incurring increasing costs of coordination over a range sufficiently wide to cover all possible cases within the limits imposed by scarcity of resources' (Ross, 1952–3, p. 154). Starbuck (1964, p. 343) imputes similar views to Andrews, albeit incorrectly,[3] and, in apparent sympathy with Ross, likewise regards the treatment by economists of these issues as entirely too narrow, and probably self-serving.

Mrs Penrose also finds this literature unsatisfactory, observing that 'whether managerial diseconomies will cause long-run increasing costs [requires that] management ... be treated as a "fixed factor" and the

2. Chamberlin (1948, pp. 249–50) objected to some aspects of the argument in his treatment of the divisibility question, but nevertheless acknowledged that problems of coordination arising from increasing complexity eventually were responsible for increasing unit costs.

3. According to Starbuck, Andrews takes the position that 'it is impossible to conceive of any human organization too vast for organized efficiency.' Andrews (1949, pp. 134–5), however, is quite specific in stating otherwise.

nature of the "fixity" must be identified with respect to the nature of the managerial task of "coordination". *This identification has never been satisfactorily accomplished*' (Penrose, 1959, p. 12; italics added). She continues to regard the issue as a vital one, however, but argues with Kaldor that it is the dynamics, not the statics of coordination, that give rise to a limitation to firm size. In their view, expansion is contingent on knowledgeable planning and skilful coordination where these are a function of internal experience. Since experience is available in restricted supply, the rate of growth is thereby necessarily restricted. Variations on this argument have since been developed, and some have come to regard the growth rate as the only limitation to firm size.[4]

It is unfortunate (although understandable) that the static limitation argument should continue to be misunderstood in this way. The difficulty is probably traceable to the distinction between truly static and quasi-static conditions. Those who reject the static-limitation argument tend to adopt the former position, while those who advocate it take the latter. This is implicit in the Kaldor–Robinson dispute cited above. Differences of this sort are especially difficult to resolve, but an effort to explicate the quasi-static position may nevertheless be useful.

The problem can be stated in terms of deterministic versus stochastic equilibrium. A steady state is reached in each. But whereas in the former the data are unchanging, in the latter the firm is required to adapt to circumstances which are predictable in the sense that although they occur with stochastic regularity, precise advance knowledge of them is unavailable. Although the deterministic condition provides circumstances in which the usual management functions can be progressively eliminated through the refinement of operations, this is the world of Kaldor's Nirvana and has limited relevance for an understanding of business behavior. Instead, customers come and go, manufacturing operations break down, distribution systems malfunction, labor and materials procurement are subject to the usual vagaries, all with stochastic regularity, not to mention minor shifts in demand and similar disturbing influences of a transitory nature. Throughout all of this, the management of the firm is required to adapt to the new circumstances: request the relevant data, process the information supplied, and provide the appropriate instructions. Coordi-

4. Thus, John Williamson takes the position that: 'One of the more discredited concepts in the theory of the firm is that of an "optimum size" firm. . . . [S]ince firms are not restricted to the sale of a single product or even a particular range of products, there is no more reason to expect profitability to decline with size than there is evidence to suggest that it does. This raises the question as to what does limit the size of a firm. The answer . . . is that there are important costs entailed in *expanding* the size of a firm, and that these expansion costs tend to increase with the firm's growth rate' (Williamson, 1966, p. 1).

nation in these circumstances is thus essential. If, simultaneously, a general expansion of operations accompanies these quasi-static adjustments, additional direction would be required. But in no sense is growth a necessary condition for the coordinating function to exist. We, therefore, take the position that bounded rationality[5] imposes a (quasi)-static limitation to firm size through the mechanism of control loss and that growth considerations act mainly to intensify this underlying condition.

In resorting to the notion of bounded rationality, we ally ourselves with Ross in his claim that economic arguments regarding a static limitation to firm size have not taken adequately into account the contributions which organization theory has made to this problem. But rather than resort to the normative literature of administrative management theory as Ross does, we turn instead to the positive theories of bureaucratic behavior. The former, as March and Simon (1958, pp. 22–32) have aptly observed, is a generally vacuous literature in which most of the interesting problems of organizational behavior are defined away. Although Ross' instincts were correct, his preference for a normative rather than a positive theory put him onto the wrong trail and inevitably led to untestable conclusions of the sort cited above.

The aspect of bureaucratic theory that we regard as particularly relevant for studying the question of a static limitation to firm size is what we will refer to as the 'control-loss' phenomenon. It is illustrated daily in the rumor-transmission process and has been studied intensively by Bartlett in his experimental studies of serial reproduction. His experiments involved the oral transmission of descriptive and argumentative passages through a chain of serially linked individuals. Bartlett concludes from a number of such studies that:

It is now perfectly clear that serial reproduction normally brings about startling and radical alterations in the material dealt with. Epithets are changed into their opposites; incidents and events are transposed; names and numbers rarely survive intact for more than a few reproductions; opinions and conclusions are reversed – nearly every possible variation seems as if it can take place, even in a relatively short series. At the same time the subjects may be very well satisfied with their efforts, believing themselves to have passed on all important features with little or no change, and merely, perhaps, to have omitted unessential matters (Bartlett, 1932, p. 175).

5. Robinson (1934, p. 254) came very close to stating it in these terms, but he failed to formalize the argument and lacked an explanation for the control-loss phenomenon. Hence, Mrs Penrose's discontent with his argument as expressed above. For a modern discussion of the notion of bounded rationality, see March and Simon (1958, chap. vi). Simon (1957a, p. xxiv) observes that 'it is precisely in the realm where human behavior is *intendedly* rational, but only *limitedly* so, that there is room for a genuine theory of organization and administration.' The theory, advanced here, attempts to make explicit the way in which intended but limited rationality operates as a limitation to firm size.

Bartlett (1932, pp. 180–81) illustrates this graphically with a line drawing of an owl which – when redrawn successively by eighteen individuals, each sketch based on its immediate predecessor – ended up as a recognizable cat; and the further from the initial drawing one moved, the greater the distortion experienced. The reliance of hierarchical organizations on serial reproduction for their functioning thus exposes them to what may become serious distortions in transmission.

Although this phenomenon is widely experienced, it was not generally regarded as having special theoretical significance until Tullock (1965, pp. 142–93) argued that not only was authority leakage possible in a large government bureau, but it was predictable and could be expressed as an increasing function of size. Downs has since elaborated the argument and summarized it in his 'Law of Diminishing Control: *The larger any organization becomes, the weaker is the control over its actions exercised by those at the top*' (1966, p. 109). The cumulative loss of control as instructions and information are transmitted across successive hierarchical levels is responsible for this result.

Thus, assuming that economies of specialization have been exhausted and that superiors are normally more competent than subordinates, a quality–quantity trade-off necessarily exists in every decision to expand. It arises for two reasons, both of which are related to the distance of the top executive from the locus of productive activity. First, expansion of the organization (adding an additional hierarchical level) removes the superior further from the basic data that affect operating conditions; information regarding those conditions must now be transmitted across an additional hierarchical level which exposes the data to an additional serial reproduction operation with its attendant losses. Furthermore, the top executive or peak coordinator (to use Papandreou's term (1952, p. 204)) cannot have all the information that he had before the expansion plus the information now generated by the new parts (assuming that he was fully employed initially). Thus, he can acquire additional information only by sacrificing some of the detail provided to him previously. Put differently, he trades off breadth for depth in undertaking the expansion; he has more resources under his control, but the quality (serial reproduction loss) and the quantity (bounded capacity constraint) of his information are both less with respect to the deployment of each resource unit. In a similar way, being further removed from the operating situation and having more subordinates means that his instructions to each are less detailed and are passed across an additional hierarchical level. For precisely the same reasons, therefore, the behavior of the operating units will scarcely correspond as closely to his objectives as it did prior to the expansion. Taken together, this loss in the quality of the data provided to the peak coordinator and in the quality of the instructions supplied to the operating units made necessary by the expansion will be referred to as 'control loss'. It will exist even if the objectives of the subordinates are perfectly consonant with those of their superiors and, a fortiori, when subordinate objectives are dissonant.

There are, of course, anti-distortion control devices that the leadership has access to, and Downs (1966, pp. 78–90) has examined a number of them. These include redundancy, external data checks, creation of overlapping areas of responsibility, counterbiases, reorganization so as to keep the hierarchy flat, coding, and so on. The problem with all of these is that they are rarely available at zero cost and invariably experience diminishing returns. Hence, eventually, increasing size encounters control loss. Our objective here is to show how this argument, initially developed in the context of the behavior of government bureaus, has relevance for the static limitation to firm size issue.[6]

2 The basic model

Consider a hierarchically organized business firm with the following characteristics:

1. Only employees at the lowest hierarchical level do manual labor; the work done by employees at higher levels is entirely administrative (planning, forecasting, supervising, accounting, and so on).
2. Output is a constant proportion of productive input.
3. The wage paid to employees at the lowest level is w_0.
4. Each superior is paid β ($\beta > 1$) times as much as each of his immediate subordinates.
5. The span of control (the number of employees a supervisor can handle effectively) is a constant s ($s > 1$) across every hierarchical level.
6. Product and factor prices are parameters.
7. All non-wage variable costs are a constant proportion of output.
8. Only the fraction $\bar{a}$ ($0 < \bar{a} < 1$) of the intentions of a superior are effectively satisfied by a subordinate.
9. Control loss is strictly cumulative (there is no systematic compensation) across successive hierarchical levels.

The first assumption can be restated as: there are no working foremen.[7] This seems quite reasonable and permits us to simplify the analysis of the

6. Monsen and Downs (1965) have used the argument that control loss varies directly with firm size to examine the self-interest seeking behavior of management in the large business firm. However, their analysis is entirely descriptive, and they pass over the optimum firm-size issue and focus instead on the implications of control loss for bureaucratic decision-making within the firm.

7. This assumption has been expressed in this way by Mayer (1960).

relation of output to input. Taken together with assumption 2 which assures that there are no economies of specialization in production (in the relevant range), we are able to express output as a constant proportion of productive input. The distinction between direct labor input and productive labor input should be emphasized. The former refers to the total labor input at the lowest hierarchical level. The latter is that part of the direct labor input which yields productive results. The latter is smaller than the former not by reason of labor inefficiencies but because of the cumulative control loss in the transmission of data and instructions across successive hierarchical levels.

Assumption 3 is innocuous; assumption 4 is plausible and appears to correspond with the facts. This is Simon's conclusion in his study (1957b) of the theory and practices of executive compensation. The constant β condition is also reported by a recent US Department of Labor study (1964, p. 8) of salary structures in the large firm, which found that 'the relationship maintained between salary rates for successive grades was more commonly *a uniform percentage spread* between grades than a widening percentage spread' (italics added). An independent check of this hypothesis is also possible from the data on executive compensation included in the Annual Reports of the General Motors Corporation from 1934 to 1942.

Assumption 5, that the span of control is constant across levels, is also employed in the wage model tested in Appendix A [appendices not reproduced here], although the cumulative distribution relation tested does not uniquely imply this relation.[8] Taken in conjunction with the Department of Labor findings on β, however, the fits reported in Appendix A also lend support to the constant span of control assumption. We nevertheless show in section 3 where this assumption can be relaxed somewhat and the basic results preserved.

Assumption 6 permits us to treat prices in the product and factor markets as parameters. As we will show, this can also be relaxed without affecting the qualitative character of our results. Assumption 7 is not critical, but permits us a modest simplification. Assumptions 8 and 9 are merely restatements of the earlier argument. They are responsible for the control-loss attributes of the model. Since much of the exposition in subsequent

8. Strictly speaking, the empirical results reported in Table A1 support the proposition that the ratio $\log s/\log \beta$ is constant across successive hierarchical levels, not that s and β are identical across levels. Letting $\log s/\log \beta = \gamma$, where γ is a constant, implies that $\beta = s^{1/\gamma}$ at every level. Thus, changes in the span of control would be accompanied by changes in the wage multiple according to the relation $\beta_i = s_i^{1/\gamma}$. That β and s are related in this way seems at least as special as to assume that they are constant across levels. Moreover, in view of the Department of Labor report that β is indeed constant across levels, the constant s condition is implied by our results. [Appendix A is not reprinted here. Ed.]

parts of the paper will be explicitly concerned with them, we will say no more about them here.

For purposes of developing a model around these assumptions, let:

s = span of control

$\bar{a}$ = fraction of work done by a subordinate that contributes to objectives of his superior $(0 < \bar{a} < 1)$; it is thus a compliance parameter.

N_i = number of employees at the ith hierarchical level = s^{i-1}

n = number of hierarchical levels (the decision variable)

P = price of output

w_0 = wage of production workers

w_i = wage of employees at ith hierarchical level

= $w_0 \beta^{n-i} (\beta > 1)$

r = non-wage variable cost per unit output

Q = output

= $\theta(\bar{a}s)^{n-1}$

R = total revenue

= PQ

C = total variable cost

= $\sum_{i=1}^{n} w_i N_i + rQ$

Without loss of generality, we assume that $\theta = 1$. The objective is to find the value of n (the number of hierarchical levels, and hence the size of the firm) so as to maximize net revenue. This is given by:

$$R - C = PQ - \sum_{i=1}^{n} w_i N_i - rQ = P(\bar{a}s)^{n-1} - \sum_{i=1}^{n} w_0 \beta^{n-i} s^{i-1} - r(\bar{a}s)^{n-1}. \qquad \mathbf{1}$$

Now

$$\sum_{i=1}^{n} w_0 \beta^{n-i} s^{i-1} = w_0 \left(\frac{\beta^n}{s}\right) \sum_{i=1}^{n} \left(\frac{s}{\beta}\right)^i,$$

where

$$\sum_{i=1}^{n} \left(\frac{s}{\beta}\right)^i = \frac{(s/\beta)^{n+1} - (s/\beta)}{s/\beta - 1} \simeq \frac{s^{n+1}}{(s-\beta)\beta^n}.$$

Thus, we have

$$R - C = P(\bar{a}s)^{n-1} - w_0 \frac{s^n}{s-\beta} - r(\bar{a}s)^{n-1}. \qquad \mathbf{1'}$$

Differentiating this expression with respect to n and setting equal to zero (and letting ln denote natural logarithm), we obtain as the optimal value for n,

$$n^* = 1 + \frac{1}{\ln \bar{a}} \left[\ln \frac{w_0}{P-r} + \ln \frac{s}{s-\beta} + \ln \left(\frac{\ln s}{\ln (\bar{a}s)} \right) \right].$$ **2**

The values of $\bar{a}$ and $w_0/(P-r)$ in this expression are both between zero and unity, while $\beta < s$ and $\bar{a}s > 1$. The condition $\beta < s$ must hold for the approximating relation to apply and is supported by the data.[9] The condition $\bar{a}s > 1$ must hold if there is to be any incentive to hire employees. Not merely diminishing but negative returns would exist were $\bar{a}s < 1$. Since $\ln \bar{a} < 0$, the expression in brackets must be negative, a condition which is virtually assured by the stipulation that the firm earn positive profits.[10] Assuming that the appropriate bounds and inequality conditions are satisfied, the following *ceteris paribus* conditions are obtained from the model:

(a) Optimal n increases as the degree of compliance with supervisor objectives ($\bar{a}$) increases.

(b) Optimal n is infinite if there is no loss of intention ($\bar{a} = 1$) between successive hierarchical levels. Only a declining product-demand curve or rising labor-supply curve could impose a (static) limit on firm size in such circumstances.

(c) Optimal n decreases as the ratio of the basic wage to the net price over non-wage variable costs ($w_0/P-r$) increases. Thus, the optimum size for an organization will be relatively small and the optimum shape relatively flat in labor intensive industries.

(d) Optimal n increases as the span of control (s) increases. Intuition would have led us to expect that flatter organizations (fewer hierarchical levels) would be associated with wider spans of control, but obviously this is not the case.[11]

(e) Optimal n decreases as the wage multiple between levels (β) increases.

9. If $\beta > s$, then $(\log s/\log \beta) < 1$ and $\bar{a}_1 = - (\log s/\log \beta) + 1 > 0$. But as the results in Table A1 show, a_1 is clearly negative, which requires that $s > \beta$, as assumed.

10. The condition that the firm earn positive profits implies that

$$(P-r)(\bar{a}s)^{n-1} - \frac{s^n}{s-\beta} w_0 > 0$$

or

$$\frac{w_0}{P-r} \cdot \frac{s}{s-\beta} \cdot \frac{1}{\bar{a}^{(n-1)}} < 1.$$

This requires that

$$\left[\ln \frac{w_0}{P-r} + \ln \frac{s}{s-\beta} + \ln \frac{1}{\bar{a}^{(n-1)}} \right] < 0.$$

Since $\ln [1/a^{(n-1)}]$ is approximately of the same magnitude as $\ln [\ln s/\ln (\bar{a}s)]$, or if anything is likely to exceed it, the condition that the firm earn positive profits is tantamount to requiring the bracketed term in equation **2** to be negative.

11. This result should be interpreted with some care. It assumes that $\bar{a}$ is unaffected

Plausible values for $\bar{a}$ can be obtained by substituting estimated values for each of the parameters into equation 2. This is done below. In addition, propositions c, d, and e can be tested empirically by observing that total employment is given by

$$N^* = \sum_{i=1}^{n^*} N_i = \sum_{i=1}^{n^*} s^{i-1}.$$ 3

The sum of this series is given by

$$N^* = \frac{s^{n^*}-1}{s-1} \simeq \frac{s^{n^*}}{s-1}.$$ 4

Taking the natural logarithm and substituting the value of optimal n^* given by equation 2, we have:

$$\ln N^* \simeq \ln\left(\frac{1}{s-1}\right) + \ln s\left\{1 + \frac{1}{\ln \bar{a}}\left[\ln\frac{w_0}{P-r} + \ln\frac{s}{s-\beta} + \ln\left(\frac{\ln s}{\ln(\bar{a}s)}\right)\right]\right\}.$$ 5

Expressing the optimal size firm in this way avoids the necessity of collecting data by hierarchical levels.

Employment among the five hundred largest industrials in the United States runs generally between one thousand and one hundred thousand employees. For values of s between 5 and 10, which is the normal range (Koontz and O'Donnell, 1955, p. 88), this implies an optimal n of between 4 and 7. If all of our assumptions were satisfied, if there were no additional factors (risk, growth, and so on) acting as limitations to firm size, and for values of β in the range 1·3 to 1·6 and $w_0/P-r$ in the range $\frac{1}{3}$ to $\frac{2}{3}$, the implied value of $\bar{a}$ is in the neighborhood of 0·90. Since other factors are likely to act as limitations to some extent, the true value of $\bar{a}$ may generally be higher than this. It is our contention, however, for the reasons given above, that values of $\bar{a}$ less than unity are typical and that the cumulative effects of control loss are fundamentally responsible for limitations to firm size.

3 Extensions

Although the basic model developed in the preceding section makes evident the critical importance of control loss as a static limitation to firm size in a way which is more precise than was heretofore available and thus both clarifies the issues and expresses them in a potentially testable form, it is obviously a highly special model and may be properly regarded with

by increasing the span of control. Within any given firm, this is possible only if the increase in the span of control results from a management or technical innovation. Otherwise, increasing the span of control would lead to an increase in control loss. With this caveat in mind, the result indicated in the text is less counter-intuitive. See part 5, Section 3.

scepticism for that reason. We attempt in this section to generalize the analysis in such a way as to make clear its wider applicability. First, the possibility of introducing economies of scale, either through the specialization of labor or in the non-labor inputs, to offset diseconomies due to control loss, is examined. Second, we develop the properties of a model in which the utility function of the firm includes both profits and hierarchical expense. Third, imperfections in the product market are permitted. Fourth, we allow for the possibility of variations in the span of control at the production level. Finally, the compliance parameter ($\bar{a}$) is expressed as a function of the span of control.

1. *Economies of scale.* We assume above that economies of scale due to specialization of labor or in the non-labor inputs have been exhausted so that diseconomies of scale due to control loss give rise to increasing average cost conditions in the range of output under consideration. These assumptions can be made more precise here. For this purpose, we express the parameter θ which converts input to output as a function of n. Over the range where economies of specialization exist $\partial\theta/\partial n > 0$, whereas when these have been exhausted $\partial\theta/\partial n = 0$. Thus, average cost can be expressed as:

$$AC = w_0 \frac{s}{s-\beta} \cdot \frac{1}{\theta\bar{a}^{n-1}} - r, \qquad\qquad 6$$

and AC will decrease so long as $\partial\theta/\partial n > \theta \ln \bar{a}$. When these two are in balance, constant returns to the labor input will prevail, but as $\partial\theta/\partial n$ declines (and eventually goes to zero), diminishing returns due to control loss will set in.

In a similar way, the non-wage variable cost per unit output parameter, r, can be expressed as a function of output, where $\partial r/\partial Q < 0$ initially, but eventually $\partial r/\partial Q = 0$. Thus, average costs will at first decline for this reason as well, but the cumulative effects of control loss will ultimately dominate and the average cost curve will rise. Implicitly, the model in section 2 assumes that both $\partial\theta/\partial n$ and $\partial r/\partial Q$ are zero, so that economies with respect to both labor and non-labor inputs are assumed to be exhausted in the relevant range. Actually, this is somewhat stronger than is necessary for control loss to impose a limitation to firm size; this result would obtain under the assumptions that $\partial^2\theta/\partial n^2 < 0$ and $\partial^2 r/\partial Q^2 > 0$. This latter, however, would lead only to changes in degree and not in kind from those derived above.

2. *A utility-maximizing version.* As we have argued elsewhere, a shift from a profit-maximizing to a utility-maximizing assumption seems appropriate where large firm size is involved, since the characteristics of the opportunity

set that the management has access to progressively favor non-profit objectives as size increases. In addition, the bureaucratic operations of a large firm may be less attractive to strictly profit-oriented managers than to managers who have broader objectives. Alternatively, if profit-directed managers are typically less adept politicians, they may simply be out-manoeuvred and displaced in circumstances which encourage or permit the pursuit of non-profit goals. In any case, only modest changes in the above model are necessary to transform it to a utility-maximizing form of the sort that we have investigated previously (Williamson, 1964). For this purpose, we assume that the management has a utility function that includes both staff (or hierarchical expense) and profits as principal components. Designating staff expense as H and treating this as all wage expense above the operating level, we have

$$H = \sum_{i=1}^{n-1} w_0 \beta^{n-i} s^{i-1} \simeq w_0 \frac{\beta s^{n-1}}{s-\beta}. \qquad 7$$

We represent the utility function by U and, given our assumption that staff and profits are the principal components, the objective becomes: maximize

$$U = U(H, R-C) = U\left[w_0 \frac{\beta s^{n-1}}{s-\beta}, P(\bar{a}s)^{n-1} - w_0 \frac{s^n}{s-\beta} - r(\bar{a}s)^{n-1} \right]. \qquad 8$$

Treating n as the only decision variable and all other variables in this expression as parameters, optimal n is now given by:

$$n^* = 1 + \frac{1}{\ln \bar{a}}\left[\ln \frac{w_0}{P-r} + \ln \frac{s-(U_1/U_2)\beta}{s-\beta} + \ln\left(\frac{\ln s}{\ln \bar{a}s} \right) \right]. \qquad 9$$

Comparing this expression with that obtained in equation 2, we observe that the only difference is the presence of a $(U_1/U_2)\beta$ term in the brackets of equation 9, where U_1 is the first partial of the utility function with respect to staff, and U_2 is the first partial with respect to profits. Obviously, if staff is valued objectively only for the contribution that it makes to profits, U_1 is zero and equation 9 becomes identical with equation 2. If, however, the management displays a positive preference for hierarchical expense so that the ratio U_1/U_2 is not zero, the optimal value of n^* in the utility-maximizing organization will be larger than in the corresponding profit-maximizing organization with identical parameters.[12]

The response of n^* to an increase in each of the parameters is identical with that given previously with the exception of β. Whether n^* will increase

12. As we argue below, it seems plausible to suppose that $\bar{a}$ will be larger in utility-maximizing organizations in which the goal of the firm represents a consensus among those managers whose preferences count.

or decrease in response to an increase in β depends on whether U_1/U_2 is greater than or less than unity respectively.

3. *Imperfection in the product market.* If product price is not treated as a parameter but instead $P = P(Q)$, $\partial P/\partial Q < 0$, we obtain the following expression for optimal n:

$$n^* = 1 + \frac{1}{\ln \bar{a}} \left\{ \ln \frac{w_0}{P(1 - 1/\eta) - r} + \ln \frac{s}{s - \beta} + \ln \frac{\ln s}{\ln (\bar{a}s)} \right\}, \qquad \mathbf{10}$$

where η is the elasticity of demand.

Obviously, in a perfect product market, where $\eta = \infty$, equation **10** is identical with equation **2**. As is to be expected, the value of optimal n decreases as demand becomes more inelastic.

4. *Variation in the span of control over operators.* It is assumed in the model developed in section 2 that the span of control is uniform throughout the organization. Although variations in the span of control among the administrative levels of the organization are generally small, this is frequently untrue between the foremen and operatives. Typically, the span of control is larger here and the reasons are quite obvious – tasks tend to be more highly routinized, and thus the need for supervision and coordination are correspondingly attenuated. Letting σ be the span of control between foremen and operatives, total employment of operatives is now given by the product of σ and the number of foremen, where this latter is s^{n-2}. Productive output is thus the product of control loss, $(\bar{a})^{n-1}$, times σs^{n-2}, or $\bar{a}\sigma(\bar{a}s)^{n-2}$. The value of optimal n derived from this version of the model is:

$$n^* = 1 + \frac{1}{\ln \bar{a}} \left\{ \ln \frac{w_0}{P - r} + \ln \left(\frac{\sigma + \beta s/s - \beta}{\sigma} \right) + \ln \left[\frac{\ln s}{\ln (\bar{a}s)} \right] \right\}. \qquad \mathbf{11}$$

Again, it is obvious by comparing this expression with equation **2** that when $\sigma = s$ they are identical and that qualitatively the properties are the same. The additional implication that obtains from this model is that as σ increases, optimal n increases. That is, for $\bar{a}$ unchanged, increasing the span of control between the foremen and operatives leads to a general increase in the number of levels and, consequently, number of employees in the hierarchical organization, a result which is completely in accord with our intuition.

5. *Compliance and span of control interaction.* The difficulties associated with the selection of an optimum span of control have been noted by Simon (1957a, p. 28) as follows:

The dilemma is this: in a large organization with interrelations between members, a restricted span of control produces excessive red tape. . . . The alternative is to increase the number of persons who are under the command of an officer. . . . But this, too, leads to difficulty, for if an officer is required to supervise too many employees, his control over them is weakened.

Granted, then, that both the increase and the decrease in span of control have some undesirable consequences, what is the optimum point?

More precisely, the dilemma can be stated in terms of compliance ($\bar{a}$) and span of control (s) interaction. Whereas the preceding analysis treats the level of compliance ($\bar{a}$) and the span of control (s) independently, in fact they are intimately related. Increasing the span of control means that while each supervisor has more productive capability responsive to him he has less time to devote to the supervision of each, and hence a loss of control results. For purposes of examining this behavior, we let

$$\bar{a} = f(s), \quad \partial f / \partial s < 0. \tag{12}$$

Given that $\bar{a}$ is a declining function of s as indicated, the question next arises: what is the optimum value of s and how is this related to size of firm? Now output is given by $Q = (\bar{a}s)^{n-1}$, so that for any particular level of output, say $\bar{Q}$, choice of n implies a value for s (and, hence, through equation 12, $\bar{a}$) and conversely.[13] To determine the relation between optimum s and $\bar{Q}$, we observe that since gross revenue is fixed given the level of output, the optimization problem can be expressed as one of minimizing labor costs subject to constraint. Thus, the objective is:

minimize

$$C_L = w_0 \frac{s^n}{s - \beta}$$

subject to

$$(\bar{a}s)^{n-1} = \bar{Q}$$
$$\bar{a} = f(s). \tag{13}$$

The standard technique for studying the behavior of this system is to formulate it as a Lagrangian and perturbate the first order conditions with respect to $\bar{Q}$.

Unfortunately, the resulting expressions cannot be signed on the basis of the general functional relation $\bar{a} = f(s)$. Assuming, however, that the function is bell-shaped on the right (which intuitively is the correct general configuration), we can replace equation 12 and, hence, the second constraint, by

$$\bar{a} = e^{-ks^2}. \tag{12'}$$

13. Actually, two values of s and $\bar{a}$ are consistent with each feasible choice of n: a high $\bar{a}$, low s pair and a low $\bar{a}$, high s pair. Of these two, the high $\bar{a}$, low s position is always preferred since, with output fixed, gross revenues are unaffected by choice of s (and the associated value of $\bar{a}$), while increasing s for a given n leads to higher employment and hence costs increase. More precisely, costs vary roughly in proportion to s^{n-1}, and the lower the value of s the lower the associated labor costs.

The value of the exponent k in this expression can be interpreted as a goal-consistency parameter. As goal consistency increases, the value of k decreases and $\bar{a}$ increases at every value of s.

The comparative statics responses of n and s (and hence $\bar{a}$) to changes in firm size (as measured by output) and goal inconsistency (k) are shown in Table 1. The direction of adjustment of any particular decision variable to a displacement from equilibrium by an increase in either of those para-

Table 1 **Comparative statics responses**

Decision variable	Shift parameter	
	Output ($d\bar{Q}$)	Goal inconsistency (dk)
Hierarchical level (dn)	+	+
Span of control (ds)	−	−
Control effectiveness ($d\bar{a}$)	+	?

meters is found by referring to the row and column entry corresponding to the decision-variable/parameter pair.[14]

That the number of hierarchical levels should increase as output increases is not surprising. That the span of control should decrease, however, is less obvious. Moreover, it contradicts what little data there are on this question. Thus, Starbuck (1964, p. 375) concludes his systematic survey of the relevant literature bearing on this issue with the observation that the 'administrative span of control . . . probably increases with organizational size.' Unless our model can be somehow extended to explain this condition, it calls seriously into question the validity of the control-loss approach to organizational behavior. Thus, one of the merits of formalizing this argument as we have is that we can go beyond mere plausibility arguments to discover the less obvious properties of the model and address the relevant evidence to them.

That an increase in k (goal inconsistency) leads to a decrease in the span of control and hence increase in n for a fixed size organization is entirely in accord with our intuition. Indeed, given that control loss is cumulative across hierarchical levels, we would expect that consistency is relatively high (k is low) and thus the span of control large in large organizations. That organizations such as the Catholic Church successfully operate with relatively flat hierarchical structures is surely partly attributable to the high degree of goal consistency that the organization possesses. Selection and training procedures obviously contribute to this result.

14. The responses to changes in k are unambiguous. Those for changes in $\bar{Q}$ hold over all relevant values of $\bar{a}$ ($\geqslant \cdot 7$) and s ($\geqslant 2$).

High goal consistency is probably also more likely in business firms that are operated as utility-maximizing rather than profit-maximizing concerns, where the utility function of the former results from the goal consensus among the management, whereas the latter represents a constraint that is rarely identical with underlying managerial objectives (Williamson, 1964, pp. 32–7, 153–60). It does not follow, therefore, that requiring strict adherence to a profit goal necessarily leads to maximum profits. Contentious discord can be expected to develop in such circumstances which implies high k and may yield low profits. We thus have the paradox that (within limits) the permissive pursuit of non-profit goals may actually lead to the realization of higher profits.

4 Conclusions

The proposition that the management factor is responsible for a limitation to firm size has appeared recurrently in the literature. But the arguments have tended to be imprecise, lacked predictive content, and consequently failed to be convincing. The present paper attempts to overcome some of these shortcomings by developing a formal model in which the control-loss phenomenon is made central to the analysis. The importance of control loss to an understanding of bureaucratic behavior in non-market organizations has been noted previously. Our use of this proposition here is based on one of the fundamental tenets of organization theory: namely, virtually all of the interesting bureaucratic behavior observed to exist in large government bureaucracies finds its counterpart in large non-government bureaucracies as well, and this is particularly true where the phenomenon in question is a result of the bounded rationality attributes of decision-makers. We, therefore, borrow from the bureaucracy literature the proposition that control loss occurs between successive hierarchical levels (and that this tends to be cumulative) and introduce it into a theory of the firm in which neither declining product-demand curves nor rising factor-supply curves are permitted to impose a static limit on firm size.

For any given span of control (together with a specification of the state of technology, internal experience, etc.) an irreducible minimum degree of control loss results from the simple serial reproduction distortion that occurs in communicating across successive hierarchical levels. If, in addition, goals differ between hierarchical levels, the loss in control can be more extensive.

The strategy of borrowing behavioral assumptions from the organization theory literature and developing the implications of the behavior observed within the framework of economic analysis would seem to be one which might find application quite generally. Thus, the organization-theory approach to problems tends frequently to be rich in behavioral insights but weak analytically, while economics generally and the theory of the firm literature in particular has a highly developed modeling apparatus but has evidenced less resourcefulness in its use of interesting behavioral assumptions. Combining these two research areas so as to secure access to the strengths of each would thus appear to be quite promising. In any case, it is the strategy followed in this paper and, to the extent we have had any success, suggests itself for possible use elsewhere.

References

ANDREWS, P. W. S. (1949), *Manufacturing Business*, Macmillan Co.

BAIN, J. S. (1956), *Barriers to New Competition*, Harvard University Press.

BARTLETT, F. C. (1932), *Remembering*, Cambridge University Press.

CHAMBERLIN, E. H. (1948), 'Proportionality, divisibility and economies of scale' *Q.J. Econ.*, vol. 62, pp. 229–62.

COASE, R. H. (1937), 'The nature of the firm', *Economica*, new series, vol. 4, pp. 386–405, reprinted in G. J. Stigler, and K. E. Boulding (eds.), *Readings in Price Theory*, Richard D. Irwin, 1952.

DOWNS, A. (1966), *Bureaucratic Structure and Decisionmaking*, (RM– 4646– PR.), Rand.

KALDOR, N. (1934), 'The equilibrium of the firm', *Econ. J.*, vol. 44, pp. 70–71.

KNIGHT, F. H. (1965), *Risk, Uncertainty and Profit*, Harper & Row.

KOONTZ, H., and O'DONNELL, C. (1955), *Principles of Management*, McGraw-Hill.

MARCH, J. G., and SIMON, H. A. (1958), *Organizations*, Wiley.

MAYER, T. (1960), 'The distribution of ability and earnings', *Rev. Econ. Stats.*, vol. 42, pp. 189–98.

MONSEN, R. J. Jr., and DOWNS, A. (1965), 'A theory of large managerial firms', *J. pol. Econ.*, vol. 73, pp. 221–36.

PAPANDREOU, A. G. (1952), 'Some basic issues in the theory of the firm', in B. F. Haley (ed.), *A Survey of Contemporary Economics*, Richard D. Irwin.

PENROSE, E. T. (1959), *The Theory of the Growth of the Firm*, Wiley.

ROBINSON, E. A. G. (1934), The problem of management and the size of firms', *Econ. J.*, vol. 44, pp. 240–54.

ROBINSON, E. A. G. (1962), *The Structure of Competitive Industry*, University of Chicago Press.

ROSS, N. S. (1952–3), 'Management and the size of the firm', *Rev. econ. Studies*, vol. 19, pp. 148–54.

SIMON, H. A. (1957a), *Administrative Behavior*, 2nd edn, Macmillan Co.

SIMON, H. A. (1957b), 'The compensation of executives', *Sociometry*, pp. 32–5.

STARBUCK, W. H. (1964), 'Organizational growth and development', in J. G. March (ed.), *Handbook of Organizations*, Rand McNally.

TULLOCK, G. (1965), *The Politics of Bureaucracy*, Public Affairs Press.

US DEPARTMENT OF LABOR (1964), *Salary and Structure Characteristics in Large Firms (1963)* (bulletin no. 1417.), Washington.

WILLIAMSON, J. (1966), 'Profit, growth and sales maximization', *Economica*, vol. 33, pp. 1–16.

WILLIAMSON, O. E. (1964), *The Economics of Discretionary Behavior: Managerial Objectives in a Theory of the Firm*, Prentice-Hall.

3 David Schwartzman

Uncertainty and the Size of the Firm

David Schwartzman, 'Uncertainty and the size of the firm', *Economica*, n. s., vol. 30, 1963, pp. 287–96.

This article examines Professor E. A. G. Robinson's idea that large firms cannot compete successfully with small firms in conditions in which there is a high degree of uncertainty (1935, p. 50). If the theory is valid, we need not rely on the concept of monopoly to explain the failure of firms to exhaust economies of scale.[1] This article discusses the effect of uncertainty on the shape of the long-run average cost (LAC) curve, giving attention to both the maximum and minimum economic size of firm. An index of uncertainty is constructed, and tests are made of some of the implications of the theory with respect to variation among industries in the sizes of leading firms, the concentration ratio, the output of small plants, and the average size of the firm.

Theory

Under a high degree of uncertainty firms are unlikely to have accurate forecasts of their sales, and executives require a relatively large amount of information at frequent intervals.[2] In addition, they make more decisions than executives in industries where a low degree of uncertainty prevails. Routine extrapolations from previous experience cannot be depended on to provide the correct responses to forecasts. Moreover, since decisions in the same firm must be consistent with each other, executives must agree on their forecasts and on the appropriate decisions. One of the advantages of depending on past budgets, ratios of stocks to sales, and other guides is that they are shared by different members of the firm and thus ensure consistency. Under a high degree of uncertainty such techniques which are economical of executives' time are less satisfactory; they must meet to consider

1. According to Marshall, firms ceased expanding despite increasing returns to scale because they supplied markets which were limited in size by tastes of consumers (1920, pp. 286–7, 316). Monopolistic conditions, however, clearly do not account for the prevalence of unspecialized processes in the shoe and women's dress industries. Shoe manufacturing plants make anywhere from 30 to several hundred designs, despite extensive duplication among plants (cf., Report of the Anglo-American Committee on Productivity (1951, pp. 15, 54, 66).

2. Fashion-goods buyers, who operate under a high degree of uncertainty, receive more frequent and more detailed reports on sales than other buyers in chain stores.

their different views of policy. Finally, flexibility and speed are important, since forecasts for any period improve as the interval decreases between the date of the forecast and the period for which it is made. The increase in the volume of information that must be received and transmitted, in the number of decisions, in the burden of communication, and in speed of decision-making raise the LAC curve under uncertainty.

The maximum economic size of the firm is the size at which the LAC curve turns up, and the argument must show why the LAC curve turns up at a relatively small size where uncertainty is high. Discussions of diseconomies of scale have stressed the rapidly increasing cost of coordinating related decisions by different persons as the number of decisions and decision-makers increases. A high degree of uncertainty has the same consequence for the number of decisions as large size, and entails the same problem of coordination. If the LAC curve turns up for these reasons with increases in size, it will turn up at a smaller size under a higher degree of uncertainty than under a lower.

Uncertainty also reduces maximum firm size by destroying some of the advantages of specialization in production. Specialization entails advance planning of production in order to permit purchasing, scheduling, arranging of machines, etc., and the resulting complex arrangement is not easily changed. Unspecialized processes by contrast employ operators and machines for a variety of tasks and they may be shifted rapidly from one product to another.[3] The need for flexibility under uncertainty reduces the gains from specialization.[4]

Since maximum firm size is not observable, the test relates instead to the aggregate size of a fixed small number of leading firms in each industry, H_{mi}, where m refers to the number of leading firms and i to the industry. The hypothesis is that H_{mi} varies among industries inversely with the degree of uncertainty. The test is based on a multiple regression analysis of variation in H_{mi}, and the independent variables are an index of the importance of technological economies of scale, industry size, and an index of uncertainty.

3. Uncertainty is low in the work-pants industry compared to the unit-price dress industry. In work-pants plants sewing is broken down into between thirty and forty different tasks, each of which is performed by a different operator. In a sample of eleven plants, five produced only one style despite considerable variety in the industry as a whole. Orders took from two weeks to one month to complete (see US Bureau of Labor Statistics, 1951, pp. 1–9). By contrast nearly all of the sewing of a unit-price dress is performed by a single operator, each firm produces a large number of styles, and orders are completed frequently in less than one week (see Disher, 1940).

4. The analysis has assumed that firms in any industry produce identical products, but firms in an observed industry typically specialize in different products. There may be no relation between size of firm and degree of specialization within observed industries, and any measure of the relation between uncertainty and maximum economic size among industries may not reflect the influence of uncertainty on degree of specialization.

Industry size is not as obviously required as the other two independent variables. Average size of firm multiplied by the number of firms equals industry size. As an industry grows, new firms enter; so average size increases less than proportionally with industry size: the elasticity of average firm size with respect to industry size typically is less than one. Unless the leading firms possess advantages over other firms, the elasticity of H_{mi} with respect to industry size also will be less than one. It will exceed zero, except in the unlikely event that the m leading firms each will have attained the maximum firm size. An additional reason for expecting a relation between H_{mi} and industry size among oligopolistic industries is that industry size is a point on the industry demand curve.

The concentration ratio is H_{mi} divided by industry size, and the concentration ratio therefore will vary inversely with uncertainty and industry size and directly with the importance of technological economies of scale.

Consider now the minimum economic size of firm, the size at which the LAC curve ceases to decline. As uncertainty increases, minimum size will decline, since the advantages of large size associated with specialization diminish. The test is based on variation among industries in the aggregate output of all *plants* below a specified 'small' size: the argument applies as much to plants as to firms, and data are available only for plants. If minimum size of plant declines with increases in uncertainty, then the total output of plants which are smaller than some fixed 'small' size will rise. In addition, the output of such plants will increase with industry size, and decline as the importance of technological economies of scale increases.

If both upper and lower limits of firm size vary inversely with the degree of uncertainty, average firm size will do likewise. By analogous reasoning we may expect average firm size to vary directly with the importance of technological economies of scale, and we have already seen that average firm size will vary directly with industry size. Since other variables such as age of industry and ease of entry probably have a powerful influence, close predictions of average size cannot be expected.

The tests

The following symbols are used:

H_{mi} = the aggregate size of the m leading firms in the ith industry
C_{mi} = the concentration ratio of the ith industry, or H_{mi}/S_i
P_{bi} = the output of all plants in industry i which are smaller than size b
A_i = average size of firm in the ith industry
U_i = the degree of uncertainty in industry i
T_i = the importance of technological scale economies in industry i
S_i = the size of industry i

The following equations describe the expected relations set out in the first section. In order to indicate that the variables are expressed in logarithms, they are represented by lower-case letters:

$$h_{mi} = a_h + b_h u_i + c_h t_i + d_h s_i, \qquad c_{mi} = a_c + b_c u_i + c_c t_i + d_c s_i,$$
$$p_{bi} = a_p + b_p u_i + c_p t_i + d_p s_i, \qquad a_i = a_a + b_a u_i + c_a t_i + d_a s_i.$$

The previous discussion leads to the following predictions: b_h, b_c, and b_a will be negative; c_h, c_c, and c_a will be positive; b_p will be positive; c_p will be negative; all the d's will be positive.

The logarithmic equations need defence. The aggregate size of the m leading firms, H_{mi}, is logarithmically related to industry size, S_i, and the concentration ratio, C_{mi}, has a similar relation, since $c_{mi} = h_{mi} - s_i$. Clearly P_{bi} and A_i are related to S_i in the same way. Although there is no theoretical basis for this, I also assume logarithmic relations between each of the dependent variables and U_i and T_i. The distributions of the logarithms of the variables are more nearly symmetrical than those of the arithmetic values, and the usual statistical tests therefore can be applied with greater confidence. Another advantage is that the regression coefficients are comparable among logarithmic equations. It should be noted that, if s_i and u_i are independent, $b_h = b_c$, $c_h = c_c$, and $d_h = d_c + 1$.

The measure of uncertainty

The selected index of uncertainty for any industry is the ratio of markdowns to total sales in the corresponding merchandise department in department stores in the United States between 1953 and 1955 (National Retail Dry Goods Association Controllers' Congress 1954, 1955 and 1956, Table 1). Total markdowns are divided by sales in order to correct for size of department.

If the sales of a line of merchandise are not adequate in relation to the stock, the price on each of the items in stock is reduced. The difference between the two prices is the markdown for a single item. Total markdowns for a department in a year is the sum of all markdowns on all items that have been in stock during the year and may still be in stock at the end of the year. The markdown ratio is the ratio of markdowns to sales, and the median markdown ratio is reported annually for each department by the National Retail Dry Goods Association (now called the National Retail Merchants Association), the trade association of department stores, on the basis of a sample of 450 stores, which is stratified by store sizes. Departments in small stores usually are less specialized than in large stores, and among large stores the merchandise mix varies in departments having approximately the same title. The NRDGA's definitions of departments therefore are in great detail in order to permit comparisons among stores.

In any case, errors arising from variation in merchandise mix are unlikely to be systematically related to variation in the markdown ratio among departments. Because markdown ratios in a single year may be dominated by the phase of the cycle, by the weather, or by other conditions specific to that year, the arithmetic mean of the medians for each department over the three years 1953–5 has been used. The departments have been matched to census manufacturing industries on the basis of comparisons of commodity lists. Many departments include more products than do corresponding industries, and industries have been grouped to match such departments.

Over-estimates of demand for whole classes of merchandise or for individual lines produce markdowns. Departmental buyers estimate the quantity of an item that would be sold at various prices during the period for which they are making a purchase. A buyer may fix an excessive price in relation to the stock which he acquires. To dispose of the resulting excess stock, markdowns will be made, and markdowns thus increase with the frequency and magnitude of over-estimates of demand. Markdowns, therefore, provide a measure of the uncertainty arising from unpredictable variations in final demand. Another virtue of markdowns as an index of uncertainty is that they increase with the cost of errors. Merchandise which does not suffer from obsolescence or deterioration in storage may be kept in stock rather than be sold at reduced prices.

An additional attraction of the selected index is that it is independent of data pertaining directly to the manufacturing firms. Thus the index would not be affected if, contrary to the major hypothesis, it were true that the ability of manufacturing firms to forecast sales improves as they grow, or that the expansion of firms occurs by way of product diversification which reduces uncertainty. Should either of these conditions be operative, the net regression coefficients b_h, b_c and b_a would probably be non-significant or positive in the present tests, rather than negative as predicted. Other possible indices of uncertainty, based on data relating directly to the manufacturing firms, would not so readily avoid bias favouring the hypothesis.

Consider now the objections that may be raised against the markdown ratio as a measure of uncertainty. Markdowns which are not the result of errors in forecasting provide a possible source of bias. Table 1 shows that fashion-goods industries are associated with high markdown ratios. While the demand for fashion-goods is uncertain it also is seasonal, and markdowns may be a method of promoting off-season sales, or of price discrimination among consumers with different preferences with respect to the timing of purchases. However, if their estimates were correct, buyers would buy at low prices between seasons when output is low and markdowns would not occur. Moreover, much of the merchandise offered during 'sales'

Table 1 Index of uncertainty: 64 manufacturing industries

S.I.C. no.	Industry	Index	S.I.C. no.	Industry	Index
2311	Men's and boys' suits and coats	6·4	2251	Full-fashioned hosiery	3·5
2321	Men's dress shirts and night-wear	3·5	2252	Seamless hosiery	3·5
2322	Men's and boys' underwear	3·5	2254	Knit underwear	4·9
2323	Men's and boys' neckwear	3·5	2271	Wool carpets and rugs	7·1
2325	Men's and boys' cloth hats	4·6	2281	Fur-felt hats and hat bodies	4·7
2328	Work shirts	3·0	2493	Mirror and picture frames	5·6
2329	Men's and boys' clothing n.e.c.	3·0	2512	Upholstered household furniture	6·7
2331	Blouses	8·7	2515	Mattresses and bedsprings	4·2
2333	Dresses, unit price	12·3	2693	Wallpaper	5·4
2334	Dresses, dozen price	9·2	2731	Books, publishing and printing	2·1
2337	Women's suits, coats and skirts	9·7	2771	Greeting cards	2·0
2338	Women's neckwear and scarfs	5·4	2851	Paints and varnishes	5·4
2339	Women's outerwear, n.e.c.	8·5	2893	Toilet preparations	3·3
2341	Women's and children's underwear	4·9	3141	Footwear, except rubber	8·4
2342	Corsets and allied garments	3·1	3151	Leather dress gloves	5·2
2351	Millinery	10·7	3161	Luggage	3·7
2361	Children's dresses	7·0	3171	Handbags and purses	5·1
2363	Children's coats	7·0	3262	Vitreous-china food utensils	6·0
2369	Children's outerwear, n.e.c.	5·5	3581	Domestic laundry equipment	6·1
2371	Fur goods	8·0	3583	Sewing machines	7·8
2381	Fabric dress gloves	5·2	3584	Vacuum cleaners	3·7
2382	Fabric work gloves	3·0	3661	Radios and related products	5·3
2384	Robes and dressing gowns	6·6	3663	Phonograph records	4·3
2387	Belts	3·9	3861	Photographic equipment	5·0
2388	Handkerchiefs	3·7	3871	Watches and clocks	4·6
2391	Curtains and draperies	6·1	3911	Jewellery	4·3
2392	House-furnishings, n.e.c.	4·8	3941	Games and toys, n.e.c.	5·3
2396	Trimmings and art goods	5·4	3949	Sporting and athletic goods	4·9
2397	Schiffli-machine embroideries	4·6	3995	Umbrellas, parasols, and canes	2·5
2398	Embroideries, except Schiffli	4·6	3931	Pianos	4·8
2274	Hard surface floor coverings	6·4	2273	Carpets and rugs, except wool	7·1
			3172	Small leather goods	5·1

Source: Computed from markdown ratios reported by National Retail Dry Goods Association.

is bought specifically for the purpose, and the 'sale' prices are original rather than markdown prices. There may, of course, be some promotional markdowns, but their value is independent of uncertainty and they will tend to produce non-significant rather than significant net regression coefficients.

A related question is presented by errors in forecasting which do not result in markdowns. Over-estimates only, and not under-estimates of demand, produce markdowns. The selected measure is based on the assumption that over-estimates are correlated with under-estimates among departments. Since variability of demand accounts for both types of errors, the assumption is realistic. It is not necessary to assume as well that errors of forecasting are unbiased.

Finally, we must note that the use of department-store markdowns limits the sample to those industries selling through department stores. The sample of 64 industries (shown in Table 1) does not include *inter alia* producers' goods industries, food industries, and automobile manufacturing, and it is heavily weighted with apparel industries. In the sample selected u_i may account for a larger proportion of the variation in c_{mi} than among all industries. The heavy representation of apparel industries reduces both the mean and standard deviation of C_{mi} and therefore the standard deviation of c_{mi}. The effect of the characteristics of the sample on the standard deviation of u_i is more difficult to assess. The standard deviation of U_i probably increases, since apparel departments have either high or low markdown ratios; but the arithmetic mean may change in either direction, and thus the standard deviation of u_i in the sample may be higher or lower than in the population of all industries. It is therefore imprudent to estimate from the sample the effect of uncertainty on maximum size of firm among all industries. Since, however, there is no bias in relation to the direction of the effect of uncertainty, the test of the hypothesis is valid despite the unrepresentative nature of the sample.

The measures of the other variables

The other independent variables are T_i, the importance of technological economies of scale, and S_i, industry size. The quantity of electricity consumed per employee by industry in 1954 is the index of T_i (US Bureau of the Census, 1957, pp. 208–21, Table 2). Large-scale techniques of production entail a high capital-labour ratio and thus large quantities of electricity relative to labour. Value-added by industry in 1954 is the measure of S_i (1957, Table 2A, pp. 4–33).

The dependent variables, C_{mi}, H_{mi}, P_{bi}, and A_i are measured as follows. In order to prevent the results reflecting an arbitrary selection among the various measures of concentration, three measures have been used. The measures of C_{mi} are the proportion of total shipments in each industry in

1954 accounted for by the four, eight, and twenty leading firms (US Senate, 1957, Table 42). The product $C_{mi} S_i$ measures H_{mi}, the aggregate size of leading firms. The variable P_{bi} is defined as the value-added of all plants below size b in industry i. For b, 9, 19, and 49 employees have been used alternatively (US Bureau of the Census, 1957, Table 1). The value of A_i, average firm size, is found by dividing value-added for each industry by the number of companies (US Senate, 1957).

The results

The net regression coefficients and their standard errors are presented in Table 2; Table 3 shows the partial correlation coefficients and the co-efficients of multiple determination. The coefficients associated with u_i are highly significant in relation to both h_{mi} and c_{mi} but not significant in relation to p_{bi} or a_i. Except in the equation for p_{9i} the signs are right, how-ever, and if the industries had been closer to the theoretical definitions, the results might have confirmed the hypotheses concerning minimum size and average size of firm.

Table 2 Net regression coefficients and standard errors (in brackets)

	u_i	t_i	s_i
c_{4i}	−0·77 (0·20)	0·43 (0·09)	−0·19 (0·07)
c_{8i}	−0·70 (0·18)	0·38 (0·08)	−0·20 (0·06)
c_{20i}	−0·60 (0·14)	0·28 (0·06)	−0·16 (0·05)
h_{4i}	−0·77 (0·20)	0·43 (0·09)	0·81 (0·07)
h_{8i}	−0·70 (0·18)	0·38 (0·08)	0·80 (0·06)
h_{20i}	−0·60 (0·15)	0·28 (0·06)	0·84 (0·05)
p_{9i}	−0·95 (1·85)	0·32 (0·78)	−0·41 (0·64)
p_{19i}	0·76 (0·98)	0·56 (0·41)	0·27 (0·34)
p_{49i}	0·42 (0·34)	−0·38 (0·15)	0·58 (0·12)
a_i	−0·45 (0·27)	0·52 (0·11)	0·22 (0·09)

Table 3 Partial correlation coefficients and coefficients of multiple determination

	u_i	t_i	s_i	R^2
c_{4i}	−0·43	0·53	−0·32	0·38
c_{8i}	−0·44	0·53	−0·38	0·40
c_{20i}	−0·46	0·50	−0·38	0·40
h_{4i}	−0·43	0·53	0·82	0·75
h_{8i}	−0·44	0·53	0·85	0·78
h_{20i}	−0·46	0·50	0·90	0 85
p_{9i}	−0·06	0·15	−0·08	0·02
p_{19i}	0·10	0·17	0·10	0·02
p_{49i}	0·15	−0·31	0·52	0·30
a_i	−0·21	0·50	0·29	0·33

The independent variable t_i, representing technological economies of scale, is highly significant in relation to h_{mi} and c_{mi}. It is also important in the explanation of a_i. On the other hand, t_i is not as successful in relation to p_{bi}. The hypothesis concerning technological economies of scale and minimum firm size is confirmed only for p_{49i}. Perhaps extremely small plants do not in general compete with larger plants in the same market but specialize in intermediate products which they supply to larger plants which are in the same census industry.

A large part of the variation in h_{mi} is explained by s_i, which represents industry size, despite the low level of concentration in most of the industries in the sample. The elasticity of the leading firms' output with respect to industry size is between 0·80 and 0·84.[5] The elasticity of average firm size is 0·22. Since $s_i = a_i + n_i$, where n_i is the logarithm of the number of firms, we may infer that the elasticity of the number of firms with respect to industry size is 0·78.[6] It is also interesting to observe that the elasticity of output of

5. A compilation bias produces an upward bias in the measured elasticity. Suppose the present census industries were redefined and grouped into arbitrarily bounded and larger industries. The average size of the m leading firms of the larger industries will exceed the average size of the m leading firms of the original industries. When a fixed number of leaders is selected from a group which increases in size, the average size of leaders will increase. Since most industries in the present sample are narrowly defined from the standpoint of the substitution possibilities either in consumption or in production, the error probably is small.

6. Evely and Little found the elasticity of the number of firms with respect to industry

plants with fewer than 49 employees with respect to industry size is 0·58. These results indicate that among the industries in the sample output increases largely through an increase in the number of firms rather than in the average size of the firm. An implication is that the maximum size of firm generally is small in relation to the size of the market. Moreover, the results indicate that for most firms the LAC curve begins to rise at a size which is not very much larger than their actual size.

Conclusion

Robinson's suggestion that uncertainty limits the size of the firm is not refuted. But the evidence concerning minimum economic size of firm and average size of firm in relation to uncertainty is not conclusive.

Subsidiary findings confirm the generally held beliefs that technological economies of scale are important in the determination of the degree of concentration. We have also observed that industry size grows largely through increases in the number of firms rather than in average size. We may infer that typically firms encounter diseconomies of scale at sizes which are small in relation to the market.

The conclusion that uncertainty limits the size of the firm has implications for the structure of markets in the future. A high degree of uncertainty restricts size because at a relatively small size of firm executives reach their capacity to communicate with associates, employees, etc., and to receive and interpret information with adequate speed and accuracy. Recent innovations in data-receiving and processing equipment have enlarged the capacity of executives and thus have weakened the uncertainty barrier to growth. The leading firms in some industries are likely to grow, and, if their markets do not grow proportionally, the general level of concentration will rise.

---

employment to be 0·79 among 219 British manufacturing industries, which is nearly identical with the present result despite the highly restricted scope of the sample in the present study and also the use of value-added in place of employment as a measure of industry size. Evely and Little's elasticity of concentration with respect to industry size was −0·29, somewhat above my equivalent finding of −0·19 (1960, p. 108).

References

DISHER, M. L. (1940), *American Factory Production of Women's Clothing*.
EVELY, R., and LITTLE, I. M. D. (1960), *Concentration in British Industry: an Empirical Study of the Structure of Industrial Production, 1935–51*, Cambridge University Press.
MARSHALL, A. (1920), *Principles of Economics*, 8th edn, Macmillan.
NATIONAL RETAIL DRY GOODS ASSOCIATION (now called National Retail Merchants Association) (1954, 1955 and 1956 edns), Controllers Congress, *Departmental Merchandising and Operating Results*.
Report of the Anglo-American Committee on Productivity (1951), *Footwear*.

Robinson, E. A. G. (1935), *The Structure of Competitive Industry*, James Nisbet.

US Bureau of the Census (1957), *US Census of Manufactures 1954*, vol. 1, summary statistics, Washington.

US Bureau of Labor Statistics (1951), *Mens Work Pants*, prepared for the Mutual Security Agency, Productivity and Technical Assistance Division, Washington.

US Senate (1957), *Concentration in American Industry*, Report of the Sub committee on Antitrust and Monopoly to the Committee on the Judiciary, 85th Congress, 1st Session.

4 Matityahu Marcus

Profitability and the Size of the Firm

Matityahu Marcus, 'Profitability and size of firm: some further evidence', *Review of Economics and Statistics*, vol. 51, 1969, pp. 104–7.

The hypothesis that the rate of return increases with the size of the firm has been developed at length by Baumol and explicitly incorporated into his model of the growth of firms (1959, ch. 5). While this may be the first attempt to integrate the hypothesis into the theory of the firm, the suggestion that mere size influences the rate of return has long intrigued economists as evidenced by the periodic studies of the subject (Alexander, 1949; Crum, 1939; Epstein, 1939; McConnell, 1945; Osborn, 1951; Stekler, 1963). These studies did not, however, provide definitive evidence on the validity of the hypothesis; they lacked consensus on their major findings, and their methodology and data were subject to several shortcomings.

The objective of the present study is the re-evaluation of the hypothesis against new data within an improved analytical framework. Coincidentally with the preparation of the present study, Hall and Weiss have also investigated the hypothesis, and their results, which strongly favor the hypothesis, have been published most recently (1967). Our own conclusion is that the hypothesis does not perform uniformly in all industries and that it cannot therefore be viewed as having general validity.

Comparison of present approach with previous studies

As Hall and Weiss correctly note, earlier studies have not always employed industry control variables when isolating the effect of size. To avoid this difficulty, some authors examined the size-profitability relationship within individual industries. However, this procedure was not adequate since the industry categories employed were far too broad. Thus, Alexander and Osborn examined the association within sectors (one-digit groupings) while Epstein and Stekler treated two-digit industries. Yet clearly, a profitability-size relationship can assume economic significance only if established within a well-defined industry context. Its presence within broad industry groupings may reflect inter-industry variations in rates of return and firms' size distributions and is not necessarily indicative of the presence of a size effect *within* narrow industry groups.

Hall and Weiss pooled observations drawn from diverse industries and sought to control for inter-industry differences by including the industry's concentration ratio as an explicit variable. There remains the possibility nonetheless that other industry differences are not taken account of in this approach; for example, traditional theory suggests that differences in rates of return among industries are also related to differences in risk, and more recent work by Comanor and Wilson indicates that rates of return will also be affected by differing advertising intensities among industries (1967). A second potential difficulty with the pooling procedure is that it presupposes equal parameters for diverse industry groups. If this *hypothesis* is incorrect, the coefficients estimated for the Hall–Weiss model cannot be interpreted unambiguously.

The hypothesis tested in the present study is not identical to the one posed in the Hall–Weiss study. In the latter, the authors interpret Baumol's hypothesis as relating to firms of 'optimal size' and consequently restrict their investigation to the very largest firms drawn from *Fortune's Directory of the 500 Largest Corporations*. In our study, on the other hand, the hypothesis is evaluated for the entire size distribution of firms. If this procedure introduces any bias, it is likely to be in favor of the Hall–Weiss results since the inclusion of 'sub-optimal' firms should strengthen any positive association between size and profitability.

One data difficulty which has plagued users of Internal Revenue Service statistics must be confronted in our study. It is widely assumed that owners of small corporations under-report their profits in order to minimize the double taxation of the fraction of profits which would have normally been distributed as dividends. The presence of such a reporting bias might, in itself, impart an apparent upward association to rates of return and size. While several procedures were used in earlier studies to remove this source of bias, their success might be questioned. We re-examined this matter against new data and concluded that the under-reporting of profits constitutes a problem only in firms with under-$500,000 in assets; these size groups will therefore be omitted from our tests.[1]

1. The method we employed to handle the small-size reporting bias relied on a 1958 change in the corporation income tax law. Starting in that year, corporations designated as small business corporations could elect to be taxed through their shareholders. The corporations using this provision, i.e. those filing Form 1120–S, are not subject to the corporation income tax, and therefore have no incentive to understate profits by exaggerating salaries. One may therefore consider this group of firms free of the 'small size bias'.

A comparison of rates of return for the 1120–S group with the 'all other' group yielded very consistent patterns up to the $500,000 size limit. In this range, the rates of return for the 1120–S group were *always* higher than the 'all other' rates. Past the $500,000 limit no systematic relationship emerged – the 1120–S series showing higher values in one half of all cases. Moreover, the *magnitude* of the differences in the rates of return between the two groups was trivial: the mean difference in rates was 0·08 per cent for the groups above $500,000 in assets against a mean difference of 4 per cent for the groups below it.

Regression analysis

The data

Our basic data source was the Internal Revenue Service *Statistics of Income Source Book* which are available on microfilm. The study extends over three years; 1959–60, 1960–61, 1961–62. All three-digit manufacturing industries with data reported for separate size classes were examined. This provided us with a sizable group of industries; 117 in 1959–60 and 1960–61; and 118 in 1961–62.

Throughout the study the rate of return is defined as the ratio of net profits (before taxes) plus interest payments to total assets. The main reason for treating interest as a component of profits is to remove variations in rates of return which may be solely due to differing equity-debt ratios.

The model

The hypothesis that size of firm exerts a separate influence on the rate of return can only be evaluated within a complete model of firms' rates of return. The literature suggests that the rate of return is influenced by:

1. The degree of monopoly power of the industry customarily measured by the concentration ratio.
2. The industry's growth rate, usually taken to represent the rate of growth of 'demand'.
3. The riskiness of the industry.
4. The 'absolute' size of the firm, the hypothesis we are testing.

The effects of industry characteristics are assumed constant *within* a given industry hence they will not affect the functional relationship of rates of return with size if it is estimated for each industry separately. This can be clearly seen from the following.

Let r_{ij} = rate of return for firms in industry i, size class j,

$i = 1, \ldots\ldots\ldots\ldots 118$

$j = 4, \ldots\ldots\ldots\ldots 12$ (first three size classes are not considered. See footnote 1)

S_j = mid-point for size class j

$c_i, g_i, z_i \ldots\ldots$ = industry characteristics such as degree of monopoly, growth rate, riskiness

u = an error term with mean zero and constant variance.

And, assume that the rate of return is determined by the equation,

$$r_{ij} = a_{i0} + a_{i1} \log c_i + a_{i2} \log g_i + a_{i3} \log z_i + a_{i4} \log S_j + u. \qquad 1$$

Table 1 **Regression results: rate of return on log size***

IRS Code	Industry description	Log size		Equation constant	$\bar{R}^2$	Number of observations
285	Perfume and cosmetics	0·114	(6·756)	−0·611	0·701	20
206	Confectionery and related products	0·101	(7·650)	−0·548	0·733	22
350	Engines and turbines	0·077	(3·020)	−0·467	0·299	20
341	Cutlery and general hardware	0·079	(3·459)	−0·404	0·323	24
358	Machinery except electrical metal-working machinery	0·066	(3·527)	−0·334	0·402	18
282	Drugs	0·064	(5·081)	−0·278	0·519	24
396	Photographic equipment and supplies	0·056	(3·711)	−0·266	0·367	23
265	Paperboard containers and boxes	0·052	(6·795)	−0·250	0·663	24
192	Malt liquors and beverages	0·048	(7·465)	−0·255	0·704	24
275	Commercial printing business forms	0·045	(3·969)	−0·186	0·391	24
368	Other electrical machinery and equipment	0·043	(3·049)	−0·175	0·274	23
327	Concrete and gypsum products	0·042	(5·339)	−0·203	0·514	27
191	Soft drinks	0·037	(3·438)	−0·105	0·323	23
321	Glass products	0·036	(2·553)	−0·121	0·175	27
209	Food and kindred products	0·036	(2·089)	−0·116	0·133	23
223	Broad woven fabric mills (wool)	0·033	(2·208)	−0·165	0·169	20
284	Paints, varnishes	0·033	(5·031)	−0·119	0·514	24
362	Electrical industrial apparatus	0·033	(2·524)	−0·100	0·212	21
288	Gum and wood chemicals	0·033	(2·826)	−0·094	0·218	26
202	Canned fruits, vegetables	0·033	(3·671)	−0·137	0·324	27
269	Converted paper and paperboard	0·032	(2·555)	−0·114	0·187	25
203	Grain mill products	0·029	(4·802)	−0·099	0·459	27
204	Bakery products	0·029	(4·043)	−0·095	0·380	26
221	Broad woven fabric mills (cotton)	0·029	(3·241)	−0·119	0·302	23
325	Structural clay products	0·028	(4·123)	−0·118	0·444	21
259	Office furniture	0·028	(2·573)	−0·076	0·248	18
251	Household furniture	0·028	(3·565)	−0·099	0·369	21
353	Metal-working equipment	0·024	(3·523)	−0·082	0·352	22

Table 1 – *continued*

IRS Code	Industry description	Log size	Equation constant	$\bar{R}^2$	Number of observations
355	General industrial equipment	0·023 (2·894)	−0·035	0·243	24
361	Electrical industrial equipment	0·022 (2·554)	−0·029	0·201	23
352	Construction handling equipment	0·021 (3·861)	−0·060	0·348	27
225	Knitting mills	0·020 (2·708)	−0·044	0·250	20
241	Logging and saw mills	0·016 (2·268)	−0·057	0·137	27
201	Dairy products	0·016 (3·056)	−0·026	0·243	27
231	Men's clothing	0·014 (3·680)	−0·009	0·385	21

* Values in parentheses are t-ratios of coefficient next to them. $\bar{R}^2$ is the coefficient of determination adjusted for degrees of freedom.

Combining constants in **1**, we obtain

$$r_{ij} = \beta_{i0} + \beta_{i1} \log S_j + u \qquad\qquad 2$$

where the new regression constant (β_{i0}) is now equal to

$a_{i0} + a_{i1} \log c_i + a_{i2} \log g_i + a_{i3} \log z_i$, and $\beta_{i1} = a_{i4}$.

Fitting equation **2** to each industry showed that the size coefficient (β_{i1}) was statistically significant at the 0·05 level in thirty-five of the 118 industries examined.[2] The results for these industries are reported in Table 1. The range of variation in the magnitude of β_{i1} is considerable; the high, in Perfume and Cosmetics, is 0·114, and the low, 0·014, is found in Men's Clothing. The mean coefficient for the thirty-five industries is 0·0405 suggesting that on the basis of this group one would expect the rate of return to rise by 1·2 per cent if size doubles, and by 4·05 per cent for a ten-fold increase in size.

Conclusions

The burden of our findings is that size of firm influences profitability in *some*, but not in all, industries; in 74 of 118 industries the null hypothesis that size has no effect on the rate of return could not be rejected at a five per cent probability level. Since profitability is ultimately determined by several complex factors – product prices, factor costs, the production function – whose relationship to size of firm might vary among industries in a manner which cannot be readily identified, it is perhaps not surprising that when offered with no qualifications, the hypothesis cannot be supported.

2. In nine industries the size coefficients were significantly negative (IRS 195, 207, 226, 272, 291, 338, 349, 404).

References

ALEXANDER, S. S. (1949), 'The effect of size of manufacturing corporation on the distribution of the rate of return', *Rev. Econ. Stats*, vol. 31, pp. 229–35.

BAUMOL, W. J. (1959), *Business Behavior Value and Growth*, Harcourt Brace & World.

COMANOR, W. S., and WILSON, T. A. (1967), 'Advertising, market structure and performance', *Rev. Econ. Stats.*, vol. 49, pp. 423–40.

CRUM, W. L. (1939), *Corporate Size and Earning Power*, Harvard University Press.

EPSTEIN, R. C. (1939), *Industrial Profits in the United States*, National Bureau of Economic Research, New York.

HALL, M., and WEISS, L. (1967), 'Firm size and profitability', *Rev. Econ. Stats*, vol. 49, pp. 319–31.

McCONNELL, J. L. (1945), 'Corporate earnings by size of firm', *Survey current Bus.*, vol. 25, no. 5.

OSBORN, R. C. (1951), 'Efficiency and profitability in relation to size', *Harvard bus. Rev.*, March, pp. 82–94.

STEKLER, H. O. (1963), *Profitability and Size of Firm*, Institute of Business and Economic Research, University of California, Berkeley.

Part Two
Entry Conditions and Entry

Mann (Reading 5) assesses the relative heights of barriers to entry into thirteen industries in the United States, using Bain's well-known classification of types of entry barrier. Comanor and Wilson (Reading 6) provide a detailed analysis of one entry barrier, that created by advertising. The product-differentiation barrier, in which advertising plays a major part, is perhaps the most controversial barrier, since a good deal of argument and empirical work revolves around the related questions of the method of operation of the barrier, its 'height' and its welfare-economic implications. (For a recent critical assessment of the available evidence, see Schmalensee (1972), especially chapter 7). Mansfield (Reading 7) explores some determinants on the rate of entry of new firms and of exit of old firms. Further, the Reading examines the hypotheses that the rate of growth of firms is independent of size of firm, and that firm sizes are log-normally distributed – hypotheses encountered also in Readings 11, 14, and 15. Stigler (Reading 8) in a few pages passes critical judgement on one aspect of the fashionable subject of 'limit pricing'.

Reference

SCHMALENSEE, R. (1972), *The Economics of Advertising*, North Holland.

5 H. Michael Mann

Entry Barriers in Thirteen Industries

Appendix A ('Classification of industries with respect to barriers to entry') of H. Michael Mann, 'Seller concentration, barriers to entry, and rates of return in thirty industries, 1950–1960', *Review of Economics and Statistics*, vol. 48, 1966, pp. 296–307.

. . . The remaining thirteen [industries] were classified according to the significance of specific entry barriers, indicated in Table 1 below by the notations 'I,' 'II,' and 'III'. These designations represent unimportant, moderately important, and very important entry barriers, respectively.

The particular rankings for each specific entry barrier were used to estimate the over-all barrier to entry for each industry. This estimate was based on intuitive judgement, not on any addition or averaging of specific barrier ranks. The lack of data or information by which to give ranks to specific entry barriers for some industries, the fact that economies of scale estimates are for plant only, and the difficulty in interpreting some of the information available precluded reliance on any procedure which did not involve use of judgement.

The information on which Table 1 depends follows. Each industry is grouped according to the judgement made about its over-all barrier-to-entry ranking.

Very high barriers to entry
Sulphur
The most important barrier to entry into the sulphur industry is the control of the natural raw material by the dominant firms. Of the twelve salt domes from which elemental sulphur (sulphur which is not combined with any other substance) was mined in the United States in 1960, Texas Gulf Sulphur and Freeport Sulphur controlled nine. The sulphur obtained from these domes is Frasch sulphur[1] and is superior to that obtained from pyrites (metal sulphides which are roasted to obtain sulphur dioxide), the major alternative source,[2] because the major consumers of sulphur

1. Frasch sulphur is so named because Dr Herman Frasch discovered the process which extracts sulphur from its underground deposits. A description of the process is contained in Federal Trade Commission, (1947, p. 20).

2. In the early 1960s, sulphur recovered from the hydrogen sulfide obtained during the sweetening of sour natural gas has become more important than pyrites as an alternative to Frasch sulphur. Furthermore, recovered sulphur is as good, if not better, in quality as Frasch sulphur.

Table 1 **Relative heights of specific entry barriers in thirteen industries**
(higher numbers denote higher entry barriers)

Industry	Scale-economy barrier	Product-differentiation barrier	Absolute-cost barrier	Capital-requirement barrier
Sulphur	n.a.	II	III	II
Nickel	n.a.	II	III	n.a.
Ethical drugs	I	III	n.a.	II
Flat glass	III	I	n.a.	II
Chewing gum	n.a.	III	II	II
Aluminium reduction	II	I	II	II
Shoe machinery	I	I	III	n.a.
Biscuits	I	II	n.a.	I
Glass containers	I	I	I	n.a.
Baking[a]	I to III	I to III	I	I
Bituminous coal	I	I	II	II
Beer	I	I	n.a.	n.a.
Textile mill products	I	I	I	I

[a] The alternative rankings refer to entry by an independent baker or by a grocery store chain. The former faces high barriers compared to the latter.

(sulphuric acid manufacturers) can derive about 30 per cent more acid from a given weight of elemental sulphur than from pyrite sulphur.

The only other source of Frasch sulphur is Mexico. Pan American Sulphur, which mined 82 per cent of Mexico's supply in 1960, entered the American market through price cutting during the years 1956 to 1958. Since that time, Pan American has behaved as an oligopolist interested in group control of price.

Sulphuric acid manufacturers prefer to receive their sulphur in a molten, rather than solid, state because the former saves the expense of melting the sulphur for pumping to the burners of the acid plants. The dominant sulphur producers have established local distribution terminals which supply either molten or solid sulphur. 'When a user becomes accustomed to using a convenient local supply of molten sulphur, an effective tie between supplier and customer is established' (Brese, 1962, pp. 45 and 47). This suggests that a moderate degree of product differentiation exists.

The facilities which provide molten sulphur are expensive. Brese estimated

However, the major source of sour natural gas is in Canada and the predictions are that recovered sulphur from Canada will only constitute about 10 per cent of United States consumption of sulphur.

that Freeport Sulphur's outlays to establish the requisite facilities exceed $20,000,000, a 'large' capital requirement.[3]

Nickel

Like the sulphur industry, the major barrier to entry into the nickel industry is the control of the natural raw material by the dominant firms. International Nickel (Inco) and Falconbridge account for over 90 per cent of the proved ore reserves of virtually the sole supplier of the United States market, Canada. Buyers have little recourse to alternative supplies because nickel has certain unique properties, particularly its toughness and non-corrosiveness, which isolate it from the competition of substitutes in many uses, notably in the production of stainless steel. Supplies of nickel recovered from scrap are a very minor portion of the market.

Although nickel is a homogeneous good, Inco apparently has a research and marketing organization which represents a formidable obstacle to a new entrant. *Business Week* states that 'Inco is vulnerable on neither product nor services' and that Falconbridge has found it quite difficult to make inroads into Inco's near complete dominance of the United States market.[4]

Ethical drugs

The first difficulty facing a potential newcomer into the ethical drug industry is the patent protection on existing drugs. Entry can occur only by being granted a license or by making some technical advance in the form of a new drug or an improvement in an existing drug. Entry by technical advance introduces the costs and risks associated with research outlays. And even if a new or improved drug is discovered, the entrant must be ready to spend large sums to promote it.[5]

3. Bain has four classes with respect to capital requirements: Very large (generally above 100 million dollars), large (generally 10 to 50 million dollars), moderate (generally 2·5 to 10 million dollars), and small (generally under 2 million dollars) (Bain, 1956, Table 13, pp. 158–9).

Further sources on sulphur: *Chemical Week* (1964); Sheehan (1960).

4. Ore reserves were estimated by taking the figures of the two dominant firms as a percentage of all Canadian firms, as found in Moody's Investors Service; Cobleigh (1956); and *Business Week* (1964).

5. One estimate indicates that, for a single drug, it requires about one million dollars to reach one-half of the physicians with one visit by a salesman. More intensive efforts, say, through additional visits, begin to be very costly (United States Senate, 1961, p. 78).

The emphasis on promotional activities can be indicated by the fact that the five companies included in this study spent, on the average, in 1958, 26 per cent of their sales revenue on advertising, the distribution of samples, and calls by salesmen upon physicians and pharmacists. The outcome of such efforts has been to emphasize brand names, which virtually insures that physicians will not treat the drugs of different companies, even if generically identical, as homogeneous commodities (Table 9, p. 31).

The capital necessary to build an efficient plant is difficult to estimate, but probably falls into Bain's moderate capital-requirement category.[6]

It is not clear how important economies of scale are, but, on balance, they do not appear to be significant. It is true that the average plant size in one major ethical drug category, antibiotics, is large relative to the industry output. However, the costs of production seem to be constant over a wide range of output.[7]

Flat glass

The evidence indicates that the technological transformation in the early 1900s from hand to machine manufacture in the flat glass industry necessitated large-scale plants for efficiency. The following table shows the change in the number of plants producing plate and sheet glass, which account for most of the flat glass output, between 1899 and 1935.

The average plant size is still very large. In 1960, Pittsburgh Plate operated four sheet and four plate glass plants. Libby–Owens–Ford operated one sheet and three plate glass plants and one which produced both plate and sheet glass. Since these firms account for about 90 per cent of the value of plate glass production and 65 per cent of the value of sheet glass output, each of their plants accounts for about 10 per cent of the value of the industry output. This information does not tell us what the shape of the plant-scale curve is, but Table 2 suggests that it is probably

Table 2 **Number of plants and total production of plate and sheet glass, selected years, 1899 to 1935**

Year	Plants (Number) Plate glass	Sheet glass	Production Plate glass (square feet)	Sheet glass boxes (50 square feet)
1899	16	100	16,884,000	4,341,000
1925	16	42	117,369,000	11,343,000
1929	8	—	118,670,136	—
1935	6	13	180,383,801	8,135,108

Source: United States Tariff Commission, (1937, Table 12, p. 49 and Table 37, p. 96).

6. One small drug manufacturer indicated that an investment of five million dollars would allow him to enter the production, assuming the research was done, of prednisone and prednisolone, two corticosteroids. On the other hand, penicillin plants cost as much as 16 million dollars to build in the early 1950s.

7. In 1956, 3,081,373 pounds of antibiotics were produced by nineteen plants. Efficient size of plant, though, appears to be variable over a range of output (Federal Trade Commission, 1958, Table 9, pp. 74–75, Table 21, pp. 98 and 118).

Other sources for the drug industry are Comanor (1964); Steele (1964); United States Senate, (1961).

steep enough to make the minimum optimal plant size very large relative to the industry output.[8]

Since plate glass and sheet glass are largely sold to manufacturers, there is little scope for much product differentiation.

The capital required for a plate glass plant is estimated to run 45 to 50 million dollars, while for a sheet glass plant, the amount runs 12 to 15 million dollars. These are 'large' capital requirements.[9]

Chewing gum

The major barrier to entry into chewing gum appears to be product differentiation. Wrigley spent, on the average, better than 8 per cent of its sales revenue on advertising from 1952 to 1960. American Chicle, between 1954 and 1960, averaged about 7 per cent of its sales revenue on advertising expenditures. Both of these percentages exceed the proportion of sales revenue spent by the dominant cigarette firms, a market where product differentiation is very important (see Henle, 1956; Jackson, 1961; *Printers' Ink*, *Advertisers' Guide to Marketing*, 1957, p. 73; 1959, p. 158; 1961, p. 343; 1963, p. 386).[10]

In addition to product differentiation, one source suggests that technical know-how and the cost of machinery also block the way of the potential entrant. Since no quantitative magnitude could be attached to the capital requirement for machinery or the degree of technical know-how involved, the absolute-cost and capital-requirement barriers were given a moderate ranking.

Substantial barriers to entry
Aluminium reduction

The ranking of aluminium reduction as having substantial barriers to entry presumes that vertical integration is not required for entry. If it is, then aluminium reduction belongs in the very high barrier class.[11]

8. Bain (1956, pp. 103–4) classifies scale economies as very important if the minimum optimal size plant or firm supplies 10 per cent or more of the market's output and if unit costs rise significantly at less than optimal scale. Moderately important scale economies occur if 4 or 5 per cent of the market's output is required for optimal size and if unit costs rise significantly at leass than optimal scale. Scale economies are unimportant if only 1 or 2 per cent of the market's output is produced at minimum optimal scale and the scale curve is relatively flat below minimum optimal size.

9. Sources for the flat glass industry are Loehwing (1963); United States Senate (1960); United States Tariff Commission (1937).

10. The figures for advertising are understated to some degree because they include only national space and time and do not include all media in some years. Sales revenue figures are from Moody's Investors Service.

11. Aluminium reduction probably ranks near the top of the substantial barrier-to-entry class because, if vertical integration is necessary, the scale-economy and capital-

Efficient plant size obtains at about 3 per cent of the industry's capacity. Although no estimate was made of the cost curve's shape below minimum optimal scale, this percentage borders on the moderately important category of scale economies. Production differentiation is unimportant in this industry.

The capital necessary to build an efficient plant is large, running at about 63 million dollars. In addition, the established firms have lower costs because new capacity is more expensive than older capacity and the latter has cheap hydropower to use (Peck, 1961, chapter 10).

Shoe machinery

The major cause of United Shoe Machinery's almost complete domination of the shoe machinery industry until 1954 was the employment of certain market practices which made it very difficult for any competitor, actual or potential, to win business. Only if a competitive machine were much better or much cheaper than a United machine would a shoe manufacturer find it worthwhile to pay the substantial costs of 'untying' from United. Therefore, the absolute-cost barrier was given the highest notation.

Economies of scale and product differentiation appear to be relatively unimportant.[12]

An antitrust case in 1954 resulted in the prohibition of many of the entry-inhibiting practices and, therefore, considerably reduced the importance of the absolute-cost barrier ranking. Before the antitrust case, then, shoe machinery might have belonged in the very high barrier group, whereas, after the case, the moderate-to-low barrier class would be appropriate. A compromise was made and shoe machinery was placed in the substantial barrier category (Kaysen, 1956).

Biscuits

Bureau of the Census data on the distribution of plant sizes in the biscuit industry, according to the number of employees, show no tendency for the smallest classes to disappear between 1947 and 1958. Since the plants in these classes account, on the average, for less than one per cent of the industry value added in 1958, economies of scale appear to be unimportant

requirement barriers would be raised to a 'III' rating. The major study of this industry in the postwar period does not reach a conclusion on the necessity of vertical integration.

12. The evidence is thin, but Carl Kaysen's examination of economies in production, distribution, service, and research do not indicate very important scale economies. United enjoys some product differentiation by virtue of its full line of machines and its marketing of supplies which are used with the machines. Apparently these advantages do not give United much edge over potential competitors (Kaysen, 1956, pp. 92–8 and pp. 229–32).

(Bureau of the Census, 1947, Table 4, p. 115; 1954a, Table 4, p. 20E–11; 1958a, Table 4, p. 20E–12).

Between 1951 and 1959, National Biscuit and Sunshine Biscuits spent about 2·3 per cent and 1·4 per cent of their sales revenue on advertising, respectively. These percentages understate their promotional efforts, however, since they do not take into account the expenditure on store displays and other kinds of promotional activity. *Barron's* reports that National Biscuit and Sunshine Biscuits invest closer to 5 per cent and 3 per cent of their sales revenue on advertising and promotion, respectively (Loehwing, 1957).

No precise estimate of capital requirements is possible. *Business Week* cites United Biscuit's new plant in Denver, Colorado as being modern and efficient and as having cost 9·5 million dollars, a moderate capital requirement (Loehwing, 1962).

The biscuit industry appears to rank near the top of the substantial barrier class. It does not make the very high barrier class, in the author's judgement, because its expenditure on sales promotion does not quite reach the proportion of sales revenue characteristic of industries with significant product differentiation (*Printers' Ink Advertisers' Guide to Marketing*, 1957, pp. 91, 97; 1959, pp. 178, 187; 1960, pp. 328, 337; 1961, pp. 360, 367; Moody's Investors' Service).

Moderate-to-low barriers to entry
Glass containers

Economies of scale do not seem to be important in the glass container industry (Bishop, 1950). Bureau of the Census data on the distribution of establishments by number of employees show no tendency for smaller plants to disappear (1947, Table 4, p. 494; 1954b, Table 4, p. 32A–7; 1958b, Table 4, p. 32A–10).[13]

Glass containers are principally producers goods. This permits little room for product differentiation.

The absolute-cost barrier, although once important, is so no longer.[14]

13. Between 1954 and 1958, there was an increase of fifteen establishments in the industry. The largest increase, seven, occurred in the 250–499 employee range. The average plant size in this class accounted for slightly less than 1 per cent of the industry value added in 1958. This suggests that the minimum optimal plant size is quite small.

The increase in establishments did not occur because of the reclassification of establishments from some other industry into the glass container industry. Both the primary product specialization and coverage ratios, which measure the degree of homogeneity of the industry's output, were nearly equal to 1·00 in 1954 and 1958. For a discussion of the measures of homogeneity, see United States Senate (1962, pp. 1–6).

14. From World War I until 1946, two firms, Owens-Illinois and Hartford-Empire, controlled, through patents, the technology of the industry. An antitrust suit ended this control, thereby removing a major barrier to entry into the industry.

Baking

The discussion of specific barriers to entry into the baking industry refers to the white bread segments of the industry, its most important branch. For entrants other than grocery chains, economies of scale are a very important barrier to entry, largely because the relevant markets are small relative to the optimal size plant.[15] The reason why grocery chains do not face such a high scale-economy barrier is that they can efficiently serve market areas much larger than independent bakers – 400 to 500 miles versus 150 miles.[16]

The leading firms spend about 4 per cent of their sales revenue on advertising, which apparently influences preferences.[17] The dominant firms also seem to have established preferential agreements with many grocery stores regarding shelf space and prominent positions for their displays. The advantages gained in these respects do not seriously hinder grocery chains since they control the shelf and the display space in their own outlets and typically charge prices for their private brands which are lower than those of established brands, thus offsetting some of the effectiveness of the large independent bakers' advertising.

Inputs and technical know-how are easily available to all potential newcomers. The capital requirement for an efficient plant appears to be small, between one and two million dollars (Slater, 1956; Walsh and Evans, 1963).

Bituminous coal

A study of the midwestern coal region finds that an underground mine exhausts economies of scale at around 500,000 tons. In 1959, this region produced over 90 million tons, of which approximately 37 million tons came from underground mines. The optimally efficient underground mine size, then, is a little over 1 per cent of the underground output.

The strip mine has a larger optimal scale, estimated to be around 5 per cent of the strip mine output, about 53 million tons in the midwestern

15. 'For example, in the Omaha market with 400,000 to 500,000 people, the required market share for entry at optimum levels of efficiency would be roughly 70–90 per cent. Given the further condition that five operating plants share the bulk of that market and operate at varying levels of under-capacity such that any two of them with nearly full plant utilization could supply the entire market, the height of the entry barrier is further raised. . . . For markets with higher or increasing population, the barrier may be somewhat less, but it is still a significant deterrent to entry at optimum levels of efficiency,' (Walsh and Evans, 1963, p. 43).

16. This is due to economies in distribution which permit full exploitation of production economies. The independent bakers' method of distribution runs into decreasing returns before the increasing returns in production are exhausted. These decreasing returns outweigh the gains from the continued expansion of production.

17. According to one consumer survey, advertising was the principal reason given for brand preferences (Walsh and Evans, 1963, p. 37).

region in 1959. For both kinds of mines, the cost curve seems to be fairly flat for some distance.

Established firms enjoy little advantage from product differentiation since coal is an industrial good. The established firms do enjoy a moderate advantage in the absolute-cost category. Although only 7 per cent of midwestern reserves are controlled by the top twenty firms, these firms control virtually all of the highest quality reserves. This is particularly true of strip reserves, an important consideration because strip mines operate at lower average costs than underground mines. Nevertheless, the absolute-cost category did not get the highest barrier ranking because there exists a strong possibility that the poorer reserves may become very valuable under the impact of the electric utilities' changing locational requirements.

A one million ton per year mine, which is larger than necessary for an efficient underground mine, requires an investment of eight million dollars. However, the optimal strip mine (about four million tons a year) would require around thirty million dollars (Moyer, 1964, especially chapters 5 and 6).

Beer

Bureau of the Census data on establishments in the beer and ale industry, distributed according to the number of employees, show a decline in the number of breweries with less than 500–999 employees between 1947 and 1958. The survivor technique suggests that this size has become the minimum optimal size. The average value-added of plants within this category in 1958 was 1 per cent of the industry value-added. This percentage is sufficiently low to suggest that economies of scale are unimportant (Bureau of the Census, 1947; Table 4, p. 132; 1954a, Table 4, p. 20G–7; 1958a, Table 4, p. 20G–11).[18]

Product differentiation does not appear to be significant. One consumer survey indicates that beer-drinkers do not show a marked preference for nationally advertised beers (Cobleigh, 1960; Grayser, 1961, pp. 136–41).

Textile mill products

Two estimates of the percentage of industry capacity accounted for by optimally efficient mills in coarse yarn and in fine cotton woven goods suggest that economies of scale are quite unimportant in the textile mill products industry. In coarse yarn, the minimum optimal size occurs at around 0·04 per cent of industry capacity. In fine cotton woven goods, the

18. A recent study concludes that the minimum optimal size brewery produces about 1,500,000 barrels per year. In 1961, 95 million barrels were produced, meaning that the size of brewery obtaining the lowest unit costs accounted for approximately 1·5 per cent of the annual production in that year (Horowitz and Horowitz, 1965, pp. 129–153).

percentage is about 0·3 per cent. More generally, small plants dominate the distribution of plants by employee-size categories and there seems to be no tendency for the small plants to disappear in favor of larger plants.[19]

Textile mill products in finished form are sold to retailers who are experts regarding the quality of the product which they are buying, permitting little opportunity for product differentiation.

Neither important patents covering the industry's technology nor tight control over raw materials exist. One economist, while making no quantitative estimate, indicates that the capital requirement is low (Weiss, 1961, chapter 4; Whitney, 1958).

19. The distribution of plants by the number of employees was compared for all the four-digit groups used in this study between 1947 and 1954, except for synthetic broad woven fabrics and converters. Bureau of the Census, (1947), Table 4, p. 159 and Table 4, p. 173; vol. II, part I, (1954a), Table 4, p. 22 B–10 and Table 4, p. 22 A–6.

References

BAIN, J. S. (1956), *Barriers to New Competition*, Harvard University Press.

BISHOP, R. L. (1950), 'The glass container industry', in W. Adams (ed.), *The Structure of American Industry*, Macmillan Co.

BRESE, W. G. (1962), *An Analysis of the Sulphur Industry in Alberta*, Edmonton, Canada.

BUREAU OF THE CENSUS (1947), *Census of Manufactures*, vol. 2, US Department of Commerce.

BUREAU OF THE CENSUS (1954a), *Census of Manufactures*, vol. 2, part 1, US Department of Commerce.

BUREAU OF THE CENSUS (1954b), *Census of Manufactures*, vol. 2, part 2, US Department of Commerce.

BUREAU OF THE CENSUS (1958a), *Census of Manufactures*, vol. 2, part 1, US Department of Commerce.

BUREAU OF THE CENSUS (1958b), *Census of Manufactures*, vol. 2, part 2, US Department of Commerce.

Business Week (1964), 'Mining new markets for nickel', 5 September.

Chemical Week (1964), 'Sulfur', 12 September.

COBLEIGH, I. V. (1956), Canadian nickel: investor slanted notes on this strategic metal', *Commercial and Financial Chronicle*, 9 August.

COBLEIGH, I. V. (1960), 'Brewing earning power', *Commercial and Financial Chronicle*, 15 December.

COMANOR, W. S. (1964), 'Research and competitive product differentiation in the pharmaceutical industry in the United States', *Economica*, vol. 31, pp. 372–84.

FEDERAL TRADE COMMISSION (1947), *Report on the Sulphur Industry and International Cartels*, Washington.

FEDERAL TRADE COMMISSION (1958), *Economic Report on Anti-biotics Manufacture*, Washington.

GRAYSER, S. A. (1961), 'Case of the befuddled brewers', *Harvard bus. Rev.*, March.

HENLE, F. (1956), 'Snap in chewing gum', *Barron's*, 28 May, pp. 13–15.

HOROWITZ, I., and HOROWITZ, A. R. (1965), 'Firms in a declining market: the brewing case', *J. indust. Econ.*, vol. 13, pp. 129–53.

JACKSON, W. S. (1961), 'American Chicle Co.', *Bankers' Monthly*, 15 March, pp. 46–9.

KAYSEN, C. (1956), *United States v. United Shoe Machinery Corporation*, Harvard University Press.

LOEHWING, D. A. (1957), 'The biscuit makers', *Barron's*, 16 December.

LOEHWING, D. A. (1962), 'Baking an assortment in one cake', *Business Week*, 29 December.

LOEHWING, D. A. (1963), 'The glass makers', *Barron's*, 11 March.

MOODY'S INVESTOR'S SERVICE, *Moody's Industrial Manual*.

MOYER, R. (1964), *Competition in the Mid-Western Coal Industry*, Harvard University Press.

PECK, M. J. (1961), *Competition in the Aluminium Industry, 1945–1958*, Harvard University Press.

Printers' Ink: Advertiser's Guide to Marketing, 1957, 1959, 1960, 1961, 1963.

SHEEHAN, R. (1960), 'The "Little Mothers" and Pan American Sulphur', *Fortune*, July.

SLATER, C. C. (1956), *Baking in America, Market Organization and Competition*, vol. 2, Northwestern University Press.

STEELE, H. (1964), 'Patent restrictions and price competition in the ethical drugs industry', *J. indust. Econ.*, pp. 198–223.

US Senate (1960), *Studies of Dual Distribution: The Flat Glass Industry Report*, Government Printing Office.

US Senate (1961), *Administered Prices, Drugs, Report*, Government Printing Office.

US Senate (1962), *Concentration Ratios in Manufacturing*, Subcommittee on Antitrust and Monopoly, Government Printing Office.

US Tariff Commission (1937), *Flat Glass and Related Products*, Report no. 123, 2nd series, Government Printing Office.

WALSH, R. G. and EVANS, B. M. (1963), *Economics of Change in Market Structure, Conduct and Performance: The Baking Industry 1947–58*, Lincoln, Nebraska.

WEISS, L. W. (1961), *Economics and American Industry*, Wiley.

WHITNEY, R. S. (1958), *Antitrust Policies*, vol. 1, The Twentieth Century Fund.

6 William S. Comanor and Thomas A. Wilson

Advertising as an Entry Barrier

Extract from William S. Comanor and Thomas A. Wilson, 'Advertising, market structure and performance', *Review of Economics and Statistics*, vol. 49, 1967, pp. 423–40.

. . . The relationship between advertising outlays and product differentiation is important for an evaluation of the competitive effects of advertising because the former reflects the policies adopted by individual firms, while the latter is a dimension of market structure.

The degree of product differentiation in a market is measured by the cross elasticities of demand and supply which exist among competing products. Low cross elasticities of demand between these products indicate that buyers prefer the products or brands of particular sellers and will not switch in significant numbers in response to small differences in price. Low cross elasticities of supply, on the other hand, signify that firms are unable to imitate the products of their rivals sufficiently well to eliminate these consumer preferences. While cross elasticities between the products of existing producers affect the character of the rivalry which exists between them, cross elasticities between the products of established firms and potential entrants influence the height of entry barriers posed by product differentiation.[1]

Product differentiation reflects two sets of factors: the basic characteristics of products within the market, and the present and past policies of established firms with respect to advertising, product design, servicing, and distribution. On the demand side, products are more likely to be differentiable when buyers are relatively uninformed about the relative merits of existing products. This is particularly important for differentiation achieved via advertising. On the supply side, differentiation is more likely where the products of rivals cannot easily be imitated and where new entrants have difficulties in producing products which are similar to those sold by successfully established firms. In producer goods industries, successful imitation requires investment in product design and adequate service facilities. In

---

1. It is important to distinguish product differentiation from product variety. The steel industry, for example, produces a great variety of products which are sold to knowledgeable buyers, but product differentiation is minimal. In contrast, the cigarette industry offers a smaller variety of products, but product differentiation – based largely on extensive advertising – is great (Bain, 1956, pp. 127–9).

consumer goods industries, successful imitation may require investment in advertising as well.

It is noteworthy that Bain, in his authoritative examination of product differentiation in twenty manufacturing industries, found advertising to be the most important source of product differentiation in the consumer goods industries in his sample. Distribution policies are also important where forward integration is prevalent, while customer services and product design play contributing but relatively minor roles.

For typical consumer goods industries, then, a persistently high level of advertising expenditures can be viewed in two ways:

1. If firms behave reasonably, high levels of advertising indicate that the product is differentiable. In this sense, advertising is a symptom of differentiation.
2. The high level of advertising is itself an important determinant of the level of differentiation which is realized by established firms vis-à-vis potential entrants. In this sense, advertising is a source of product differentiation.

Provided that firms act reasonably, observed advertising expenditures provide a useful measure of the extent of product differentiation. We write reasonably rather than rationally since, in an oligopolistic market, rational policies are not unambiguous. What is rational policy for the group acting in concert is not rational policy for the individual firm expecting to gain a march on its rivals. It is quite possible, moreover, that rivalry via advertising among established firms is carried to the point of diminishing returns in terms of group profit rates. However, even in this case, the result of extensive advertising rivalry may be to permit the achievement of higher future profits for the group by raising entry barriers.

Although advertising is only one source of product differentiation, it is especially important in a number of consumer goods industries where it has a strong direct impact on entry barriers (Bain, 1956, pp. 114–43). In these industries, new entrants generally are forced to sell at a price below the established brands or else incur heavy selling costs. This explains the phenomenon of unbranded products selling at prices substantially below those of highly advertised products even where there is little 'real' difference between them. On this account, established firms can set prices above existing cost levels, including advertising and other selling expenses, without inducing entry.

Product differentiation via advertising affects entry barriers in three ways, each of which is analogous to the other determinants of overall entry barriers. First, high prevailing levels of advertising create additional costs for new entrants which exist at all levels of output. Because of buyer inertia and loyalty, more advertising messages per prospective customer must be supplied to induce brand switching as compared with repeat buying. Since the market which prospective entrants must penetrate is made up largely of consumers who have purchased existing products, advertising costs per customer for new entrants will be higher than those of existing firms who are maintaining existing market positions. Moreover, the costs of penetration are likely to increase as output expands and customers more inert or loyal need to be reached.[2] This effect of advertising creates an absolute cost advantage for established producers, since they need not incur penetration costs.

In addition, the effect of advertising on firm revenues is subject to economies of scale which result from the increasing effectiveness of advertising messages per unit of output as well as from decreasing costs for each advertising message purchased. The first source of economies will exist whenever the effect of advertising on consumer decisions is sufficiently important that a threshold level of advertising is required for a firm to stay in the market and maintain its current market share. In such a situation, larger firms have the advantage of being able to spread this cost over more units of output and thereby spend less per unit sold. This advantage creates economies of scale at the firm level, since an established firm does not have to spend twice as much on advertising to maintain a market share which is twice that of a rival. Higher output levels are associated with lower unit costs.[3] As a result, smaller firms, including most entrants, are placed at a strong disadvantage.[4]

Economies of scale in advertising also result when the cost per advertising message declines as the number of messages supplied increases. An increased use of some forms of advertising leads to a lower cost per message, and available evidence suggests that this is very important for advertising on national television and in national magazines.[5]

2. These penetration costs depend on past as well as current advertising outlays by established firms. The importance of past outlays is examined by Palda who concludes that 'distributed lag models both give a better fit to the Pinkham data and forecast better than the models which do not incorporate lagged effects' (1964).

3. In the automobile industry, for example, the two smaller firms during the 1950s were forced to spend more than twice as much on advertising per car sold as did either Ford or General Motors. Between 1954 and 1957 Studebaker and American Motors spent annually on national advertising approximately $64.04 and $57.89, respectively, per automobile sold while G.M. spent $26.56 per unit and Ford spent $27.22 per unit. Chrysler was in an intermediate position, spending $47.76 per unit (Weiss, 1961, p. 342).

4. This result occurs *within* the relevant market. When a firm in a regionally segmented market expands its national market share by moving into new geographic areas, unit advertising costs do not decline.

5. The extent of discounts given to large advertisers is documented in *Federal Trade Commission vs. The Procter & Gamble Company*, (1966) Brief for the Federal Trade Commission in the Supreme Court of the United States, pp. 12–13.

If advertising in a particular industry is characterized by economies of scale for either of these reasons, an entrant will suffer an additional cost disadvantage if he enters at a relatively small scale. If he enters at a scale sufficient to realize available economies of scale in advertising, however, his actions are likely to influence the price or advertising policies of the established firms. The possible reactions of established firms increase the costs and risks of entry.

Finally, if economies of scale exist either in production or in advertising, the need to obtain funds for advertising will give rise to capital requirements over and above those needed for physical plant and equipment. Furthermore, this investment in market penetration will involve a particularly risky use of funds since it does not generally create tangible assets which can be resold in the event of failure. The required rate of return on such capital will therefore be high.

These various effects are illustrated diagrammatically in Figure 1. Curve APC represents average production costs for established and prospective firms, and MESP is minimum efficient scale in production. Curve AAC describes average advertising costs for existing firms as well as for new entrants after they have become established. It denotes unit advertising outlays which are required in order to maintain a firm's market position and to preserve a given volume of sales once it has been established. This will depend on both the total level of advertising outlays and their distribution among established firms, and therefore, it describes prospective

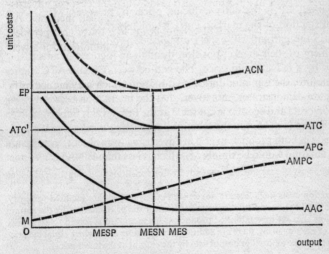

Figure 1 Advertising and entry barriers

advertising costs for entrants only if existing firms do not react to any loss of market share. To the extent that they do respond, required advertising outlays will be higher. Curve ATC, the vertical sum of these two curves, represents average total costs for established firms.[6] MES denotes the minimum efficient scale in both production and advertising for an established firm with a given market share.

In addition, curve AMPC describes average market penetration costs for new entrants. Penetration costs represent an investment in establishing a market position and therefore depend on the opportunity cost of capital as well as on total penetration expenditures.[7] This schedule therefore denotes the required rate of return on capital invested in market penetration times the total expenditure required to establish a given volume of sales, all divided by the number of units sold. The figure illustrates the case where average penetration costs rise throughout the relevant range of output. This assumes that the growing difficulty involved in winning over customers with stronger preferences for the products of established firms, reinforced by rising required rates of return as the absolute amount of capital required for penetration increases with the scale of entry, is not fully offset by economies of scale in advertising or by bandwagon effects for the new entrant's products.

Curve ACN represents average costs, including penetration costs, for new entrants, and MESN is the most efficient scale for entry if the reactions of established producers are neglected. From this, it follows that EP is the *minimum* price at which entry will occur. If MESN is a negligible fraction of the market, EP is the entry-inducing price. If, however, MESN is a significant fraction of the market, entry is unlikely to occur even at price EP because the entrant will expect established producers to contest the encroachment of their market position through an increase in advertising outlays or by a reduction in price. The gap between EP and ATC′ represents, therefore, the minimum price–cost margin which may induce entry.

This figure demonstrates, moreover, that the interaction between rising penetration costs and economies of scale at the firm level is important even if no allowance is made for the reactions of existing producers. If economies of scale in both production and in advertising were absent, the relevant price–cost margin would be simply M, which is less than EP–ATC′.

6. For simplicity, we assume here that advertising constitutes the only form of selling expense.

7. Penetration costs include extra advertising outlays which are required for entry. These outlays will represent total penetration costs if the price charged by the entrant is the same as that set by established producers. If the entrant is forced to set a price below that of existing firms, there are additional penetration costs which equal the price differential times the amount of output sold by the entrant at the lower price.

References

BAIN, J. S. (1956), *Barriers to New Competition*, Harvard University Press.
PALDA, K. S. (1964), *The Measurement of Cumulative Advertising Effects*, Prentice-Hall.
WEISS, L. W. (1961), *Economics and American Industry*, Wiley.

7 Edwin Mansfield

Entry, Exit and Growth of Firms

Edwin Mansfield, 'Entry, Gibrat's law, innovation, and the growth of firms',
American Economic Review, vol. 52, 1962, pp. 1023–51.

Because there have been so few econometric studies of the birth, growth
and death of firms, we lack even crude answers to the following basic
questions regarding the dynamic processes governing an industry's structure. What are the quantitative effects of various factors on the rates of
entry and exit? How well can the growth of firms be represented by Gibrat's
law of proportionate effect? What have been the effects of successful
innovations on a firm's growth rate? What determines the amount of
mobility within an industry's size structure?[1]

This paper provides some tentative answers to these questions. First, it
constructs some simple models to estimate the effects of an industry's
capital requirements, profitability, and other such factors on its entry and
exit rates. Second, it investigates how well Gibrat's law of proportionate
effect can represent the growth of firms in each of the industries for which
we have appropriate data. Although this law has played a prominent role
in models designed to explain the size distribution of firms, it has been
tested only a few times against data for very large firms. Third, we estimate
the difference in growth rate between firms that carried out significant
innovations and other firms of comparable initial size. The results help to
measure the importance of successful innovation as a cause of inter-firm
differences in growth rates, and they shed new light on the rewards for such
innovations. Fourth, the paper presents and tests a simple model to explain
inter-industry and temporal differences in the extent to which firms change
relative positions in the size distribution.

1. With regard to the effects of various factors on the rates of entry and exit, there has
been considerable theorizing (Bain, 1956; Hoggatt, 1959; Marshall, 1916; Triffin, 1941)
and a few relevant empirical studies (Bain, 1956; Churchill, 1959), but there has been
no systematic attempt to estimate the quantitative effect of various factors. With regard
to the growth of firms, there have been several studies of Gibrat's law (Ferguson, 1960;
Hart and Prais, 1956; Hymer and Pashigian, 1959; Simon and Bonini, 1958) based only
on the largest firms (one of which dealt in part with the determinants of the amount of
mobility) and an analysis (Collins and Preston, 1961) of the size structure of the largest
firms in the economy. There are no previous studies (as far as I know) of the effects of
innovation on a firm's growth rate.

1 Determinants of rates of entry and exit

A Entry, profitability, and capital requirements

Entry can be defined as the net change in the number of firms in an industry. Alternatively, it can be defined as the extent to which new owners of productive facilities become established in an industry either through the construction of new plants or the purchase of existing firms. Each concept has its own set of uses. The first concept is useful in analyzing problems regarding market structure and industrial concentration, since the number of firms in an industry is a significant factor in such problems. The second concept is useful in measuring the ease with which new entrepreneurs can become established in an industry and the extent to which they do so. For this purpose, it would be misleading to ignore those that entered by purchasing existing concerns.[2]

The second of these concepts is employed in the present subsection; the first will be employed in the next one. Regardless of which concept is used, perhaps the most obvious measure of the amount of entry into the ith industry during the tth period is E_{it}' – the number of firms that entered during the period as a proportion of the number of firms in the industry at the beginning of the period. But the available data force us to use E_{it} – the number of firms that entered during the period and survived until the end as a proportion of the original number of firms. Since E_{it}' and E_{it} should be highly correlated, this discrepancy is probably not too important for our purposes.[3]

2. Of course, the second concept of entry is somewhat slippery, since it is sometimes difficult to define and detect a significant change in the ownership of a firm. This is particularly true in the case of large companies. In practice, we generally use changes in company names as indicators of changes in ownership (see the Appendix), but this is very crude. This problem also occurs in the next subsection and in Sections 2 and 3.

A third definition of entry would be useful for some purposes. This would measure the number of firms that entered with new plant, regardless of the number of firms that scrapped their plant during the period. That is, it would be a gross measure of entry. Bain's discussion (1956, p. 4ff.) generally runs in these terms. The available data do not permit us to measure this gross concept of entry. See the Appendix.

3. Other measures might be used: e.g., the absolute number of entrants. But the establishment of two new firms would seem to mean one thing if there previously were two firms and something else if there previously were 100. Moreover, one would expect that ease of entry would be directly related to the number of firms in the industry (Oxenfeldt, 1943). Although it is somewhat arbitrary, it seems sensible to follow the Department of Commerce's procedure (Churchill, 1959) and to normalize in this way for the original number of firms.

The size of the entrants – as well as their number – might be very important for some problems. Although we ignore this aspect of the problem, it could be included fairly easily. Note too that, in comparisons of the values of E_{it}, differences in length of the period might be important. Although we tried to obtain periods of equal length, this

Letting C_{it} be the investment required to establish a firm of minimum efficient size in the ith industry during the tth period and letting Π_{lt} be the average ratio of the rate of return in the ith industry to that in all manufacturing during this period, we assume that

$$E_{it} = f(\Pi_{it}, C_{it}, \ldots). \qquad 1$$

Increases in Π_{it} – because of their presumed effect on profit expectations – make entry more attractive, and increases in C_{it} make it more difficult. Thus, E_{it} should be directly related to Π_{lt} and inversely related to C_{lt}.[4]

More specifically, since the effects of these variables are likely to be multiplicative, we assume that

$$E_{it} = a_0 \Pi_{it}^{a_1} C_{it}^{-a_2} Z_{it}, \qquad 2$$

where Z_{lt} is a random error term and the a's are presumed to be positive. To estimate the a's, data are needed on E_{lt}, Π_{lt}, and C_{lt}. Table 1 shows the values of E_{it} during various periods in the history of the steel, petroleum refining, rubber tire, and automobile industries. It also contains corresponding estimates of Π_{lt} and C_{lt}, the latter being based on Bain's figures (1956) and the assumption that the ratio of the minimum efficient size to the average size of firm remained constant over time in each industry.

---

was not always feasible. However, when introduced into equations 3, 7, and 16, this factor has no significant effect on E_{lt}, R_{it}, or P_{lt}. See Section 4 A.

Having only the transition matrices in the Appendix, we had no choice, but to use E_{lt}. So long as the survival rate for new firms is relatively independent of E_{lt}' or positively correlated with it, E_{lt} should be a reasonably good surrogate. Moreover, if one believes that we should only be concerned with entrants that survive for some specified length of time, E_{lt} may be closer to what we want then E_{lt}'. Finally, E_{lt} has the advantage that it equals $D_{lt} + R_l$ (see Section 1 B).

4. As a first approximation, it may not be too unreasonable to assume that the profit expectation of potential entrants during the period is a function of Π_{lt}. But many other factors are obviously of importance – the variability of the industry's profits during the period, the absolute level of profits, the probability that new processes or related new products will be developed, the outlook with regard to factor prices, etc. Note too that C_{lt} may vary, depending on whether the entrant is an existing firm in a related industry or an entirely new enterprise; that C_{lt} should be measured in real terms; and that the effect of C_{lt} will depend on the ease with which a given amount of capital can be obtained.

Equation 2 should be much more effective in explaining changes in the number of new firms with new plant than changes in the numbers of firms that are bought. For example, if Π_{lt} is relatively high, relatively few firms may be sold. But, since new firms with new plant are a large percentage of the total number of entrants included in E_{lt} (about two-thirds of the total in recent years, according to Churchill, 1959), equation 2 is a reasonable first approximation. (However, one might argue from this that the error term is additive.) Unfortunately, the data are such that one cannot treat the entrants with new plant separately from those that bought existing plant.

Although these data are very rough they should be useful first approximations.[5]

Taking logarithms of both sides of equation **2** and using these data to obtain least-squares estimates of the a's, we find that

$$\ln E_{it} = 0{\cdot}49 + 1{\cdot}15 \ln \Pi_{it} - 0{\cdot}27 \ln C_{it} \qquad 3$$
$$\qquad\quad (0{\cdot}43) \qquad\quad (0{\cdot}14)$$

where the quantities in parentheses are standard errors and $\ln Z_{it}$ is omitted. As one would expect, there is considerable variation about equation **3**, the coefficient of correlation (corrected for degrees of freedom) being about $0{\cdot}70$ (Figure 1). The residuals reflect the effects of differences in the capacity of a firm of minimum efficient size as a per cent of the total market, availability of raw materials, and other important factors that are omitted.[6]

The estimates of a_1 and a_2 have the expected signs and are both statistically significant ($0{\cdot}05$ level). Because of the small number of observations, they have fairly large standard errors, and because of errors in the exogenous variables and the probable effects of $\ln E_{it}$ on $\ln \Pi_{it}$ (cf. section 4 A), they are probably biased somewhat toward zero. But despite these limitations, they shed new light on the effects of Π_{it} and C_{it} on E_{it}. For example, if the bias is in the expected direction, one can be reasonably sure that the average value of E_{it} would increase by at least 60 per cent if Π_{it} doubled and that it would decrease at least 7 per cent if C_{it} doubled. Lower bounds of this sort are obviously useful.[7]

5. The Appendix describes the data on entry for each industry and explains how the data regarding C_{it} and Π_{it} were derived. It also points out the difficulties in these measures. I suspect that the true values of C_{it} (and $\tilde{S}_{it}/\overline{S}_{it}$) for petroleum in 1921–7 and 1927–37 were substantially lower than those shown in Table 1 and that the true values of C_{it} (and $\tilde{S}_{it}/\overline{S}_{it}$) for steel in 1916–26 and 1926–35 were somewhat higher than those shown in Table 1. Errors of this sort, assuming they are randomly distributed, are taken into account in the analysis below.

6. For an elementary account of some of the factors omitted here, see Papandreau and Wheeler, 1954. For a discussion of the automobile industry, see Vatter, 1952. Of course, the influence of the Second World War (with controls of various sorts) should not be overlooked either.

7. The tests described above are one-tailed tests – which are appropriate here. Our primary purpose is to estimate the effects of Π_{it} and C_{it} on E_{it}, rather than to see if they have any effect. They almost certainly do have an effect but research to date provides little or no clue regarding its magnitude.

For a discussion of the biases due to measurement errors and least-squares, see Section 4 A and note 31 in particular. If there were no bias, the likelihood that the lower bounds in the test would be exceeded would equal $0{\cdot}85$. Given the probable bias, it should be much higher.

The percentage change in the average value of E_{it}, given a doubling of Π_{it}, is $2^{a_1}-1$. The effect of doubling C_{it} is given by substituting $-a_2$ for a_1. Of course, one could get lower bounds for the effects of a 10, 20, ... per cent change in Π_{it} and C_{it} in exactly the same way.

Table 1 **Values of exogenous and endogenous variables in equations 3, 7, and 16, steel, petroleum, rubber tire, and automobile industries, selected periods**[a]

Industry and time period	E_{it}	Π_{it}	C_{it}	R_{it}	V_{it}^2	$\bar{S}_{it}/\hat{S}_{it}$	P_{it}	A_{it}	n_{it}
Steel									
1916–26	0·57	1·38	228	0·20	18	1·15	0·20	271	90
1926–35	0·08	0·38	214	0·46	20	1·15	0·17	281	122
1935–45	0·20	0·73	423	0·16	12	1·15	0·17	290	76
1945–54	0·17	0·77	465	0·15	9	1·15	0·26	300	81
Petroleum									
1921–27	0·66	0·84	93	0·59	11	0·17	0·36	62	314
1927–37	0·46	0·60	138	0·65	13	0·17	0·42	68	335
1937–47	0·78	0·82	231	0·42	15	0·17	0·35	78	269
1947–57	0·25	1·01	238	0·71	21	0·17	0·26	88	366
Tires									
1937–45	0·45	0·84	11	0·31	8	1·18	0·30	41	49
1945–52	0·68	0·88	22	0·46	10	1·18	0·26	49	57
Autos									
1939–49	0·20	0·94[b]	316	0·20	3	1·00	—	—	—
1949–59	0·10	0·36[b]	575	0·50	4	1·00	—	—	—

[a] Symbols: E_{it} is the number of firms that entered the ith industry during the tth period (and survived until the end of the period) as a proportion of the number in the industry at the beginning of the period; Π_{it} is the average ratio of the rate of return in the ith industry during the tth period to that in all manufacturing; C_{it} is the investment (in millions of dollars) required to establish a firm of minimum efficient size in the ith industry during the tth period; R_{it} is the proportion of the firms in the ith industry at the beginning of the tth period that left during the period; V_{it} is the coefficient of variation of the firm sizes in the ith industry at the beginning of the tth period; $\bar{S}_{it}/\hat{S}_{it}$ is the ratio of the average size of firm to the minimum efficient size of firm in the ith industry at the beginning of the tth period; P_{it} is the probability that a randomly drawn firm in the ith industry will be smaller at the end of the tth period than another firm drawn randomly from those 60–70 per cent of its size at the beginning of the tth period; A_{it} is the age of the ith industry (in years) at the beginning of the tth period; and n_{it} is the number of firms in the ith industry at the beginning of the tth period. For a discussion of some of the difficulties in these measures, see the Appendix and notes 3, 26 and 27.
[b] See the Appendix, p. 111 and 112, for some discussion of these figures.
Source: See the Appendix p. 107.

B Exit rates and changes in the number of firms

This subsection estimates the effects of several factors on the rate at which firms leave an industry, and it takes up the effects of these, and related, variables on the amount of entry defined in terms of changes in the number of firms – the first of the two concepts of entry defined at the beginning of this section. We use R_{it} – the proportion of firms in the ith industry at the beginning of the tth period that had left by the end – as a measure of the exit rate. Both firms that scrapped their plant and those that sold out are counted as departures.

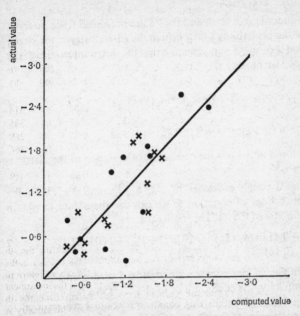

Figure 1 Plot of actual values of ln E_{it} and ln R_{it} against those computed from equations 3 and 7, steel, petroleum, rubber tire, and automobile industries, selected periods[a]

[a] The dots represent ln E_{it} and the Xs represent ln R_{it}. E_{it} is the number of firms that entered the ith industry during the tth period (and survived until the end of the period) as a proportion of the number in the industry at the beginning of the period. R_{it} is the proportion of the firms in the ith industry at the beginning of the tth period that left during the period

Source : Table 1 and equations 3 and 7. The line is a 45° line through the origin

Letting $R_{it}(S)$ be the proportion of firms of size S (at the beginning of the period) that left during the period, we assume that

$$R_{it}(S) = g(S/\hat{S}_{it}, \Pi_{it}, \ldots),$$
4

where $\hat{S}_{it}$ is the minimum efficient size of firm at the beginning of the period. As a firm becomes smaller relative to the minimum efficient size, its chance of survival decreases; and as the industry becomes less profitable relative to others, firms become more likely to leave. Thus, $R_{it}(S)$ should be inversely related to both $S/\hat{S}_{it}$ and Π_{it}.[8]

Since their effects are likely to be multiplicative, we assume that

$$R_{it}(S) = v_0(S/\hat{S}_{it})^{-v_1}\Pi_{it}^{-v_2}Z'_{it} \qquad 5$$

where Z'_{it} is a random error term and the v's are presumed to be positive. Letting $\rho_{it}(S)$ be the probability that a firm in the ith industry at the beginning of the period is of size S and assuming that the distribution of firms by size is log-normal,[9] we have

$$R_{it} = \int_0^\infty R_{it}(S)\rho_{it}(S)dS = v_0\left[\int_0^\infty (S/\hat{S}_{it})^{-v_1}\rho_{it}(S)dS\right]\Pi_{it}^{-v_2}Z'_{it}, \qquad 6$$

$$R_{it} = v_0[\bar{S}_{it}/\hat{S}_{it}]^{-v_1}(1+V_{it}^2)^{v_1(v_1+1)/2}\Pi_{it}^{-v_2}Z'_{it}$$

where $\bar{S}_{it}$ is the mean and V_{it} is the coefficient of variation of the distribution of firm sizes.

Table 1 contains rough estimates of R_{it}, $\bar{S}_{it}/\hat{S}_{it}$, and V_{it}^2.[10] Taking logarithms of both sides of equation 6, we can use these data to obtain least-squares estimates of the v's. The results are

$$\ln R_{it} = -1{\cdot}68 - 0{\cdot}41\ln(\bar{S}_{it}/\hat{S}_{it}) + 0{\cdot}10\ln(1+V_{it}^2) - 0{\cdot}60\ln\Pi_{it}, \qquad 7$$
$$\quad\;\;(0{\cdot}14)\qquad\qquad\quad(0{\cdot}25)\qquad\qquad\;(0{\cdot}33)$$

where the quantities in parentheses are standard errors and $\ln Z'_{it}$ is omitted. For simplicity, the coefficient of $\ln(1+V_{it}^2)$ was not constrained to equal $\hat{v}_1(\hat{v}_1+1)/2$ – although this constraint would have resulted in somewhat better estimates of the v's. Figure 1 shows that there is considerable variation about equation 7, the coefficient of correlation (corrected for degrees of freedom) being $0{\cdot}70$.[11]

8. Of course, the sale of a firm need not mean that it was a failure. Equation 4 is likely to represent the scrappage or abandonment rate better than the rate at which firms are sold. But the former is likely to be a large part of the total and hence equation 4 is likely to represent R_{it} fairly well. The data are such that firms which scrapped their plant cannot be separated from those that sold out. See the Appendix (p. 107).

9. The log-normal distribution seems to provide a reasonably good (but by no means perfect) fit to the distribution of firms by size (Hart and Prais, 1956). Note that we assume only that it is a serviceable approximation from an empirical point of view. Some other distribution (e.g., the Yule distribution) may be more appropriate, but, if it can be approximated by a log-normal, this is good enough for present purposes. The Appendix (p. 107) gives the units in which a firm's size is measured.

10. The sources and limitations of the data regarding R_{it}, $\bar{S}_{it}/\hat{S}_{it}$, and V_{it}^2 are discussed in the Appendix (p. 107).

11. The residuals reflect the effects of various important variables that are omitted – the extent to which the plants in the industry can be adapted for other uses, the adaptability and mobility of the management and the work force, the liquidity of the firms,

The estimates of v_1 and v_2 have the correct signs and are statistically significant. Although they contain fairly large sampling errors and are probably biased somewhat toward zero (because of errors in the exogenous variables and the probable effects of $\ln R_{it}$ on $\ln \Pi_{it}$), they provide useful information regarding the effects of $\bar{S}_{it}/\hat{S}_{it}$ and Π_{it} on R_{it}. For example, if the bias is in the expected direction, one can be reasonably sure that the average value of R_{it} would decrease by at least 15 per cent if Π_{it} or $\bar{S}_{it}/\hat{S}_{it}$ doubled. Lower bounds of this sort can easily be computed for the effects of other percentage increases in Π_{it} or $\bar{S}_{it}/\hat{S}_{it}$.[12]

We are now in a position to consider the first, and probably for most purposes the more important, definition of entry. A reasonable measure in this case is D_{it} – the change in the number of firms during the period as a proportion of the number at the beginning. Since the number of firms bought during the period must equal the number sold,

$$D_{it} = E_{it} - R_{it} . \qquad\qquad 8$$

Taking antilogs of both sides of equations 3 and 7, multiplying the resulting right-hand-side of each equation by $e^{\sigma^2/2}$ (where σ^2 is the variance of Z_{it} or Z'_{it}) to obtain an unbiased estimate of E_{it} or R_{it}, and inserting the results into equation 8, we can estimate the change in the number of firms, given that the values of Π_{it}, C_{it}, $\bar{S}_{it}/\hat{S}_{it}$, and V_{it}^2 are given.

Of course, such estimates are likely to be rough because of the crudeness of the estimates of the a's and v's and the likelihood that there will be considerable variation about the expected value of D_{it}. (In the twelve cases for which we have data, the correlation between the actual and computed values of D_{it} is $0 \cdot 60$.) Nonetheless, they may be of use as first approximations in estimating D_{it} and in estimating the effects of changes in Π_{it}, C_{it}, $\bar{S}_{it}/\hat{S}_{it}$ and V_{it}^2 on the average value of D_{it}.

Two further points should be noted. First, it would be preferable to combine equations 2 and 6, obtain D_{it} as a function of Π_{it}, C_{it}, etc., and

the durability of their equipment, the rate at which costs rise when firms are less than minimum efficient size, etc.

12. The procedure used to obtain these figures is just like that described in note 7. Again, our primary purpose is to estimate the effects of the exogenous variables, not to test whether they have any effect. Almost certainly, they have some effect on R_{it}.

This model also suggests a technique for estimating the minimum efficient size of firm in an industry. Suppose that $\hat{S}_{it}$, rather than R_{it}, were regarded as the 'dependent' variable. If data regarding R_{it}, $\bar{S}_{it}$, Π_{it} and V_{it}^2 were obtained for some new industry or time period, they could then be used to estimate $\hat{S}_{it}$. This technique is likely to be rough, but some work might be carried out to see how accurate it is and to sharpen it. Of course, this presumes that the long-run average cost curve is J-shaped and consequently that a minimum efficient size of firm exists in the new industry. For another technique that is somewhat similar in spirit, see Stigler (1958).

estimate the a's and v's all at once. But the difference between equations **2** and **6** is awkward to work with. [Perhaps future work will show that some other form of equations **2** and **6** that is more convenient in this respect will fit as well.] Second, the empirical results in this section, like those in section 3, pertain to periods of 7–10 years. They should not be applied to periods much longer or shorter than this.

2 The process of firm growth

A · Gibrat's law and the growth of firms

Gibrat's law is a proposition regarding the process of firm growth. According to this law, the probability of a given proportionate change in size during a specified period is the same for all firms in a given industry – regardless of their size at the beginning of the period. For example, a firm with sales of \$100 million is as likely to double in size during a given period as a firm with sales of \$100 thousand. Put differently, Gibrat's law states that:

$$S_{ij}{}^{t+\Delta} = U_{ij}(t, \Delta)S_{ij}^{t} , \qquad\qquad 9$$

where S_{ij}^{t} is the size of the jth firm in the ith industry at time t, $S_{ij}{}^{t+\Delta}$ is its size at time $t+\Delta$, and $U_{ij}(t, \Delta)$ is a random variable distributed independently of S_{ij}^{t}.

Since this law is a basic ingredient in many mathematical models designed to explain the shape of the size distribution of firms and since this law has interesting implications regarding the determinants of the amount of concentration in an industry, some importance attaches to whether or not it holds. This section provides tests based on data for practically all firms – large and small – in three individual industries: the steel, petroleum, and rubber tire industries. The automobile industry is omitted because, with only a handful of firms, it is unlikely to provide much evidence regarding a proposition of this sort.[13]

A simple way to test Gibrat's law is to classify firms by their initial size (S_{ij}^{t}), compute the frequency distribution of $S_{ij}{}^{t+\Delta}/S_{ij}^{t}$ within each of these classes, and use a χ^2 test to determine whether the frequency distributions are the same in each class. We rely heavily on this test, but supplement it with others. The basic data used in these tests are described and presented in the Appendix.

Gibrat's law can be formulated in at least three ways, depending on the

13. For a discussion of the use of Gibrat's law in explaining the size distribution of firms, see Gibrat (1931); Hart and Prais (1956); Simon and Bonini (1958). For previous tests, see also Ferguson (1960); Hymer and Pashigian (1959). In connection with Simon and Bonini (1958), see note 17.

treatment of the death of firms and the comprehensiveness claimed for the law. First, one can postulate that it holds for all firms – including those that leave the industry during the period. If we regard the size (at the end of the period) of each of these departing firms as zero (or approximately zero), this version can easily be tested. The results – shown in Table 2 – indicate that it generally fails to hold. In seven of the ten cases, the observed value

Table 2 Observed value of χ^2 criterion, estimated slope of regression of ln $S_{ij}^{t+\Delta}$ on ln S_{ij}^t, and ratio of variances of growth rates of large and small firms, steel, petroleum, and rubber tire industries, selected periods[a]

Item	Steel				Petroleum				Tires	
	1916–1926	1926–1935	1935–1945	1945–1954	1921–1927	1927–1937	1937–1947	1947–1957	1937–1945	1945–1952
χ^2criterion:										
Including deaths	9·0	17·0[b]	22·5[b]	7·8	29·2[b]	44·9[b]	25·6[b]	42·7[b]	9·3	22·9[b]
Excluding deaths	7·1	3·3	9·5[b]	3·4	2·8	22·1[b]	17·7[b]	8·9	6·3	6·6[b]
Degrees of freedom (χ^2 tests):										
Including deaths	6	6	6	6	6	6	6	6	6	4
Excluding deaths	4	4	4	4	4	4	4	4	4	2
Estimated slope:[c]										
Excluding deaths	0·88[b]	0·99	0·92[b]	1·00	0·94	0·88[b]	0·99	0·94	0·97	0·97
Large firms only	0·94	0·96	1·00	0·98	0·99	0·98	0·93	1·10	1·07	0·89
Standard error of slope:										
Excluding deaths	0·05	0·04	0·03	0·4	0·05	0·04	0·03	0·04	0·05	0·04
Large firms only	0·16	0·16	0·07	0·06	0·24	0·14	0·07	0·07	0·10	0·05
Number of firms:										
Excluding deaths	72	66	64	69	128	116	156	106	34	31
Large firms only	7	9	11	12	7	11	16	17	11	12
Ratio of variances of growth rates of large and small firms:[d]										
Excluding deaths	8·96[b]	0·80	37·40[b]	5·06[b]	43·27[b]	19·25[b]	63·56[b]	147·1[b]	16·16[b]	0·31
Large firms only	0·63	161·00[b]	0·90	8·50[b]	3·50	7·75[b]	4·00[b]	3·6[b]	39·25[b]	8·67

[a]Symbols: S_{ij}^t is the size of the jth firm in the ith industry at time t, and $S_{ij}^{t+\Delta}$ is its size at time $t+\Delta$. For the classification of firms by size and the classification of $S_{ij}^{t+\Delta}/S_{ij}^t$ used in each industry in the χ^2 tests, see the Appendix. The number of degrees of freedom equals $(a=1)(b=1)$ where a is the number of size classes and b is the number of classes of $S_{ij}^{t+\Delta}/S_{ij}^t$ in the contingency table.

[b] For χ^2 criteria and ratios of variances, this means that the probability is less than 0·05 that a value would be this large (or larger) if Gibrat's law held. For estimated slopes, this means that they differ significantly from unity (0·05 significance level).

[c] The number of firms in each regression is shown under 'Number of firms'.

[d] The firms regarded as 'small' and 'large' in the first row are as follows: In steel, small firms have 4,000–16,000 and large firms have 256,000–4,096,000 tons of capacity. In petroleum, small firms have 500–999 and large firms have 32,000–511,999 barrels of capacity. In tires, small firms have 80–159 and large firms have 640–5,119 employees. The firms regarded as 'small' and 'large' in the second row are described in note 18.
Source: See the Appendix (p. 107).

of χ^2 exceeds the critical limit corresponding to the 0·05 significance level.[14]

Why does this version of the law fail to hold? Even a quick inspection of the transition matrices in the Appendix [not reproduced here, Ed.] shows one principal reason. The probability that a firm will die is certainly not independent of its size. In every industry and time interval, the smaller firms were more likely than the larger ones to leave the industry. For this reason (and others indicated below), this version of the law seems to be incorrect.[15]

Second, one can postulate that the law holds for all firms other than those that leave the industry. Hart and Prais (1956) seem to adopt this version. Omitting such firms, we ran another series of χ^2 tests, the results of which are shown in Table 2. In four of the ten cases, the evidence seems to contradict the hypothesis, the observed value of χ^2 exceeding the limit corresponding to the 0·05 significance level.

To see why this version must be rejected, note that equation 9 implies that

$$\ln S_{ij}{}^{t+\Delta} = V_i(t, \Delta) + \ln S_{ij}^t + W_{ij}(t, \Delta), \qquad 10$$

where $V_i(t, \Delta)$ is the mean of $\ln U_{ij}(t, \Delta)$ and $W_{ij}(t, \Delta)$ is a homoscedastic random variable with zero mean. Thus, if $\ln S_{ij}{}^{t+\Delta}$ is plotted against $\ln S_{ij}^t$, the data should be scattered with constant variance about a line with slope of one. Table 2 contains the least-squares estimate of the slope of each of these lines. In half of the cases where the law was rejected the slope is significantly less than one.

In addition, the variance of $S_{ij}{}^{t+\Delta}/S_{ij}^t$ tends to be inversely related to S_{ij}^t. Taking in each case a group of small firms and dividing the variance of their values of $S_{ij}{}^{t+\Delta}/S_{ij}^t$ by the variance among a group of large firms, we obtain the results shown in Table 2. In eight of the ten cases the variances differed significantly. Thus, contrary to this version of the law smaller firms often tend to have higher and more variable growth rates than larger firms.[16]

14. The size classes and the cut-off points for $S_{ij}{}^{t+\Delta}/S_{ij}^t$ used in these tests are described in the Appendix.

15. The way mergers are handled here (see the Appendix) may help to produce an inverse relationship between a firm's size and its probability of death. But this alone cannot account for this result. Such a relationship has often been noted before (e.g. see Adelman, 1958; Oxenfeldt, 1943).

16. These results differ in part from those of Hart and Prais (1956); Simon and Bonini (1958); Ferguson (1960); Hymer and Pashigian (1959). The latter conclude that there was no tendency for the smaller firms to grow more rapidly than the large ones. But this was due to the fact that they included only very large firms. With regard to the larger variation in growth rates among smaller firms, our findings agree with those in Ferguson (1960), and Hymer and Pashigian (1959), but differ from those in Simon and Bonini (1958). There is no treatment of this in Hart and Prais (1956).

All firms that survived during the period are included in these regressions. Note that

Third, one can postulate that the law holds only for firms exceeding the minimum efficient size in the industry – the size (assuming the long-run average cost curve is J-shaped) below which unit costs rise sharply and above which they vary only slightly. This is the version put forth by Simon and Bonini (1958), although it seems to be a stronger assumption than they require.[17] One is faced once again with the problem of whether or not to include firms that die. We excluded them, but the major results would almost certainly have been the same if they had been included.

This version was tested in two ways. First, we estimated the slope of the regression of $\ln S_{ij}^{t+\Delta}$ on $\ln S_{ij}^t$, but included only those firms that were larger than Bain's (1956) estimate of the minimum efficient size. The results are quite consistent with Gibrat's law (the slopes never differing significantly from one). Second, we used F tests to determine whether the variance of $S_{ij}^{t+\Delta}/S_{ij}^t$ was constant among these firms. Contrary to Gibrat's law, the variance of $S_{ij}^{t+\Delta}/S_{ij}^t$ tends to be inversely related to S_{ij}^t in six of the ten cases.[18]

Thus, regardless of which version one chooses, Gibrat's law fails to hold in more than one-half of these cases. What sort of mechanism produced

---

all crude capacity – domestic and foreign – is included for each firm in the petroleum industry. The data on foreign capacity had to be obtained from the individual firms.

In one case in steel, the slope is significantly less than one but this does not show up in the χ^2 test – largely because of the incomplete coverage in the latter. See the Appendix. One-tailed F tests are used to determine whether the variances differ. In several cases, the variances differ significantly, but it does not show up in the χ^2 tests.

17. Simon informs me that the version of Gibrat's law they used in Simon and Bonini, 1958 is not required to obtain the Yule distribution and that their proof will hold if the expected value of $S_{ij}^{t+\Delta}/S_{ij}^t$ does not vary with S_{ij}^t regardless of whether or not the variance of $S_{ij}^{t+\Delta}/S_{ij}^t$ depends on S_{ij}^t. Our results do not contradict these weaker assumptions for firms above the minimum efficient size and consequently they do not contradict their findings based on them. But they do contradict the version of Gibrat's law in Simon and Bonini (1958).

18. The χ^2 tests had to be abandoned here because of the small number of firms. Firms with more than 64,000 barrels of capacity (petroleum), 1,000,000 net tons of capacity (steel), or 0·8 per cent of total employment (tires) were included in the regression. The number included in each case is shown in Table 2. The fact that none of the slopes differs significantly from one indicates that there is no evidence that among these firms the average growth rate depended on a firm's initial size.

In the variance ratio tests we divided these firms into two size (S_{ij}^t) groups, the dividing line being 150,000 barrels of capacity (petroleum), 3,000,000 tons of capacity (steel), and 30,000 employment (tires). Then F tests were used to determine whether the variances of $S_{ij}^{t+\Delta}/S_{ij}^t$ differed. This test is not too robust with regard to departures from normality, but it should perform reasonably well here.

Note that in petroleum and tires we include firms that are more than one-half of the minimum efficient sizes given in the Appendix. According to Bain (1956), the cost curve is quite flat back to one-half of those sizes. Thus, it seemed acceptable to include the additional firms and to increase the power of the tests in this way.

the observed departures from this law? The reasons for the inverse relationships between a firm's chance of death and its initial size seem fairly obvious, but why should the data for the survivors show that the smaller firms tend to have higher and more variable growth rates than the larger ones?[19]

One very simple model that might help to account for this is as follows. Consider the distribution of growth rates of firms of size S_{ij}^{t} that would have resulted if none had left the industry. It is not unreasonable to suppose that above some minimum value of S_{ij}^{t} the average of this distribution would have been about the same in each size class and that it would have exceeded the average growth rate that would have been experienced by firms that left the industry. For simplicity, we assume that the difference between these averages was the same in each size class. Moreover, because each large firm can be viewed as a collection of somewhat independent smaller firms, the variance of this distribution would be expected to be inversely related to S_{ij}^{t}.[20]

Then, under the fairly reasonable assumption that the actual growth rate of each survivor is proportional to what it would have been if all firms had survived, one can show that

$$\sigma_s^2(S) = \mu^2 \left\{ \sigma_t^2(S) - \frac{P(S)K^2}{[1-P(S)]^2} \right\},$$

where $\sigma_s^2(S)$ is the variance of the growth rates of the survivors (originally of sizes S_{ij}), $\sigma_t^2(S)$ is the variance of the growth rates of all firms (originally of size S_{ij}^{t}) that would have resulted if all had survived, K is the difference between the average growth rate of all firms (if none had left) and the average growth rate that would have been experienced by those leaving the industry, $P(S)$ is the probability of death for firms initially of size S_{ij}^{t} and μ is the ratio of a survivor's actual growth rate to what it would have been if all had survived. (This assumes that if they had not left, the firms origin-

19. Note that the inverse relationship between S_{ij}^{t} and the average growth rate shows up only when all firms are included. There is no evidence of this among firms exceeding the minimum efficient size. (The inverse relationship between S_{ij}^{t} and the variability of growth rates shows up in both cases.)

20. The growth rate of a large firm can be viewed as the mean of the growth rates of its smaller 'components' (e.g. plants). This point has also been made in Hymer and Pashigian (1959). Note that, if the growth rates of the components (plants or otherwise) were independent, the standard deviation would be inversely proportional to the square-root of a firm's size. But, since they tend to be located in the same region and have other similarities, one would expect the growth rate of such components to be positively correlated. Thus, the standard deviation would not be expected to decrease as rapidly with increases in size as the square-root formula suggests. In fact, this expectation turns out to be true.

ally of size S_{ij}^t that left the industry would have had growth rates with a variance of $\sigma_t^2(S)$.)

In addition, one can show that the average growth rate of the survivors originally of size S_{ij}^t equals

$$\bar{S}(S) = \mu \left\{ \bar{\iota} + \frac{P(S)K}{1-P(S)} \right\},$$

where $\bar{\iota}$ is the average growth rate for all firms of size S_{ij}^t if none had left the industry. Note that we, in the same spirit as Simon and Bonini (1958), are stipulating only that $\bar{\iota}$ will be constant above some minimum size.

Thus, if $\sigma_t^2(S)$ is inversely related to S_{ij}^t (for the reason discussed in note 20) and if $P(S)$ is inversely related to S (which certainly is true), it follows that $\sigma_s^2(S)$ will be inversely related to S_{ij}^t so long as $P(S) > 1/3$ or $d\sigma_t^2(S)/dS_{ij}^t$ is large in absolute terms relative to $dP(S)/dS_{ij}^t$. Moreover, it follows that $\bar{S}(S)$ will be inversely related to S_{ij}^t.

Thus, if this highly simplified model should be at all reliable, one would often expect to observe departures from Gibrat's law of the sort found in Table 2. Research should be carried out to develop and study more sophisticated models of the growth process. Although Gibrat's law is very convenient from an analytical point of view, it does not seem to hold up very well empirically. It seems to be a rather unreliable base on which to rest theories of the size distribution of firms.

B Successful innovation and the growth of firms

How much of an impact does a successful innovation have on a firm's growth rate? In another study (Mansfield, 1963a), I presented a list of the firms that were first to introduce the significant new processes and products that emerged since the First World War in the steel and petroleum refining industries. (See the Appendix for a brief description of this list.) A comparison of their growth rates – during the period in which the innovation occurred – with those of other comparable firms should help to indicate how great the pay-off is (in terms of growth) for a successful innovation.

For each period for which we have data, Table 3 estimates the average annual growth rate of

1. Firms that carried out significant innovations during the period.
2. Other firms that were equal in size to the successful innovators at the beginning of the period.

There is a marked difference between the two groups. In every time interval and in both industries, the successful innovators grew more rapidly than the others; and in some cases, their average rate of growth was more than twice that of the others.[21]

Taking each innovator separately, the difference between its growth rate and the average growth rate of other comparable firms seems to have been inversely related to its size. As one would expect, a successful innovation had a much greater impact on a small firm's growth rate than on a large firm's. The fact that fewer of the successful innovators in more recent periods were small firms probably accounts in part for the decrease over time in the average difference (in Table 3) between the two groups.[22]

Each growth rate in Table 3 pertains to the entire period indicated in the caption – whereas the innovations occurred sometime within the period. Consider the period from time t to time $t+\Delta$. Suppose that the jth successful innovator in this period introduced its innovation at time t_j, that its average annual growth rate from time t to time t_j exceeded that of other comparable firms by e_j, and that its average annual growth rate from time t_j to time $t+\Delta$ exceeded that of other comparable firms by e_j+d_j. What were the average values of e_j and d_j? If the innovators grew more rapidly than other firms because of certain characteristics associated with the innovation, but not because of the innovation itself, and if these characteristics had approximately the same effect throughout the period, the average value of d_j would be expected to be zero.

Letting $S_j^{t+\Delta}$ be the size (i.e. capacity) at time $t+\Delta$ of the jth innovator and $Q^{j+\Delta}$ be the average logarithm of the sizes at time $t+\Delta$ of the other

21. Note:
1. We are not comparing innovators with non-innovators, since some of the 'other firms' may have been unsuccessful innovators. Because we can only include successful innovators (the data being what they are), it is not surprising that they have higher growth rates, and we are much more interested in the size of the difference than in its existence.
2. Some of the innovators introduced more than one innovation during the period. Thus, the difference in growth rates is not due entirely to a single innovation. But in the subsequent analysis (involving $\bar{d}$) only cases involving a single innovation are included.
3. It would be interesting to see how an innovation's effects depended on its character, but we have too little data to attempt this.
4. The way in which the average annual growth rate of the 'other firms' in Table 3 was computed is described in the Appendix (p. 107).
22. If the innovators in steel are divided into two groups – those above 1,000,000 tons and those less than (or equal to) 1,000,000 tons at the beginning of the period – the average difference between their growth rates and the growth rates of other comparable firms differs considerably between the groups. Among the larger firms, the average difference is generally about 0·5 points whereas it is 3–10 points among the smaller ones. Similarly, if the innovators in petroleum are divided into two groups – those above 32,000 barrels and those less than (or equal to) 32,000 barrels at the beginning of the period – the average difference is practically zero among the larger firms but 6–24 points among the smaller ones.

firms that were equal in size to the jth innovator at time t, one can show that

$$(\ln S_j^{t+\Delta} - Q_j^{t+\Delta})/\Delta = e_j + [1 - (t_j - t)/\Delta]d_j.$$

$\qquad$ **11**

Table 3 **Average annual growth rates of successful innovators and other firms (of comparable initial size), computed values of $\bar{e}$ and $\bar{d}$, and regressions (excluding innovators) of $\ln S_{ij}^{t+\Delta}$ on $\ln S_{ij}^t$, steel and petroleum refining industries, selected periods**[a]

Item	Steel				Petroleum			
	1916–1926	1926–1935	1935–1945	1945–1954	1921–1927	1927–1937	1937–1947	1947–1957
Average annual growth rate (per cent):								
Innovators	13·7	6·5	3·4	3·2	13·1	7·9	3·6	6·7
Other firms	3·7	3·3	2·0	2·4	6·6	4·1	3·6	4·2
Computed value of:[b]								
$\bar{e}$ (per cent)	—	0·7	0·7	—	—	4·2	−2·5	−2·8
$\bar{d}$ (per cent)	—	3·9	5·2	—	—	5·7	3·6	13·4
Regression (excluding innovators) of $\ln S_{ij}^{t+\Delta}$ on $\ln S_{ij}^t$:								
Intercept (a_i)	1·68	0·55	1·34	0·18	1·10	1·68	0·41	1·27
Slope (b_i)	0·88	0·97	0·90	1·01	0·93	·84	0·98	0·90

[a] Symbols: S_{ij}^t is the size of the jth firm in the ith industry at time t; $S_{ij}^{t+\Delta}$ is its size at time $t+\Delta$; $\bar{e}$ is the average value of e_j, where e_j is the difference between the average annual growth rate of the jth innovator during the period from time t to time t_j and that of 'other firms' of equivalent size (at time t) during the same period; and $\bar{d}$ is the average value of d_j, where $e_j + d_j$ is the difference between the average annual growth rate of the jth innovator during the period from time t_j to time $t+\Delta$ and that of 'other firms' of equivalent size (at time t) during the same period. See the Appendix for the way in which the regressions described here are used to estimate the figures in the second row of this table.

[b] No figures are computed in cases where there were only a few innovators. See note 23 and the Appendix for a discussion of the derivation of these figures.

Source: See the Appendix and Mansfield, (1963a).

To see this, consider the kth 'other firm' of the same size as the jth innovator at time t. If r_{1k} is its average rate of growth between time t and time $t+j$, r_{2k} is its average rate of growth between time t_j and time $t+\Delta$, and $S_{jk}^{t+\Delta}$ is its size at time $t+\Delta$,

$$\ln S_{jk}^{t+\Delta} = \ln S_j^t + r_{1k}(t_j - t) + r_{2k}(t+\Delta - t_j).$$

Thus, if r_1 is the average value of r_{1k} and r_2 is the average value of r_{2k},

$$Q_j^{t+\Delta} = \ln S_j^t + r_1(t_j - t) + r_2(t+\Delta - t_j).$$

But by the definitions of e_j and d_j,

$$\ln S_j^{t+\Delta} = \ln S_j^t + (r_1+e_j)(t_j-t) + (r_2+e_j+d_j)(t+\Delta-t_j).$$

Thus,

$$\ln S_j^{t+\Delta} - Q_j^{t+\Delta} = e_j\Delta + d_j(t+\Delta-t_j),$$

and equation **11** follows.

Letting $\bar{e}$ and $\bar{d}$ be the average values of e_j and d_j and assuming that $(e_j-\bar{e})$ and $(d_j-\bar{d})$ are statistically independent of $(t_j-t)/\Delta$, we have

$$(\ln S_j^{t+\Delta} - Q_j^{t+\Delta})/\Delta = \bar{e} + [1-(t_j-t)/\Delta]\bar{d} + W_j, \qquad \textbf{12}$$

where W_j can be treated as a random error term. Using equation **12** we can apply least-squares to obtain $\bar{e}$ and $\bar{d}$.[23]

The results (in Table 3) indicate that $\bar{d}$ was always positive, but that the sign of $\bar{e}$ varied. This means two things. First, in the period immediately before they introduced the innovations, there was no persistent tendency for the successful innovators to grow more rapidly than other comparable firms. In some cases they grew more rapidly, but in others they did not. Thus, their higher growth rate cannot be attributed to their pre-innovation behavior. Second, in the period after they introduced the innovations their mean growth rate consistently exceeded that of other comparable firms by more than it had before their introduction – which is what one would expect.

If one makes the crude assumption that the pre-innovation difference in average growth rate between successful innovators and other firms would have been maintained from time t to time $t+\Delta$ if the innovations had not been introduced, $\bar{d}$ measures the average effect of these successful innovations on a firm's growth rate during the relevant period. Based on this

23. To estimate $Q_j^{t+\Delta}$, we use the procedure described in the Appendix. In computing $\bar{e}$ and $\bar{d}$, innovators that introduced more than one innovation had to be excluded (except in a few cases where the innovations were all introduced at the same time). These relatively few omissions are ignored, and we act as if we had the entire population of innovators in the analysis.

Of course, the assumption that $(e_j-\bar{e})$ and $(d_j-\bar{d})$ are statistically independent of $(j-t)/\Delta$ is rather bold. Some bias may result if d_j is higher immediately after the introduction of an innovation. If so $(d_j-\bar{d})$ and $1-(t_j-t)/\Delta$ may be negatively correlated, and we would probably overestimate $\bar{e}$ and underestimate $\bar{d}$.

Where there were only a few innovators, this assumption (and the one in the previous paragraph) seemed particularly risky and we did not compute values of $\bar{e}$ and $\bar{d}$. But some preliminary work suggested that, had we done so, the results would have been much the same.

assumption, their average effect was to raise a firm's growth rate by 4–13 percentage points, depending on the particular time interval and industry. In view of the widespread interest in measures of the pay-off from successful innovation, these estimates, despite their crudeness, should be useful. Of course, estimates of the effects of successful innovation on a firm's profits would be even more useful, but they lie outside the scope of this paper.[24]

3 Mobility within an industry's size structure

In recent years, economists have become quite interested in the amount of mobility in an industry – i.e. the extent to which firms change their relative positions in the size distribution. The importance of this characteristic of an industry has been pointed out by Adelman (1958), Hart and Prais (1956), Simon and Bonini (1958), and others (Miller, 1955; Stigler, 1955). This section measures the amount of mobility in several industries and constructs a simple model to help explain its observed variation. The results shed additional light on the process of firm growth, since the amount of mobility is obviously related to the amount of interfirm variation in growth rates.[25]

To measure the amount of mobility in the ith industry during the tth period, suppose that we have a list of all firms that were in existence at both the beginning and end of the period. Suppose that a firm is chosen at random from this list. Then suppose that another firm is chosen at random from those that were 60–70 per cent as large as the first firm at the beginning of the period. The probability that the second (initially smaller) firm will be bigger than the first (initially larger) firm at the end of the period is

24. Note that the successful innovators tend to be the large spenders on research. (For evidence on this score and discussions of the imitation process, see Mansfield (1961; 1963b; 1964), Mansfield and Hensley (1960).)

If we had complete, year-by-year data on each firm's size, we could compute $\bar{e}$ and $\bar{d}$ without making the assumption discussed in note 23. The differences in growth rates shown in Table 3 are averages over periods of 1–10 years after an innovation was introduced. Obviously, the effects of an innovation decrease as time goes on.

Finally, for the reason cited in note 23, the estimates of $\bar{d}$ may be biased downward. On the other hand, in the petroleum industry in 1947–57, $\bar{d}$ may be unduly affected by one firm and is probably too high. Note, too, that the observed differences in growth rate may still be due in part to other factors that are associated with a firm's willingness to innovate and the timing of the innovation.

25. If Gibrat's law held and if $W_{ij}(t, \Delta)$ were normally distributed, the amount of mobility would be solely a function of the latter's variance. For this reason, its variance has sometimes been suggested as a measure of the amount of mobility. But, since Gibrat's law generally does not hold and the normal distribution is only an approximation, the measure discussed below seems preferable.

a rough measure of the amount of mobility. Let this probability be P_{it}.[26]

Table 1 contains estimates of P_{it} for various periods in the history of the steel, petroleum refining, and rubber tire industries. Because of the small number of firms, it was impossible to obtain meaningful estimates for the automobile industry. To help explain the considerable variation in P_{it}, we assume that

$$P_{it}(S) = h(S/(n_{it}\overline{S}_{it}), A_{it}, S_{it}^*/\widetilde{S}_{it}, n_{it}, \ldots),$$ 13

where $P_{it}(S)$ is the probability that a firm of size S at the beginning of the period will be smaller at the end of the period than a firm originally of size $0 \cdot 6S - 0 \cdot 7S$, n_{it} is the number of firms in the industry at the beginning of the period, $\overline{S}_{it}$ is their mean size, $\widetilde{S}_{it}$ is their median size, S_{it}^* is the size of firm such that firms exceeding it accounted for one-half of the market, and A_{it} is the age of the industry.

What are the effects of these variables? First, the smaller firm's chance of overtaking the larger one will be inversely related to the initial difference between their market shares – which is proportional to $S/(n_{it}\overline{S}_{it})$. Second, as an industry grows older, stronger ties are established between firms and their customers, the technology becomes more settled, and the industry's structure tends to become more rigid. Thus, A_{it} – which is a proxy variable for these factors – is likely to be important.[27] Third, $P_{it}(S)$ is likely to be inversely related to the amount of concentration in the industry. Thus, n_{it}

26. The choice of 60–70 per cent is arbitrary. We could have experimented with alternative ranges, but the amount of clerical work involved would have been prohibitive. Note that this measure is based on all firms; if one were interested in the amount of mobility among the larger firms only, the measure could easily be modified to that end.

This measure is based solely on firms that survived until the end of the period. If we included all firms – regardless of whether or not they survived – the results would depend heavily on the death rate. Because the latter was already taken up in section 1 it seemed preferable to use this measure. If one is interested in results that include deaths, it is relatively easy to combine the findings in this section with those in section 1.

Let $P_{it}'(S)$ be the probability that a firm initially of size S will be smaller at the end of the period than – or as small as – a firm that initially was 60–70 per cent of its size. If a firm dies, let its size be zero. Then

$P_{it}'(S) = R_{it}(S) + [1 - R_{it}(S)][1 - R_{it}(S')]P_{it}(S),$

where $R_{it}(S')$ is the probability that a firm of initial size, $0 \cdot 6S - 0 \cdot 7S$, will die during the period. Since section 1 B takes up $R_{it}(S)$ – and $R_{it}(S')$ – and this section analyses $P_{it}(S)$, together they provide information regarding $P_{it}'(S)$.

27. The age of an industry is a somewhat slippery concept. In 1896, Goodyear made the first US tires for commercial vehicles. In 1859, oil production began in the United States. The production of iron began here in 1645. Using these years as estimates of the dates of birth of the industries, A_{it} was derived by subtracting them from the initial year of the tth period. Although the results seem reasonable their crudeness should be obvious.

and $S_{it}^*/\tilde{S}_{it}$ (a convenient measure of the amount of inequality among firm sizes) are included.[28]

Since the effects of these variables are likely to be multiplicative, we assume that

$$P_{it}(S) = \beta_0[S/(n_{it}\,\bar{S}_{it})]^{-\beta_1} A_{it}^{-\beta_2}(S_{it}^*/\tilde{S}_{it})^{-\beta_3} n_{it}^{\beta_4} Z_{it}'' \qquad 14$$

where Z_{it}'' is a random error term and the β's are presumed to be positive. Assuming again that the distribution of firms by size is log-normal, we have:

$$P_{it} = \int_0^\infty P_{it}(S)\rho_{it}(S)dS$$

$$= \beta_0\left[\int_0^\infty S^{-\beta_1}\rho_{it}(S)dS\right]\bar{S}_{it}^{\beta_1} A_{it}^{-\beta_2}(S_{it}^*/\tilde{S}_{it})^{-\beta_3} n_{it}^{\beta_4+\beta_1} Z_{it}''$$

$$P_{it} = \beta_0(1+V_{it}^2)^{\beta_1(1+\beta_1)/2-\beta_3} A_{it}^{-\beta_2} n_{it}^{\beta_4+\beta_1} Z_{it}''. \qquad 15$$

To see how well this model can represent the data, we take logarithms of both sides of equation 15, and using the data in Table 1, we obtain least-squares estimates of the coefficients. The results are:

$$\ln P_{it} = -0.55 - 0.57\ln(1+V_{it}^2) - 0.15\ln A_{it} + 0.29\ln n_{it}, \qquad 16$$
$$\phantom{\ln P_{it} = -0.55} (0.20) \qquad\qquad (0.07) \qquad\quad (0.08)$$

where the quantities in parentheses are standard errors and $\ln Z_{it}''$ is omitted Figure 2 shows that equation 16 can explain much of the variation in $\ln P_{it}$, the coefficient of correlation (corrected for degrees of freedom) being about 0.90. All of the regression coefficients have the expected signs and are statistically significant at the 0.05 level. Thus, what evidence we have seems

28. Since we assume that the distribution of firms by size is log-normal, the obvious measure of their inequality is the variance of the logarithms of the firm sizes. It can be shown that the latter is equal to $\ln(S_{it}^*/\tilde{S}_{it})$. Thus, our measure – which is convenient because it allows some terms in equation 15 to be collected – is a monotonic increasing function of the variance.

The chief reason for using a measure of inequality of firm sizes plus the number of firms as a measure of concentration is convenience. For some disadvantages in the use of such measures, see Adelman (1959). For some evidence that increases in concentration are associated with decreases in mobility, see Hymer and Pashigian (1959). Of course, one would expect this variable to be important because where markets are highly concentrated it is more likely that discipline can and will be maintained to see to it that firms remain in about the same relative positions. E.g., there may be explicit or tacit agreements to share markets, each firm maintaining a certain per cent of the total.

to be quite consistent with the model. Indeed, it fits the data surprisingly well.[29]

4 Concluding remarks

A Limitations

Some of the limitations of this study are the following: First, the empirical results in sections 1 and 3 are based on relatively few observations. Considerable work was required to obtain even this small number because each observation is based on a large amount of relatively inaccessible data. But regardless of the reasons, the small number of industries and time periods results in fairly substantial sampling errors and obvious dangers of bias.

Second, the basic data in Table 1 are often very rough. The estimates of E_{it}, R_{it}, C_{it}, Π_{it}, A_{it}, and $\bar{S}_{it}/\hat{S}_{it}$ are based on the rather crude assumptions described in the Appendix. Unfortunately, no better data could be found. To the extent that they are distributed randomly, the errors of measurement in the exogenous variables tend to bias the estimates of the coefficients in equations 3, 7, and 16 toward zero.

Third, the models in sections 1 and 3 are obviously oversimplified. The small number of observations, as well as measurement problems and lack of data, limited the number of explanatory variables that could be included. One other explanatory variable – the length of the time period – was used initially in equations 3, 7, and 16, and its effect turned out to be nonsignificant.[30] Note too that the residuals in these equations may not be entirely independent because of the effects of factors that persist in a given industry or time period.

29. The expression in equation 15 is not a very obvious one. E.g., it is not obvious (at least to me) that $\ln P_{it}$ should be a linear function of $\ln (1 + V_{it}^2)$. Consequently, it is all the more satisfying that this function turns out to be such a good representation of the data.

There is some evidence that the variability of firm growth rates increases with the industry's over-all rate of growth (Hymer and Pashigian, 1959). Of course, A_{it} and the industry's growth rate are liable to be related in general. But in the cases used here, there is no correlation between the two variables. Consequently, the observed effects of A_{it} are not mere reflections of the effects of the industry's growth rate.

Another factor that may be important is the extent to which the smaller firms tend to be the innovators. In addition, Hart and Prais (1956) provide some evidence that there is more mobility during depressions, but this may be due to the differences among industries in the extent to which sales fall during a recession. Our data – which do not lump all industries together – do not show any obvious signs of such a tendency.

In deriving equation 15, we presume that $P_{it}(S)$ exists for all S. But in some cases there are no firms 60–70 per cent as large as another firm. Thus, strictly speaking, we should use the size distribution of firms where it exists.

30. Of course, the exclusion of important factors can create biases of various sorts, e.g. it is possible that C_{it} is correlated with other barriers to entry and that consequently its effects on E_{it} are overstated.

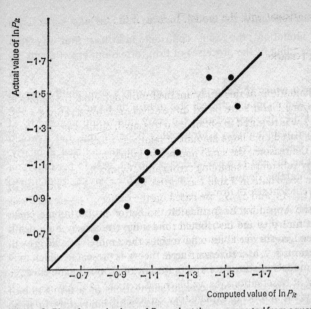

Figure 2 Plot of actual values of P_{it} against those computed from equation 16, steel, petroleum, and rubber tire industries, selected periods
Source : Table 1 and equation 16. P_{it} is the probability that a randomly drawn firm in the ith industry will be smaller at the end of the tth period than another firm drawn randomly from those 60–70 per cent of its size at the beginning of the tth period.

Fourth, the estimating procedures are sometimes rough. In section 2, the computed values of $\bar{e}$ and $\bar{d}$ are based on a rather bold assumption. In section 1, there is probably some least-squares bias toward zero in the estimates of the a's and v's because Π_{it} is inversely related to E_{it} and directly related to R_{it}. But in the case of a_2 and v_2, this bias should not be very large, and considering the quality of the basic data, it did not seem worthwhile to use more complicated estimating procedures.[31]

31. For an elementary discussion of least-squares bias of this sort, see Bronfenbrenner (1953). To evaluate the bias, we first formed a complete system of equations by adding to equations 3 and 7 a third equation in which ln Π_{it} is represented as a linear function of ln E_{it}, ln R_{it}, ln $\Pi_{i(t-1)}$, an unspecified exogenous variable, and an error term. As noted in the text, the coefficient of ln E_{it} in the third equation is assumed to be negative and the coefficient of ln R_{it} is assumed to be positive. What we have in mind is that the rate of change of Π_{it} (i.e. $\Pi_{it}/\Pi_{i(t-1)}$) is an increasing function of R_{it}, a decreasing function of E_{it} and a function of some other (unspecified) exogenous variable. Next, we assumed that the residuals in the equations were uncorrelated (which is consistent with the data we have), and we assumed for simplicity that the covariances of the exogenous variables were all zero.

B Summary and conclusions

Despite their limitations, the results contribute in at least four ways to a better understanding of the processes of firm formation, growth, and decline.

1. They help to gauge the effects of an industry's profitability, capital requirements, and minimum efficient size of firm on its rates of entry and exit. For example, they suggest that the entry rate would increase by at least 60 per cent if an industry's profitability doubled and that it would decrease by at least 7 per cent if its capital requirements doubled. Similarly, they suggest that the exit rate would decrease by at least 15 per cent if an industry's profitability doubled or if the ratio of the average size of firm to the minimum efficient size of firm doubled.

2. The tests of several variants of Gibrat's law of proportionate effect reveal that, contrary to the law, smaller firms have relatively high death rates and those that survive tend to have higher and more variable growth rates than larger firms. Moreover, a simple theory is presented which may help to account for these deviations from the law of proportionate effect.

3. Evidence as to the effects of successful innovations on a firm's rate of growth indicate that on the average the successful innovators in these industries grew about twice as rapidly as other comparable firms during the relevant period.[32] In terms of short-term growth, the rewards for successful innovation seem to have been substantial, particularly for smaller firms.

4. A simple model is presented to help explain variation among industries and over time in the extent to which firms change their relative positions in the size distribution of an industry. Our tentative findings indicate that the amount of mobility in an industry depends significantly on its age and its market structure, the model fitting data for several industries surprisingly well.

In recent years, economists have begun to study in a systematic way the changes over time in an industry's composition and structure, but because so little econometric work has been carried out, they have had relatively little to go on in constructing models to represent the relevant dynamic processes. For this reason and others, they have not proceeded far beyond the simplest sorts of stochastic models, e.g. Markov processes with con-

---

Under these conditions we found that the asymptotic bias in the estimates of the a's and v's was always towards zero and that it was likely to be a small percentage of the estimates of a_2 and v_2. But this only holds in the limit and our assumptions are obviously rough.

32. The average growth rate in the first row of Table 3 is approximately double the average growth rate in the second row.

stant transition probabilities based on Gibrat's law.[33] By providing some of the necessary econometric results, this paper should contribute to the development of a richer theory of the dynamic aspects of industrial structure.

Appendix: data and methods

First, this Appendix presents the basic data regarding the birth, growth, and death of firms in the steel, petroleum refining, and rubber tire industries. (The data for the automobile industry pertain to only a small number of firms and are readily available in the annual statistical issues of *Automobile Industries*.) These data can be summarized most easily in the form of transition matrices – shown in Appendix Tables 1, 2, and 3. If all firms are classified into n size classes, the ijth element of the transition matrix for a particular period $(i, j = 1, \ldots, n)$ is the number of firms in the ith class at the beginning of the period that were in the jth class at the end. Despite the pioneering work of Hart and Prais (1956) and Adelman (1958), few such transition matrices have been constructed.

Appendix Table 1 contains transition matrices for the steel industry for 1916–26, 1926–35, 1935–45, and 1945–54; Table 2, for petroleum refining for 1921–27, 1927–37, 1937–47, and 1947–57; Table 3, for the rubber tire industry for 1937–45 and 1945–52. Some of these periods were dictated by the availability of data; others were chosen rather arbitrarily. A firm's size is measured in terms of gross tons of ingot capacity (steel), daily crude capacity (petroleum), or employment (tires). In steel and petroleum, all firms with ingot capacity or crude capacity are included. In rubber tires, all firms cited in the *Rubber Red Book* as manufacturers of rubber tires are included.

The basic data were derived from the American Iron and Steel Institute 1916, 1926, 1935, 1945, 1954, Bureau of Mines bulletins 1937, 1947, 1957, the *Petroleum Refiner*, the *Rubber Red Book*, *Moody's Industrials*, and correspondence with particular firms. To construct each matrix, we obtained from these sources complete lists of the firms in the industry at the beginning and end of the period and the size of each firm at both points in time. With this information at hand, it was a simple matter to construct each matrix.

Four points should be noted regarding these data:

1. When a firm's name appeared on a list for the first time, we assumed that

33. Judging by our results and the transition matrices in the Appendix, the assumption – sometimes made – that the transition probabilities are constant over time is likely to be a poor one; e.g. the extent of 'mixing' (Simon and Bonini, 1958) seems to decrease with time.

Appendix Table 1 Transition matrices for the steel industry, 1916–26, 1926–35, 1935–45, and 1945–54[a]

Capacity (tons) at beginning of the period	Total	Disappearances	Ingot capacity (tons) at end of the period						
			Under 4,000	4,000– 15,999	16,000– 63,999	64,000– 255,999	256,000– 1,023,999	1,024,000– 4,095,999	Over 4,095,999
[Number of firms] 1916–26									
Entrants	51	—	10	10	15	12	4	0	0
Under 4000	10	2	4	3	1	0	0	0	0
4000–15,999	17	5	1	6	4	1	0	0	0
16,000–63,999	14	1	0	1	11	1	0	0	0
64,000–255,999	31	6	0	0	0	16	8	1	0
256,000–1,023,999	10	2	0	0	0	0	7	1	0
1,024,000–4,095,999	7	2	0	0	0	0	4	0	1
Over 4,095,999	1	0	0	0	0	0	0	0	1
1926–35									
Entrants	10	—	0	4	2	2	2	0	0
Under 4000	14	11	3	0	0	0	0	0	0
4000–15,999	20	11	1	7	1	0	0	0	0
16,000–63,999	30	17	0	1	10	1	1	0	0
64,000–255,999	31	12	0	0	1	13	5	0	0
256,000–1,023,999	19	5	0	0	0	0	11	3	0
1,024,000–4,095,999	6	0	0	0	0	0	1	4	1
Over 4,095,999	2	0	0	0	0	0	0	0	2

1935–45

	total	Under 4000	4000–15,999	16,000–63,999	64,000–255,999	256,000–1,023,999	1,024,000–4,095,999	Over 4,095,999
Entrants	15	—	2	7	3	3	0	0
Under 4000	4	4	0	0	0	0	0	0
4000–15,999	12	0	5	6	1	0	0	0
16,000–63,999	14	4	1	6	3	0	0	0
64,000–255,999	16	0	0	0	14	2	0	0
256,000–1,023,999	19	3	0	0	0	14	1	1
1,024,000–4,095,999	8	1	0	0	0	1	5	1
Over 4,095,999	3	0	0	0	0	0	0	3

1945–54

	total	Under 4000	4000–15,999	16,000–63,999	64,000–255,999	256,000–1,023,999	1,024,000–4,095,999	Over 4,095,999
Entrants	14	—	1	6	4	3	0	0
Under 4000	0	0	0	0	0	0	0	0
4000–15,999	9	2	4	3	0	0	0	0
16,000–63,999	20	1	0	14	4	1	0	0
64,000–255,999	21	6	0	1	12	2	0	0
256,000–1,023,999	20	3	0	0	1	12	4	0
1,024,000–4,095,999	7	0	0	0	0	0	3	4
Over 4,095,999	4	0	0	0	0	0	0	4

[a] The first column (labeled 'total') contains the number of firms in each size class at the beginning of the period. For each beginning-of-period size class (i.e. each row), the remaining columns show the end-of-period size distribution.

Appendix Table 2 **Transition matrices for the petroleum refining industry, 1921–27, 1927–37, 1937–47, and 1947–57[a]**

Daily capacity (bbls.) at beginning of the period	Daily capacity (bbls.) at end of the period							
	Total	Disap-pearances	Under 1000	1000–3999	4000–15,999	16,000–63,999	64,000–255,999	Over 255,999
[Number of firms] 1921–27								
Entrants	207	—	75	92	36	4	0	0
Under 1000	58	34	13	6	4	1	0	0
1000–3999	173	119	3	34	15	2	0	0
4000–15,999	61	29	1	5	17	9	0	0
16,000–63,999	15	4	0	0	0	7	4	0
64,000–255,999	6	0	0	0	0	0	6	0
Over 255,999	1	0	0	0	0	0	0	1
1927–37								
Entrants	153	—	44	62	43	3	1	0
Under 1000	92	74	8	8	2	0	0	0
1000–3999	137	94	1	27	14	0	1	0
4000–15,999	72	40	1	6	19	6	0	0
16,000–63,999	23	11	0	1	2	5	4	0
64,000–255,999	10	0	0	0	0	0	6	4
Over 255,999	1	0	0	0	0	0	0	1
1937–47								
Entrants	210	—	83	75	43	9	0	0
Under 1000	54	26	21	6	1	0	0	0
1000–3999	104	53	4	34	13	0	0	0
4000–15,999	80	30	1	7	27	15	0	0
16,000–63,999	14	3	0	0	2	8	1	0
64,000–255,999	12	1	0	0	0	0	8	3
Over 255,999	5	0	0	0	0	0	0	5
1947–57								
Entrants	90	—	7	33	31	16	3	0
Under 1000	109	98	4	5	2	0	0	0
1000–3999	122	95	0	16	10	1	0	0
4000–15,999	86	54	0	3	22	7	0	0
16,000–63,999	32	13	0	0	2	12	5	0
64,000–255,999	9	0	0	0	0	0	5	4
Over 255,999	8	0	0	0	0	0	0	8

[a] See note a, Appendix Table 1. Both domestic and foreign capacity owned by firms are included.

it entered the industry during the preceding period. Similarly a firm is regarded as having left the industry when its name disappeared from the lists. Although we tried to keep track of mere changes in company names (where changes in ownership were not involved), some were undoubtedly missed and hence the entry and exit rates may be inflated. But on the other hand, they may also be underestimated because some firms may have kept the same names despite a change in ownership. (Of course, for large corporations, changes in ownership occur to some extent all the time and are not very important unless changes in the control of the firm are involved.)

Unfortunately, the available data force us to use a firm's name as an indicator of its ownership. But one would certainly expect the resulting rates of entry and exit to be closely related to the actual ones. Of course, if they are proportional on the average, there is no problem. But this is unlikely.

2. When mergers occurred, they were treated as if the largest firm involved in the merger bought the others. That is, the resulting firm was regarded as a continuation of the largest of its components, and the other parties to the merger were treated as if they went out of business. This procedure is arbitrary, but no other seems clearly preferable. Fortunately, it should not affect the results very substantially. Note too that some of the entrants may have 'purchased' existing facilities by merging with established firms.

3. Some members of the industry did not provide data regarding their size at some of these points in time, and there was no choice but to omit them during the relevant periods. This should be of little consequence because only a few such cases were encountered. Note that this accounts for the fact that the number entering a particular size class sometimes differs from the number in that size class at the beginning of the next period.

4. The steel data pertain to all firms with ingot capacity (open hearth, bessemer, or electric) and the petroleum data pertain to all firms with crude capacity (operating or shut-down). For some purposes, it might have been preferable to have excluded electric furnaces and shut-down capacity.

Second, we describe the way in which the data in Table 1 in the text (p. 88) regarding Π_{lt}, C_{tt}, V_{it}^2, and $\bar{S}_{lt}/\hat{S}_{lt}$ were derived. To estimate Π_{lt}, we needed figures on profits after taxes as a percentage of net worth in each industry. For rubber tires, the data came from the *Statistics of Income*. For petroleum, they came from Epstein (1934), De Chazeau and Kahn (1959), and the *Statistics of Income*. For steel, they came from Schroeder (1953), but some adjustment was made for differences in concept. The data for automobiles came from *Moody's* and pertained to the largest five firms. The 1925–57 data for all manufacturing came from the First National City Bank of NY (as reported in the 1959 *Petroleum Facts and Figures*). The earlier data for all manufacturing came from Epstein (1934).

In many respects, the data are rough. An unweighted average of the profit rates of firms above the minimum efficient size would seem appropriate here. But judging by Bain's figures (1956), there is little correlation between size and profit rate in steel, petroleum, and tires; and firms above the minimum efficient size account for almost all of the assets. Thus the weighted averages that we use should be fairly good approximations. In autos, there seems to be some correlation of this sort and consequently we use an unweighted average. This results in a much lower figure for autos

Appendix Table 3 **Transition matrices for the rubber tire industry, 1937–45 and 1945–52[a]**

Number of people employed at beginning of the period	Number employed at end of the period								
	Total	Disappearances	Under 40	40–159	160–639	640–2,559	2,560–10,239	10,240–40,959	Over 40,959
[Number of firms] 1937–45									
Entrants	22	0	4	12	4	2	0	0	0
Under 40	6	4	0	2	0	0	0	0	0
40–159	13	6	0	3	4	0	0	0	0
160–639	13	2	0	0	5	6	0	0	0
640–2,559	11	2	0	0	0	6	3	0	0
2,560–10,239	2	1	0	0	0	0	1	0	0
10,240–40,959	3	0	0	0	0	0	0	0	3
Over 40,959	1	0	0	0	0	0	0	0	1
1945–52									
Entrants	39	0	16	15	6	2	0	0	0
Under 40	4	4	0	0	0	0	0	0	0
40–159	17	14	0	2	1	0	0	0	0
160–639	12	3	0	1	6	2	0	0	0
640–2,559	14	5	0	0	1	7	1	0	0
2,560–10,239	6	0	0	0	0	0	6	0	0
10,240–40,959	0	0	0	0	0	0	0	0	0
Over 40,959	4	0	0	0	0	0	0	0	4

[a] See note a, Table 1. In each year a few firms had to be excluded because the *Rubber Red Book* provided no employment figures for them.

than the weighted average that is generally published. For 1949–59, the figure seems much too low, but it could be appreciably higher without affecting the results substantially.

To obtain C_{it} in each industry, we multiplied Bain's estimate (1956) of the required investment by the ratio of the average size of firm at the beginning of the tth period (measured in terms of capacity in steel and petroleum, production in automobiles, and employment in tires) to the average size of firm in 1945 (steel), 1947 (petroleum), 1949 (autos), or 1945 (tires). (By Bain's estimate we mean the average of the upper and lower limit he gives. It includes initial losses in the case of the automobile industry.) If the ratio of the average size to the minimum efficient size of firm remained constant over time in each industry and if the necessary investment varied in proportion to the minimum efficient size, this would be all right. This is probably as sensible as any of the simple, operational assumptions we could make, but its crudeness is obvious.

Note that C_{it} – even if it were accurately measured – would not necessarily be the minimum investment for an entrant because the typical entrant was below the minimum efficient size. For the same reason, the typical entrant could not expect to earn profits of Π_{it}. But it seems reasonable that the expected profitability of the typical entrant would be closely related to Π_{it}. And since the average size of an entrant is a relatively constant proportion of the minimum efficient size in these cases, it is pretty certain that the average capital requirements would be closely related to C_{it}.

The estimates of V_{it}^2 were obtained from the frequency distributions in Appendix Tables 1–3 and from *Moody's* figures on assets of automobile firms. To estimate the ratio of the average size of firm to the minimum efficient size, we divided Bain's estimate (1956) of the minimum efficient size in each industry into the average size of firm in 1947 (petroleum), 1945, (steel and tires), or 1949 (autos). The estimates of the minimum efficient size were 1,000,000 net tons of capacity (steel), 120,000 barrels of capacity (petroleum), $1\frac{1}{2}$ per cent of total employment (tires), and 10 per cent of total production (autos). The average size of firm in each case came from Tables 1–3 and *Automotive Industries*. Then we assumed that this ratio was constant over time. Note that the minimum efficient size for the production of specialty items (and in certain locations) may be less than this. This may be quite important. For further comments, see note 18. The crudeness of these estimates of $\overline{S}_{it}/\hat{S}_{it}$ is obvious.

Third, we describe the way in which firms were classified by S_{ij}^t and $S_{ij}^{t+\Delta}/S_{ij}^t$ in the χ^2 tests in Table 2 (in the text, p. 93). In the tests where deaths were included, the following size classes were used. In steel, we classified by their value of S_{ij}^t into four classes: 4000–15,999 tons, 16,000–63,999 tons, 64,000–255,999 tons, and 256,000–4,096,000 tons. In tires, we used four classes: 20–79 men, 80–159 men, 160–639 men, and 640–5119 men. And in petroleum, there were four classes: 500–999 barrels, 2000–3999 barrels, 8000–15,999 barrels, and 32,000–511,999 barrels. To cut down the computations involved, only firms in these classes were included. Thus, some of the largest and smallest firms were omitted in steel and tires, and some small, medium-sized, and large firms were excluded in petroleum. But had all firms been included, the results would almost certainly have been much the same.

In all cases, the firms in a size class were divided into three groups – those where $S_{ij}^{t+\Delta}/S_{ij}^t$ was less than 0·50, between 0·50 and 1·50, and 1·50 or more. These classes were chosen so that the expected number of firms in each cell of the contingency table would be five or more. (According to a well-known rule of thumb, the expected number in each cell should be this large.) This did not always turn out to be the case, but further work showed that the results would stand up if cells were combined.

With the following exceptions, these same classifications were used in the tests where deaths were excluded. In steel and tires, the two smallest size classes were combined. In some cases, firms were classified into groups where $S_{ij}^{t+\Delta}/S_{ij}^t$ was less than 1·00, between 1·00 and 2·00, and 2·00 or more. These changes were made to meet the rule of thumb noted above. Despite these changes, the expected number of firms in some cells was not quite five, but the results would not be affected if some cells were combined.

Fourth, we describe the way in which the innovators in Section 2 *B* were identified. The first step was to write trade associations and trade journals in each industry and to ask for a list of the important processes and products first introduced in the industry since 1918. Usable questionnaires were filled out and returned by one trade association and three trade journals. There was evidence that the respondents went to considerable pains in preparing them. The number of innovations of each type (process and product) that were provided ranged from about twenty to forty. In all, about 150 innovations were listed in the replies.

The second step was to determine what firm first introduced each innovation commercially and when this took place. To determine the date and to identify the innovator, articles in trade and technical journals were consulted. When doubts arose, letters were sent to equipment producers and members of the industry to determine whether the information was correct. Members of the Carnegie Institute of Technology engineering faculty were also consulted. Ultimately, the required information was obtained for over 80 per cent of the innovations. These data appear in Mansfield (1963a).

Finally, we describe the way in which the average annual growth rate of the 'other firms' in Table 3 (in the reading) was computed. If the innovator was smaller than the sizes given in the second sentence in note 18, we used the following technique to estimate the average annual growth rate of the other firms of its initial size. We assumed that, for the jth 'other firm' in the ith industry, $\ln S_{ij}^{t+\Delta} = a_i + b_i \ln S_{ij}^t + Z_{ij}'''$, where Z_{ij}''' is a random error term. An equation of this form fits the data for the smaller firms quite well. We then obtained least-squares estimates (shown in Table 3 in the text, p. 99) of a_i and b_i; and taking each innovator, we used this regression to estimate the average value of $\ln S_{ij}^{t+\Delta}$ for the 'other firms' corresponding to its value of S_{ij}^t. Deducting its value of $\ln S_{ij}^t$ from this computed average value and dividing the result by Δ, we obtain an estimate of the average annual growth rate of 'other firms' of the same original size as this innovator.

If the innovator was larger than the sizes given in note 18, we had to use another method because the regressions do not always fit the larger firms very well. In these cases, we used the average annual growth rate of the 'other firms' larger than the sizes given in note 18. Finally, to obtain the figures in the second row of Table 3 (in the text, p. 99), we took the resulting average growth rate for the 'other firms' corresponding to each innovator during the period (whether or not it was above the sizes in note 18) and averaged them.

References

ADELMAN, I. (1958), 'A stochastic process analysis of the size distribution of firms', *J. Amer. stat. Assoc.*, vol. 58, pp. 893–904.

ADELMAN, M. (1959), 'Differential rates and changes in concentration', *Rev. Econ. Stats.*, vol. 41, pp. 58–69.

AMERICAN IRON AND STEEL INSTITUTE, (1916, 1926, 1935, 1945 and 1954), *Directory of Iron and Steel Works in the United States*, New York.

BAIN, J. S. (1956), *Barriers to New Competition*, Harvard University Press.

BRONFENBRENNER, J. (1953), 'Source and size of least-square bias in a two-equation model', in W. C. Hood, and T. C. Koopmans (eds.), *Studies in Econometric Method*, New York.

BUREAU OF MINES, (1937, 1947 and 1957), *Petroleum Refineries, including Cracking Plants in the United States*, Washington.

CHURCHILL, B. (1959), 'Rise in the business population', *Survey curr. Bus.*, vol. 39, pp. 15–19.

COLLINS, N., and PRESTON, L. (1961), 'The size structure of industrial firms, 1909–58', *Amer. econ. Rev.*, vol. 51, pp. 986–1011.

DE CHAZEAU, M., and KAHN, A. (1959), *Integration and Competition in the Petroleum Industry*, New Haven.

EPSTEIN, R. (1934), *Industrial Profits in the United States*, New York.

FERGUSON, C. (1960), 'The relationship of business size to stability: an empirical approach', *J. indust. Econ.*, vol. 19, pp. 43–62.

GIBRAT, R. (1931), *Les inégalités économiques*, Paris.

HART, P., and PRAIS, S. (1956), 'The analysis of business concentration: a statistical approach', *J. Roy. stat. Soc.*, Series A., vol. 119, pp. 150–81.

HOGGATT, A., (1959), 'A simulation study of an economic model', in *Contributions to Scientific Research in Management*, Los Angeles.

HYMER, S., and PASHIGIAN, B. (1959), 'Firm size and rate of growth (abstract)', *Econometrica*, vol. 27, p. 615.

MANSFIELD, E. (1961), 'Technical change and the rate of imitation', *Econometrica*, vol. 29, pp. 741–66.

MANSFIELD, E. (1963a), 'Size of firm, market structure and innovation', *J. polit. Econ.* vol. 71, pp. 556–76.

MANSFIELD, E. (1963b), 'The speed of response of firms to new techniques', *Q.J.Econ.*, vol. 77, pp. 290–311.

MANSFIELD, E. (1964), 'Industrial research and development expenditures', *J. polit. Econ.*, vol. 72, pp. 319–40.

MANSFIELD, E., and HENSLEY, C. (1960), 'The logistic process: the stochastic epidemic curve and applications', *J. Roy. stat. Soc.*, Series B., vol. 22, pp. 332–7.

MARSHALL, A. (1916), *Principles of Economics*, Macmillan.

MILLER, J. (1955), 'Measures of monopoly power and concentration: their economic significance', *Business Concentration and Price Policy*, Princeton.

OXENFELDT, A. (1943), *New Firms and Free Enterprise*, Washington.

PAPANDREAU, A. and WHEELER, J. (1954), *Competition and its Regulation*, New York.

PENROSE, E. (1959), *The Theory of the Growth of the Firm*, New York.

SCHROEDER, A. (1953), *The Growth of the Major Steel Companies*, Baltimore.

SIMON, H., and BONINI, C. (1958), 'The size distribution of business firms', *Amer. econ. Rev.*, vol. 48, pp. 607–17.

STIGLER, G. (1955), 'Introduction', *Business Concentration and Price Policy*, Princeton.

STIGLER, G. (1958), 'The economies of scale', *J. Law Econ.*, vol. 1, October, pp. 54–71.

TRIFFIN, R. (1941), *Monopolistic Competition and General Equilibrium Theory*, Cambridge.

VATTER, H. (1952), 'The closure of entry in the American automobile industry', *Oxford econ. Papers*, vol. 4, pp. 213–34.

8 George J. Stigler

A Note on Potential Competition

George J. Stigler, *The Organization of Industry*, Richard D. Irwin, 1968, Addendum 3 to chapter 2, pp. 19–22.

The leading exponent of the importance of potential competition in protecting the community from exploitation by trusts was J. B. Clark. In a characteristic passage, he wrote:

When prices are unduly high, owing to the grasping policy of some trust, what happens? New competition usually appears in the field. Capital is seeking outlets, but it has become hard to find them. Readily, and sometimes almost recklessly, does it build new mills and begin to compete with trusts, when these consolidated companies do not know enough to proceed on a conservative plan. Let any combination of producers raise the prices beyond a certain limit, and it will encounter this difficulty. The new mills that will spring into existence will break down prices; and the fear of these new mills, without their actual coming, is often enough to keep prices from rising to an extortionate height. The mill that has never been built is already a power in the market: for if it will surely be built under certain conditions, the effect of this certainty is to keep prices down (1901, p. 13).

Clark's only fear was that unfair tactics (selective price cutting, pre-emption of dealers, and railroad rebates) would stop potential competition, and he wished to restrict public policy to eliminating such tactics. He believed trusts were efficient and inevitable and also that potential rivals were an efficient check upon trusts – and made no effort to reconcile these views.

The 'limit-price' theory of Bain (1956 and 1958), subsequently elaborated by Modigliani (1958), is essentially a refurnished theory of potential competition. It differs from the traditional versions chiefly in being more precise.

In Modigliani's restatement, the analysis turns on economies of scale (although it could be adapted to a true barrier to entry)[1]. In Figure 1, let D be the industry demand curve, C the average cost curve of a potential entrant, and P_c the level of minimum costs for the existing firms (of optimum size). Shift the cost curve C to the right until no part of it lies below the demand curve, and the axis of ordinates with respect to which it is

1. [Stigler defines a barrier to entry as 'a cost of producing (at some or every rate of output) which must be borne by a firm which seeks to enter an industry but is not borne by firms already in the industry' (1968, p. 67). Ed.].

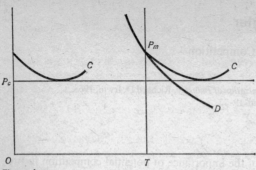

Figure 1

drawn shifts to T. The demand curve P_mD is that which faces the new entrant if the existing firms

1. Sell output OT at price P_m, and
2. They will persist in selling this amount if the potential entrant actually enters.

The price P_m, so determined, is then the maximum price which, on these assumptions, will exclude entry.

Bain believes that such a price will tend to exclude new entrants for two reasons. The lower profits are less likely to be detected and invite entry. And the price so arrived at will be interpreted as evidence that the existing firms do not welcome new rivals and may possibly combat them by active price competition[2]. The analysis does not guarantee low profits to existing firms, but presumably they are lower than they would be without regard to entry.

This theory raises questions faster than it answers them. Four are particularly troublesome:

1. Why should it be more profitable to exclude all entrants than merely to retard their rate of entry? Suppose at a price 10 per cent above P_m (Figure 1), a new entrant will appear in seven years – may this not be more profitable?[3]

2. Why should a prospective entrant believe that after his entry a colluding group will not revise its policy so that all will earn returns above the competitive level? (The theory predicts the disappearance of more than competitive returns after a single firm enters.)

3. If the industry's demand is growing over time, how is the prospective

2. I so interpret the sentence: '[the potential entrant] may view the price which the established firm(s) currently charge as a partial indicator of the rival price policy he will face after entry.' (Bain, 1958, p. 225).
3. Bain notes the possibility (1958, p. 230).

entrant to be persuaded that he can have no share of the increments of demand?

4. Industry structure is irrelevant. The ability of the oligopolists to agree upon and police the limit price is apparently independent of the sizes and numbers of oligopolists. The theory of oligopoly is solved by murder.

No empirical evidence has been offered for the theory, which is not surprising.

The interesting question, from the viewpoint of both the theory of oligopoly and the measurement of concentration, is: how does one measure potential competition? The number of potential entrants is necessarily greater than the number of actual entrants (per unit of time); indeed the number of potential entrants is perhaps at a maximum in a *declining* industry such as agriculture.

The answer can be given at two levels. If we are asked, in an antitrust case, to determine whether Procter & Gamble was likely to enter the household bleach industry, we shall proceed by examining

1. The entry of other soap companies into bleaches.
2. The similarity of bleaches to the other products (industries) into which soap companies enter.

One can form a defensible estimate, and one which can be improved as our understanding of firm product structures develops.[4]

But if we are asked to identify the number of potential entrants of an industry, we must ultimately resort to the actual rate of entry when the industry was an attractive field for investment. Only when an industry has had substantial profits in excess of the competitive level and for a substantial period can we assume that potential entrants would seek to become more than potential. But then we are in effect using the magnitude and duration of monopoly profits as our main (inverse) measure of the number of potential entrants. Unless this measure can be replaced by another, potential competition has no *explanatory* value in dealing with monopoly price or monopoly profit.

4. The Federal Trade Commission and the Supreme Court found entry to be likely, but on the basis only of casual intuition.

References

BAIN, J. S. (1956), *Barriers to New Competition*, Harvard University Press.
BAIN, J. S. (1958), 'A note on pricing in monopoly and oligopoly', reprinted in R. B. Heflebower and G. W. Stocking (eds.), *Readings in Industrial Organization and Public Policy*, Richard D. Irwin.
CLARK, J. B. (1901), *The Control of Trusts*, New York.
MODIGLIANI, F. (1958), 'New developments on the oligopoly front', *J. polit. Econ.*, vol. 66, pp. 215–32.

Part Three
Concentration

The seven readings on concentration, a major issue of public policy in many countries, are concerned primarily with attempts to explain or account for levels of concentration in different industries, and for changes in concentration over time. Pryor (Reading 9) establishes that the ranking of industries by concentration is much the same in a number of different countries, a finding which suggests the importance of underlying cost and market conditions. In the course of a study of the effects of advertising expenditures on the size distribution of firms, Guth (Reading 10) examines the influence on concentration of production scale economies and capital requirements. Kamerschen (Reading 11) looks into the relationship between changes in the extent of the market and changes in concentration. Weiss (Reading 12) analyses in detail the changes in concentration in six industries. Stein (Reading 13) considers a model in which market uncertainty and a simple learning process can account for high concentration. Weiss (Reading 14) discusses and examines the hypothesis that market uncertainty, in the case of goods in which design, style or fashion elements are important, leads to increases in concentration. Finally, Scherer (Reading 15) develops a model which shows that random influences alone can generate increases in concentration over time.

Part Three
Concentration

9 Frederic L. Pryor

An International Comparison of Concentration Ratios

Frederic L. Pryor, 'An international comparison of concentration ratios', *Review of Economics and Statistics*, vol. 54, 1972, pp. 130–40.

Introduction

Up to now empirical research on industrial monopoly utilizing comparative data for several countries has focused primarily on relative concentration levels in certain specified industries. The purpose of this article is to supplement these analyses by investigating from international data what we can learn about overall concentration as well as concentration in every manufacturing industry. This is accomplished by comparing the degree of industrial concentration in twelve nations on both an aggregate level and on the individual industry level. For the major industrial nations I show not only that the average levels of concentration in the manufacturing sector are the same, but also that concentration ratios are roughly the same in any specified four-digit industry.

After a short discussion of several important relationships, the empirical analysis is started with an examination of weighted averages of four-firm four-digit concentration ratios for various nations. This is followed by a regression analysis of individual concentration ratios for specified industries for pairs of nations. An attempt is made to interpret these results in the following section and the study ends with a brief summary of the most important implications of the empirical results. Technical matters including the sources of data and their adjustment are in the appendix (pp. 138–41).

Several preliminary remarks

An implicit or explicit assumption in many discussions about international aspects of the 'monopoly problem' is that industrial concentration is lower in the United States than in other countries having smaller domestic markets.[1] Underlying this assumption are the arguments that a single minimum efficient scale (MES) or optimal size enterprise may produce more than enough to supply the domestic market of a small nation, while in the

1. For instance, in an introduction to a presentation of French concentration ratios, Loup (1969) expressly notes that the United States concentration ratios are lower but does not bother to carry out any actual empirical comparisons which would, in point of fact, show the reverse conclusion (see Table 2).

United States, domestic consumption is equal in many cases to the production of many MES or optimal size firms; further, the minimum efficient or optimal scale of an enterprise is roughly the same in all developed nations; and finally, the relevant market facing the enterprise is related to the domestic GNP, and foreign trade is an irrelevant consideration.

These views have come under attack on several fronts. The minimum efficient or optimal scale (in terms of output) may depend on relative factor prices; or it may also depend on size of the domestic market.[2] Further, since many United States industries are regional, not national, the average degree of concentration in the United States is much higher than previously suspected when this phenomenon is properly taken into account;[3] and the European industrial concentration data do not look so out of line with the American results. Foreign trade considerations also seem too important to omit as many analysts have done. Although attempts have been recently made to construct coherent models taking all these various factors systematically into account, we have far to go to reach a satisfactory explanation.

In the industrial organization literature one finds scattered comments about the degree to which given industries in different nations have similar degrees of concentration. Although it seems likely that more concentrated industries in one nation might also be more concentrated in another, a satisfactory model of this phenomenon has not yet been presented either, and primary efforts have focused on explaining differences in industrial concentration between the United States and the United Kingdom.

Any type of complete theoretical statement on these matters must take into account the following empirical observations:

1. Average sizes of manufacturing establishments among nations are strongly correlated with indicators of market size of these nations.[4] Data illustrating this relationship are presented in Table 1 for various types of measures of average establishment size for the manufacturing sector as a whole; similar relationships hold for narrowly defined industries as well.

2. The degree to which economies are characterized by multi-establishment enterprises is correlated also with indicators of the market size of nations.[5]

2. This point was emphasized to me in correspondence by Pashigian; for a detailed analysis of certain other critical aspects of the relationships between market size and monopoly, see Pashigian (1968; 1969).

3. This is argued by Shepherd (1970).

4. This relationship is argued from theoretical considerations and is also found empirically to hold true in Pryor (1972). Other alleged determinants of establishment size such as the level of development of the economy were tested and did not seem to be correlated with establishment size, at least in my sample of twenty-three developed or semideveloped economies during the 1960s.

5. Data and theoretical justifications for this relationship are presented in Pryor, (1973).

Table 1 Average employment sizes of establishments and enterprises in manufacturing[6]

Establishments	S	R^2
$\ln A = 2 \cdot 805 + 0 \cdot 166^* \ln Y + 0 \cdot 093 \ \ln X$ $\quad\quad\quad (0 \cdot 035) \quad\quad\quad (0 \cdot 084)$	23	$0 \cdot 36^*$
$\ln E = 1 \cdot 070 + 0 \cdot 273^* \ln Y + 0 \cdot 241^* \ln X$ $\quad\quad\quad (0 \cdot 049) \quad\quad\quad (0 \cdot 117)$	23	$0 \cdot 61^*$
$\ln N = 1 \cdot 843 + 0 \cdot 508^* \ln Y + 0 \cdot 481^* \ln X$ $\quad\quad\quad (0 \cdot 082) \quad\quad\quad (0 \cdot 193)$	23	$0 \cdot 67^*$

Enterprises		
$\ln A = 1 \cdot 882 + 0 \cdot 173^* \ln Y + 0 \cdot 065 \ \ln X$ $\quad\quad\quad (0 \cdot 060) \quad\quad\quad (0 \cdot 138)$	10	$0 \cdot 63^*$
$\ln E = -3 \cdot 203 + 0 \cdot 541^* \ln Y + 0 \cdot 087 \ln X$ $\quad\quad\quad (0 \cdot 121) \quad\quad\quad (0 \cdot 279)$	10	$0 \cdot 82^*$
$\ln N = -7 \cdot 785 + 0 \cdot 919^* \ln Y + 0 \cdot 682^* \ln X$ $\quad\quad\quad (0 \cdot 105) \quad\quad\quad (0 \cdot 243)$	10	$0 \cdot 93^*$

$*$ = statistical significance at the $0 \cdot 05$ level.

A = arithmetic average employment size of production units in manufacturing. E = entropy index of employment sizes of production units in manufacturing. N = Niehans index of employment sizes of production units in manufacturing. Y = GNP calculated with dollar price weights in 1000 dollars. X = ratio of nonagricultural merchandise exports to value-added in manufacturing and mining. S = number of nations in sample. R^2 = coefficient of determination.

6. The regressions come from the sources cited in footnotes 4 and 5. In the regressions two measures of 'market size' are used: the total GNP (with the dollar value of the GNP calculated with purchasing power exchange rates) and the relative importance of nonagricultural exports. When the latter variable is omitted from the regressions, the other calculated regression coefficients remain roughly the same. The standard errors are shown in parentheses below the calculated coefficients.

For the employment size variables, only establishments or enterprises with labor forces of 20 or more are included in the calculations. . . . The formula for the entropy index is $\log E = \log L - \sum s_i \log (1/s_i)$; and the formula for the Niehans index is $N = \sum s_i L_i$, where E = entropy index; N = Niehans index; s_i = share of labor force of a particular production unit in the total labor force; L = total labor force; and L_i = labor force in the production unit.

For the foreign trade variable I am assuming that the ratio of value added in non-agricultural export good production to total value added in manufacturing is roughly in the same proportion in all nations to the ratio of total value of nonagricultural exports to value added in manufacturing, an approximation for which some evidence exists.

Regressions such as those shown in the table have also been calculated for individual industries and, in most cases, show roughly similar results. Other regression experiments using the entire manufacturing sector but assuming a constant composition of output for all nations were also carried and the results were very similar to those presented in the above table.

This relationship holds not only for manufacturing as a whole but also for narrowly defined industries as well.

3. Given the above two empirical relationships, it should not be surprising that average size of industrial enterprises among nations is strongly correlated with indicators of market size. Data illustrating this relationship are also presented in Table 1 for various types of measures of average enterprise size for the manufacturing sector; similar empirical results can be obtained for narrowly defined industries as well.

Since the purpose of this Reading is to present the results of an empirical study of concentration, exploration of the theoretical factors underlying the above described relationships would lead us too far from the central focus. In addition, consideration of alternative theories linking enterprise size and market size (e.g. theories that link product variety to enterprise size and size of domestic market to product variety) must also be left to others. Whatever the theoretical explanations underlying the results presented in Table 1, the empirical relations shown must be noted carefully before the empirical comparisons of monopoly presented below can be correctly interpreted.

The average degree of monopoly

Our empirical knowledge about relative industrial concentration is small, especially since most international comparisons have been limited to the United States and the United Kingdom.[7] Using some newly released data, we can now extend such international comparisons.

The statistic used below to measure industrial concentration is the four-firm concentration ratio, i.e. the percentage of the value of shipments or production accounted for by the top four enterprises in a narrowly defined industry. In certain cases, which are designated below, the concentration ratios are based on the percentage of employment in a particular industry that is accounted for by the largest four enterprises in an industry. Although there are certain well-known objections to the use of concentration ratios as a measure of monopoly, they provide the only available data with which any comparisons can be made.[8] The concentration ratios are calcu-

7. Two recent international comparisons dealing with more than the United States and the United Kingdom deserve mention: Bain (1966); and Adelman (1966). In neither study are global comparisons of industrial concentration calculated.

8. One objection to the use of four-firm concentration ratios is that the relative concentration in two industries might be reversed if a different cutoff point is used; empirical investigations using United States data show this objection of little consequence. Another criticism is that concentration ratios may understate concentration in regional industry since they are calculated on a national level; I try to make corrections in my analysis for this factor. Finally, many have argued that the four-digit classifications are too broad and that industries must be more narrowly defined. In many cases this is a quite valid objection but unfortunately this empirical investigation is limited by the data at hand.

lated primarily for industries corresponding to the four-digit classification in the United States industrial statistics reporting system; in certain cases, however, concentration ratios for five-digit industries (i.e. industries defined more narrowly) are used after appropriate adjustments are made.

From pairs of concentration ratios for similarly defined industries of the United States and a given foreign country there were computed weighted averages of overall concentration for each. The results for all countries were then standardized by setting the weighted United States concentration ratios equal to 1·00 and recalculating the foreign weighted average so that the derived ratio was obtained. The number of such pairs of concentration ratios in the indices varied, ranging from 24 (the United States–Netherlands comparisons) to 107 (the United States–Sweden comparisons), and depended on the number of similarly defined industries for which concentration data could be found.

The indices (or weighted averages) were actually calculated in a two-step procedure because of weighting difficulties.[9] Where concentration ratios based on value of shipments were available, value-added weights were used to consolidate the ratios of individual industries into weighted averages for classes corresponding to the International Standard Industrial Classification (ISIC) two-digit branches of manufacturing. These two-digit branch averages were then combined using value-added weights for the entire branch to calculate the aggregate measure for the entire manufacturing sector.[10] Where only concentration ratios from employment data are available, a similar two-step procedure was carried out using employment in individual industries and in the two-digit industrial branches as weights instead. For France both types of concentration ratios were available and the results were roughly the same.

There is, of course, an index-number problem in the choice of the national weights in the individual comparisons between the United States and different foreign nations. And, moreover, problems of interpretation arise whatever weights are selected. In order to gauge quantitatively the magnitude of this problem, three different sets of indices were calculated for the two-country comparisons: one using United States value-added weights for the individual industries and two-digit branches; another using United States value-added weights for the individual industries but foreign

9. Weighted averages or indices of concentration have been analysed and used by a number of economists. For a theoretical analysis of their construction see Weiss (1963, pp. 231–54).

10. Greater details on the construction of the averages are given in the appendix. Value-added weights are used to aggregate concentration ratios within the two-digit branches in order to minimize differences in definition between weights that might occur because the degree of vertical integration of a particular industry is defined differently in the various national statistics.

Table 2 Weighted four-firm, four-digit aggregate average concentration ratios as a ratio of weighted concentration ratios in the United States[11]

Country	Date	Type of concentration ratio	Size of 'basic sample'	Sub-branch weights / Branch weights — US v.a. or employment / US v.a. or employment	US v.a. or employment / Other nation v.a. or employment	Other nation v.a. or employment / Other nation v.a. or employment
(a) No adjustments						
United States	1963	both		1·00	1·00	1·00
Belgium	1963	shipments	54	1·66	1·52	N.A.
Canada	1948	employment	48	1·38	1·35	1·34
France	1963	shipments	70	0·93	0·95	0·92
West Germany	1963	shipments	89	0·94	0·92	N.A.
Italy	1961	employment	56	0·89	0·86	0·83
Japan	1962	shipments	70	1·14	1·11	N.A.
Netherlands	1963	shipments	24	1·23	1·25	N.A.
Sweden	c. 1965	shipments	107	1·54	1·55	1·41
Switzerland	1965	employment	61	1·63	1·68	1·71
United Kingdom	1951	shipments	101	1·20	1·13	1·14
Yugoslavia	1963	shipments	42	1·47	1·41	N.A.

(b) Omitting US 'regional industries'

United States	1963	both		1·00	1·00	1·00
Belgium	1963	shipments	37	1·54	1·35	N.A.
Canada	1948	employment	37	1·34	1·31	1·29
France	1963	shipments	47	0·85	0·87	0·85
West Germany	1963	shipments	67	0·91	0·93	N.A.
Italy	1961	employment	38	0·82	0·76	0·79
Japan	1962	shipments	46	1·02	1·02	N.A.
Netherlands	1963	shipments	16	1·10	1·10	N.A.
Sweden	c. 1965	shipments	74	1·42	1·45	1·49
Switzerland	1965	employment	39	1·51	1·69	1·72
United Kingdom	1951	shipments	72	1·07	1·03	1·13
Yugoslavia	1963	shipments	29	1·33	1·28	N.A.

11. For the 'type of concentration ratio' I have distinguished for simplicity only between those based on shipments and employment. In the former class I include those based on production, sales, and shipments and defined in either value or quantity terms. The 'basic sample' designates the number of comparable industries included in the comparison with the United States using United States weights for both sub-branch and branch weights. The number of comparable industries using foreign sub-branch weights is somewhat greater since a number of five-digit industries are included. N.A. means not available. To give some idea of the absolute values involved in the comparisons, the following data on United States weighted concentration ratios (using 427 four-digit industries) may be of interest (with weighted concentration ratios based on employment data in parentheses): no adjustments to the raw data, 0·39 (0·30); adjustments made by excluding United States regional and local industries, 0·44 (0·33). Shepherd (1961) makes different adjustments by including the regional and local industries, but increasing their concentration ratios and, in addition, adjusting the concentration ratios of certain industries to take into account the fact that they are too widely or narrowly defined. If we follow Shepherd's adjustments, the United States weighted concentration ratio rises to 0·58 (0·44); this procedure is not, however, followed in the text. Sources of data and methods of calculation are given in the appendix.

value-added weights for the two-digit branches; and a third using foreign value-added weights for both individual industry and industrial branch weights. Much less data are available for the third comparison but, as shown below, the results for all three calculations are roughly the same, so that we can draw relatively unambiguous conclusions without worrying unduly about index-number effects.

A final problem arises in the treatment of regional industries and several choices of method are available. Rather than adjust the concentration ratios for each country to reflect whether regional industries are involved, I have chosen to omit from the indices those industries that can be classified as regional in the United States.[12] This procedure considerably reduces the size of the samples and, in order to give some perspective on the effect of this measure, comparisons based on the raw data without such adjustments for regional industries are also presented.

The data in Table 2 show that three nations, France, West Germany, and Italy, have weighted concentration ratios somewhat lower than the United States, while an additional three, Japan, the Netherlands, and the United Kingdom, have weighted concentration ratios only slightly higher than the United States. In only five nations are concentration ratios clearly higher, namely, Belgium, Canada, Sweden, Switzerland, and Yugoslavia. It is also noteworthy that concentration in Yugoslavia, a socialist nation which some have believed to be highly monopolized, has about the same degree of concentration as Sweden and Switzerland.

Unfortunately, no convenient tests of statistical significance can be performed on these doubly weighted averages in order to determine whether or not the differences are important. Nevertheless, the unweighted averages yield results quite similar in most cases to the weighted averages and for these we can perform significance tests. Some relevant data for the various nations excluding United States regional industries are presented in Table 3; similar results are obtained when other samples are used.

The data in Table 2 show that there are no statistical differences at the 0·05 level in the average aggregate concentration ratios of the United States and France, West Germany, Italy, Japan, the Netherlands, and the United Kingdom. In the remaining five nations the overall levels of concentration are higher.

From Table 2 it should be clear that the aggregate degree of concentration is related in some way to the overall market size, rather than level of

12. I have followed the designation of these industries (with several minor modifications) that is made by Shepherd (1970), appendix Table 8. It should be added that in the choice of comparable United States and United Kingdom industries, I also partly followed Shepherd's designation (1961) but included industries with low concentration ratios as well.

Table 3 Unweighted averages of aggregate, four-firm, four-digit concentration ratios (excluding United States 'regional industries')[13]

Country	Size of sample	Ratio of foreign mean to US mean	Difference between absolute levels of mean concentration ratios, stated as percentages
Belgium	37	1·46	18·41*
Canada	37	1·52	20·94*
France	47	0·90	− 5·26
West Germany	67	0·98	− 0·84
Italy	38	0·97	− 1·20
Japan	46	1·05	2·76
Netherlands	16	1·17	6·77
Sweden	74	1·58	27·63*
Switzerland	39	1·49	17·47*
United Kingdom	72	1·04	1·78
Yugoslavia	29	1·50	26·93*

* Designates statistical significance at 0·05 level.

economic development. The countries fall quite naturally into two groups: those with large dollar values of gross national production (United States, France, West Germany, Italy, Japan, and the United Kingdom); and those with small dollar values of gross national production (Belgium, Canada, the Netherlands, Sweden, Switzerland, and Yugoslavia). The countries in the first group have roughly the same concentration ratios; further, their overall levels of concentration are much lower than those for the nations in the second group (with the exception of the Netherlands). Dividing the groups of nations into those with relatively high and low per capita income admits of many more exceptions to any generalization. Using regression techniques to analyse the data yields the same conclusions.[14]

In interpreting these results one caveat must be emphasized: the data related only to structural characteristics and not to the functioning of the individual economies. Before we can generalize from such structural information to the state of competition, we must have information about other considerations such as the degree of cartelization (or collusion) and

13. Sources of data are the same as the previous table. The concentration ratios for each pair of comparisons are added without weighting one industry more than another.

14. I calculated a number of such regressions, of which a typical one is: $\ln C = 1·712 − 0·218^* \ln Y$; $R^2 = 0·71$; $S = 11$ (United States excluded) and where $C = $ average (0·047) aggregate concentration ratio, regional industries excluded, United States weights for both sub-branches and branches; and the rest of the symbols are the same as in Table 1. Changing the form of such regressions or adding additional independent variables does not substantially change the results.

the role of foreign trade. Since foreign trade plays a more important role in most foreign nations than in the United States, imports may provide an additional competitive element in those economies vis-à-vis the United States (assuming that tariff barriers are roughly similar); on the other hand, cartelization may be more important in these foreign nations as well. Credible conclusions about the relative state of competition in various nations can only be drawn from highly detailed studies in which these various factors can be properly weighted.[15]

Concentration within particular industries

The first step of the analysis is to rank the various two-digit manufacturing branches in each of the twelve nations of the sample according to their weighted average concentration. The average rankings of such weighted average concentration estimates are presented in Table 4.

A very distinct pattern of relative concentration emerges and the concordance coefficient, which designates the degree to which the rank orderings of the various nations are similar, is statistically significant at the 0·01 level. Concentration in all nations is highest among the industries in the tobacco, transport equipment, machinery and petroleum and coal product branches and lowest in the furniture, lumber products (except furniture) and clothing branches.

A more detailed comparison can be made by examining the relationship between individual comparable concentration ratios for the United States and each of the foreign nations and the results of one set of such calculations is presented in Table 5.

The calculations show that in all cases there is a statistically significant (0·05 level) relationship between the four-firm, four-digit concentration ratios in the United States and the various foreign nations. The amount of variation of the foreign concentration ratios that is 'explained' by variation in comparable United States ratios ranges from 26 to 67 per cent.

The most striking results occur for France, West Germany, Italy, Japan and the Netherlands; for these nations we cannot reject the hypothesis (at the 0·05 level of significance) that the concentration ratios in particular

15. Foreign trade considerations can be partly taken into account by calculating concentration ratios so as to include imports (Shepherd, 1972), which uses this approach) or by calculating international concentration ratios, so as to be able to take into account multinational enterprises (see Miller, forthcoming, which uses this approach). Nevertheless, we also need information concerning the degree to which tariffs protect domestic markets and the substitutability of foreign and domestic trade before the competitive effect of foreign trade can be fully judged. Quantitatively determining the effect of formal and informal collusion, cartelization, and other such devices dampening the forces of competition is even more difficult. Effects of both foreign trade and domestic market considerations are analysed in one manner by Esposito and Esposito (1971).

Table 4 Average rank orderings of weighted concentration ratios[16]

ISIC number	Industry	
20	Food processing	13
21	Beverages	15
22	Tobacco products	1
23	Textiles	16
24	Clothing and shoes	18
25	Lumber products export furniture	19
26	Furniture and fixtures	20
27	Paper products	14
28	Printing and publishing	8
29	Leather products	17
30	Rubber products	6
31	Chemicals	5
32	Petroleum and coal products	4
33	Stone, glass, glass products	10
34	Primary metals	12
35	Metal products except machinery	11
36	Machinery except electric and transport	3
37	Electrical equipment	7
38	Transportation equipment	2
39	Miscellaneous	9
	Concordance coefficient	0·51
	Number of nations in sample	12

industries are numerically the same as in the United States, i.e., that the regression equation is: foreign concentration ratio for industry $X = 0·0 +1·0 \times$ United States concentration ratio for industry X! Thus, for five out of the six nations that have similar overall levels of concentration as the United States, the results appear because the concentration ratios for individual industries are similar as well. (The United Kingdom is the only exception.) These results are particularly impressive because there is a statistical bias in the regressions that leads to slopes less than unity, a positive constant coefficient, and an *underestimation* of the degree of equality

16. Weighted two-digit, four-firm concentration ratios were calculated for the twelve nations and then ranked; the average ranks for the manufacturing sector for the individual two-digit industries are presented in the table. The sources for the data are the same as the previous table.

The concordance coefficient, which ranges from 0·00 to 1·00, designates the degree to which the various rank orderings are similar; the coefficient presented in the table is significant at the 0·01 level, i.e. the rankings in the various nations comprising the sample are quite similar. This coefficient is defined and analysed by Kendall (1962).

Table 5 Relationships between foreign and US four-firm, four-digit concentration ratios (excluding United States 'regional industries')[17]

Country			S	R^2
Belgium	$F =$	$0.283* + 0.752* U$	37	$0.26*$
		(0.095) (0.216)		
Canada	$F =$	$0.220* + 0.973* U$	37	$0.59*$
		(0.063) (0.138)		
France	$F =$	$0.009 + 0.918* U$	47	$0.55*$
		(0.073) (0.125)		
West Germany	$F =$	$0.088 + 0.807* U$	67	$0.53*$
		(0.053) (0.095)		
Italy	$F = -0.019 + 1.017* U$		38	$0.67*$
		(0.053) (0.118)		
Japan	$F =$	$0.162 + 0.754* U$	46	$0.37*$
		(0.088) (0.149)		
Netherlands	$F =$	$0.195 + 0.674* U$	16	$0.36*$
		(0.107) (0.241)		
Sweden	$F =$	$0.444* + 0.652* U$	74	$0.46*$
		(0.044) (0.083)		
Switzerland	$F =$	$0.290* + 0.674* U$	39	$0.37*$
		(0.061) (0.145)		
United Kingdom	$F =$	$0.227* + 0.541* U$	72	$0.26*$
		(0.056) (0.110)		
Yugoslavia	$F =$	$0.557* + 0.469* U$	29	$0.36*$
		(0.073) (0.119)		

$F =$ foreign four-firm, four-digit concentration ratio. $U =$ US four-firm/four-digit concentration ratio. $S =$ number of concentration ratios of different four-digit industries in sample. $R^2 =$ coefficient of determination. Asterisks denote a statistical difference from zero at the 0.05 level.

between foreign and United States concentration ratios because concentration ratios are bounded between 0.00 and 1.00.[18] Investigation of the individual industries in which concentration ratios in the five nations differed significantly from those of the United States yielded no very interesting results.

17. Standard errors are placed below the calculated regression coefficients; asterisks denote statistical significance at the 0.05 level. The source of data is the same as in previous tables.

18. The nature of this bias can be seen most clearly by starting with the full form of the calculated regression: $F = a + bU + u$, where u is a random disturbance. If U is very small, u will tend to be positive since F cannot be less than 0.00; if U is very large, u will tend to be negative since F cannot be greater than 1.00. This will lead to a positive intercept and a slope less than unity, even when the true relation is $F = 0.00 + 1.00$ U. Certain complicated statistical techniques such as probit analysis can be employed to get around this difficulty but for the purposes at hand these did not seem necessary.

For Belgium and Canada we cannot reject the hypothesis (at the 0·05 level) that the individual concentration ratios are equal to the individual United States ratios plus a constant; and, comparing Tables 2 and 3, the constant in the regression is roughly equal to the difference between the overall levels of concentration in these nations and the United States. Thus, for seven out of the eleven nations under examination (Belgium and Canada plus the five nations discussed in the previous paragraph) the slope co-efficient relating the United States and foreign concentration ratios for individual industries is not statistically different from unity.

For the remaining four nations (Sweden, Switzerland, the United King-dom, and Yugoslavia), the pattern of relationship with United States con-centration ratios is statistically significant but less easy to interpret, since, for a given industry, their concentration ratios are greater than those in the United States for industries with low concentration, and are lower than those in the United States for highly concentrated industries.[19]

The results show clearly that forces making for monopoly in a particular industry are similar in the twelve nations. A considerable amount of empirical work has been devoted to explaining the impact of forces such as barriers to entry on industrial concentration in the United States and much work needs to be done on other nations as well. The available international data do not permit adequate derivation of measures of barriers to entry that are independent of the concentration variable that we are trying to ex-plain.[20] I did try to test a recently proposed hypothesis by L. G. Telser that

Several experiments were made to test the strength of the bias, e.g. the regressions were recalculated, omitting from the sample all industries in which the concentration ratio of one or both nations is a prespecified distance from 0·00 and 1·00. These seemed in most cases to yield roughly the same results as those presented in Table 5 above. The samples did not seem large enough to be able to be used to discriminate between different func-tional forms of the relationship between the concentration ratios of pairs of nations and, therefore, I chose the most simple relationship.

19. Pashigian (1968) argues that the difference in concentration ratios for individual industries in the two nations can be explained by the relative sizes of the individual markets for these two countries.

20. I did find significant correlations between the rank order of concentration (Table 4) and rank orders of fixed capital in average size enterprises in the two-digit industries, or of workers and employees in average size enterprises. Unfortunately, since absolute and relative enterprise size are highly correlated, such measures of barriers to entry are quite inadequate. From United States and Swiss industrial censuses, I found data on the ratio of research and development personnel to total personnel in the industry; and these data give some indication of the 'degree of technical intensiveness' of an industry which, in turn, might reflect an important barrier to entry. Although such a rank order-ing of industries is significantly correlated with the average rank ordering of concentra-tion, the measure of this technological barrier is sufficiently imperfect to make inter-pretation of the results very uncertain.

the nature of the competitive process is such that concentration is related to the capital intensiveness of production by calculating a rank order correlation coefficient between relative concentration (Table 4) and relative capital–labor ratios,[21] but the calculated coefficient was low and not statistically significant. A quantitative international study of forces encouraging monopoly in particular industries must be put on the agenda of future research if we wish to fully understand industrial organization from a world standpoint.

Some interpretative remarks

For those who believe that the degree of industrial concentration is inversely related to market size, the results presented in this Reading provide an interesting paradox. The following remarks are intended to provide assistance in unraveling this problem.

1. The empirical results of this study are consistent with the proposition presented above that average enterprise sizes (both in the manufacturing sector as a whole and also in individual industries) vary according to the market size in aggregate. If we look closely at the various indicators of enterprise size in the regressions reported in Table 1, we note that the greater the weight placed on the largest enterprise (the Niehans index places greater weight on the largest sized enterprises than the entropy index; and the entropy index places greater weight on these large enterprises than the arithmetic average), the closer the calculated elasticity coefficient of average enterprise size to total GNP is to unity. It thus appears from the regressions in Table 1 that the sizes of the largest enterprises vary in the same proportion as total GNP, and this is quite consistent with the results that the average degrees of industrial concentration for many nations are roughly the same. The rise in industrial concentration in nations with small GNPs would, according to this interpretation, reveal a non-linearity that is not reflected in the specification of the regressions in Table 1. Although questions about the functional form and the numerical value of coefficients linking average enterprise size and GNP cannot be resolved with the small sample of nations with comparable data with which we have to work, the existence of a relationship between enterprise size and GNP seems crucial to interpret the empirical results presented in the last two sections of this study.

2. The approach used in this essay focuses the search for an explanation of the similarity of four-firm, four-digit concentration ratios in the largest

21. This proposition has been argued on the basis of an interesting model of business behavior by Telser (1966). The capital–labor ratios come from a multi-national comparison contained in Pryor (1973).

industrial nations on those factors underlying the positive correlation between enterprise size and total GNP, namely, the positive relationships between total GNP and average establishment size and also the degree to which industries are characterized by multi-establishment enterprises in nations with different GNPs.

3. Alternative approaches toward an explanation that rely on the impact of differential tariffs or that start from Markov analyses of the growth of enterprises show little promise for helping us understand the results. Trying to explain the results of this study from the empirical analyses of concentration in a single country (that show an inverse relationship between market size and industrial concentration), with the addition of one or two more explanatory variables to take into account 'international effects', does not seem very promising to me either. One explicitly acknowledged difficulty in all of these more intensive studies of market size and concentration is the difficulty in obtaining an adequate measure for market size.

4. The results of this study of concentration may have one important implication for the analysis of production functions, namely, that the optimal or minimum efficient sizes of enterprises may not be invariant in all nations but may vary with size of the GNP. If the link between these results and production functions is denied, then some alternative explanation for the correlation between enterprise size and the GNP must be specified. One possible alternative explanation that resorts to differences in relative factor prices to explain the conclusions about concentration was casually examined by the author, but my empirical results to examine this hypothesis seemed sufficiently unpromising to discourage any greater efforts along these lines.

5. The empirical results in this Reading, especially those showing great similarity in the degree of concentration in the group of largest nations, are the cross-section analog to results reported by others showing that for individual nations, the degree of concentration has not changed greatly over long periods of time.[22] This numerical similarity of concentration at several points in time has never been adequately explained but implies a distinct relationship between average enterprise and market size, a relation that seems crucial to the above reported results as well. It must be added

22. Pryor (1973). For the United States the key study is Adelman (1951). The relevant data are reprinted by Bureau of Census (1960, p. 573). A study of the more recent period is Shepherd (1968). For the United Kingdom, data on these matters are analysed in Evely and Little (1960). Studies of the more recent period include Shepherd (1966), and George (1967). The Norwegian case is examined by Wedervang (1964, chapter 6).

In short run the degree of industrial concentration has apparently changed considerably in some nations, e.g. in Yugoslavia over a nine-year period, average concentration markedly declined. (Such data are analysed by Sacks, 1972).

that neither the time-series nor the cross-section comparisons of industrial concentration give insight into the exact nature of this relation between enterprise and market size, but merely demonstrate the existence of such a relation. But recognizing the existence of some force is an important step in trying to assess its nature.

6. The similarity of industrial concentration in the largest nations at one point in time and the similarity of industrial concentration in particular nations over time make us wonder whether or not anti-trust legislation and enforcement, particularly in the United States, has been very effective.[23]

A brief summary

The data show that the average four-firm, four-digit concentration ratios among large industrial nations are roughly the same; and also that concentration in these nations is less than among smaller nations.

The data also show that the rank order of concentration ratios by specific industries is roughly the same in all nations. Indeed, for most of the larger industrial nations, such concentration ratios are roughly the same for individual four-digit industries. And for the rest of the nations, simple relationships between such individual four-firm, four-digit concentration ratios and those in the United States can be easily established.

Underlying the results is a previously determined empirical relationship showing that average enterprise size (both for manufacturing as a whole and for individual industries) and total market size appear to be highly correlated. And this correlation appears to be the result of the fact that establishment size and the degree to which industries are characterized by multi-establishment enterprises are correlated with GNP. Although the exact form and parameters of these various relationships have not been accurately determined because of the limited number of degrees of freedom of the samples on which they were derived, such relationships nevertheless appear to be the key to unlocking the meaning of the empirical results on industrial concentration in twelve nations that are presented in this Reading.

Appendix
Sources

United States: The concentration ratios come from US Senate (1966); the branch weights in manufacturing come from Bureau of the Census (1966).
Belgium, West Germany, Netherlands: The concentration ratios were calculated by the European Economic Community (EEC) and presented by Houssiaux (1969). These data were supplemented in several cases by esti-

23. This question has also been raised in the context of a comparison between the United Kingdom and the United States concentration by Stigler (1966).

mates made by Joseph Miller. The branch weights come from EEC (1967).

Canada: The concentration ratios come from Rosenbluth (1957, p. 90 and Appendix A). Those ratios given for just three firms were adjusted in the following manner: three- and four-firm concentration ratios by individual industries that were given by Rosenbluth were compared and a curve was fitted. This relationship was then used to adjust those three-firm ratios for which four-firm ratios were not given. Branch weights were estimated from data from: United Nations (1963); and Dominion Bureau of Statistics (1957).

France: The concentration ratios come from Houssiaux (1969), and Loup (1969, pp. 17–239). For the concentration ratios based on value of shipment, the two-digit averages were calculated with value of shipment weights, rather than value-added weights which were not available. The branch weights come from EEC (1967). For the value-added weights enterprise rather than establishment data had to be used since the latter were not available.

Italy: The concentration ratios were calculated from employment data by size class following a technique described by Bain (1966, pp. 27–29). The basic data come from Istituto Centrale di Statistica (1966). The branch weights come from EEC (1967).

Japan: The concentration ratios come from Iinkai (1964). The branch weights come from United Nations (1967).

Sweden: The concentration ratios come from Statens offentliga utredningar, Finansdepartementet (1968). The basic set of statistics are ratios by industrial branches, Table 2, pp. 86–95; these were supplemented by ratios for products according to the Brussels classification, Table 3, pp. 95–110. The former were based on value of shipment and had value-added weights supplied; the latter were based on physical shipments and had gross-sales information. The gross-sales data were converted into value-added weights by applying the United States ratios of these magnitudes. Certain estimates were also made in those cases where concentration ratios for more than four firms were presented. The branch weights come from Statistiska Centralbryan (1965).

Switzerland: The concentration ratios were calculated according to the Bain method from employment data by size group presented in Eidgenössisches Statistisches Amt (1967; Heft 409, Reihe Df–1). The data are not completely comparable with those of the other nations because of the Swiss practice of isolating those firms that produce products in a great many industries and placing them in a special category entitled 'Verbindung', a procedure that may greatly affect the calculated concentration ratios in the machinery branches. The branch weights are from Band 2, Heft 410, Reihe Df-2 in the same series.

United Kingdom: The basic data on concentration ratios come from Evely and Little (1960), Appendix B. Where three-firm concentration ratios are given, estimates for four-firm ratios are made using the relationship found for Canada and described above; where five- and six-firm concentration ratios are presented, estimates of four-firm ratios were made using the Bain method. Branch weights were estimated from data from: United Nations (1963) and Central Statistical Office (1959).

Yugoslavia: The concentration ratios come from Dirlam (1969). Although the original source could not be located, a similar table is published by Drutter (1964, Table 13). One misprint was corrected. Branch weights come from Savezni zavod za statistiku (1966).

A detailed description of the calculation of the weighted averages

The basic data were comparable concentration ratios for a number of four- and five-digit industries for eleven foreign nations plus a complete set of four- and five-digit concentration ratios for the United States. In order to simplify discussion, the following symbols are used:

$UC5_i$ = the concentration ratio in a five-digit industry i in the United States.

$FC5_i$ = the concentration ratio in the foreign country that is comparable to $US5_i$.

$UC4_i$ = the concentration ratio in a four-digit industry that includes industry i in the United States.

$FC4_i$ = the concentration ratio in the foreign country that is comparable to $US4_i$.

$UU2$ = weighted two-digit concentration ratio for the United States for the particular sample, using United States value-added weights.

$FU2$ = weighted two-digit concentration ratio for the foreign nation for the particular sample, using United States value-added weights.

$UUT2$ = weighted two-digit concentration ratio for the United States for all industries in that classification, using United States value-added weights (one set of these were calculated using all industries, another set excluding regional industries).

For each country the foreign five-digit ratios were first 'converted' into four-digit ratios by using a simple method. For those industries in which only one pair (i.e. comparable United States and foreign ratios) of five-digit concentration ratios was available, the foreign ratio was adjusted by multiplying by $(UC4_i/UC5_i)$ and was then paired with $UC4_i$. Where several pairs of five-digit ratios were available, a weighted average (using value-of-shipment weights) was first calculated and then the foreign weighted average was adjusted by multiplying by ($UC4_i$/United States weighted five-digit average).

The calculated two-digit weighted averages give the desired relationship between the United States and foreign ratios, but they cannot be considered to reflect satisfactorily the absolute degree of concentration since the sample of industries is not necessarily representative. Therefore, both the $UU2$ and the $FU2$ data were adjusted by multiplying by ($UUT2/UU2$). The results were then used to calculate the final weighted averages.

When the averages using the foreign weights were calculated, one additional problem arose since we had no complete set of foreign ratios with which to calculate an aggregate corresponding to $UUT2$. If we assume that the adjusted $FU2$ average (i.e. $FU2 \times UUT2/UU2$, which I designate by the letter X) reflects the *level* of concentration for the whole two-digit branch, then we can adjust both the foreign-weighted United States and foreign two-digit weighted averages by multiplying both by X/foreign-weighted foreign two-digit weighted average. While this procedure is the best we can do with the available data, it does leave something to be desired if we are interested only in this result alone. However, the reason for the exercise is to gain some idea of possible index number effects by comparison with the United States weighted results and, therefore, the major purpose is served.

References

ADELMAN, M. A. (1951), 'The measurement of industrial concentration', *Rev. Econ. Stats,* vol. 33, pp. 269–96.

ADELMAN, M. A. (1966), 'Monopoly and concentration: comparisons in time and space', in T. Bagiotti (ed.), *Essays in Honor of Marco Fanno,* University of Padua.

BAIN, J. S. (1966), *International Differences in Industrial Structure,* Yale University Press.

BUREAU OF THE CENSUS (1960), *Historical Statistics of the United States, Colonial Times to 1957,* US Government Printing Office.

BUREAU OF THE CENSUS (1966), *1963 Census of Manufactures,* vol. 1, US Government Printing Office.

CENTRAL STATISTICAL OFFICE (1959), *The Index of Industrial Production,* HMSO.

DIRLAM, J. (1969), 'Tables to accompany statement', Subcommittee on Antitrust and Monopoly of the Committee on the Judiciary, *Economic Concentration,* part 7a, US Government Printing Office.

DOMINION BUREAU OF STATISTICS (1957), *General Review of Manufacturing Industries of Canada, 1954,* Ottawa.

DRUTTER, I. (1964), 'Tržišni aspekti koncentracije', *Problemi privedne Koncentracije,* Economski Institut, Zagreb.

EEC (1967), *Industrial Statistics J–A.*

EIDGENÖSSISCHES STATISTISCHES AMT (1967), *Eidgenössische Betriebszählung, September 1965,* Band 1, Berne.

ESPOSITO, L. and ESPOSITO, F. F. (1971), 'Foreign competition and domestic industry profitability', *Rev. Econ. Stats,* vol. 53, pp. 343–53.

EVELY, R., and LITTLE, I. M. D. (1960), *Concentration in British Industry,* Cambridge University Press.

GEORGE, K. D. (1967), 'Changes in British industrial concentration, 1951–1958', *J. indust. Econ.*, vol. 15, pp. 200–211.

HOUSSIAUX, J. (1969), 'Annex I to statement', Subcommittee on Antitrust and Monopoly of the Committee on the Judiciary, US Senate, *Economic Concentration*, part 7a, US Government Printing Office.

IINKAI, T. (1964), *Nihon no sangyo shucho*, Tokyo.

ISTITUTO CENTRALE DI STATISTICA (1966), *4° Censimento generale dell' Industriae del Commercio*, vol. 3, Industria Tomo 1, Rome.

KENDALL, M. G. (1962), *Rank Correlation Methods*, Hafner.

LOUP, J. (1969), 'La concentration dans l'industrie française d'après le recensement industriel de 1963: la structure des marchés', *Études et Conjoncture*, vol. 24.

PASHIGIAN, P. (1968), 'Market concentration in the United States and Great Britain', *J. Law Econ.*, vol. 11, pp. 299–329.

PASHIGIAN, P. (1969), 'The effect of market size on concentration', *Int. econ. Rev.*, vol. 10, pp. 291–314.

PRYOR, F. L. (1972), 'The size of production establishments in manufacturing', *Econ. J.*, vol. 82, pp. 547–66.

PRYOR, F. L. (1973), *Property and Industrial Organisation in Communist and Capitalist Nations*.

ROSENBLUTH, G. (1957), *Concentration in Canadian Manufacturing Industries*, Princeton University Press for National Bureau of Economic Research.

SACKS, S. R. (1972), 'Changes in industrial structure in Yugoslavia, 1959–1968', *J. pol. Econ.*, vol. 80, pp. 561–74.

SAVEZNI ZAVOD ZA STATISTIKU (1966), 'Jugoslavenska Industrija 1963', *Statisticki biltin*, no. 421.

SHEPHERD, W. G. (1961), 'A comparison of industrial concentration in the United States and Britain', *Rev. Econ. Stats.*, vol. 18, pp. 70–75.

SHEPHERD, W. G. (1966), 'Changes in British Industrial concentration 1951–1958', *Oxford econ. Papers*, vol. 18, pp. 126–33.

SHEPHERD, W. G. (1968), 'Trends of concentration in American manufacturing industry, 1947–58', *Rev. Econ. Stats*, vol. 46, pp. 200–212.

SHEPHERD, W. G. (1970), *Market Power and Economic Welfare*, Random House.

SHEPHERD, W. G. (1972), 'The elements of market structure', *Rev. Econ. Stats*, vol. 54, pp. 25–37.

STATENS OFFENTLIGA UTREDNINGAR, FINANSDEPARTMENTET (1968), *Industrins struktur och konkurrens förhållanden*, Koncentrationsutredningen, vol. 3, Stockholm.

STATISTISKA CENTRALBRYAN (1965), *Industri 1965*, Stockholm.

STIGLER, G. (1966), 'The economic effects of the antitrust laws', *J. Law Econ.*, vol. 9, pp. 225–58.

TELSER, L. G. (1966), 'Cutthroat competition and the long purse', *J. Law Econ.*, vol. 9, pp. 259–77.

UNITED NATIONS (1963), *The Growth of World Industry 1938–1961*, New York.

UNITED NATIONS (1967), *The Growth of World Industry*, vol. 1.

US SENATE (1966), *Concentration Ratios in Manufacturing Industry, 1963*, Subcommittee on Antitrust and Monopoly of the Committee on the Judiciary, US Government Printing Office.

WEDERVANG, F. (1964), *Development of a Population of Industrial Firms*, Universitets forlaget, Oslo.

WEISS, L. W. (1963), 'Average concentration ratios and industrial performance', *J. indust. Econ.*, vol. 11, pp. 237–54.

10 Louis A. Guth

Some Determinants of Market Structure

Louis A. Guth, 'Advertising and market structure revisited', *Journal of Industrial Economics*, vol. 19, 1971, pp. 179–98.[1]

The effect of advertising on competition, particularly on market structure has been heatedly debated of late. (See Telser (1964), Backman (1967), Mann, *et al.* (1967), Edwards (1968). See also Comanor and Wilson (1967), Simon (1967)). Nicholas Kaldor has noted: 'That advertising promotes the concentration of economic power cannot reasonably be doubted. . . .' (1950–51, p. 15). A recent study by Mann, *et al.* concluded:

. . . enough of the variance in concentration is explained by advertising intensity to raise an issue for public policy (1967, p. 38).

On the other hand, extensive analysis by Telser failed to find a relationship between advertising expenditures and market structure:

There is little empirical support for an adverse association between advertising and competition, despite some plausible theorizing to the contrary (1964, p. 558).

A recent paper by Comanor and Wilson (1967) supplied ample empirical support for the contrary position. Using similar data to that of Telser, Comanor and Wilson observed that:

. . . advertising has a statistically significant and quantitatively important impact upon profit rates which provide a measure of market performance as well as indicate the existence of market power (p. 423).

This paper continues the analysis by presenting an empirical study of the relationship between advertising expenditures and the relative size structure of firms in an industry. The primary finding is that advertising also has a statistically significant and quantitatively important impact upon the size distribution of firms in an industry. Since the sample used here is for the most part the same as Telser's and the basic data on advertising outlays are

1. Since this article was written, a number of papers dealing with the advertising-concentration controversy have appeared. Among these are four papers in a Symposium on Advertising and Concentration (1969), Ekelund and Gramm (1970); and Schnabel (1970). These papers refine the statistical aspects of relating advertising and concentration measured by share of the market held by (usually) four biggest firms. They do not affect the argument developed in this paper.

the same, the findings also have direct implications for the Telser findings.

In the first section of this paper, I discuss the theoretical basis for a relationship between advertising and the size distribution of firms. Then I consider the nature of the variables used in the multivariate analysis, the nature of the sample and the use of the Lorenz Coefficient as a summary measure of the size distribution of firms. Finally, the empirical results are presented.

Advertising and the size distribution of firms in theory

The argument that advertising should lead to high levels of concentration – defined as the market share of the four leading (largest) firms in an industry – may be simply summarized. Advertising increases the product differentiation in an industry. This relationship has been explored at length by Comanor and Wilson. Bain (1956) has found that advertising is the leading factor in product differentiation. Now, increased product differentiation leads to higher barriers to entry for new firms – and also for small firms attempting to increase market share. This results from higher penetration costs of new firms, consumer inertia, and economies of scale in advertising available to larger extant firms.[2] Thus, the distribution of consumer preferences is shifted toward those firms with successfully differentiated products and the resources to further exploit advertising media.[3]

The argument may be summarized by the following three relationships,

$$\partial P/\partial A > 0, \qquad\qquad 1$$

$$\partial B/\partial P > 0, \qquad\qquad 2$$

$$\partial C/\partial B > 0, \qquad\qquad 3$$

where P = level of product differentiation in an industry, A = level of advertising in that industry, B = barriers to entry in that industry, C = degree of concentration in that industry.

Such an argument makes for plausible theory as Telser suggests, but it ignores the feedback effect that aspects of performance may have on structure. In particular, it ignores the empirical observations of Comanor and Wilson that advertising expenditures are consistent with high rates of return. Now, classical economic theory of the firm is predicated upon the fact that resources (firms) will distribute themselves among industries in accord with the distribution of returns to be earned. Therefore, it is reasonable to expect that, at the same time that advertising is promoting product differentiation leading to high price–cost margins, these high margins

2. For a discussion of selling costs as a barrier to entry, see Bain (1956) and Williamson (1963).

3. The above points are made in detail by Comanor and Wilson (1967, pp. 425–7).

should attract new firms to the industry.[4] The ability of these firms to succeed in the industry will be limited, however, by the advertising barrier.

Consideration of this feedback mechanism causes us to add two additional relationships to the above model,

$$\partial \pi / \partial A > 0, \qquad\qquad\qquad 4$$

$$\partial E / \partial \pi > 0, \qquad\qquad\qquad 5$$

where π = rate of return for the industry, E = rate of entry for the industry.

What might we expect to be the net impact of these forces?[5] They suggest that the barrier to entry raised by advertising can be, for the most part, a *barrier to significant entry*. While many firms of fringe size might survive in the industry because of the general excess profit margins that permit higher unit costs, cut rate pricing, etc., on low volume, few can compete for significant market shares because of the heavy burden of large selling costs such an attempt imposes upon the firm.

Size distribution of firms in an industry with heavy advertising expenditures should show concentration of output in the hands of a few large firms, *tempered by the growth of a large number of small, fringe firms*. Pashigian (1968) has found that concentration tends to be negatively associated with the number of firms in an industry.[6] The above argument suggests that advertising should tend to offset this sort of relationship.[7]

Therefore, all other things equal, the hypothesis of the relation between advertising and the relative sizes of firms in an industry may be restated as the following:

Advertising expenditures raise barriers to significant entry, or, all other things equal, the share of the top firms will be greater where advertising expenditures are great, given the number of firms in the industry.[8]

4. Of course, to the extent that the technical cost disadvantage of economies of scale faced by these new firms is severe, the feedback mechanism will be retarded. This cost disadvantage does not appear to be severe, however. The simple correlation between minimum efficient size of firm and advertising expenditures as a per cent of sales (variables defined as in the text) was 0·10 for 1958 and 0·16 for 1963.

5. The purpose of this system of equations is to illustrate the above hypothesis and does not represent a full system of market relationships.

6. To a certain extent, this is true by definition. The number of firms in an industry, n, determines the minimum concentration ratio for that industry, $4/n$.

7. Else (1966) regresses the industry ad/sales ratio on sales and number of products. He adjusts the results for competitive conditions measured by a three-firm concentration ratio. It is interesting to note that in industries where high advertising expenditures are not associated with high levels of concentration, Else finds a tendency for substantially larger number of products.

8. Naturally, this could be as easily expressed as an increase in the number of firms, holding the share of the top firms constant.

This suggests that advertising, increasing at the same time barriers to entry and profit incentives for entry, affects the skewness of the overall size distribution of firms. Thus, I shall test the validity of a positive association of advertising expenditures with skewness in this distribution.

Nature of the sample

The analysis consists of cross-section data for two years, 1958 and 1963. These years were chosen to provide one year of overlap with the Telser data and also to take advantage of the most recent data available.

In order to have the analysis conform as closely as possible to that of Telser and Comanor and Wilson, a similar sample was used. This basic sample consists of the Telser list of consumer goods in industries, based upon the 'minor industries' classifications of the Internal Revenue Service. This industry classification scheme corresponds to the three-digit level of SIC industry groups.[9] From the Telser list of forty-four industries, nine have been excluded for various reasons. First, the two regional industries – bakery products and dairy products – were removed, since the analysis hinges on the distribution of firms and thus is highly sensitive to the total number of firms in an industry. Detailed information on all variables for regional markets was not available. Second, three industries were excluded because of the difficulty in constructing corresponding data for 1958 and 1963 due to the change in the SIC classification scheme in 1957. These were household appliances, household and service machinery, and professional

Table 1 Comparisons of regressions of concentration ratios, Y, and advertising expenditures, X, for original Telser sample and revised sample, 1958[a]

		Means		Multiple correlation coefficient
Sample	Regression of Y on X	Y	X	
Telser	$Y = 34 \cdot 32 + 1 \cdot 150 X$	37·67	2·907	0·169**
	$(1 \cdot 057)$	(19·17)	(2·824)	
Revised	$Y = 33 \cdot 66 + 1 \cdot 198 X$	37·31	3·045	0·172*
	$(1 \cdot 148)$	(20·49)	(3·013)	

[a] Y = Market share of shipments of four largest firms (per cent).

X = Advertising expenditure over sales revenue (per cent).

* Indicates coefficient statistically significant at the 95 per cent level.

** Indicates coefficient statistically significant at the 99 per cent level.

9. Telser, Mann, *et al.*, and others have pointed out the shortcomings of this data as representative of economic 'industries'. Nevertheless, this is the most comprehensive source on advertising expenditures per dollar of gross sales, and it was felt more was gained in making the analysis directly comparable with Telser and Comanor and Wilson, than was lost in the weaknesses of the data.

and scientific instruments. Third, two industries were removed by Telser – motor vehicles and parts and accessories – as they did not have comparable concentration and advertising data. Finally, petroleum refining was removed because of general distortions caused by tax depletion allowances,[10] and other tobacco products (including cigarettes) was excluded because of the very small number of firms in the cigarette industry and the problems this causes for the distributional analysis.

The removal of these industries did not bias the results, relative to Telser, in any appreciable way. Table 1 compares the Telser analysis on forty-two industries with the same analysis on the thirty-five industries used in the revised sample. Clearly, no appreciable difference exists.

Variables considered in the analysis
Dependent variables

In order to provide some basis for comparison, it was decided to analyse relationships explaining both behavior of four-firm concentration ratios – as is conventionally done – and the behavior of some characteristics of the size distribution of firms.

While the four-firm concentration ratio is probably the most widely used summary measure of market structure and competition, it is not a perfectly inclusive measure of these.[11] Nevertheless, it is useful to employ this measure as a standard of comparison, and also because of its measurement of the approximation of the industry to the monopoly – or more correctly small-group oligopoly – model.

Since the hypothesis on the effect of advertising on the size distribution of firms was generated by considerations of concentration relative to the total number of firms in the industry, the use of a Lorenz analysis seems appropriate.[12] The Lorenz Curve, Figure 1, in this case gives the joint cumulation, both of the market shares of firms and of the fraction of firms included. If market output is equally distributed among all the firms in the industry, then the Lorenz Curve is just the 45-degree line. On the other hand, if one firm in the industry has all industry sales, then the curve is composed of the two axes. The degree of inequality (skewness) of the distribution, therefore, is represented by the extent to which the Lorenz Curve bends away from the diagonal toward the axes. This suggests the summary measure for the distribution, namely, the Lorenz Coefficient. The Coefficient is composed of the ratio of the area between the diagonal and the Lorenz Curve (shaded in Figure 1) and the total area under the diagonal.

10. This industry is also removed by Comanor and Wilson for this reason.

11. Comanor and Wilson indicate shortcomings of this measure (1967, p. 424).

12. For a discussion of this analysis see Lorenz (1905), and Aitchison and Brown (1963).

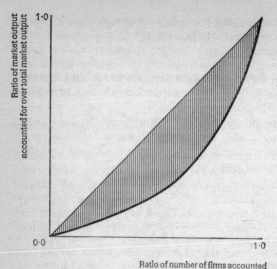

Figure 1 Lorenz curve for distribution of firm sizes

This latter area is, of course, equal to $\frac{1}{2}$. The Lorenz Coefficient varies from 0 to 1 as the degree of inequality in the distribution increases. Thus, it is suited for comparison with the concentration ratio.

The Lorenz Coefficient of a given four-digit level SIC industry in a given year was computed on the basis of concentration data for that year.[13] These data include the market shares of the largest four, eight, twenty, and fifty firms. Thus, they compose four points on the Lorenz Curve, plus a fifth point for the observation that all firms in the industry comprise all industry output.[14]

Several structural forms were used in attempting to fit these data for the large number of four-digit industries relevant to the study. It was decided to avoid using a common distribution – the lognormal immediately comes to mind – since such distributions are known to be only moderately success-ful as general measures of size distribution of firms.[15] In order for the structural form used to be a reasonable approximation of a Lorenz Curve, however, it was necessary that the equation pass through the two extreme

13. See the Appendix for a discussion of the sources of construction of the data. As noted there, the four-digit industries were combined in weighted averages to form the results for the IRS industries.

14. Where the industry was composed of fifty firms or less (but more than twenty) only four points were observed on the given Lorenz Curve.

15. See, for example, Silberman (1967), and Quandt (1966).

points, 0, 0 and 1, 1. This called for some form of constraint on the coefficients employed in the model. The final form decided upon was:

$$Y = X/(a+bX), \qquad\qquad 6$$

where Y is the market share, in natural units, of the first X firms relative to the total number of firms; the firms are arrayed in ascending order; $a+b$ must equal one.

The normal equations for this form[16] may be derived using the fact that the expression is equivalent to $Y' = b+aX'$, where Y' and X' are the reciprocals of Y and X. This form has the advantage of being able to fit observations for values of X between 0·9 and 1·0 better than other forms tried.[17] Figure 2 compares this form in one case, the cosmetics and perfumes industry (SIC 2844), with the form $Y = X^b$ also constrained to pass through the 1, 1 point by having a zero intercept on log form. Table 2 summarizes the ratio of explained variance in Y' to total variance in Y' for 214 four-digit industries adjusted for degrees of freedom.

Table 2 **Distribution of per cent of explained variance to total variance in functional form used to estimate Lorenz coefficients of 214 industries, 1958 and 1963[a]**

	Frequency	
Range	1958	1963
95–99·99%	73	73
90–94·99	14	19
85–89·99	7	6
80–84·99	4	2
70–79·99	5	2
Less than 70	5	4
Total	108	106

[a] Includes all four-digit SIC industries used in the regression analysis plus additional four-digit SIC industries dropped from the later analysis.

16. For a discussion of regression under linear constraint on the coefficients, see Williams (1959). The normal equations are derived by minimizing $L = (Y'-b-aX')^2 = \lambda(a+b-1)$ with respect to a, b, and λ. It was decided to use only this form as it was felt that consistent use of one structural form permitted better comparison of the resulting Lorenz Coefficients.

17. For any industry with over 200 firms, at least four of the five observed points fall into this range. That the form, $Y = X/(a+bX)$, fits well in this region is a result of its steep, and steeply accelerating, slope. The first derivative at $X = 1·0$, given that $a+b = 1·0$, equals a. The second derivative, again at $X = 1·0$, equals $-2ab$ or $2a(a-1)$. Since a is presumably much greater than 0, this implies a steep slope. This is further corroborated by the fact that since $a > 0$ and $b < 0$, the function approaches infinity as X approaches a/b, equal to $a/(1-a)$, which for large values of a, occurs very close to 1·0.

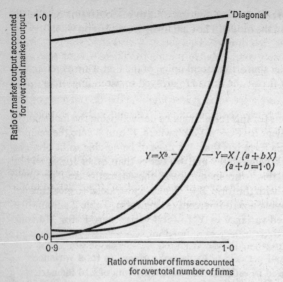

Figure 2 Lorenz curve for cosmetic industry SIC 2844

Finally, it is worth noting that the two dependent variables are only mildly associated, with a simple correlation coefficient of 0·43 in both years.

Independent variables

In order to provide useful comparisons on the explanation of the concentration ratio and the Lorenz Coefficient, it was decided to employ the same independent variables in both cases in conjunction with the advertising expenditures to sales ratio used by Telser, Comanor and Wilson, and Mann *et al.* The two independent variables decided upon were minimum efficient plant scale (*MES*) and absolute capital requirements (*K*). There were a number of reasons for using these variables. In the first place, minimum efficient scale of plant defines the number of efficient-sized plants that can simultaneously coexist in an industry. Thus, it should directly relate to concentration and, perhaps, to size distribution. In addition, these two variables, in conjunction with product differentiation (largely represented by the advertising variable), make up the dominant set of considerations in Bain's landmark study of barriers to entry. Furthermore, empirical analysis has tended to confirm the important effect these variables have on market structure.[18]

The calculation of minimum efficient plant scale proceeded in the same

18. See, for example, Bain (1956) and Mansfield (1962).

fashion as that employed by Comanor and Wilson. The average plant size, in terms of value output, of the largest plants composing 50 per cent of the industry output was determined. This figure was then divided by total industry output to determine relative minimum efficient plant scale. An alternative technique, known as the Survival Technique and employed by Weiss, was considered and rejected by Comanor and Wilson on the basis of inferior performance relative to Bain's studies.[19] For the purpose of this paper, it is sufficient to say that the Survival Technique does not provide determinate answers in all cases (Weiss, 1964, pp. 258–9) and thus was discarded at apparently little cost.

The absolute capital requirements also were computed by the Comanor and Wilson technique. This involves multiplying the average size of the largest plants, in terms of value of output, that explain 50 per cent of industry output, by the total asset to gross sales ratio.

Result of the analysis

The two relationships, then, to be considered in the analysis are

$$Conc = f_1(MES, K, Ad/Sales) \qquad\qquad 7$$
$$L = f_2(MES, K, Ad/Sales) \qquad\qquad 8$$

where $Conc$ = four-firm concentration ratio, L = Lorenz Coefficient, MES = minimum efficient plant scale, K = absolute capital requirements, $Ad/Sales$ = advertising expenditures over gross sales.

An important consideration – not always considered – in the analysis of concentration ratios is that the value is bounded from above by $1 \cdot 0$. The same is true about the Lorenz Coefficient which is bounded above by $1 \cdot 0$. And naturally, both variables are bounded below as well by $0 \cdot 0$. This should reduce the effectiveness of linear forms as explanations of their behavior. In particular, this holds true for the Lorenz Coefficient. As noted in Table 3, the mean of this value exceeded $0 \cdot 8$ in both years; thus extreme conditions in the other three variables had limited effect on the Lorenz Coefficient – misspecified by the linear form – due to the upper bound.

One should expect, therefore, that nonlinear structural forms of the relationships 7 and 8 – such as logarithmic transformations – should fit the data better than linear forms.

The results of the regressions explaining four-firm concentration ratios for 1958 and 1963 are summarized in Table 4. The results of the regression explaining the Lorenz Coefficients for 1958 and 1963 are summarized in Table 5.

19. The concept of the 'survival' principle was popularized by Stigler (1958). Weiss (1964) used this technique to measure optimal-sized plants in industries and the extent of suboptimality in plant size in the economy. See also Saving (1961).

Table 3 Arithmetic means and standard deviation of variables

	1958		1963	
	Mean	Standard deviation	Mean	Standard deviation
Concentration – share of top four firms in per cent	36·1743	19·6138	34·6971	18·4563
Lorenz coefficient	0·825445	0·094269	0·833864	0·099521
Minimum efficient plant scale in per cent of total industry output	2·888	3·57338	2·60714	2·81209
Absolute capital requirements in dollars	$11,346,300	$12,832,100	$15,925,500	$19,594,200
Advertising expenditures to gross sales in per cent	2·97706	3·02855	3·04286	3·07057

Table 4 Regressions of concentration ratios[a]

Year	Case and partial correlation coefficient[b]	Constant term	Independent variables[c] MES[d]	K[e]	Ad/sales[f]	R̄²	R̄² for concentration on estimated concentration[g]
1958	I Linear	21·903	2·70651**	0·000670691**	−0·387981	0·521599**	
	t-ratio		3·90421	3·27569	−0·473851		
	II Linear in logs	1·6828	0·278414**	0·187973**	−0·0137512	0·6723**	0·598274**
	t-ratio		3·27601	2·80794	−0·177131		
	Partial correlation coefficient concentration ratio with		0·25717	0·20272	0·0010124		
1963	I Linear	18·6804	4·13514**	0·000195637	0·695806	0·548894**	
	t-ratio		5·12103	1·55923	0·917259		
	II Linear in logs	2·16172	0·328107**	0·121631*	0·0184824	0·713489**	0·648687**
	t-ratio		4·26649	2·10384	0·27233		
	Partial correlation coefficient concentration ratio with		0·36996	0·12494	0·002389		

[a] Market share of shipments of four largest firms (per cent).
[b] Partial Correlation Coefficient,

e.g. $r_{12.34} = 1 - \dfrac{1 - R^2{}_{1.234}}{1 - R^2{}_{1.34}}$ Partials are only given for best fitting form.

[c] For sources of data, see Appendix.
[d] Minimum efficient plant scale in per cent of industry output.
[e] Absolute capital requirements in thousands of dollars.
[f] Advertising expenditures/sales (per cent).
[g] Given only where dependent variable has been transformed.
* Indicates coefficient is statistically significant at the 95 per cent level.
** Indicates coefficient is statistically significant at the 99 per cent level.

Table 5 Regressions of Lorenz coefficients[a][b]

Year	Case and partial correlation coefficient	Constant term	Independent variables			$\bar{R}^2$	$\bar{R}^2$ for coefficient on estimated coefficient
			MES	K	Ad/sales		
1958	I Linear	0.758926	0.004584	2.11541×10^{-6}	0.0098346*	0.255278*	
	t-ratio		1.10281	1.72293	2.00301		
	II Linear in logs	0.71867	0.0255177	0.058667**	0.0429363**	0.532823**	0.555348**
	t-ratio		1.3862	4.04592	2.255334		
	Partial correlation coefficient Lorenz coefficient with		0.058367	0.34557	0.17376		
1963	I Linear	0.762163	0.00692362	1.03364×10^{-6}	0.0122215*	0.27248*	
	t-ratio		1.25213	1.20302	2.34938		
	II Linear, but reciprocal of Ad/sales	0.853927	0.0064821 2*	$1.31311 \times 10^{-6*}$	−0.0721857**	0.65941**	
	t-ratio		1.71303	2.39769	−6.85624		
	Partial correlation coefficient Lorenz coefficient with		0.097874	0.15656	0.60260		

[a] Expressed in decimals.
[b] For source of data see Appendix; for definitions of variables, see Table 4.
* Indicates coefficient is statistically significant at the 95 per cent level.
** Indicates coefficient is statistically significant at the 99 per cent level.

One should note first that in all four cases the argument for non-linearity is substantiated by the results. Both the concentration ratio and the Lorenz Coefficient would seem to be affected by the upper and lower bounds, though the effect is much more pronounced on the Lorenz Coefficient because of its higher mean value.

The results on concentration ratios indicate a consistent positive relationship between this variable and minimum efficient size of plant and absolute capital requirements. Roughly 60 per cent of the variance in concentration ratios among industries is explained by this model for each of the two years. Residuals were not associated with any of the independent variables. This finding parallels those reported by Comanor and Wilson (1967, pp. 434–5). In both 1958 and 1963, the minimum efficient size provides most of the explanation of the variance in concentration, followed by capital requirements, with little explanatory power in the ad–sales variable.[20]

While the effect of advertising on the four-firm concentration ratio is insignificant, this is clearly not the case for the Lorenz Coefficient. Again, roughly 60 per cent of total variance in the dependent variable is explained by the model and residuals are well-behaved. For 1958, a log-linear structural form provides the best fit (as measured by the coefficient of determination between the estimated values of the Lorenz Coefficient and the actual values). In this case, the scale economies variable has a spurious coefficient, and the ad–sales variable is statistically significant. Most of the explanatory power of the model lies in the absolute capital variable and the ad–sales variable.

The 1963 data are best fitted by a linear model except for the introduction of the ad–sales variable as a reciprocal.[21] In this case, the role reversal of the three explanatory variables is complete. Where the descending order of importance in explaining four-firm concentration is minimum efficient scale of plant, absolute capital requirements, and ad–sales, it is now the exact opposite for the Lorenz Coefficient. In fact, the ad–sales variable

20. As indicated by these partial correlation coefficients and those for the explanatory variables in the Lorenz Coefficient model present, there was some multicollinearity. As one would expect, this was the case between minimum efficient plant scale and absolute capital requirements. These had a simple correlation coefficient of roughly 0·35 for each of the two years. But this was not of prime concern to the investigation. Absolute capital requirements and advertising expenditures/gross sales were also linearly related with simple correlation coefficients in the two years of 0·35 to 0·40. (Comanor and Wilson report a similar relationship.) This would seem to indicate that the advertising expenditure should, in some sense, be thought of as an investment.

21. Since the advertising–sales (ad–sales) ratio appears as a reciprocal in the 1963 relationship, multicollinearity is reduced, the simple correlation of advertising with absolute capital requirements being 0·15. The coefficient of advertising in this case is insensitive to alternative specifications of the model.

dominates the relationship, as evidenced by the partial correlation coefficients.[22]

The findings of a reversal in the order of importance of the explanatory variables should not be surprising in light of the discussion of the theoretical relationships prevailing. While relatively large advertising would seem to represent an important barrier to entry, this influence is not reflected in interindustry comparisons of concentration ratios because of a second effect, namely, the coincidence of relatively large advertising outlays in an industry with high rates of return. But the advertising barrier does tend to prevent smaller firms from capturing significant portions of the market, thus leading to a skewness in size distributions reflected in the Lorenz Coefficient.

Causality

As noted by Simon (1967), studies of the relationship between market structure and advertising have failed to firmly establish the direction of causality. In this Reading I have established a strong relationship between the size distribution of firms in an industry as measured by the Lorenz Coefficient and the advertising behavior of the industry. Throughout, the direction of causation has been assumed to run from advertising to behavior to size structure. Is this assumption warranted?

With regard to the analysis of advertising and four-firm concentration ratios, the problem of establishing causality is profound. For while advertising may create advantages for some firms and increase concentration, it is equally true that once pre-eminence is established, firms may advertise to create barriers to entry.[23]

There are several reasons for believing that, here, causality runs in the direction assumed. In the first place, if causality ran the other way, one would expect to find that industries with skewed distributions due to other factors would have large advertising expenditures. In fact, this is not the case, as evidenced by the low correlations of advertising with the other independent variables. A second reason, advanced by Comanor and Wilson, (1967, p. 437) is that these cross-section results tend to emphasize the

22. One might argue that, if nonlinearity is important in explaining variation in the Lorenz Coefficient across industries, the result for 1963 is forced in favor of the ad-sales variable since it is the only one introduced in a non-linear fashion. But, in fact, all log and reciprocal specifications tried yielded the same result with regard to the full role reversal of the explanatory variables. For example, a log-linear specification yields a partial correlation coefficient between the Lorenz Coefficient and ad-sales of 0·34041; between the Lorenz Coefficient and capital requirements of 0·10839; and between the Lorenz Coefficient and minimum efficient size of plant of 0·017389.

23. See Williamson's formal development of selling costs as a strategy toward increasing barriers to entry (1963).

structural differences among industries rather than their behavior over time. Finally, the partial correlation coefficients for 1963 indicate that the bulk of the skewness in distributions is 'explained' by the advertising–sales ratio. One might then reasonably ask, 'How do firms and industries arrive at such skewed distributions in the first place if the skewness *then* leads to advertising?' Since the relationship of minimum efficient plant scale and advertising is so weak, there would seem to be no answer other than that the pre-eminent firms achieved their positions through product differentiation, including the effect of advertising.

Conclusion

The empirical findings of this paper do not indicate whether an industry that increases its advertising output will grow more or less concentrated. I have not specified conditions that make substantial advertising an attractive behavior pattern for firms in an industry. The findings do indicate advertising has a definite impact upon the present differences in the size structure of firms in the industries studied. The larger the role of advertising industry-wide, all other things equal, the greater the inequality of the size distribution of firms. The largest firms' market share is *greater* relative to the number of firms in the industry.

What is the quantitative impact of this effect? Telser has pointed out, based on his analysis, that '... a 1 per cent increase in the ratio of advertising to sales is associated with only a 0·08 per cent increase in concentration (1964, p. 544).' Now, the advertising elasticity of the Lorenz Coefficient is only 0·108.[24] But this does not truly reflect the impact of the advertising variable. For, in fact, that variable, with a standard deviation larger than its mean, is likely to be much further removed than 1 per cent from the mean of the sample in those industries where advertising is a significant portion of gross sales.[25]

Table 6 indicates the effect of a 5 per cent advertising–sales ratio as opposed to the mean value of this variable, holding constant minimum efficient plant scale and absolute capital requirements at their mean values. The effect is to increase L by 5·2 per cent. Two extreme cases are illustrated in the table. In the first instance, it is assumed that the number of firms remains constant at 245. For the mean value of L, this number is consistent with a four-firm concentration ratio of 34·7, the mean value for 1963. In this case, the 5·2 per cent increase in L is consistent with over a 10-point

24. Assuming mean values of the variables, the elasticity of the advertising effect equals $0·072/((\text{ad–sales}) (\text{Lorenz Coefficient}))$.

25. Put another way, the elasticity measure underestimates the impact of the ad–sales ratio on industry structure – represented by the Lorenz Coefficient – since the coefficient of variation (σ/μ) of the former (in reciprocal form) is 1·19, while the coefficient of the variation of the latter is only 0·12.

rise in concentration, a 30·3 per cent increase. On the other hand, if the concentration ratio is held constant, the number of firms must increase by 133, or 54·3 per cent, in order for the concentration ratio to be consistent with the increase in L.

The actual result, yielding the new Lorenz Coefficient, will presumably be a combination of these two extreme cases. But even if the effect works predominantly through adjustments in the number of firms, the necessary implication is that new firms, attracted by higher returns, are not able to decrease the market share of the leading firms in the industry.

Table 6 **Impact of advertising on structure: an example using Lorenz coefficient relationship estimated for 1963**

| | Independent variables[a] | | | | | |
Case	MES	K (000)	Ad/Sales	L	Number of firms[c]	Conc.[c]
1	2·60714%	$15925·5	0·891755[b]	0·833864	245	34·7
2	2·60714%	15925·5	0·20000	0·877302	or $\begin{cases} 245 \\ 378 \end{cases}$	45·2 34·7

[a] For definition of variables, see Table 4. Values used are at mean of sample except for ad/sales in case 2.

[b] Mean value of reciprocal.

[c] For case 2, results are extreme cases with number of firms or concentration held constant.

Now, it is quite true that the connection between the value of a Lorenz Coefficient and expected market performance is not as decisive as that between high levels of concentration and performance. Thus, while the control of 80 per cent of a market by an absolutely small number of firms has direct implications for interdependence and performance, the existence of a similarly large share of output in the hands of a *relatively* small number of firms would seem to have more imprecise implications.[26] But the empirical finding of this paper relating behavior to structure is supported by the Comanor–Wilson relation of behavior to performance. This paper has shown that advertising affects the distribution of firm sizes in an industry; they have shown that advertising increases the industry average profit level. The coexistence of these two effects suggests that advertising places some barriers around the market shares of the leading firms in the industry.

Comanor and Wilson report:

26. For example, Phillips (1962), has argued that the degree of interfirm rivalry increases with the number of firms but decreases with skewness in the distribution of power. The net result of the increase in the Lorenz Coefficient would seem to depend on the relative strengths of these two cross-influences.

Appendix Table 1 **1958 variables**

Industry	Market share of top 4 firms	Lorenz coefficient	Minimum efficient size (per cent of industry output)	Absolute capital requirements ($000)	Advertising expenditure over gross sales
Beer and malt	29·0	0·784166	1·91	16,898·0	6·872
Wines	35·0	0·789072	2·12	4,900·1	4·395
Distilled liquor	60·0	0·907789	3·12	20,295·2	2·408
Meats	28·4	0·910436	0·40	6,160·8	0·610
Canning	31·0	0·859591	1·90	10,218·9	2·658
Grain-mill	32·0	0·871676	1·93	8,507·8	1·695
Sugar	65·1	0·610154	4·75	28,144·0	0·280
Confections	37·2	0·828025	8·23	16,628·6	3·543
Cereals	83·0	0·941180	15·15	28,934·3	4·845
Misc. foods	41·2	0·917593	0·52	6,036·2	4·073
Cigars	54·0	0·921365	3·05	7,583·0	2·370
Knits	18·9	0·714440	0·98	2,147·8	1·075
Carpets	51·4	0·853404	7·65	11,909·3	2·052
Hats	63·2	0·716253	1·39	973·1	2·124
Men's clothing	14·6	0·773583	0·48	1,596·9	0·928
Women's clothing	9·6	0·784183	0·15	356·5	1·263
Millinery	6·0	0·598693	0·26	203·0	0·326
Furs	5·0	0·676200	0·22	252·7	0·916
Misc. apparel	23·6	0·675602	0·99	450·0	1·269
Furniture	18·4	0·800535	0·43	1,339·2	1·451
Periodicals	31·0	0·929139	1·51	17,002·9	0·304
Books	16·0	0·847251	0·89	6,307·7	2·702
Drugs	30·4	0·934682	2·98	46,124·4	10·280
Soaps	63·0	0·924313	2·14	17,207·2	7·938
Cosmetics	29·0	0·919150	2·13	14,010·8	14·723
Paints	35·4	0·873957	1·43	7,098·4	1·450
Tires and tubes	74·0	0·916845	2·81	54,984·9	1·885
Footwear	26·5	0·783768	0·29	1,915·4	1·326
Other leather	25·3	0·739340	1·10	1,302·3	1·204
Hand tools	33·3	0·844781	1·99	7,794·0	3·791
Communications	44·3	0·906173	4·35	27,235·1	2·034
Motorcycles	58·0	0·867628	14·56	6,370·4	1·078
Clocks	48·9	0·892416	5·62	11,332·5	5·629
Jewelry	32·4	0·807818	3·06	4,272·3	2·202
Costume jewelry	12·0	0·769377	0·59	657·7	2·498

Sources of data: 1958

Variables	Sources
1. Market Share–Concentration	Telser (1964)
2. Lorenz Coefficient	Bureau of the Census (1961)
3. Minimum Efficient Plant Scale (*MES*)	Bureau of the Census (1961)
4. Absolute Capital Requirements	Bureau of the Census (1961); Internal Revenue Service, (1962)
5. Advertising	Telser (1964)

Appendix Table 2 **1963 variables**

Industry	Market share of top 4 firms	Lorenz Coefficient	Minimum efficient size (per cent of industry output)	Absolute capital requirements $000	Advertising expenditure over gross sales
Beer and malt	34·3	0·831369	2·09	22,610·2	6·8
Wines	44·0	0·810271	2·39	6610·4	5·4
Distilled liquor	58·0	0·855441	4·17	31,860·2	2·4
Meats	25·6	0·915016	0·41	6421·2	0·6
Canning	33·6	0·858152	1·53	11,406·5	2·8
Grain-mill	33·8	0·894856	1·86	9585·5	2·7
Sugar	61·0	0·554527	4·48	31,304·5	0·2
Confections	36·1	0·858484	7·46	18,731·8	3·2
Cereals	86·0	0·944377	12·02	32,396·1	6·1
Misc. foods	25·2	0·893289	0·67	3622·9	6·0
Cigars	59·0	0·958258	1·91	4799·1	2·8
Knits	20·6	0·750176	1·10	3210·4	1·0
Carpets	38·0	0·752320	4·16	12,794·0	1·0
Hats	31·0	0·750574	1·34	936·6	1·7
Men's clothing	19·2	0·770919	0·54	2400·7	1·1
Women's clothing	10·5	0·792403	0·24	657·7	0·8
Millinery	9·0	0·603714	0·32	211·7	0·3
Furs	5·0	0·679369	0·22	299·3	0·7
Misc. apparel	21·9	0·705811	1·02	599·8	0·9
Furniture	14·3	0·816525	0·40	1646·2	1·1
Periodicals	28·0	0·944179	2·20	33,799·4	2·1
Books	19·7	0·865549	1·31	15,651·2	3·4
Drugs	26·1	0·940793	3·52	88,453·3	9·0
Soaps	60·7	0·919765	3·02	31,589·5	10·1
Cosmetics	38·0	0·931266	1·72	19,128·6	13·8
Paints	23·0	0·878544	0·37	5664·7	1·7
Tires and tubes	70·0	0·958561	2·95	66,139·0	2·1
Footwear	24·7	0·776444	0·30	2230·9	1·4
Other leather	21·3	0·738928	1·44	1636·5	0·9
Hand tools	38·4	0·868728	3·20	20,215·6	3·3
Communications	43·1	0·909790	3·72	41,939·4	1·5
Motorcycles	56·0	0·941079	11·48	7973·1	0·9
Clocks	46·7	0·892042	4·94	16,362·8	5·3
Jewelry	35·6	0·834307	2·06	3747·2	1·7
Costume jewelry	17·0	0·789406	0·69	855·3	1·7

Sources of data: 1963

Variables	Sources
1. Market Share-Concentration	Bureau of the Census (1966a)
2. Lorenz Coefficient	Bureau of the Census (1966a)
3. Minimum Efficient Plant Scale (MES)	Bureau of the Census (1966b)
4. Absolute Capital Requirements	Bureau of the Census (1966b); Internal Revenue Service (1962)
5. Advertising	Troy (1966)

These empirical results suggest that factors which promote product differentiation may be as important as those which influence the size distribution of firms in terms of their effect upon the achievement of market power (1967, pp. 437, 438).

On the basis of these results, it would seem that factors which promote product differentiation may *themselves* be important influences on the size distribution of firms and through that influence, affect the achievement of market power.

Appendix: data sources and adjustments

The industry data used in this study are aggregated to SIC three-digit groupings, which correspond roughly to IRS 'minor industries'. In the calculation of the variables it is necessary to establish a relationship between the Census and the IRS data. This is done on the basis of procedures suggested in the Census Link Project (Bureau of the Census, 1958, part 3.) A more complete statement on development of the data is available from the author. The data for the variables are presented in Appendix Tables 1 and 2, see pp. 159–60.

References

AITCHISON, J., and BROWN, J. A. C. (1963), *The Lognormal Distribution*, 2nd edn, Cambridge University Press.

BACKMAN, J. (1967), *Advertising and Competition*, New York University Press.

BAIN, J. S. (1956), *Barriers to New Competition*, Harvard University Press.

BORDEN, N. W. (1942), *The Economic Effects of Advertising*, Richard D. Irwin.

BUREAU OF THE CENSUS (1958), *Enterprise Statistics*, US Government Printing Office.

BUREAU OF THE CENSUS (1961), *1958 Census of Manufactures*, US Government Printing Office.

BUREAU OF THE CENSUS (1962), *Concentration Ratios in Manufacturing Industry, 1958*, US Government Printing Office.

BUREAU OF THE CENSUS (1966a), *Concentration Ratios in Manufacturing Industry, 1963*, US Government Printing Office.

BUREAU OF THE CENSUS (1966b), *1963 Census of Manufactures*, US Government Printing Office.

COMANOR, W. S., and WILSON, T. A. (1967), 'Advertising market structure and performance', *Rev. Econ. Stats*, vol. 49, p. 423.

EDWARDS, D. C. (1968), 'Advertising and competition', *Bus. Horizons*, February, p. 59.

EKELUND, R. B., and GRAMM, W. P. (1970), 'Advertising and concentration: some new evidence', *The Antitrust Bull.*, vol. 15, pp. 243–9.

ELSE, P. K. (1966) 'The incidence of advertising in manufacturing industries', *Oxford econ. Papers*, vol. 18, p. 88.

INTERNAL REVENUE SERVICE (1962), *Corporate Tax Returns*, US Government Printing Office.

KALDOR, N. (1950–1951), 'The economic aspects of advertising', *Rev. econ. Stud.*, vol. 18, p. 6.

LORENZ, M. O. (1905), 'Methods of measuring the concentration of wealth', *Publications of the American Statistical Association*, n.s., vol. 70, p. 209.

MANN, H. M., HENNING, J. A., and MEEHAN, J. W. Jr. (1967), 'Advertising and concentration: an empirical investigation', *J. indust. Econ.*, vol. 15, p. 34.

MANSFIELD, E. (1962), 'Entry, Gibrat's law, innovation and the growth of firms', *Amer. econ. Rev.*, vol. 52, p. 1023.

PASHIGIAN, P. (1968), 'Market concentration in the United States and Great Britain', *J. Law Econ.*, vol. 11, p. 299.

PHILLIPS, A. (1962), *Market Structure, Organization and Performance*, Harvard University Press.

QUANDT, R. E. (1966), 'On the size distribution of firms', *Amer. econ. Rev.*, vol. 56, p. 416.

SAVING, T. R. (1961), 'Estimation of the optimum size plant by the survivor technique', *Q.J. Econ.*, vol. 75, p. 569.

SCHNABEL, M. (1970), 'A note on advertising and industrial concentration', *J. polit. Econ.*, vol. 78, pp. 1191–4.

SILBERMAN, I. H. (1967), 'On lognormality on concentration', *Amer. econ. Rev.*, vol. 7, p. 807.

SIMON, J. L. (1967), 'The effect of the competitive structure upon expenditures for advertising', *Q.J. Econ.*, vol. 81, p. 610.

STIGLER, G. J. (1958), 'The economies of scale', *J. Law Econ.*, vol. 1, p. 54.

SYMPOSIUM ON ADVERTISING AND CONCENTRATION (1969), *J. indust. Econ.*, vol. 18, pp. 76–100.

TELSER, L. G. (1964), 'Advertising and competition', *J. polit. Econ.*, vol. 72, p. 537.

TROY, L. (1966), *Manual of Performance Ratios*, Prentice-Hall.

WEISS, L. (1964), 'The survival technique and the extent of suboptimal capacity', *J. polit. Econ.*, vol. 72, p. 246.

WILLIAMS, E. J. (1959), *Regression Analysis*, Wiley.

WILLIAMSON, O. E. (1963), 'Selling expense as a barrier to entry', *Q.J. Econ.*, vol. 77, p. 112.

11 David R. Kamerschen

Market Growth and Industry Concentration

David R. Kamerschen, 'Market growth and industry concentration', *Journal of the American Statistical Association*, vol. 63, 1968, pp. 228–41.

Introduction

In recent years there have been two excellent empirical studies testing the hypothesis that market growth leads to reduced sellers' concentration. In these studies both Nelson (1960)[1] and Shepherd (1964)[2] lend positive though not conclusive support to this hypothesis. Nelson's study (1960) for 1947–1954 used the increase in the value of shipments as the measure of growth of *industry groups* and *product classes* while Shepherd's study (1964) for 1947–1958 used employment as the measure of the growth of *industry groups*.[3] Recently, the Census Bureau's set of concentration ratios for 1963 has become available (US Senate, 1966). This new 'Report' also contains comparable data for 1947, 1954, and 1958. The present study uses these new

1. Also see Nelson's comments as a witness to the *Hearings on Economic Concentration* (1964) which in turn were primarily based on his book (1963, especially chapter 3, pp. 38–58). Although Nelson presented some regressions using a sample of product classes, his comprehensive and disaggregated regressions for industries represent the more definitive work.

2. Also see Shepherd's comments as a witness to the *Hearings on Economic Concentration* (1965).

3. A Federal Trade Commission study analysing 76 industries for the period 1935 to 1947 also found a negative association between market growth and concentration change. See US Federal Trade Commission (1954, pp. 54–7). Similarly, Dr Mueller's paper (1967) supports a negative association between the level of industry concentration and industry growth rates. However, his analysis differs from the Nelson–Shepherd findings in that he compared the average (apparently unweighted) concentration change for several arbitrary classes of industries with different growth rates instead of applying regression techniques. These results are presented in the Appendix's Table 3. Mueller (1967, p. 78) interprets these results as follows: 'These relationships suggest that although fundamental economic forces peculiar to particular industries determine the level and change in concentration, industry growth rates also have an impact in some industries. One of the reasons for this is that, other things being the same, it is easier to enter rapid growth industries than slow growth industries because new entrants need take less business away from established firms. Similarly, small firms already in an industry may find it easier to grow and prosper when an industry is growing rapidly. This supports the generalization that not only does small business have an especially high stake in a rapidly growing economy, but that rapid economic growth can play an important pro-competitive effect on industrial structure.'

data to both re-examine the Nelson–Shepherd findings for the earlier periods and to extend the analysis through 1963. On the basis of an examination of these new data I make the diffident suggestion that in contrast to the above two studies there was no significant relationship between changing concentration and industry growth in both the period between 1954 and 1963, and between 1958 and 1963. While there does seem to be a significant inverse relationship between 1947 and 1958 (as was found by Nelson and Shepherd in different time periods), the (negative) association appears to have declined steadily in significance over time since the 1947 period.

Evaluation of data

Both the Nelson and Shepherd studies suffer from imperfections of the available data. Both authors readily admit this. Nelson comments:

While the hypothesis receives support from the experience of the seven-year period 1947–54, there is a question as to whether the period itself is appropriate for such a test. Certainly one could place more confidence in tests based on a period much longer than seven years, as the processes of market growth and structure change are much longer-run processes. For this reason alone the tests permit no drawing of final conclusions. There is yet another reason for questioning the appropriateness of the period, and this is its beginning year 1947, a year of postwar readjustment. This may be especially important in interpreting the effect of product diversification on concentration change. If wartime production controls narrowed the product-mix of establishments and companies, the immediate postwar year of 1947 may still have reflected the forced specialization of production rather than a more diversified peacetime pattern. To the degree this is true this paper may be more a description of an aspect of war-to-peace economic readjustment than of the evolution of free markets (1960, p. 649).

Similarly, Shepherd makes the following comment:

It must be noted that the 1947–1958 period contains many abnormal features, particularly the existence of demand backlogs in many important industries in the early postwar years. Yet there appears to have been an association between growth and changes in concentration, and between growth and the number of firms in individual industries. . . . *By 1958, the 1947 SIC system had grown obsolescent in some areas;* but in order to permit comparisons over time, the Census prepared ratios for both years based on the 1947 system (pp. 208, 203, note 12, italics not in original).[4]

The admitted abnormality of the time periods investigated in both these studies is particularly unfortunate. In addition, however, the Nelson study suffers from the difficulty that a seven-year period is relatively short for

4. Yet in some respects the 1947–1958 period in Shepherd's sample and the 1947–1963 period in my sample are more significant since they come closest in duration to reflecting long-term trends.

identifying trends. The Shepherd study suffers from the fact that the industrial classification used was obsolete for the period for which it was employed.

The present study reflects in a sense a combination of the Nelson and Shepherd analyses, in that value of shipments are exclusively used to measure growth à la Nelson, and the industry rather than the product approach is exclusively used à la Shepherd. But since the Shepherd study is of later vintage and more especially since it explicitly presents the relevant regressions, the direct comparisons of regressions presented here will be with that study. (The reader is warned that some of the same statistical problems that mar Shepherd's, and to a lesser extent Nelson's, study – especially multicollinearity – are no doubt present in this study.) However, any general comparisons made with the Shepherd study would be approximately correct for the Nelson study as well.

The 1963 concentration ratios employed in the present study are based on the revised 1957 Standard Industrial Classification (SIC) Manual as modified in 1963. (The four-digit grouping contains approximately 415 industries.) While this classification system represents a substantial revision from the previous 1945 classification, the concentration ratios in 1958 were tabulated on the (modified) 1945 system to preserve comparability to prior years. In addition establishments in Alaska and Hawaii were not included in 1958 since these states did not attain statehood until 1959. Thus, 'data and ratios for 1958 and prior years are shown in this [1963] report only if the industry definitions are so closely comparable that the concentration ratios could not be affected by the shifting of plants due to industry classification changes or by the change in treatment of Alaska and Hawaii (US Senate, 1966, footnote 1, p. 38).'

The Census Bureau officially explains its position on this as follows:

The latest revision of the Standard Industrial Classification was made in 1957 and used in the 1958 census. In preparing the concentration ratios based on the 1958 census, the application of these revisions would have made it impossible to compare, for a considerable number of industries, their concentration ratios in 1958 with those of 1954 and 1947. Because of the importance of showing for as many industries as possible the change in concentration over time, it was then decided to derive the concentration ratios within each industry according to the classification system as it existed in 1954. As a result, historical comparability from 1947 to 1958 was maintained in the 1958 Concentration Report for virtually all of the approximately 430 four-digit industries. But it would have been inappropriate and mechanically impossible to continue to use the classification system of 1954 in deriving concentration ratios for 1963. The 1963 concentration ratios are based on the revised 1957 Standard Industrial Classification as modified in 1963. An inevitable cost of this use of the more recent classification system is that comparability can be maintained with earlier years for only about one-half of the industries; i.e., those whose definitions were not significantly affected by the revision. It is not feasible to retabulate the 1958 concentration ratios on the current industrial classification basis because of the possibility of disclosing individual company data for 1958 (US Senate, 1966, p. xiii).

Thus, in contrast to the 366 industries (expanded to 426 by employing 1954 data in the absence of one or two figures for 1947 in 60 industries) for which Shepherd was able to get complete data from 1947 to 1958 or the 399 product classes used by Nelson between 1947 and 1954, the present study contains only 177 industries for the 1947–63 period, 198 industries for the 1954–63 period and 212 industries for the 1958–63 period. Despite the notable drop in sample size the more recent data are superior in the use of a more recent and more relevant classification system. Thus, out of the, e.g., 213 industries listed as comparable by the FTC (see note 3), only 177 had complete data for all the variables with which we were concerned. We see no reason to expect any systematic bias due to these exclusions in any of the time periods. (More complete data for just concentration ratios are contained in Table 6). Of course, the same general limitations in the use of concentration ratios apply in all cases (US Senate, 1966, pp. xv–xvii; Shepherd, 1964, p. 200, note 1; Kamerschen, 1966, pp. 351–3, 1955; Singer, 1965, pp. 851–78).[5] However, since all three studies are concerned with employing the ratios in time-series analysis of changes in industry structure rather than cross-sectional analysis these limitations are less serious.

. . . the limitations will generally tend to have less effect on the use of the ratios to show changes in concentration over time than in depicting the level of concentration in the market at a given point of time. This is because the factors making for under- or over-statement are usually present both at the beginning and the end of the time span for which the change is measured (US Senate, 1966, p. xvii).

The concentration ratios used in the present study are those based on the industry approach. Under the industry approach the entire shipments of the plant are assigned to the particular four-digit industry to which it is classified. Thus, the output includes primary products or products classified in the industry and secondary products or products classified in other industries as well as miscellaneous receipts and resales. The concentration ratios are derived by calculating the total value of shipments (or employment) belonging to the largest firms as a percentage of the value of shipments (employment) of all firms in the industry. While concentrations based on value of shipments are available for 1935, 1947, 1954, 1958, and 1963, ratios based on employment are not available for 1947. Since the two

5. On the limitations of the industry concept relative to the product concept see Nelson (1960, pp. 642–3); Conklin and Goldstein (1955, pp. 15–36); Bock (1959, chapter 2).

measures generally yield similar results, one measure is about as satisfactory (or unsatisfactory) as the other. Only the ratios based on value of shipments are used in the present study.[6]

Variables employed

In this study the following variables were employed:

1. The level of the value of shipments concentration (C_i, $i = 4, 8, 20$) and the change in value of shipments concentration (ΔC_i, $i = 4, 8, 20$) for the four-firm, eight-firm, and twenty-firm ratios were used as the 'concentration' variables.[7]

2. The percentage change in the value of shipments (ΔVS) was employed as the 'growth' variable.

3. The percentage change in the total number of companies or firms (ΔNF) was used to represent the 'net entry' conditions.

4. The 'coverage ratio' (CR) and the absolute change in the 'coverage ratio' (ΔCR) were used as explanatory variables for changes in concentration and growth respectively. Since the coverage ratio 'measures the extent to which the products primary to an industry are shipped by plants classified in that industry' (US Senate, 1966, p. xv)[8] (as distinct from shipments produced in plants classified in other industries), it is an

6. Shepherd sometimes employs both methods. While both measures have their difficulties, in Shepherd's study 'the change in employment variable consistently showed clearer association with structural indicators than did the shipments variable,' (1964, p. 204). The likely upward bias in employing value of shipments (because of changes in the price level) in measuring growth, compared to the likely downward bias in using employment (because of changes in productivity) was felt to be the lesser of the two evils during the period under investigation. It should also be mentioned that the use of a VS concentration ratio and VS as a measure of industry growth can lead to spuriously high positive or negative correlations. VS appears in both variables and, to the degree that there are errors in the VS data for the industry and for the leading firms, one can get spurious correlations. See, for example, Nelson (1963), pp. 55–6, footnote 14.

7. The 50-firm ratios, while generally included in the 1963 study, are empirically incomplete and theoretically unsatisfactory and therefore are not utilized. Professor Shepherd, in a private communication dated 2 December, 1966 explained his reason for using ΔC (and ΔCR below) in absolute and not percentage terms. He said he measures ΔC_4 in absolute terms because he thinks 'a change from 90 per cent to 100 per cent in the 4-firm ratio is at least as significant as from 9 per cent to 19 per cent, and far more than from 9 per cent to 10 per cent.'

8. On p. 38, note 6 the coverage ratio is defined as measuring 'the extent to which all shipments of primary products of an industry are made by plants classified in the industry, as distinguished from secondary producers elsewhere; that is, value of shipments of the primary products made by plants classified in the industry is expressed as a ratio of the total shipments of primary products made by all producers, both in and out of the specified industry.'

(inverse) measure of the degree of potential entry from firms already producing the products. Thus, the lower is the coverage ratio the higher is the entry potential by already existing firms who currently have their primary products in another industry.

Utilizing these variables, two hypotheses are tested relating sellers' concentration (as cause or effect) with market growth (or contraction). The influence of entry conditions in the industry is also considered. The first test concerns itself with the relationship between an industry's rate of growth (or shrinkage) and its subsequent concentration level. The second test reverses the direction of the possible causality and investigates whether an industry's initial level of concentration affects its subsequent growth rate.

Influence of industry growth rates (ΔVS) on concentration (ΔC_i)

There are a number of possible theoretical explanations for the Nelson–Shepherd conclusion that 'concentration seems more likely to decline in growing industries and to rise in shrinking industries, than *vice versa*' (Shepherd, 1964, p. 203 and Mueller, 1967, see footnote 3). For instance, the rapid entry of new firms into growing industries tends, *ceteris paribus*, to weaken existing pockets of concentration. Furthermore, static diseconomies of scale and numerous dynamic factors and bottlenecks all adversely affect a dominant firm's ability to grow (see Penrose, 1959; and Baumol, 1962). According to Stigler (1952, p. 222–43), dominant firms in oligopolistic industries are further disposed to yield market shares in order to maximize long-run profits. Gort (1962), Nelson (1960) and Penrose (1959) also point out that firms may choose to diversify their product lines, for numerous reasons such as overall stability, rather than increase or even maintain their shares in given markets. Nelson ably summarizes the existing theory favoring contraction of market shares as growth takes place as follows:

As markets grow in size, at least for the growth stages beyond the periods of industry formation and early acceleration, one might expect an increasing divergence between the individual market and the firm's part of it. There are a number of reasons for this. For one thing there may be limits on the optimum size of plants, and growth may then take the form of increasing the number rather than the size of plants producing a given product. Multi-plant operation may involve increasing costs of coordination and control, putting an upper limit on the number of plants a firm can economically administer. However, even if substantial economies of administration, marketing, and finance are to be gained through multiplant operation, there may be good reasons for growing by diversification rather than by increasing or maintaining one's share of a given product market. A greater opportunity to achieve over-all stability in sales, and a larger number of more profitable new product lines into which it is possible to diversify may accompany the growth of the economy. This, together with a fear of anti-trust prosecution may lead a firm to diversify rather than grow in its traditional market. Stated more broadly the growth of an economy, and its markets, may make feasible a greater exploitation of the division of labor along both industry and functional lines, and lead to lower concentration levels (1960, p. 641).

Empirical results

The empirical results presented in this Reading in Table 1 suggest that the Penrose, Stigler, *et al.*, theoretical notions as well as the Nelson–Shepherd empirical findings regarding growth and subsequent concentration may not always hold. More specifically, the equations numbered 1–3 – correlating $\Delta C_i(i = 4, 8, 20)$ with ΔVS – for the three time periods, show a steadily declining negative association from the 1947–63 sample. In fact, in what is usually considered the most relevant case – the four-firm concentration ratio – the association eventually becomes positive albeit insignificant. Thus, while Shepherd's results are (negatively) significant at the 0·01 level for the 1947–58 period, our coefficients show 0·05 level significance for 1947–63, and are not significant for the other two periods. (Since Nelson did not present comparable regressions only the Shepherd results are summarized in Table 1.)

One possible interpretation of these results is that a definite trend is under way that is tending to negate the previous inverse association between growth and concentration. On the other hand, it is possible that our results are consistent with the Nelson–Shepherd results in the sense that during short periods of time, say under five or even under ten years, rapidly growing industries may be better able to gain monopoly power – or more precisely become more concentrated; but in the longer run, perhaps over ten years, some of the above mentioned theoretical factors may be effective. That is, it is suggested that in short periods, rapidly growing industries may well be able to gain in concentration while these gains are attenuated in the longer run. The monotonic decline in significance and even a change of signs from negative to positive as the time periods become shorter from 1947–63 (seventeen years) to 1954–63 (ten years) to 1958–63 (six years) could be interpreted in such a fashion. But this interpretation does not explain why Nelson found a negative association over a relatively short period (seven years). Either interpretation indicates that the Nelson–Shepherd conclusions are more tentative than they suggested. They must be reformulated if the second interpretation is correct or abandoned altogether if the first is correct.

In Shepherd's sample, the 'net entry' variable (ΔNF), equations 4–6, is closely correlated (negatively) with changing concentration for ΔC_4, ΔC_8,

Table 1 Results of simple and multiple regressions for all industries

Equation number	Dependent variable	Independent variable(s)	Shepherd's results: 1947-58 (N = 436) Simple r² and (t-value)	Multiple R² and (F value)	Our results 1947-63 (N = 177) Simple r² and (t-value)	Multiple R² and (F value)	1954-63 (N = 197) Simple r² and (t-value)	Multiple R² and (F value)	1958-63 (N = 212) Simple r² and (t-value)	Multiple R² and (F value)
1.1	ΔC_4	ΔVS	0.038 (−4.11)		0.034 (−2.48)		0.001 (−0.37)		0.002 (0.69)	
2.1	ΔC_8	ΔVS	0.047 (−4.57)		0.047 (−2.94)		0.007 (−2.16)		0.001 (−0.06)	
3.1	ΔC_{20}	ΔVS	0.032 (−3.72)		0.028 (−2.26)		0.014 (−1.66)		0.006 (−1.09)	
4.1	ΔC_4	ΔNF	0.140 (−8.31)		0.105 (−4.52)		0.098 (−4.60)		0.016 (−1.84)	
5.1	ΔC_8	ΔNF	0.172 (−9.39)		0.228 (−6.28)		0.141 (−5.64)		0.016 (−1.86)	
6.1	ΔC_{20}	ΔNF	0.160 (−8.98)		0.205 (−7.19)		0.165 (−6.20)		0.007 (−1.23)	
7.1	ΔC_4	ΔVS	(−1.11)	0.143 (35.18)	0.009 (−1.24)	0.112 (11.03)	0.027 (2.30)	0.122 (13.49)	0.004 (−0.94)	0.020 (2.14)
		ΔNF	(−7.17)		0.081 (−3.92)		0.121 (−5.18)		0.018 (−1.95)	
8.1	ΔC_8	ΔVS			0.009 (−1.30)	0.192 (20.64)	0.018 (1.92)	0.157 (17.99)	0.000 (0.18)	0.016 (1.75)
		ΔNF			0.152 (−5.58)		0.151 (−5.86)		0.016 (−1.87)	
9.1	ΔC_{20}	ΔVS			0.000 (−0.32)	0.228 (25.79)	0.013 (1.59)	0.175 (20.61)	0.004 (−0.94)	0.011 (1.19)
		ΔNF			0.206 (−6.72)		0.163 (−6.16)		0.006 (−1.10)	

			(1)		(2)		(3)		(4)	
10-1	ΔVS	C_4 (of base period)	0.006 (1.58)		0.009 (1.26)		0.001 (−0.43)		0.000 (0.12)	
11-1	ΔVS	C_8 (of base period)	0.005 (1.42)		0.006 (1.02)		0.001 (−0.47)		0.000 (−0.03)	
12-1	ΔVS	C_{20} (of base period)	—		0.005 (0.92)		0.001 (−0.52)		0.000 (0.10)	
13-1	ΔVS	ΔNF	0.160 (8.99)		0.096 (4.31)		0.261 (8.31)		0.017 (1.90)	
14-1	ΔVS	CR (of base period)	0.024 (−2.97)		0.012 (−1.48)		0.042 (−2.92)		0.131 (−5.64)	
15-1	ΔVS	ΔCR	—		0.005 (0.97)		0.038 (2.76)		0.139 (5.82)	
16-1	ΔVS	ΔNF	n.s. (8.64)		0.093 (4.21)		0.258 (8.20)		0.019 (2.00)	
		ΔCR	n.s. (4.03)	0.191 (49.97)	0.001 (0.32)	0.097 (9.41)	0.033 (2.56)	0.285 (38.75)	0.140 (5.85)	0.155 (19.18)
17-1	ΔVS	C_4 (of base period)	n.s. (1.81)		0.011 (1.42)		0.000 (−0.71)		0.001 (0.37)	
		CR (of base period)	n.s. (−3.29)	0.031 (6.68)	0.015 (−1.62)	0.023 (−2.11)	0.041 (−2.88)	0.042 (4.24)	0.132 (−5.64)	0.132 (15.89)

Source: US Senate (1962 and 1966); Shepherd (1964).

n.s. Means the correlation coefficient was not shown in Shepherd (1964).

and ΔC_{20} respectively – all three coefficients being significant at the 0·01 level. However, he notes 'these two [NF and ΔC_i] variables are in large part jointly determined by growth conditions, and possibly by other influences (1964, p. 205).' In addition, the ΔNF variable usually dominates his (as well as our) multiple regressions. However, the simple correlation results in our three samples with but one exception (equation 4.1 in the 1947–63 period compared to the 1954–63 period) become progressively less significant over time. The coefficients for the 1947–63 and 1954–63 period are statistically significant at the 0·01 level but the 1958–63 coefficients are not significant at the 0·05 level. Apparently entering firms in the 1958–63 period were rather small relative to the size of existing firms – at least relative to the largest ones included in the concentration index in question.

Equation sets 7–9 show the multiple regressions of the simple variables reported in 1–6[9]. In general, the 'net entry' variable dominates over the growth variable in these results. However, our results certainly do not lend strong support to the previous findings. Looking at 7.1 with ΔC_4 the dependent variable we find in the 1947–63 sample the results are about the same as Shepherd's – *viz.*, the ΔVS and ΔNF coefficients are both negative with only ΔNF significant. In the 1954–63 period the negative *t*-value for the ΔNF coefficient is roughly 50 per cent higher than in the 1947–63 sample. However, the ΔVS coefficient is now positively significant at the 0·05 level. In the 1958–63 sample the coefficients for both independent variables are insignificant. In fact, the coefficients for this period are also insignificant for equation sets 8–9 (with ΔC_4 and ΔC_8 as the dependent variables respectively) and occasionally even have positive signs. Once again we have to conclude that the previous hypotheses must either hold only for long-run periods – all coefficients being insignificant for the 1958–63 period in equations 7–9 (as well as in equations 1–6) – or only in the past and not recently.

Regressions for subsets of industries

In addition to testing the 'growth leads to declining concentration' thesis for all industries, it is possible to test it for subsets of industries. A sample of 'concentrated' industries – those with a C_4 in the base period of 50 per cent or higher – is one possibility. Shepherd did this and found the coefficients were quite similar to the coefficients for the overall sample except that the concentrated sample coefficients were generally somewhat more

9. Incidentally, while Shepherd does not show his exact simple association between changes in concentration (ΔC) and the 'coverage ratio' (CR), he does state that the coefficients are positive and not quite statistically significant. Our results in Table 5 (p. 179) show inconsistency both as to sign and significance.

statistically significant, *in r^2 terms*[10] (save equation set no. 5). The 'concentrated' sample results are contained in Table 2. The equation sets are the same as in Table 1 with only the number after the decimal now 2 instead of 1 to distinguish the results – e.g., equation set 3.2 in Table 2 corresponds to 3.1 in Table 1.

In summary, our results in Table 2 are not as uniform as Shepherd's. The first six equation sets are more significant in the 'overall' sample than in the 'concentrated' sample for the 1947–63 period. For the 1954–63 period the 'concentrated' sample coefficients are more (less) significant for equation sets numbered 1–3 (4 – 6). Finally, in the 1958–63 period the 'concentrated' sample results are more significant except for equation set no. 6.[11] These inconsistent empirical results perhaps mirror the lack of theoretical support for any *a priori* expectations regarding the differential association using the 'concentrated' rather than the 'overall' sample. While it is obviously true that the higher the initial concentration level, the more likely C_i is to go down than up since it has an upper bound of 100 per cent concentration, there is little 'economic' basis for expecting the 'concentrated' sample to show greater association.

Another possible subset are industries which are 'growing', i.e. those where employment increased by 15 per cent or more and those which are 'shrinking,' i.e. those where employment declined by 15 per cent or more. This was tried for value of shipments rather than employment without success. The sample sizes for 'shrinking' industries were simply too small.[12] Apparently those industries whose SIC classification did not change sufficiently to force a new classification are generally the 'growing' industries. And since in Shepherd's study the 'growing' industries had more significant coefficients than the 'shrinking' industries (except for equation set no. 6), the reader should note our results are biased to this extent. Unfortunately, this was the only form in which the 1963 data are printed.[13]

10. He does not show the *t*-values for these subsets but only the r^2. In this study, significance shall be measured in terms of *t*-values rather than r^2. While the interpretation is identical, it is easier to remember the importance of sample size in determining significance when *t*-values are used.

11. However, equation set number 1 differs in sign; but both are insignificant.

12. Shepherd (1964, p. 206, note 6) notes that the value of shipments growth rate would have been much higher for his sample, too.

13. Although no further disaggregation was attempted in our sample, Nelson did compute industry regressions between the growth rate and concentration. In addition, Mueller (1967) does present some figures for comparable producer goods and consumer goods industries as well as the overall statistics. Using simple, apparently unweighted, averages of percentage point changes of 4-digit industry concentration ratios, he found: 1. Concentration increased in the consumer goods industries ($N = 81$) and declined in the producer goods industries ($N = 132$) resulting in a relatively unchanged concentration overall ($N = 213$) during the 1947–63 period; and 2. More precisely,

Table 2 Results of simple and multiple regressions for 'concentrated' industries*

Equation Number	Shepherd's results r^2 1947–58 ($N = 141$)	Our results r^2 or R^2 and (t-value or F value) 1947–63 ($N = 50$)	1954–63 ($N = 55$)	1958–63 ($N = 66$)
1.2	0·056	0·038 (−1·37)	0·034 (−1·37)	0·009 (−0·78)
2.2	0·039	0·073 (−1·95)	0·069 (−1·98)	0·039 (−1·61)
3.2	0·013	0·015 (−0·85)	0·089 (−2·28)	0·020 (−1·14)
4.2	0·201	0·094 (−2·23)	0·103 (−2·46)	0·129 (−3·08)
5.2	0·238	0·177 (−3·21)	0·208 (−3·72)	0·245 (−4·56)
6.2	0·189	0·082 (−2·08)	0·458 (−6·70)	0·013 (−0·92)
7.2		0·115 (3·04) 0·023 (−1·04) 0·080 (−2·02)	0·107 (3·11) 0·004 (−0·47) 0·075 (−2·05)	0·130 (4·68) 0·000 (0·09) 0·121 (−2·94)
8.2		0·218 (6·55) 0·050 (−1·57) 0·156 (−2·94)	0·215 (7·12) 0·010 (−0·71) 0·157 (−3·11)	0·248 (10·38) 0·003 (−0·47) 0·217 (−4·18)
9.2		0·088 (2·26) 0·006 (−0·53) 0·074 (−1·94)	0·460 (22·07) 0·002 (−0·29) 0·406 (−5·96)	0·026 (0·83) 0·013 (−0·90) 0·006 (−0·61)
10.2		0·004 (−0·46)	0·002 (0·35)	0·012 (−0·87)
11.2		0·016 (−0·87)	0·003 (0·43)	0·026 (−1·30)
12.2		0·001 (−0·23)	0·002 (−0·30)	0·001 (−0·22)
13.2		0·029 (1·20)	0·161 (3·19)	0·089 (2·51)
14.2		0·002 (−0·33)	0·000 (0·14)	0·136 (−3·17)
15.2		0·000 (0·14)	0·087 (2·24)	0·274 (4·91)
16.2		0·030 (0·71) 0·029 (1·19) 0·000 (0·11)	0·207 (6·80) 0·132 (2·81) 0·055 (1·71)	0·340 (16·24) 0·092 (2·52) 0·275 (4·89)
17.2		0·007 (0·16) 0·005 (−0·47) 0·002 (−0·34)	0·002 (0·06) 0·002 (0·33) 0·000 (0·91)	0·143 (5·25) 0·008 (−0·70) 0·133 (−3·10)

* 'Concentrated' industries are those industries with 4-firm concentration ratios of 50 per cent or more in the base period.

The coding for the equation numbers is given in Table 1. Thus, equation 1·2 here corresponds to equation 1·1 in Table 1.

Source: US Senate (1962 and 1966) and Shepherd (1964).

Influence of concentration (C_i) on industry growth rates (ΔVS)

It is of course possible to reverse the causality and test if the initial concentration level influences the growth rate either positively or negatively. The traditional static theory of monopoly suggests that monopolies restrict output as compared with levels reached in more competitive industries. Of course, this does not imply that monopolies will restrict the rate of growth of output. The latter question concerns the rate at which firms with market power react to changed market conditions, and it *might* be the case that these firms will react quicker than their competitive counterparts. However, the usual presumption is that the association between initial concentration and subsequent growth is negative. On the other hand, a positive association is postulated by the Schumpeterian dynamic theory of monopoly that emphasizes reinvestment and innovation. An intermediate group of theories – including Bain's 'limit pricing' and Baumol's 'sales maximization' – suggest concentrated firms are less (more) restrictive than the traditional (Schumpeterian) theory would suggest.

On the basis of a frequency distribution of 1947 concentration and subsequent changes in industry employment (1947–58), Shepherd concludes that there is a negative relationship between initial concentration and subsequent growth – i.e. the declining industries were more highly concentrated than the advancing industries.[14] However since the present study is concerned with output and not employment growth, no revision or extension of his table is attempted. Instead, a comparison of output growth regressions is made.

In Table 1 equation sets 10–17 bear on the question of concentration and subsequent growth. In Shepherd's sample no significant, or even systematic, association was found between concentration, C_4, C_8, C_{20},[15] and growth measured by either output or employment.[16] The insignificant relationship between C_i and ΔVS was also present in the multiple correlations which

---

average concentration fell by 0·4 percentage points in both the 1947–54 and 1954–8 periods but rose sharply by 1·1 percentage points from 1958–63. The producer goods (consumer goods) industries experience decreases (increases) in concentration in each of the periods: 1947–63, −1·0 (+0·55); 1954–8, −0·76 (+·08); and 1958–63, −0·29 (+2·5). The change in concentration results according to whether concentration, increased, decreased, or remained the same are given in Table 4 (p. 178).

14. However, the most rapidly growing industries had higher initial concentration levels than the less rapidly growing industries. But non-concentration factors explain a good part of this association.

15. In the text he states C_{20} and growth were not significantly related but he does not table the precise coefficients.

16. The employment results are not presented here. While both growth variables were insignificant, the employment coefficient was generally negative and the output coefficient generally positive.

Table 3 Comparison of industry growth rates and change in industry concentration

| | Total industries | Average concentration change[b] | Industry growth between 1947 and 1963[a] | | | | | | | |
| | | | 200 per cent or more | | 100–199 per cent | | 25–99 per cent | | Under 25 per cent | |
			No. of industries	Average concentration change	No. of industries	Average concentration change	No. of industries	Average concentration change	No. of industries	Average concentration change
All industries	205[c]	0·3	41	−2·5	68	0·4	61	1·9	35	2·3
Producer goods	127	−1·5	29	(−)3·8[d]	50	(−)1·1[d]	29	−0·2	19	−1·1
Consumer goods	78	3·4	12	0·7	18	0·4	32	3·8	16	6·4

[a] Percentage change in value of shipments.
[b] Simple average change of 4-firm concentration ratios.
[c] Comparable industries between 1947 and 1963 for which data were available.
[d] Although these signs are not in the source's table, the text clearly states that the signs should be negative.
Source: Mueller, (1967, Table 17, p. 77).

included coverage and entry explanatory variables (equation sets 16 and 17).

The simple correlation results of growth (ΔVS) against initial concentration (C_4, C_8, and C_{20}) presented in 10.1, 11.1, and 12.1 respectively reinforce the Shepherd finding of no association. In fact, the t-values are always lower than his and the signs are negative in 4 of 9 cases (always being negative in the 1958–63 sample). Equation 13.1 relating ΔVS with ΔNF shows a definite (positive) association in all the samples. However, the 1958–63 coefficient is only significant at the 0·01 level. Since there is some question as to direction of the causality and to other 'outside' influences the association is not very meaningful.

Equation 14.1 is interesting in that the observed negative association between CR – the inverse of potential entry from existing firms – and subsequent growth (ΔVS) is confirmed in all the samples. In addition, the relationship became stronger over time as the t-ratios roughly doubled from 1947–63 to 1954–63 and again from 1954–63 to 1958–63. This rise in significance is particularly interesting since Shepherd noted that his negative association may 'merely reflect *special postwar conditions*, or other peculiarities of the concept and measure of coverage ratios (1964, p. 208).'[17] While his associations 'explain' but 2 to 6 per cent of the actual growth, the 1958–63 result 'explains' over 13 per cent. Thus, actual or threatened entry appears to make existing firms grow faster than otherwise. Equation 15.1 showing the simple correlation between ΔVS and changes in $CR(\Delta CR)$ is also consistent with the above findings. Potential entrants turning into actual entrants apparently stimulated growth. And what is more this pattern is becoming stronger over time.

The multiple correlations using the ΔVS, ΔCR, ΔNF, C_4, and CR variables are presented in equations 16.1 and 17.1.[18] Equation 16.1 correlates ΔVS with ΔNF and ΔCR jointly. The 1947–58 sample shows the association between ΔVS and ΔCR definite even when 'net entry' (ΔNF or change in the total number of firms in the industry) is included. From the 1947–63

17. While not shown, he stated that his correlations on subsets of industries for growing, shrinking, and high concentration are not significant. Our 'high concentration' results in Table 2 show that equation 14.2 is also insignificant for the 1947–63 and 1954–63 periods but is significant at the 0·01 level for 1958–63. This reinforces our above notion that this last period is important.

18. An anonymous referee suggested and I concurred that the ΔNF and CR have something to be desired as explanatory variables. The ΔNF variable is subject to a considerable instability because the Census finds it necessary to classify large numbers of small one-plant firms and it often has to do so quite arbitrarily. On the coverage ratio, it can only be interpreted in the context of comparing concentration on a product versus industry basis, as Nelson attempted to do. Moreover, changes in the homogeneity ratio might also be considered, as this might reflect opportunities for leading firms to expand into new products.

Table 4 Percentage of comparable industries by change in four-firm concentration ratios, 1947–63, 1947–54, 1954–58 and 1958–63

Per cent of industries

Industry type	Total	1947–63 In which concentration ratios:			1947–54 In which concentration ratios:			1954–58 In which concentration ratios:			1958–63 In which concentration ratios:		
		In-creased	Stayed the same[a]	De-creased	In-creased	Stayed the same[a]	De-creased	In-creased	Stayed the same[a]	De-creased	In-creased	Stayed the same[a]	De-creased
All industries	100	38	22	40	29	37	34	22	47	31	34	43	23
Producer goods	100	29	24	47	26	36	38	22	45	33	27	43	30
Consumer goods	100	53	17	30	33	38	29	22	49	29	47	42	11

[a] Change less than 3 percentage points.

Source: US Senate, (1966) cited 'n Mueller (1967'Table 15, p. 69). Mueller's figures given here for 1947–63 and 1958–63 in percentages are not the same as those he gives in Appendix A for the same years. I was not able to find anywhere in his paper how he reconciles these two sets of figures.

sample to the 1958–63 sample, the ΔCR coefficient grew progressively more significant. It is statistically insignificant in 1947–63 and significant at the 0·02 and 0·01 levels in 1954–63 and 1958–63 respectively. On the other hand the ΔNF coefficient is significant at the 0·01 level for the first two periods but only at the 0·05 level in the 1958–63 period. The 1954–63 period results are quite similar to Shepherd's. The only conclusion that emerges from this

Table 5 Comparison of changes in concentration and the coverage ratio

Independent variable	Dependent variable CR		
	1947–63	1954–58	1958–63
	Simple correlation coefficient (and t-value)		
ΔC_4	0·052(0·694)	−0·157(−2·221)	−0·033(−0·480)
ΔC_8	0·107(1·419)	−0·210(−2·999)	0·031(0·456)
ΔC_{20}	0·154(2·061)	−0·237(−3·414)	0·059(0·856)

pattern is the apparent rising importance over time of changes in CR on industry growth. Equation 17·1 relates ΔVS with the base period's C_4 and CR. This equation corroborates the 1947–58 finding that the base period CR is negatively and significantly associated with subsequent growth, even after allowing for the influence of the base period concentration. Furthermore, the impact of CR on growth appears to grow over time. In contrast, the C_4 coefficient is progressively less significant over time and even has a negative sign in the 1954–63 period.[19]

On the basis of his broad findings discussed above, Shepherd challenged the general hypothesis that firm sizes are lognormally distributed. This law of proportionate effect says that that rate of firm growth is independent of firm size. His assertion is based on his association between growth (ΔVS) and changes in concentration (ΔC_i) and between growth (ΔVS) and changes in the number of firms (ΔNF). Since the first of these associations is either disappearing over time or only true for long-run periods, such a challenge appears inappropriate. Although the relationship between ΔVS and ΔNF in the present study is much less impressive in the 1958–63 period both for simple and multiple correlations, Shepherd's suggestion that the birth rate of new firms is a variable rather a constant is more substantiated than the concentration and growth nexus. However, since Shepherd himself noted

19. Table 2 also contains our results for equations 7–16 for 'concentrated' industries (Shepherd's published results did not include comparable figures). In general these results are very similar to the 'overall' results as to sign but the 'concentrated' results are generally less significant – the exceptions chiefly occurring in the 1958–63 sample.

that the period he investigates, the 1947–58 period, 'contains many abnormal features, particularly the existence of demand backlogs in many important industries in the early postwar years' (Shepherd 1964, p. 208),[20] the reduced statistical significance in the perhaps more 'normal' 1958–63 period for both the ΔVS on ΔC_i coefficients and for the ΔNF on ΔVS coefficients suggests his challenge does not possess a serious threat to the proportionate effect thesis.

Table 6 **Concentration levels for all manufacturing industries**

	1947	1954	1958	1963
C_4	37·3	38·9	37·6	36·2
Number of industries	199	216	238	408
C_8	49·1	51·2	51·0	48·7
Number of industries	200	216	240	413
C_{20}	63·7	66·7	66·2	63·8
Number of industries	200	214	226	415

These concentration ratios are weighted averages of the concentration ratios for the four digit subindustries the weights being the total value of shipments for the subindustries. This Table maximizes the number of observations for each variable as given in US Senate (1966).

Summary and conclusions

The present paper is primarily an empirical revision and extension of several important papers, particularly by Nelson and Shepherd, on the relationship between market growth and seller's concentration. While it has been suggested that the data employed here are better – because, e.g. they incorporate a meaningful SIC classification, and focus on a more appropriate time period, etc. – they suffer, in comparison to the earlier studies, in that the sample size was substantially reduced. In addition, none of the regressions 'explains' very much of the actual changes in the dependent variables. However, the important conclusion does emerge that the Nelson–Shepherd finding that market growth leads to lower levels of industry con-

20. Of course, I do not mean to imply that the 1958–63 period was necessarily 'normal' in any business-cycle sense. But it is clear that the stage of the business cycle may have an important effect on the results. Both the Nelson and Shepherd analyses have final years that were recessions. In other words, they examine developments from mid-prosperity (1947) to recession (1954 or 1958). On the other hand, my 1954–63 and 1958–63 analyses examine developments from recession to mid-prosperity. It is really only the 1947–63 analysis that contains beginning and terminal years of comparable business cycle stages. Thus, both the cyclical and trend factors give reason for paying more attention to the 1947–63 period.

centration does not receive positive support.[21] Unfortunately, this conclusion as well as all of the above findings are, of course, quite tentative in view of the limited sample of industries for which comparisons could be made and of related statistical problems, but they suggest avenues for further research.

21. Although I have based this conclusion on regressions only (largely reruns of Shepherd's), there is other evidence that also undercuts the growth hypothesis, such as Shepherd's Hearings testimony, see footnote 2 above. A referee suggested that Pashigian at Chicago has also developed some additional results, not yet published. On the other hand, when and if Mueller's manuscript cited earlier is put in final form and published it will be necessary to give it a careful perusal in order to reconcile his conclusions with mine. With the vastly superior data at his disposal I would, *ceteris paribus*, be inclined to give his study greater weight than mine.

References

BAUMOL, W. J. (1962), 'On the theory of the expansion of the firm', *Amer. econ. Rev.*, vol. 52, pp. 1078–87.

BOCK, B. (1959), *Concentration Patterns in Manufacturing*, National Industrial Conference Board Studies in Business Economics, no. 65, chapter 2.

CONKLIN, M. R., and GOLDSTEIN, H. T. (1955), 'Census principles of industry and product classification manufacturing industries', in *Business Concentration and Price Policy*, National Bureau of Economic Research.

GORT, M. (1962), *Diversification and Integration in American Industry*, National Bureau of Economic Research.

KAMERSCHEN, D. R. (1966), 'Conglomerate concentration coefficients', *Antitrust Bull.*, vol. 11, pp. 351–73.

MUELLER, W. F. (1967), Statement before Select Committee on Small Business, US Senate, Washington, 15 March.

NELSON, R. L. (1960), 'Market growth, company diversification and product concentration, 1947–54', *J. Amer. stat. Assn*, vol. 55, pp. 640–49.

NELSON, R. L. (1963), *Concentration in the Manufacturing Industries of the United States: A Midcentury Report*, Yale University Press.

NELSON, R. L. (1964), testimony, US Senate, Committee on the Judiciary, Subcommittee on Antitrust and Monopoly, Hearings, *Economic Concentration*, part 1, US Government Printing Office.

PENROSE, E. T. (1959), *The Theory of the Growth of the Firm*, Wiley.

SHEPHERD, W. G. (1964), 'Trends of concentration in American manufacturing industries, 1947–58', *Rev. Econ. Stats*, vol. 66, pp. 200–212.

SHEPHERD, W. G. (1965), testimony, US Senate, Committee on the Judiciary, Subcommittee on Antitrust and Monopoly, Hearings, *Economic Concentration*, part 2, US Government Printing Office.

SINGER, E. (1965), 'Census concentration: a critical analysis', *Antitrust Bull.*, vol. 10, pp. 851–78.

STIGLER, G. J. (1952), 'The theory of oligopoly', in *The Theory of Price*, Macmillan Co.

US FEDERAL TRADE COMMISSION (1954), *Changes in Concentration in Manufacturing 1935–1947 and 1950*, US Government Printing Office.

US SENATE (1962), *Concentration Ratios in Manufacturing Industries, 1958*, Bureau of the Census, US Government Printing Office.

US SENATE (1966), *Concentration Ratios in Manufacturing Industries, 1963*, part 1, Bureau of the Census, US Government Printing Office.

12 Leonard W. Weiss

Mergers and Concentration in Six Industries

Leonard W. Weiss, 'An evaluation of mergers in six industries', *Review of Economics and Statistics*, vol. 47, 1965, pp. 172–81.

Economists have long attacked horizontal merger for its role in increasing concentration and defended it as a relatively painless means of attaining economies of scale and/or inter-regional entry. This Reading attempts to evaluate these divergent views using the experience of six large industries. In part 1, the data and definitions used are explained. In part 2, an attempt is made to measure the role of merger and of various other factors in concentration change. Part 3 examines the proportion of acquired capacity that is sub-optimal in scale, and part 4, the proportion that is inter-regional. Part 5 contains some brief conclusions.

1

The data used consist of plant and firm sizes reported at regular intervals by industry directories or similar sources for six industries: steel, automobiles, petroleum refining, cement, flour, and brewing.[1] The industries and periods chosen were dictated by the availability of data. These are almost the only large industries that regularly publish information on the size of identified plants and firms. Plant sizes were recorded for four years at approximately ten-year intervals in steel, automobiles, refining, cement, and flour and for two such years in brewing.[2] The exact dates used appear in appendix Table A1. Size was measured in operating capacities[3] in all

1. The sources used were as follows: steel – American Iron and Steel Institute (1926–57); automobiles – *Automotive News* (1962); petroleum refining – Bureau of Mines (1928–58); cement – *Pit and Quarry* (1932–58), and correspondence with four major producers; flour – *Northwestern Miller* (1932–59); brewing – *Modern Brewery Age* (1947–58).

2. Data were also collected for twenty-seven shorter but more irregular periods averaging about six years in length. The results were about the same as for the long periods.

3. Shipments might have been better than capacity, but they were not ordinarily available. Capacity does have the advantage of avoiding temporary fluctuations. The defects of capacity are lessened by the exclusion of shutdown plants. Concentration, measured in capacity, was similar to that based on industry shipments in most cases. The 1954 and 1958 Census four-firm concentration ratios compare with those computed from the capacity data used in this study as follows (Census figures from US Senate, 1962, Table 2):

cases except automobiles where registrations were used. Plant scale was measured in a strictly horizontal dimension in each case – e.g. steel plants were reported at ingot capacities ignoring blast furnace or finishing capacities. A plant was defined as the total capacity owned by a firm at a particular address except for automobiles where the combination of facilities associated with a 'make' was treated as a plant.

A 'merger' was recorded whenever a plant in operation at the beginning of a period was operated by a different, previously-existing firm at the end of the period. Regardless of the formal transaction, the larger firm was always treated as acquiring the smaller one. Acquisitions by firms new to the industry were treated as name changes rather than mergers unless the new firm acquired the plants of more than one previously-existing firm, in which case the largest acquired firm was treated as changing its name (no merger) and acquiring the other plants involved (merger). Most mergers were first detected in industry directories, but they were checked in *Moody's Industrial Manual* whenever possible. Mergers were dated when the locus of control appeared to change. For instance, Tidewater 'acquired' Skelly in 1948–58 when *Moody's* first indicated that the Getty interests held a majority of Tidewater stock, but Shell did not 'acquire' Roxana in 1929–39 because *Moody's* showed Shell as having a majority interest earlier. Since only changes between the starts and ends of periods were observed, mergers followed by exits, or mergers following entries, were not always recorded.[4]

An 'exit' was recorded if some of a firm's plants were operating at the start of a period but all of its plants were either shut down or not listed at the end of the period. No exit was recorded so long as any of a firm's plants continued to operate, even if some plants closed or even if all the continuing plants had been acquired by other firms.

	Steel	Petroleum refining	Cement	Flour	Beer
1958 concentration ratios					
by census industry shipments	55 (by v.a.)	33	31	40	27
by directory capacities	59·6	34·0	32·4	29·7	22·2
1954 concentration ratios					
by census industry shipments	53 (by v.a.)	32	32	38	28
by directory capacities	52·8	32·4	31·2	35·7	23·3

4. The one important merger missed in this way was US Steel's acquisition of the RFC's 1,283,000 ton Geneva Steel Plant in 1938–48. All the conclusions of this paper would hold if this had appeared as a merger rather than as internal growth. Two other important mergers, the acquisitions of Packard and of Hudson by Studebaker-Packard and American Motors in 1948–58, were recorded by the device of giving the Packard and Hudson makes nominal values in 1958.

An 'entry' was recorded if a firm had no capacity at the start of a period and if at the end of the period it had at least one plant that was not operating previously. 'Entry' required both a new firm and a new plant, though the new firm may have existed previously in a different industry. No entry was recorded if the name of a firm with a previously-operating plant was changed or if a new firm acquired the previously operating plants of a single firm.[5]

This paper focuses on the roles of merger and various other influences in changes in the four- and eight-firm concentration ratios. Effects on the shares of other numbers of leading firms (hereafter 'majors') were also investigated, but they showed no important differences from the results for four and/or eight majors.

Any attempt to measure the change in concentration due to merger requires some assumption about the probable effect of other factors if merger had not occurred. Some previous studies have measured the effect of merger on the growth of firms by taking the size of acquired assets as a percentage of total firm growth.[6] If used as an indicator of the effect of merger on concentration, this would involve the assumptions that acquired plants would not have changed in absolute size if left independent and that acquiring firms would have built the same absolute amount of new capacity without merger that they did with merger.

The main alternative is to measure acquisitions by their percentages of industry capacity at the times that the transactions occur. The resulting percentages are directly comparable to the conventional concentration ratios we are attempting to analyse. This approach involves the assumptions that the acquired plant would survive and grow at the same rate as the industry does if left independent and that acquiring firms would build new capacity no faster or slower if prevented from merging than they in fact do when merger occurs. At least in growing industries this second approach ordinarily makes merger seem more important than the first.

5. This definition contrasts with that of Mansfield who identified entries by the change in a firm's name (1962, pp. 1024–26). It seems to me that entry carrying with it the appearance of new capacity comes much closer to the meaning usually assigned the term in economic analysis than entry which reflects only a change in corporate organization. For instance, Mansfield's concept resulted in a substantial entry rate in automobiles in the 1950s due to the 'entry' of American Motors.

An arbitrary convention had to be adopted in the case of the large numbers of small oil refineries in the Long Beach and East Texas areas in the late 1920s and early 1930s. It was impossible to trace particular plants, so each plant was treated as continuing in existence with neither entry nor exit so long as there were enough refineries listed in a town at the start of a period to cover those listed at the end of a period. Only changes in the numbers of refineries in a town could involve entry or exit.

6. See, for example, Schroeder (1952, pp. 79–94).

It is not unusual to find that mergers account for only a small part of the total absolute growth of large firms, though few such firms have been able to increase their market shares by much more than the market shares of their acquisitions (Weston, 1953, p. 48 and Appendix E). We will use this second, market share approach.

The following notation is useful in expressing the elements of concentration changes: X – total capacity assignable to exits; N – total capacity assignable to entries; M – total capacity assignable to mergers; F – total capacity assignable to the four (or eight) majors, and TC – total industry capacity.

These symbols will bear the subscripts 1 or 2 indicating whether capacities are measured at the start or end of a period. The symbols F and M will bear the additional subscripts a or b indicating whether the majors involved are among the four (eight) leaders at the start (a) or the end (b) of the period It follows that $F_{a1} \geq F_{b1}$ and $F_{a2} \leq F_{b2}$. Using this notation, the concentration ratio at time one is F_{a1}/TC_1. A major purpose of this paper is to explain the change in the concentration ratio over the period. This change is

$$\frac{F_{b2}}{TC_2} - \frac{F_{a1}}{TC_1}.$$

The change in concentration during a period can be wholly accounted for by merger, internal growth, and 'displacement' if these are defined as follows:

The effect of merger – the percentage of initial industry capacity assignable to plants acquired by the four (eight) largest firms at the end of the period (hereafter 'time two majors'),

$$\frac{M_{b1}}{TC_1}, \qquad\qquad 1$$

the effect of internal growth by time two majors – the amount by which they were able over the period to increase the share of total industry capacity assignable to their plants and acquisitions,

$$\frac{F_{b2}}{TC_2} - \frac{F_{b1} + M_{b1}}{TC_1}, \qquad\qquad 2$$

and the effect of 'displacement' – the portion of the growth of the time two majors' share of total capacity which went into catching up with time one majors and therefore did not increase concentration,

$$-\frac{F_{a1}-F_{b1}}{TC_1}.\qquad\qquad\qquad\qquad 3$$

The algebraic sum of these three expressions is the change in concentration. However, these expressions ignore the effects of entry and exit, or more accurately, they assign to internal growth and merger variable elements of concentration change that might better be separately identified. Mergers and/or internal growth do not directly cause entries and exits. The changes in concentration due to entry and exit can be distinguished by finding the differences between the majors' shares of total capacity and their shares of total capacity of surviving firms (excluding exits at time one and entries at time two) as follows:[7]

The effect of exit,

$$\frac{F_{a1}}{TC_1-X_1}-\frac{F_{a1}}{TC_1},\qquad\qquad\qquad 4$$

the effect of entry,

$$\frac{F_{b2}}{TC_2}-\frac{F_{b2}}{TC_2-N_2}.\qquad\qquad\qquad 5$$

For consistency, the effects of merger, internal growth, and displacement must be expressed as percentages of capacity of surviving firms excluding exits from the denominator when concepts are measured at time one and excluding entries when they are measured at time two:

The effect of merger,

$$\frac{M_{b1}}{TC_1-X_1},\qquad\qquad\qquad\qquad 6$$

the effect of internal growth of time two majors,

$$\frac{F_{b2}}{TC_2-N_2}-\frac{F_{b1}+M_{b1}}{TC_1-X_1},\qquad\qquad 7$$

and the effect of displacement of time one majors by time two majors,

$$-\frac{F_{a1}-F_{b1}}{TC_1-X_1}.\qquad\qquad\qquad\qquad 8$$

Expressions **4** to **8** add up to the total change in concentration again. The effect of merger appears greater using expression **6** than using expression **1** because M_{b1} is divided by a smaller denomination in expression **6**.

7. More complex formulations would be necessary if majors were themselves to enter or exit. In the industries studied, none of the top eight firms entered or exited in a period in which they were majors.

2

Values for expressions **1** to **3** and **4** to **8** appear for four and eight firm concentration ratios for each industry and period in appendix Table A1, and annual average rates for each period in appendix Table A2. Text Table 1 shows annual averages for each expression taking all industries and periods together. By definition, the effects of merger (**1** and **6**) and exit (**4**) are positive, and the effects of displacement (**3** and **8**) and entry (**5**) are negative. Only internal growth by time two majors (**2** and **7**) can have either sign.

Table 1 hides a good deal of information, but a few of the generalizations suggested there seem to fit the more detailed tabulations in the Appendix. Entry seldom had much effect in these industries. The four largest firms experienced an erosion of the market shares of only 0·11 percentage points per year as a result of entry – 0·07 per year if the temporary entry of Kaiser into automobiles in 1946 and of many small refiners in East Texas in the early 1930s were excluded. Only in automobiles and steel in the 1940s (both mainly due to Kaiser enterprises) was the effect of entry net of exit enough to reduce the four leaders' market share by as much as one percentage point in a decade.

Concentration was more likely to increase at the eight-firm than at the four-firm level. It rose even more at the twenty-firm level (not shown).

Table 1 **Average annual changes in concentration ratios due to various influences**

Factor affecting concentration	All industries		Automobiles excluded	
	4 Majors	8 Majors	4 Majors	8 Majors
Ignoring exit and entry				
1. Merger	0·19	0·29	0·21	0·32
2. Internal growth	0·12	0·12	−0·001	0·06
3. Displacement	−0·11	−0·13	−0·08	−0·06
Total change in concentration ratios per year	0·20	0·28	0·13	0·32
Explicitly allowing for exit and entry				
4. Exit	0·21	0·26	0·20	0·31
5. Entry	−0·11	−0·15	−0·09	−0·14
6. Merger	0·22	0·33	0·23	0·36
7. Internal growth	−0·02	−0·01	−0·13	−0·13
8. Displacement	−0·11	−0·14	−0·09	−0·07
Total change in concentration ratios per year	0·20	0·28	0·13	0·32

The element of concentration change that increases most as the number of majors grows is the effect of merger.

The fairly common notion that concentration would increase very little except for merger[8] seems to be borne out in Table 1. Without merger, and with other factors in Table 1 unchanged, concentration would apparently have decreased by a quarter or a third in steel, petroleum, and cement over the three decades covered, but this result is misleading on several counts.

First, merger involving time two majors was often associated with displacement of time one majors, so that the net increase in concentration was less than the merger figures in Table 1 show. Seven of the eight displacements of time one majors observed at the four-firm level and six of the eight at the eight-firm level coincided with important mergers by the new majors. All the exceptions were in the automobile industry. Correlation coefficients relating concentration change due to displacement and those due to merger (excluding automobiles) are 0.6549 at the four-firm level, 0.6029 at the eight-firm level, and 0.8220 at the twenty-firm level ($N = 13 - 2 = 11$). The relationship between merger and displacement partially explains the greater importance of merger as the number of majors increases. Displacement seldom results in much decline in the market shares of displaced time one majors. If some firm succeeds in merging into the ranks of the top four, the share of the four leaders may not grow, but the share of the top eight firms almost certainly will.

The effect of merger is further exaggerated by Table 1 since increases and decreases due to internal growth cancel out. Table 2 shows coefficients of determination relating overall concentration change to each of its elements in turn. All the extreme values for concentration change appear in automobiles, so correlation coefficients have been computed with and without that industry.

With exit and entry ignored, internal growth of time two majors is more closely related to concentration change than is merger, but much of this is because the effect of exit is included in 'internal growth'. Explicitly allowed for, exit is more closely related to concentration change than any other influence. Entry is still unimportant. Internal growth is more closely related to concentration change than merger at the four-firm level, but not at the eight-firm level. Allowing for the interaction between merger and displacement, the net correlation between merger and concentration change is significant only at the eight-firm level. At the four-firm level, merger, like entry, though often present, is not significantly more important in cases where concentration increases sharply than in others.

8. See House Select Committee on Small Business (1962, pp. 11–12), and sources cited there.

Table 2 Coefficients of determination relating overall concentration change to concentration change due to particular causes

Factor affecting concentration	All industries ($N-2 = 14$)		Automobiles excluded ($N-2 = 11$)	
	4 Majors	8 Majors	4 Majors	8 Majors
Ignoring exit and entry				
1. Merger	0·1478	0·3764[b]	0·1864	0·4678[c]
2. Internal growth	0·8926[c]	0·6431[c]	0·8442[c]	0·8111[c]
3. Displacement	0·4666[c]	0·0230	0·2601	0·3456[a]
Allowing for exit and entry				
4. Exit	0·6551[c]	0·5994[c]	0·7245[c]	0·6249[c]
5. Entry	0·2636[a]	0·0568	0·0132	0·0164
6. Merger	0·3472[b]	0·4885[c]	0·2981	0·6082[c]
7. Internal growth	0·5281[c]	0·0417	0·5624[c]	0·3956[a]
8. Displacement	0·5355[c]	0·0334	0·3676[a]	0·4184[b]
Partial correlation coefficients	($N-3 = 13$)		($N-3 = 10$)	
$r_{c6 \cdot 8}$	0·2097	0·4982[c]	0·0615	0·4108[a]
$r_{c7 \cdot 8}$	0·1400	0·0119	0·4816[b]	0·1444

[a] Significant at 5 per cent level.
[b] Significant at 2 per cent level.
[c] Significant at 1 per cent level.

3

The role of merger in concentration change may still be overstated if merger is an alternative to exit for the absorbed firm. To test this possibility, an attempt was made to determine what portion of acquired plants was sub-optimal in scale.

No method for estimating minimum efficient scale is perfect.[9] This paper uses the Stiglerian survival technique (Stigler, 1958, pp. 61–7; and Saving, 1961, pp. 569–607) because it is feasible with the data at hand and offers a basis for estimating differing minimum efficient scales for different periods. The technique seems on safest grounds when used as it is here to estimate *minimum* efficient scales of *plants*. At any rate, the minimum efficient scale estimates coincide with those made by Bain for the early 1950s (1956, pp. 227–49). Estimates appear in the first column of Table 3. Survival technique estimates show decreasing minimum efficient scales in most industries during the World War II period, possibly reflecting a temporary advantage of small plants in a setting of shortages and controls. The lower of prewar or postwar estimates are substituted for these temporary lows. In most cases, a single minimum efficient scale was easy to

9. See comments of Smith (1955) and Friedman (1955, pp. 213–38).

identify but in petroleum refining two such scales seem to show up. The larger corresponds to Bain's estimate which he explicitly identified with diversified plants at coastal locations (1956, p. 233). The lower estimate is associated with more specialized plants usually, though not always, at inland locations. Two sets of figures reflecting the two estimates are shown in Table 3.[10]

Any single-valued estimate of minimum efficient scale is necessarily rough. Optimal scales for individual plants may differ because of the raw material sources or management skills available, and sub-optimal plants may be viable in small regional or specialized product markets. However, there seems to be no reason to expect deviations from industry-wide estimates to be biased either upward or downward for the group of plants acquired in mergers.

Table 3 shows total capacity acquired in all mergers and the percentage of it which was sub-optimal at the start of the period in which the merger took place. All the acquisitions in automobiles and steel, and more than half of the acquired capacity in other industries, were sub-optimal. An unweighted average of the sixteen periods shows 82·9 per cent of all acquired capacity as sub-optimal when the low estimate of minimum efficient scale in petroleum refining is used and 91·1 per cent sub-optimal when the high estimate is used.

If they had not been acquired, the sub-optimal plants would not necessarily have disappeared, but a large proportion of sub-optimal plants do disappear in most periods. The sixteen periods were examined for exits by firms whose total capacity in all plants was below that of a single, optimal plant. An unweighted average of all periods showed 28·7 per cent of such 'sub-optimal firms' with 17·3 percent of initial sub-optimal capacity exiting each period (27·8 per cent and 15·1 per cent respectively if high estimates for petroleum refining are used). The percentage of sub-optimal firms exiting reached 55 per cent in refining in the 1930s and flour in the 1950s, representing 54 per cent and 46 per cent of sub-optimal capacity, respectively. Most exits were by sub-optimal firms, the only exceptions being two cement and twenty-four flour companies. All of these 'supra-optimal' exits were near minimum efficient scale except for one in flour in the 1930s.

4

Some of the supra-optimal mergers that did occur had limited effect upon competition in that they represented diversification into new regions or products by acquiring firms. To estimate the extent of such mergers, the

10. More extensive discussion of and support for estimates used here appears in Weiss (1964, p. 249).

Table 3 Sub-optimal acquisitions

Period	Minimum efficient scale	Capacity acquired by all firms			Percentage of capacity acquired by majors that was sub-optimal	
		Total	Sub-optimal total	Percentage sub-optimal	4 majors	8 majors
Small specialized petroleum refineries (thousands of bbls. per day)						
1929–1939	5·8	297·3	77·5	26·1	27·0	21·0
1939–1948	30·0	106·0	106·0	100·0	100·0	100·0
1948–1958	30·0	386·7	256·3	66·3	100·0	47·1
Large diversified petroleum refineries (thousands of bbls. per day)						
1929–1939	67·0	297·3	297·3	100·0	100·0	100·0
1939–1948	100·0	106·0	106·0	100·0	100·0	100·0
1948–1958	150·0	386·7	386·7	100·0	100·0	100·0
Steel (thousands of tons per year)						
1930–1938	2250	4777	6188	100·0	100·0	100·0
1938–1948	2250	2332	2332	100·0	100·0	100·0
1948–1957	2250	2043	2043	100·0	100·0	100·0
Automobiles (thousands of units per year)						
1929–1939	160	0	0			
1939–1948	160	0	0			
1948–1958	640	207	207	100·0	100·0	100·0
Cement (thousands of bbls. per year)						
1933–1939	1800	0	0			
1939–1948	1800	13,626	11,626	85·3	48·7	83·9
1948–1958	2300	18,920	18,920	100·0	100·0	100·0
Flour (hundredweight per day)						
1932–1942	2250	86,739	49,989	57·6	35·8	39·3
1942–1948	2250	40,376	27,440	68·0	33·3	37·4
1948–1958	5000	88,952	71,752	80·7	61·3	61·3
Beer (thousands of bbls. per year)						
1947–1958	1000	14,980	13,980	93.3	100·0	100·0

six industries were subdivided into regions (price classes in the case of automobiles),[11] and inter-regional mergers were distinguished from those combining plants in the same region. An inter-regional merger was said to occur when a pre-existing firm acquired plants in regions in which it had no capacity at the start of the period. Where an acquisition involved

11. A list of the regions used will be supplied by the author upon request directed to him in care of the Economics Department, University of Wisconsin, Madison, Wisconsin 53706.

Table 4 Extent and growth of inter-regional mergers by major firms

Industry and period	Inter-regional acquisitions as a percentage of all acquired capacity		Inter-regional mergers and/or sub-optimal[a] mergers as percentages of all acquired capacity		Inter-regional mergers as percentage of national capacity of industry in time 1		Increase from time 1 to time 2 in percentage of national capacity of inter-regional mergers	
	by 4 majors 1	by 8 majors 2	by 4 majors 3	by 8 majors 4	by 4 majors 5	by 8 majors 6	by 4 majors 7	by 8 majors 8
Petroleum refining[a]								
1929–1939	4·0	22·0	27·0	39·9	0·12	1·05	0·03	—0·07
1939–1948	43·9	46·4	100·0	100·0	0·14	0·40	0·03	0·04
1948–1958	0	0	100·0	100·0	0	0		
Steel								
1926–1938	66·6	69·6	100·0	100·0	3·93	4·51	0·13	0·30
1938–1948	100·0	100·0	100·0	100·0	1·19	1·24	—0·30	—0·25
1948–1958	0	0	100·0	100·0	0	0		
Cement								
1933–1939	27·2	64·3	100·0	100·0	0·41	3·12	0·21	1·98
1939–1948	82·9	67·0	100·0	100·0	2·37	3·38	—0·77	—0·78
1948–1958								

Table 4 – continued

Automobiles								
1929–1939								
1939–1948								
1948–1958	0	47·2	100·0	100·0	0	5·75		−5·75
Flour								
1932–1942	57·2	59·5	82·5	83·4	0·84	0·92	0·40	0·64
1942–1948	42·7	30·7	76·1	68·1	0·40	0·40	−0·03	−0·03
1948–1959	7·4	7·4	61·3	61·3	0·33	0·33	0·29	0·29
Brewing								
1947–1958	29·5	51·6	100·0	100·0	0·69	3·20	0·39	0·83

[a] Using minimum efficient scale for small, specialized refineries.

plants in both old and new regions, only those in the new regions were included in the volume of inter-regional merger. Where a new firm acquired a number of firms, the largest acquired firm was considered the 'old' firm and only acquisitions in regions new to it were treated as inter-regional mergers.

The percentages of the majors' acquired capacity in new regions are shown in columns 1 and 2 of Table 4. Unweighted averages of these percentages show 35·5 per cent of the capacity acquired by the four leading firms and 43·5 per cent of that acquired by the eight leaders to have been in regions new to the acquiring firms. Columns 3 and 4 show the percentages of acquisitions that were inter-regional or sub-optimal or both. The unweighted averages are 88 per cent and 89 per cent respectively.

Inter-regional merger may serve as a means of inter-regional entry, the larger firms using their acquisitions as starting points from which to expand in the new regions. As a partial check on this, industry shares of inter-regional acquisitions at the start and end of the periods in which the mergers occurred were compared. The time one shares are shown in columns 5 and 6 and the absolute increases in those shares by time two in columns 7 and 8 of Table 4. Columns 7 and 8 probably understate the internal growth of the merging firms in the new regions because new plants built after the merger in the new region are not included, because inter-regional shipments by the acquired or acquiring firm before merger are not recorded, and because much of the internal growth may occur in subsequent periods. On the other hand, some of the growth of acquired plants may have occurred before the mergers since only sizes at the start and end of the period are used.

Despite these deficiencies in the data, it is quite clear that inter-regional merger was not invariably a vehicle of inter-regional entry. It clearly was not in the case where the acquired plants' shares of national capacity declined sharply as in the 1950s in steel, cement, and particularly automobiles (the Studebaker-Packard merger). By contrast, industry shares of inter-regional acquisitions increased substantially (usually by more than 50 per cent in a decade) in cement in the 1940s, in flour in the 1930s and 1950s, and in brewing in the 1950s. All of these periods of strikingly 'successful' inter-regional merger were marked by slow growth or actual decline in national capacity in the industries involved. A possible interpretation is that in such stagnant industries merger becomes a more attractive – perhaps the only attractive – means of inter-regional entry. At the same time the chances of survival for a plant merged into a national major are better than for an independent in the face of stagnation. This is particularly likely if the national majors acquire the most promising independents in the new regions. There may be room for debate about whether inter-regional entry is beneficial in stagnant industries, especially if it accelerates the exit of independents, but to the extent that it is considered desirable, inter-regional merger does seem to facilitate such entry into such markets.

Inter-regional merger may have some anti-competitive effects. For one thing, regional boundaries are inevitably arbitrary, and a good deal of inter-regional competition occurs. Some of the boundaries used in this paper would probably not stand up in court in a merger case. Secondly, the development of national chains may facilitate gentlemen's agreements. US Steel's acquisition of a major Western plant and its construction of a major Eastern plant certainly enhanced its leadership qualities. With FOB mill prices and freight absorption, quasi-isolated plants might find periodic changes in base prices attractive, but with US Steel in every major market, such independent local pricing decisions seem less likely. Again, a group of oligopolists who must deal with one another in several markets may be more likely to reach agreements than groups of independent majors in each market. Most of the petroleum refiners in the mountain states were independent of the national majors in 1928. Today the area has roughly the same degree of concentration as before, but the leaders are mainly national majors. A live-and-let-live policy might be more likely under present circumstances because the leaders are apt to have varying relative power in the different markets in which they meet. A major making an unpopular move in a market where it is large or low cost may face retaliation in another where it is weaker.

Finally, inter-regional merger may be an alternative to inter-regional entry. If Bethlehem is prevented from buying a Chicago plant, it may build one. Both the acquisition and the construction of the new plant increase national concentration, but the acquisition leaves regional concentration unchanged while the inter-regional entry reduces regional concentration if there is no offsetting exit.

5

This study is based on only sixteen observations of six industries, so little claim of generality can be made for any conclusions. Moreover, the minimum efficient scales and regional boundaries used are necessarily arbitrary at the border lines, so that only rough generalizations, which are incorrect in some individual instances, are possible for the limited group of cases observed.

Within the limits set by the data, however, the common defenses of merger seem to be more solidly supported by the experience of these industries than the usual attacks upon it. Internal growth and exit, both traditionally attributed to economies of scale, are much more closely related to change in concentration at the four-firm level than is merger. There were mergers at this level, but they were distributed among industries and periods in a fairly random way and offered little explanation of the net changes in concentration that actually occurred. Merger did become important in concentration change when more majors were considered, but at the eight- or twenty-firm levels, mergers are much more likely to represent 'rationalization' and less likely to represent attempts to create monopoly. In any event, the bulk of the acquired capacity did in fact turn out to be of sub-optimal scale. Some of the acquired plants might reasonably be expected to have disappeared without mergers, and even if they had not, merger provided a means of their expansion to or replacement by lower cost scales of plant. The inter-regional mergers were more equivocal in competitive effect, but their facilitation of inter-regional entry in at least some cases and the possibility of multi-plant economies would often tend to offset the somewhat problematical impediments to competition in such mergers. Altogether, it seems certain that most mergers since the 1920s in these industries can be defended as at least harmless and probably socially useful developments.

All of this occurred in the presence of laws restricting merger for monopoly. Even before the Celler-Kefauver Act, the anti-trust laws surely put limits on merger by such firms as US Steel and Standard of New Jersey, Columbia Steel notwithstanding. It does not follow from the evidence in this paper, therefore, that anti-merger laws were unnecessary, but simply that their objectives were largely accomplished in the industries and periods covered. Before any generalization could be drawn from this sort of study, a much larger sample of industries would have to be examined on similar terms.

Appendix
Table A1 Total change in four-firm concentration ratios by period

Industry and period	1 Merger	2 Internal growth	3 Displacement	4 Exit	5 Entry	6 Merger	7 Internal growth	8 Displacement	Total change
Petroleum refining									
1929–1939	2·99	1·09	−1·84	2·70	−3·57	3·24	1·38	−1·51	2·24
1939–1948	0·25	−0·56	0	1·70	−1·10	0·26	−1·17	0	−0·31
1948–1958	0·34	−1·46	0	1·34	−0·44	0·36	−2·38	0	−1·12
Steel									
1930–1938	5·90	−3·90	−1·58	0·41	−0·44	5·94	−3·90	−1·58	0·42
1938–1948	1·19	−2·22	0	0·08	−1·60	1·20	−0·70	0	−1·03
1948–1957	0·38	−3·63	0	0·02	−0·92	0·38	−2·73	0	−3·25
Cement									
1933–1939	0	−2·36	0	0·19	−0·04	0	−2·50	0	−2·36
1939–1948	1·52	0·79	−1·44	1·45	−0·85	1·60	0·19	−1·51	0·87
1948–1958	2·86	−3·68	0	0·19	−0·53	2·87	−3·36	0	−0·82
Automobiles									
1929–1939	0	10·56	−3·81	1·09	0	0	9·52	−3·86	6·75
1939–1948	0	−6·71	0	0·16	−5·01	0	−1·85	0	−6·71
1948–1958	3·04	13·28	−2·64	5·41	0	6·12	4·95	−2·82	13·67
Flour									
1932–1942	1·46	0·43	−1·18	3·76	−1·01	1·69	−3·23	−1·37	−0·15
1942–1948	0·95	0·34	−0·62	1·81	−0·37	1·02	−1·11	−0·66	0·69
1948–1959	4·48	7·55	−0·96	5·92	−0·34	5·55	1·13	−1·19	11·07
Beer									
1947–1958	2·34	8·34	−1·72	4·86	0	3·13	3·26	−2·30	8·95

Table A1 Total change in eight-firm concentration ratios by period – *continued*

Petroleum refining									
1929–1939	4·76	−0·82	−0·16	4·41	−5·84	5·15	0·23	−0·17	3·78
1939–1948	0·78	−0·68	0	2·80	−1·84	0·82	−1·69	0	0·09
1948–1958	0·72	−0·50	0	2·23	−0·75	0·75	−2·01	0	0·22
Steel									
1930–1938	6·48	−0·91	−0·55	0·48	−0·56	6·53	−0·87	−0·56	5·02
1939–1948	1·24	−2·80	0	0·10	−2·01	1·24	−0·89	0	−1·56
1948–1957	0·51	−1·66	0	0·02	−1·20	0·51	−0·48	0	−1·15
Cement									
1933–1939	0	−2·83	0	0·26	−0·06	0	−3·03	0	−2·83
1939–1948	4·86	2·03	−2·91	2·05	−1·28	5·08	1·13	−3·00	3·98
1948–1958	5·05	−5·12	0	0·29	−0·82	5·08	−4·62	0	−0·07
Automobiles									
1929–1939	0	4·69	−1·22	1·23	0	0	3·47	−1·24	3·46
1939–1948	0	−0·81	−0·55	0·17	−5·79	0	4·81	−0·55	−1·36
1948–1958	5·75	6·15	−10·36	0·01	0	6·13	6·44	−11·04	1·54
Flour									
1932–1942	1·55	0·05	0	4·99	−1·41	1·79	−3·77	0	1·60
1942–1948	1·32	1·73	−0·70	2·29	−0·49	1·42	−0·12	−0·75	2·36
1948–1959	4·48	9·27	−0·81	8·62	−0·47	5·55	0·25	−1·00	12·94
Beer									
1947–1958	6·21	9·55	−2·40	7·96	0	8·28	0·31	−3·21	13·35

Table A2 Annual rates of change, four-firm concentration ratios

Industry and period	1 Merger	2 Internal growth	3 Displacement	4 Exit	5 Entry	6 Merger	7 Internal growth	8 Displacement	Total change
Petroleum refining									
1929–1939	0·299	0·109	−0·184	0·270	−0·357	0·324	0·138	−0·151	0·224
1939–1948	0·028	−0·062	0	0·189	−0·122	0·029	−0·130	0	−0·034
1948–1958	0·034	−0·146	0	0·134	−0·044	0·036	−0·238	0	−0·112
Steel									
1930–1938	0·738	−0·488	−0·198	0·051	−0·055	0·742	−0·488	−0·198	0·052
1938–1948	0·119	−0·222	0	0·008	−0·160	0·120	−0·070	0	−0·103
1948–1957	0·042	−0·403	0	0·002	−0·102	0·042	−0·303	0	−0·361
Cement									
1933–1939	0	−0·393	0	0·032	−0·007	0	−0·417	0	−0·393
1939–1948	0·169	0·088	−0·160	0·161	−0·094	0·178	0·021	−0·168	0·097
1948–1958	0·286	−0·368	0	0·019	−0·053	0·287	−0·336	0	−0·082
Automobiles									
1929–1939	0	1·056	−0·381	0·109	0	0	0·952	−0·386	0·675
1939–1948	0	−0·746	0	0·018	−0·557	0	−0·206	0	−0·746
1948–1958	0·304	1·328	−0·264	0·541	0	0·612	0·495	−0·282	1·367
Flour									
1932–1942	0·146	0·043	−0·118	0·376	−0·101	0·169	−0·323	−0·137	−0·015
1942–1948	0·158	0·057	−0·103	0·302	−0·062	0·170	−0·185	−0·110	0·115
1948–1959	0·407	0·686	−0·087	0·538	−0·031	0·505	0·103	−0·108	1·006
Beer									
1947–1958	0·213	0·758	−0·156	0·442	0	0·285	0·296	−0·209	0·814

Table A2 Annual rates of change, eight-firm concentration ratios – *continued*

Petroleum refining									
1929–1939	0·476	−0·082	−0·016	0·441	−0·584	0·512	0·023	−0·017	0·378
1939–1948	0·087	−0·076	0	0·311	−0·204	0·091	−0·188	0	0·010
1948–1958	0·072	−0·050	0	0·223	−0·075	0·075	−0·201	0	0·022
Steel									
1930–1938	0·810	−0·114	−0·069	0·060	−0·070	0·816	−0·109	−0·070	0·628
1939–1948	0·124	−0·280	0	0·010	−0·201	0·124	−0·089	0	−0·156
1948–1957	0·057	−0·184	0	0·002	−0·133	0·057	−0·053	0	−0·128
Cement									
1933–1939	0	−0·472	0	0·043	−0·010	0	−0·505	0	−0·472
1939–1948	0·540	0·225	−0·323	0·228	−0·142	0·564	0·126	−0·333	0·442
1948–1958	0·505	−0·512	0	0·029	−0·082	0·508	−0·462	0	−0·007
Automobiles									
1929–1939	0	0·469	−0·122	0·123	0	0	0·347	−0·124	0·346
1939–1948	0	−0·090	−0·061	0·019	−0·643	0	0·534	−0·061	−0·151
1948–1958	0·575	0·615	−1·036	0·001	0	0·613	0·644	−1·104	0·154
Flour									
1932–1942	0·155	0·005	0	0·499	−0·141	0·179	−0·377	0	0·160
1942–1948	0·220	0·288	−0·117	0·382	−0·082	0·237	−0·020	−0·125	0·393
1948–1959	0·407	0·843	−0·074	0·784	−0·043	0·505	0·023	−0·091	1·176
Beer									
1947–1958	0·565	0·868	−0·218	0·724	0	0·753	0·028	−0·292	1·214

References

AMERICAN IRON AND STEEL INSTITUTE (1926–57), *Directories of Iron and Steel Works in the United States and Canada (1926–57)*.

AUTOMOTIVE NEWS (1962), *Almanac Issue*.

BAIN, J. S. (1956), *Barriers to New Competition*, Harvard University Press.

BUREAU OF MINES (1928–58), 'Petroleum refineries including cracking plants in the United States', *Information Circulars*.

FRIEDMAN, M. (1955), 'Comment', *Business Concentration and Price Policy*, Princeton University Press.

HOUSE SELECT COMMITTEE ON SMALL BUSINESS (1962), *Mergers and Super-Concentration*.

MANSFIELD, E. (1962), 'Entry, Gibrat's law, innovation and the growth of firms', *Amer. econ. Rev.*, vol. 52, pp. 1030–34.

Modern Brewery Age, Blue Books, 1947–58.

Northwestern Miller, a list of Flour Mills in the United States and Canada (1932–59).

Pit and Quarry, Directory of Non-Metallic Minerals Industries, (1932–58).

SAVING, T. R. (1961), 'Estimation of optimal scale of plant by the survival technique', *Q.J. Econ.*, vol. 75, pp. 569–607.

SCHROEDER, G. (1952), *The Growth of the Major Steel Companies, 1900–1950*, Johns Hopkins University Press.

SMITH, C. A. (1955), 'Survey of the empirical evidence on economies of scale', *Business Concentration and Price Policy*, Princeton University Press.

STIGLER, G. (1958), 'The economies of scale', *J. Law Econ.*, vol. 1, pp. 54–71.

US SENATE (1962), *Concentration Ratios in Manufacturing Industry, 1958*, Bureau of the Census for the Subcommittee on Antitrust and Monopoly of the Committee on the Judiciary, US Government Printing Office.

WEISS, L. W. (1964), 'The survival technique and the extent of sub-optimal capacity', *J. polit. Econ.*, vol. 72, pp. 246–61.

WESTON, J. F. (1953), *The Role of Mergers in the Growth of Large Firms*, University of California Press.

13 Jerome L. Stein

Oligopoly in Risk-Bearing Industries with Free Entry

Jerome L. Stein, 'Oligopoly in risk-bearing industries with free entry', *Economica*, vol. 30, 1963, pp. 159–64.

An intriguing phenomenon

Professional risk-bearers are the focal points of the foreign exchange market, and the over-the-counter-market in corporate and government securities. They make primary markets by quoting bid and ask prices at which they are ready to buy and sell for their own accounts. They are not brokers, who match incoming bids and offers, but principals in every transaction. By taking positions for their own accounts, in various maturities, and by maintaining inventories they help to provide prompt execution of orders with a minimum of disorderly price movements. Profits, when they exist, do not arise mainly from the spread between the bid and ask prices but rather from the management of positions. The assumption of positions, by failing to match incoming bids and offers at every moment of time, involves risk.[1]

A few firms account for the major fraction of the volume in each of the risk-bearing industries in question. In effect, there are only six major dealers who operate in volume in all maturity sectors of the government bond market (*Treasury-Federal Reserve Study*, 1959, p. 24). A handful of banks account for the major volume of transactions in the foreign exchange

1. This is vividly illustrated by events which occurred in the foreign exchange market.
   On the Friday prior to the revaluation of the D-mark in 1961 (from 4·2 to 4·0 marks to the US dollar) several banks in New York found themselves oversold on D-marks. During the day their customers and other banks purchased more D-marks than they sold to the banks in question. The bank traders expected to cover their sales by purchasing D-marks in Germany on Saturday morning. If they sold dollars at the Bundesbank's buying price for dollars (i.e. selling price for D-marks), they would have made profits on the transactions. Revaluation was 'in the air': it had been expected for months. But traditionally, exchange rate changes had been made after the close of business on Saturdays. So, they were confident that they could buy their marks on Saturday morning. Moreover, a high authority in the Bundesbank said, in a speech to a small group of bankers on Thursday that revaluation would not occur. On Saturday morning the traders placed buy orders with the German commercial banks. The German commercial banks went to the Bundesbank, which was the only buyer of dollars at that time. Contrary to previous practice, the Bundesbank refused to sell; and it revalued the mark. Instead of a trading profit a capital loss was suffered.

market in New York. This dominance of a few firms, trading in a homogeneous commodity, is intriguing in view of the relatively free entry into these risk-bearing industries. No legal barriers obstruct entry. Any bank or brokerage house could solicit foreign exchange business or offer to buy and sell government bonds for its own account. Among the existing risk-bearers, competition for business is extremely keen[2] and there is no evidence of collusive behaviour. Why, then, is the risk-bearing industry dominated by a few firms?

I show that success and failure in these risk-bearing industries are formally similar to gambling successes and failure. Then, using the theory of gambler's ruin (Feller, 1957, chapter 14) I prove that oligopoly – the dominance of a few firms – will tend to occur.

A proposed explanation based upon gambler's ruin theorems
Assumptions and their plausibility

Assume that

1. Initially, there are n firms with C_1, C_2,... C_n units of capital. Every C_i is less than \$$a$.

2. Either the firm makes a profit or a loss of \$1 per transaction in the commodity traded (e.g. foreign exchange, corporate or government securities).

3. Initially, the professional risk-bearers who take positions have the same ability (or inability) to forecast price, when the quote bid and ask prices. Thus the probability p of making a profit on a transaction is $1 > p > 0$ for each risk-bearer. The probability q of making a loss on a transaction is $1-p$.

4. When the firm survives to augment its capital[3] to \$$a$, the probability of making a profit rises to p', $1 > p' > p$. A *once and for all change* in the probability of making a profit occurs when the firm succeeds in augmenting its capital by \$$(a-C_i)$. Let p' exceed $1/2$. The probability of a loss q on any transaction depends upon the maximum attained capital of the firm, as described in Figure 1. Initially, C_1, C_2,... C_n were less than \$$a$. Any firm which succeeds in accumulating \$$(a-C_i)$ of profits can lower its q to $1-p'$, for all time. Learning is irreversible. If the firm's capital rises to a and then falls back to C_i, the probability of a gain per transaction remains at p'.

The rationale of assumption 4 is that the trader (dealer) who survives to accumulate $a-C_i$ of profits learns how to forecast price better than he did initially. Or, the firm that survives to accumulate $a-C_i$ of profits

2. This view is generally held by the customers of the professional risk-bearers.
3. Assume that all profits are re-invested.

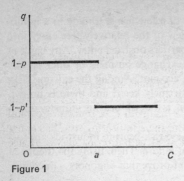

Figure 1

establishes a sufficiently wide clientele as to provide it with better channels of information than it had initially. The senior traders, in the foreign exchange and over-the-counter corporate and government securities market located in New York, told me that it takes a few years to evaluate whether a trainee has the potentialities to be a senior trader; and it takes about five years until he earns his salary. It is in the spirit of this observation that I built a learning-process in the model, whereby the probability of making a profit rises when the firm accumulates $a - C_i$ of profits.

A quotation from the *Treasury-Federal Reserve Study* (1959) further supports the assumption that there is a learning process that must be an integral part of the model.

When queried why there had not been more entrants into the dealer market, consultees mentioned as a principal deterrent the small supply of qualified specialists to staff new firms. One banker stated that in his opinion the most logical candidates for entry were the established and well-capitalized firms already operating in other financial areas, particularly the underwriters of corporate and municipal securities. Discussants representing firms of the latter type stated that they have periodically reviewed the pros and cons of entering the government securities business, but have been discouraged mainly by the scarcity of experienced personnel.

Very little is known concerning the learning function described above. Under ideal conditions, the shape of this function could be determined. Classify firms by the size of the highest values of capital (plus surplus) plus distributed profits ever attained. If assumption 4 is correct, the probability of making a profit per transaction (p) should differ between the size of classes. Conceivably, there are several 'steps' in the learning (step) function. If so, the probability p would assume more than two values. Alternative learning functions could be tested, and the one most compatible with the data could be used as assumption 4.

The oligopoly theorem

Given assumptions 1–4, I prove the following,

Theorem: A few firms will dominate the risk-bearing industry when a exceeds a^*, where a^* is a finite positive number.

Proof: When a firm has a capital of zero it is ruined and leaves the industry; but when its capital grows to $\$a$ it succeeds to raise its probability of profit to p'. Define q_c as the probability that a firm with $C < a$ units of capital will be ruined. After the first transaction, the risk-bearing firm has either gained $\$1$ with a probability p or has lost $\$1$ with a probability q. Hence the probability of being ruined is

$$q_c = pq_{c+1} + qq_{c-1}. \qquad \textbf{1}$$

q_c is the sum of the probabilities that a firm, with $C+1$ or with $C-1$ units of capital after the first transaction, will be ruined. Recall that p is the probability of gaining $\$1$ and q is the probability of losing $\$1$ on a transaction. By definition, $q_0 = 1$: the probability of being ruined is unity for a firm with no capital. *Success* is defined as the situation whereby the firm has gained $a - C_i$ of earnings. Hence $q_a = 0$: the probability of being ruined is zero for a firm which achieves $\$a$ of capital (plus surplus). At this stage of the argument, ruin and success are mutually exclusive phenomena and are the only possibilities.

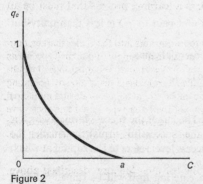

Figure 2

The solution of difference equation **1**, subject to the boundary conditions $q_0 = 1$ and $q_a = 0$, is curve q_c in Figure 2. The probability of ruin (q_c) decreases at a decreasing rate as the initial capital C increases towards a, the success level. If C is close to a, ruin is not very probable.

Mathematically, there are two solutions to the difference equation **1**, given the boundary conditions. When $p = q = 1/2$, then the solution is

$$q_c = 1 - (C/a). \qquad \textbf{2·1}$$

When $(q/p) \equiv R$ is *not* unity, the solution is

$$q_c = (R^a - R^c)/(R^a - 1). \qquad 2 \cdot 2$$

Both solutions produce a q_c curve as described in Figure 2: a convex, decreasing function of C.

It has been proved, so far, that initially larger firms have smaller probabilities of ruin than do the initially smaller firms. For example, when $p = 1/2$, the probability of ruin for a firm with an initial capital equal to 50 per cent of a is $1/2$. For a firm with an initial capital equal to 25 per cent of a, the probability of ruin is $3/4$.

Consider the set of firms which have survived to achieve success, i.e. a capital (plus surplus) of at least \$$a$. These firms have a probability of a gain equal to $p'(1 > p' > p > 0)$, which will not be changed until they are ruined. Learning is irreversible. If their capital rises to a and then falls back to C_i, the probability of a gain remains at p'. Let p' exceed $1/2$. The firms which achieved capitals of (at least) \$$a$ can, of course, be ruined. Define *ultimate ruin* as the situation whereby a firm which once achieved \$$a$ of capital is ruined, i.e. loses \$$a$ plus any other subsequent profits.

The probability of ultimate ruin, Q, is simply the solution of difference equation **1** with the following changes.

(a) The firm starts with \$$a$ of capital.

(b) The relative probability of loss and gain (q'/p') is less than unity but greater than zero.

(c) There is no upper bound on the potential gains.

The probability Q of ultimate ruin is

$$Q + (q'/p')^a, \qquad 4$$

which is graphed in Figure 3 below. The larger the success level a (which is the starting amount of capital for the 'successful' firms) the smaller the chance of being ruined. The term success level refers to the capital at which the probability of gain rises to $p' > p$.

Is it more probable that: (1) an entering firm will be ruined *before* it achieves success (i.e. raises its probability of a profit per transaction to p') or (2) a successful firm will be ruined?

Figure 3 contains two curves which permit a graphic answer to this question. The Q curve, as explained, is the probability of ultimate ruin as a function of the success level a. The larger the success level, the larger the starting amount of capital for the successful firms. The larger the starting amount of capital, the smaller the probability of being (ultimately) ruined.

The q_c curve is similar to the one described in Figure 2, but there is one

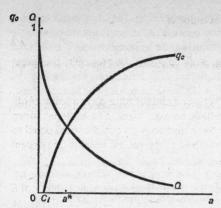

Figure 3

change. There, q_c was regarded as a function of C; here, q_c is regarded as a function of a: and C is given. Hence, given the initial capital of an entering firm (C_i), the probability of ruin increases at a decreasing rate as a increases. The more distant the success level (i.e. the greater the value of a relative to C_i), the higher the probability of ruin (q_c).

In Figure 3 there is a critical success level $a = a^*$. For smaller values of a the probability of ruin is less than the probability of ultimate ruin. But, for larger values of a, the probability of ultimate ruin is smaller than the probability of ruin for the entering firms.[4]

An $a = a^*$ has been produced which proves the oligopoly theorem. For $a > a^*$, two conclusions follow. First, the probability of success is greater for the initially large firms than for the initially small firms. Second, the survivor rates are greater for the successful firms than for the entering firms. It is less probable that an entering firm will achieve 'success' than it is that a successful firm will be ruined. As a consequence the initially large firms tend to have the greatest survivor rates, and the industry tends towards oligopoly.

Returns to scale and the learning function

Whenever we find an industry where small firms have high mortality rates and large firms flourish, we say that there are returns to scale; larger

4. *Proof:* for a close to C: q_c is in the neighbourhood of zero, and $q_c < Q$. But for large values of a, e.g. $a = \infty$ $(q'/p')^a$ is in the neighbourhood of zero and q_c is in the neighbourhood of unity. Hence $q_c > Q$. Both functions q_c and Q are continuous on a. Hence $(q_c - Q)$ is continuous on a. By the intermediate value theorem $(q_c - Q)$ takes on all values in between $(q_c - Q)$ (c) and $(q_c - Q)$ (∞). The first number is negative and the second number is positive. Hence there exists an a between c and ∞ at which $q_c - Q = 0$. Call this value a^*.

firms are relatively more efficient (Stigler, 1952, p. 144). In the risk-bearing industries, the returns to scale arise because the larger firms are better able to withstand the losses that occur during the learning period, i.e. the time when the probability of making profit is $p < p'$. As a result, the larger firms have better chances of completing their educations and raising the probability of making a profit to p'. In these industries, the learning function postulated in assumption 4, above, indirectly produces the increasing returns to scale.

References

FELLER, W. (1957), *An Introduction to Probability Theory and its Applications*, 2nd edn, Wiley.

STIGLER, G. J. (1952), *The Theory of Price*, revised edn, Macmillan Co.

Treasury-Federal Reserve Study of the Government Securities Market (1959), Washington D.C., vol. 1.

14 Leonard W. Weiss

Factors in Changing Concentration

Leonard W. Weiss, 'Factors in changing concentration', *Review of Economics and Statistics*, vol. 45, 1963, pp. 70–77.

This Reading is an attempt to account for changes in industrial concentration in terms of the varying risks of competition from industry to industry. A hypothesis will be developed and checked against observed changes in concentration between 1947 and 1954.

The hypothesis

Several recent analyses of concentration (Kalecki, 1945; Hart and Prais 1956; Hart, 1957; Prais, 1958; Simon and Bonini, 1958)[1] have been based on the 'law of proportionate effect' – the assumption that the chance of any given *proportional* change in firm size is equal for all firms. If F_1 represents the logarithm of some firm's size (measured in shipments, assets, or any other absolute term) at time t_1, and F_2 represents the logarithm of its size at time t_2, then $E(F_2-F_1)$ is assumed to be independent of F_1. This implies that the F's will tend toward a normal distribution. The variance of these values (that is, $\sigma^2{}_F$) would then provide a measure of inequality of firm size. By itself the variance does not measure concentration in an economically very meaningful way because it takes no account of the number of firms.[2] Inequality does play a role in concentration, however. *Given the number of firms*, an increase in $\sigma^2{}_F$ would tend to mean an increase in concentration at some level. Since the variances are expressed in logs, they are comparable over time or between industries, regardless of the mean values of F. Higher variances will therefore always mean greater inequality, and hence greater concentration, if the number of firms do not change.

It has been shown that the law of proportionate effect implies constantly

1. Edwin Mansfield (1962) has recently shown that the assumption of Gibrat's law is not wholly justified. His conclusion implies that the analyses in this and other studies oversimplify industrial experience. However, his finding that the variance of firm growth rates is relatively high for small firms would seem to re-enforce the hypothesis developed below, since it means particularly high exit rates for small firms.

2. This is only one of several difficulties. See Blair (1956) and his discussion with Prais (1957). Also Adelman (1959). Adelman and Preston (1960). and comments by Hart (1961) and Prais (1961).

increasing variances over time (Kalecki, 1945, pp. 161–2; Hart and Prais, 1956, p. 172; Prais, 1958, pp. 268–72). If F_1 and $(F_2 - F_1)$ both tend toward normal distributions and if $(F_2 - F_1)$ is independent of F_1, the relationship between the variances is simply additive:

$$\sigma^2_{F_2} = \sigma^2_{F_1} + \sigma^2_{(F_2 - F_1)}.$$

It follows that concentration would increase continuously, given no change in the number of firms (no exit or entry) and equal proportional effects.

The main point of emphasis of this paper is that the increase in variance is greater, the greater the variance of the logs of firm size changes. Concentration is more likely to increase, the greater the dispersion of relative firm size changes.

This conclusion is not completely destroyed when the assumptions of no exit, no entry, and proportional effects are relaxed. In fact, allowing exit would strengthen it, since a high dispersion of firm size changes would mean that relatively many firms would fall to uneconomical scales in each period. If entry occurs, decreasing concentration in the economic sense of the term would be possible. Even then, however, given the rate of entry, an increase would be more likely or a decrease would be less likely, the greater the value of $\sigma^2_{(F_2 - F_1)}$.

If the assumption of equal proportional effects is removed – that is, if F_1 and $(F_2 - F_1)$ are related, an interaction term must be introduced. Then,

$$\sigma^2_{F_2} = \sigma^2_{F_1} + \sigma^2_{(F_2 - F_1)} + 2\rho\sigma_{(F_2 - F_1)}\sigma_{F_1},$$

where ρ is the coefficient of correlation relating F_1 and $(F_2 - F_1)$. If ρ is positive, the earlier statements still hold, but if ρ is negative, concentration might decrease without entry. This, of course, is what one would expect where small firms grow faster than large ones. Even here, however, σ^2_F will grow more or decrease less, the greater the value of $\sigma^2_{(F_2 - F_1)}$ provided that $\sigma_{(F_2 - F_1)} > 2\rho\sigma_{F_1}$. In reality the ρ's are likely to differ in value and even in sign from industry to industry. As a result the relationship between the dispersion of firm size changes and changes in concentration cannot be stated with certainty in inter-industry comparisons. But there remains some reason to expect concentration to increase more or decrease less, the greater the dispersion of relative firm size changes.

High risks for individual firms do not *necessarily* imply high values of $\sigma^2_{(F_2 - F_1)}$. For instance, a depression that cut sales of all firms in an industry by half would involve little dispersion of relative firm size changes. For $\sigma^2_{(F_2 - F_1)}$ to be large the risks borne by firms within an industry must be high *and* the gains and losses must fall on different firms unequally.

The prevailing type of competition seems more promising than general business fluctuations as a determinant of the variance of firm growth rates. Four types of competition might be distinguished:

1. Price competition.
2. Promotional expenditures.
3. Types of quality competition that involve changes in product design either to satisfy fashion or to incorporate technological modifications; and
4. Other types of quality competition where small changes can be made at any time such as competition in credit terms, delivery time, or materials used.

There are some *a priori* grounds for predicting that competition in product design will be both more severe and less predictable in its effects on particular firms than other types of competition, at least in markets with some degree of recognized interdependence among firms. The uncertain effect of non-price moves is a familiar explanation of active non-price competition where price competition is suppressed. It will be argued presently that uncertainty is especially great in model or style changes. In addition, the long gestation periods involved in many design changes offer an innovator a substantial period of advantage, even if ultimate retaliation is inevitable. Finally, in the case of durables or semi-durables, where most of the regular style or model change occurs, the existence of a stock of previously produced goods might well result in new automobile models or new editions of introductory texts, even in the presence of perfect collusion.

Casual observation seems also to show style or model change to be especially unpredictable in its effect on the fortunes of particular firms. It is difficult to imagine cases where at least the *direction* in which volume will change in response to a change in price, promotion, or observable quality cannot be predicted. Yet it appears quite common for firms to miscalculate this completely in deciding on new automobile bodies or text books.

These considerations suggest that concentration is most likely to increase or least likely to decrease, other things being equal, in those industries where the prevailing form of competition is style or model change – that is, in the industries which produce differentiated durable or semi-durable goods. The rest of this Reading will be devoted to the evaluation of this proposition.

This hypothesis could be consistent with low concentration in certain industries if entry rates were high, as might be true where minimum optimum scales are small or where the market is growing rapidly. Nor does this hypothesis necessarily conflict with the role usually assigned to minimum optimum scales and market size in determining concentration if, as is widely supposed (Bain, 1956, pp. 61–5; Stigler, 1958, p. 61–67), long-run cost curves decline to some critical scale and thereafter remain constant over a wide range. It would be in this area of indeterminacy that differentiation and durability of product might affect concentration.

The sample

The changes in concentration in census four-digit industries between 1947 and 1954[3] will be analysed to provide a partial test of this hypothesis. To avoid weighting problems and to reduce the difficulties in estimating plant scales later on, only industries with shipments in excess of $500 millions in 1947 or 1954 will be considered. There were 134 such industries in 1954, accounting for about 77 per cent of manufacturing shipments, but a number of these were dropped from the sample:

1. Twenty-four industries where comparable concentration figures were not provided for 1947 and 1954;

2. Six others with the phrase 'not elsewhere classified' in their titles;

3. Eleven others where coverage or primary product specialization ratios fell below 75 per cent;

4. Four others where the sources used explicitly warn that inter-census comparisons are apt to mislead; and

5. Newspapers, where large scales relative to local markets make all the measures used here doubtful.

6. In addition, 'motor vehicles and parts' and 'bread and related products' had to be excluded in a subsequent regression analysis because of difficulties in estimating plant size.

The remaining sample of eighty-seven and eighty-five industries accounted for about 55 per cent and 51 per cent of 1954 manufacturing shipments. It may be mildly biased against the rapidly growing industries and those producing particularly complex goods where industry definitions are changeable, but a casual review of the excluded items suggests that the bias is not severe.[4] When the tests used in this study were applied to a larger sample (making only the unavoidable exclusions in 1 and 6 above), they yielded similar, though slightly less reliable, results.

3. The figures used in this study were derived from Bureau of the Census (1958) and from US Senate (1960, Table 42).
4. The writer will be happy to supply upon request a list of industries excluded from the sample and a tabulation of the industries covered with pertinent observed values, classifications, and computed residuals. Requests should be addressed to the Economics Department, University of Wisconsin, Madison, Wisconsin 53706.

Concentration change will be measured by the share of the four largest firms in industry shipments in 1954 expressed as a percentage of the four largest firms' share in 1947. The variance of the logs of firm sizes was used earlier to show a plausible basis for a relationship between concentration change and the dispersion of relative firm size changes. The question now is whether the type of competition does, in fact, significantly affect changes in concentration. For this purpose the *economically* most significant measure of concentration seems appropriate. The weight of previous comment appears to hold that this requires a measure which takes explicit account of the share of some absolute number of leading firms.[5] Concentration must be measured in terms of industry rather than product shipments because the latter are not available for 1947. Industries with low coverage or specialization ratios are excluded to reduce the errors that might result. The four-firm concentration ratio is used to minimize the cases of initial concentration ratios near 100 where concentration can only change in one direction.[6]

Differentiation and durability of product

The eighty-seven industries are next classified as to durability and differentiation of product. The durability classification of the National Resources Committee (1939, pp. 264–9) will be followed except that 'books, publishing and printing' will be treated as durable rather than semi-durable. The distinguishing mark of differentiated durables in this Reading is their competition in product design, certainly an outstanding characteristic of book publishing. Thorp and Crowder give some basis for this reclassification when they treat book paper as a durable good (1941, p. 525).

The product differentiation grouping is open to more question. To avoid a large number of questionable judgements this paper will use the consumer good, producer good distinction. Producer durables will be subdivided into durable equipment and durable materials and parts. Consumer goods and durable equipment will be treated as relatively differentiated, and materials and parts as relatively undifferentiated. Most of the questionable cases are in the durable equipment class. While it includes such clearly differentiated items as tractors, aircraft, and computing equipment, it also contains a number of items commonly produced to specifications which competing firms can meet equally well and where strong loyalties seem unlikely, such as transformers or pumps and compressors.

5. Blair (1956), Adelman (1959), Adelman and Preston (1960); even one of the main defenders of 'statistical' measures agrees that the variances of the logs of firm sizes give an adequate picture of industry structure *only* when a second variable such as the number of firms is introduced. Prais (1957, p. 250).
6. Three industries in the eighty-seven industry sample had initial concentration ratios of ninety or more. Eight had initial concentration ratios of seventy-five or more.

The directions of concentration change and the average 1954 concentration ratios as percentages of 1947 concentration ratios are tabulated for the seven industry classifications in Table 1.

Table 1 **Direction of concentration change and average 1954 concentration ratios as percentages of 1947 concentration ratios by durability of product and type of buyer**

| Industry classification | Numbers of industries | | | Mean value of 1954 C R as percentage of 1947 C R |
	with rise in C R*	with decline in C R	Total	
Consumer durables	7	2	9	119·6
Consumer semi-durables	6	1	7	112·9
Durable equipment	9	7	16	104·6
Sub-total	22	10	32	110·6
Consumer non-durables	5	11	16	95·9
Durable materials	5	15	20	91·6
Semi-durable materials	2	4	6	94·0
Non-durable materials	8	5	13	99·4
Sub-total	20	35	55	95·0
Total sample	42	45	87	100·7

* Includes those with no change in concentration ratios.

The three groups of industries producing relatively differentiated durable or semi-durable goods show increases in concentration, on the average, while other groups tended to show declines. The increase in concentration is greatest in consumer durables where products are most clearly subject to severe style or model competition. The increase is weakest and least consistent in durable equipment where the classification used is least reliable. The differences between the two sub-total means in Table 1 are compared in Table 2, using analysis of variance.

Table 2

Nature of variability	Sum of squares	DF	Mean square	F-ratio	F_{99}
Between the two groupings in Table 1	4,961	1	4,961		
Within the two groupings in Table 1	27,730	85	326	15·22	6·94
Total	32,691	86			

The observed differences in concentration change between the differentiated durable and semi-durable goods industries, where competition in product design change is generally important, and other industries where it is not, would not occur by chance as often as one time in a hundred.

Minimum optimum plant scale and market size

The conventional explanation of concentration emphasizes optimum scale relative to market size. Differentiation and durability of product are presumed to have an effect over and above these traditional factors. To further test this hypothesis, the statistical relationship between plant and market size changes and concentration changes will be derived and the residuals examined for consistent effects of durability and differentiation.

Since direct estimates of minimum optimum scale are seldom available, this study, like others (FTC, 1950; Evely and Little, 1960, pp. 158–9, and 165–73), must rely on observable establishment sizes. The use of such information implies an assumption that the main economies of scale occur within the plant. Bain's finding that multi-plant economies were either small or non-existent in most industries for which he had information (1956, pp. 88–9) offers some basis for such an assumption.

Accurate estimates of minimum optimum scale on the basis of existing plants are difficult because of establishments of more or less than minimum optimum scale in many industries. The index of plant scale used here will be selected to minimize this difficulty.

Bain reports that in the industries in his study the largest several plants were typically of more than minimum optimum scale (1956, p. 110). If the same is true of other industries, it would seem wise to avoid indexes such as the plant concentration ratio which depend on the largest establishments in an industry. While it is probable that the *minimum* optimum scale of plant is important in determining concentration, it would be difficult to assign such a role to the observed sizes of plants in excess of that minimum. The line of causation is reversed, if anything. Big firms offer an explanation for plants larger than the minimum dictated by technology, not the other way around.

Plants of less than optimum scale accounted for 10 to 30 per cent of total output in industries for which Bain had information (1956, p. 185), and since his sample was avowedly biased in favor of large and concentrated industries, one might expect a higher percentage, if anything, in other fields. These inefficiently small establishments should not be allowed to affect the scale index either. For this reason, both the mean and median will be rejected. The mean can be either too small or too large depending on the number of sub-optimal plants and the size of supra-optimal plants.

Going by Bain's figures, the median would ordinarily fall at less than optimum scale since the smallest half of the plants almost always produce less than 30 per cent of total industry output and usually less than 10 per cent. Both measures can shift unpredictably due to changes in the economically unimportant *number* of plants.

This study will attempt to avoid the deficiencies of other indexes by using the size of the 'mid-point' plant, that is, the hypothetical plant at the mid-point of the output array. Half of the output of an industry comes from plants larger than its mid-point plant and half from smaller plants. This index avoids both extremes of the plant array. It is less arbitrary than the mean or median since a change in the number of small plants cannot alter it if industry output is not appreciably affected. It is larger than the median plant and is unlikely to be sub-optimal, especially when the sample is limited to large industries as in this case. The 'mid-point' plant is obviously not a precise index of optimum scale, but it should make better use of the information available than other indexes.

No index derived from the array of plant scales existing at one time can dependably represent the minimum optimum scale at that time because of changes in optimum scale over the period in which the existing plant was built. However, *changes* in mid-point plant sizes should show the direction and magnitude of optimum plant scale changes in most cases.[7] Since the variable to be accounted for in the present study is the *change* in concentration, the change in mid-point plant size is an appropriate 'explanatory' variable.

It is the change in optimum scale *relative to industry* size which would affect concentration. A 20 per cent growth in the midpoint plant size might tend toward a decrease or an increase in concentration depending on whether the industry grew by more or less than 20 per cent during the same period. Following this reasoning, the independent variable used to 'explain' concentration change in this paper will be:

$$P = \frac{1954 \text{ mid-point plant size}}{1954 \text{ industry size}} \bigg/ \frac{1947 \text{ mid-point plant size}}{1947 \text{ industry size}}$$

Both mid-point plant size and industry size and industry size will be measured in value added terms because shipments are not available by establishment size for 1947. The use of these ratios obviates any deflation of plant or industry output and probably reduces the inaccuracy of plant scale

7. The main exception is where a new plant concentration curve crosses the old one. This would happen if large and small plants both grow or both decline relative to middle-sized plants. When they both grow the fault probably lies more with the industry definition than with the index. When the mid-point plant grows in relative importance, however, the present index will show a spurious increase in scale.

estimates since parallel errors are apt to occur for 1947 and 1954 and to cancel out.[8]

The concentration variable is the same as before,

$$C = \frac{1954 \text{ four-firm concentration ratio}}{1947 \text{ four-firm concentration ratio}}$$

A simple least squares regression relating C and P for eighty-five industries yields the following equation:

$$C = 0 \cdot 295P + 70 \cdot 19 \quad r = 0 \cdot 51$$
$$(0 \cdot 094)$$

The relationship has the expected sign and is significant at the 1 per cent level. The 'unexplained' residual values of C are shown in Table 3 tabulated

Table 3 **Residual values of C by durability of product and type of buyer**

Industry classification	Number of industries			Mean residual
	with positive residuals	with negative residuals	total	
Consumer durables	8	0	8	20·0
Consumer semi-durables	4	3	7	6·2
Durable equipment	9	7	16	3·9
Sub-total	21	10	31	8·6
Consumer non-durables	4	11	15	−9·2
Durable materials	7	13	20	−2·9
Semi-durable materials	2	4	6	−5·1
Non-durable materials	5	8	13	−3·3
Sub-total	18	36	54	−5·0
Total sample	39	46	85	0·0

8. The mid-point plant size was estimated as follows: cumulative totals of value added by employment size classes were computed to find the class containing the mid-point plant, and the employment size of that plant was estimated by interpolation. Its value added was then estimated by multiplying its number of employees by the value added per employee in its size class. When the mid-point fell in the open ended 'more than 2500 employees' class (in nine industries) the assumption is made that the mean and the median of that size class coincide. When the mid-point plant fell in two or more size classes which had been combined by the Census to avoid disclosure (in twelve industries), a minimum employment size for the upper class is used, based on either the number of establishments in the upper class times lowest number of employees per plant in that class or the number of establishments in the lower class times the largest number of employees per plant in that class. Since the variable used in this study is the ratio of 1954 to 1947 plant sizes, errors tend to cancel out.

by durability and type of buyer once more. On the average the groups of industries in which periodic design changes are important had greater increases or smaller decreases in concentration than could have been predicted on the basis of plant and industry size changes, while the other industries showed negative residuals.

An analysis of the variance between the two sub-total means in Table 3 appears below in Table 4:

Table 4

Nature of variability	Sum of squares	DF	Mean square	F-ratio	F_{99}
Between the two groupings in Table 2	3637	1	3637		
Within the two groupings in Table 2	19,476	82	238	15·28	6·94
Total	23,113	83			

The difference in 'unexplained' concentration changes between the differentiated durable and semi-durable goods industries and other industries is statistically significant. Again, the most clearly differentiated durables show the most consistent tendency for concentration to rise. Every consumer durable showed a positive residual after plant and industry size were taken into account.

Other hypotheses

A variety of other influences undoubtedly play a role in concentration change, but those examined in this study all proved to be not significant for the 1947–54 period. The initial (1947) concentration ratio and 1954 deflated shipments expressed as percentages of 1947 shipments were introduced as additional independent variables in the regression but neither proved to be statistically significant.[9]

The local, regional, and national character of markets was examined on the hypothesis that concentration ratios would show a rise for local or regional industries due to the rapid growth of large metropolitan areas, the apparently more lenient policy of authorities toward chain mergers than toward other horizontal mergers, and the relatively low cost of transportation services in the 1947–54 period. In fact, the expected relation-

9. Let I stand for initial concentration and S stand for 1954 deflated shipments as percentages of 1947 shipments. For a smaller, more reliable sample (fifty-seven observations): $r_{CI \cdot PS} = -0·21$, $r_{CS \cdot PI} = -0·22$ and $r_{CP \cdot SI} = 0·43$. For a larger, less reliable sample (ninety-seven observations) $r_{CI \cdot PS} = -0·06$, $r_{CS \cdot PI} = -0·12$ and $r_{CP \cdot SI} = 0·42$. Neither partial correlation coefficient for either I or S is significant at even the 5 per cent level.

ship was reversed. The local and regional industries showed negative residuals, on the average, while national industries showed a slight tendency toward positive residuals, but the difference between the two was not statistically significant.[10]

Residuals were also compared for all industries within the sample for which Bain made single-valued estimates of the barriers to entry. Surprisingly, the industries with lower barriers showed a greater tendency for concentration to increase after plant and industry size were taken into account, but again the difference was not statistically significant.[11]

The size of industry shipments, the initial concentration ratio, the local character of industry, and the conditions of entry, certainly cannot all be rejected as influences on concentration on the basis of this evidence. Probably their effects differ in importance and even sign from industry to industry and period to period. Still, none of them offers any conflict with the role proposed for differentiation and durability.

In general, the 1947–54 concentration statistics yield the results that might have been predicted on the basis of the initial hypothesis, but a great deal of variability remains to be 'explained' even after plant and industry size and the durability and differentiation of products have been taken into account. Such high degrees of residual variability seem to be inherent in broad cross-section analyses of concentration change (Evely and Little, 1960, pp. 164–5, 175, 341).[12]

While the statistics presented support the hypothesis of this paper, other hypotheses can account for the same phenomena.

1. The increase in concentration among differentiated durables and semi-durables may be due to the economies of large-scale promotion. The simultaneous decrease in concentration in the consumer non-durable class argues against a general tendency for promotional economies to increase in this period, but a change in the promotion of durables is still a possibility. Firms producing such goods often require large volume to support market-wide systems of dealer and service facilities. The 1947–54

10. Local and regional industries were those classified by the National Resources Committee (1939, pp. 265–9) as located near consumers, located near resources, or 'regional'. The nineteen local and regional industries had mean residuals of -4.6 against $+1.1$ for the other sixty-six. ($F = 1.27$, $F_{95} = 3.96$.)

11. Estimates of 'aggregate' entry barriers are given for fourteen of the industries in our sample (Bain, 1956, p. 170), but farm machinery and footwear, where Bain gave different estimates for sub-industries, were left out. Mean residuals were $+4.9$ for industries with low or moderate barriers and -4.7 for those with substantial or high barriers. ($F = 3.65$, $F_{95} = 4.96$.)

12. It has been possible to 'account for' a much larger proportion of variability in concentration from industry to industry at a given time. See Rosenbluth (1957, pp. 28–37, 45–9 and 52–3) and Evely and Little (1960, pp. 109–14 and 334).

period was the era of the discounter when margins on differentiated durables in particular were falling. As a result, larger scale may have been required for effective distribution.

2. The post-war shortages which were particularly severe in the durables and semi-durables may offer another explanation. Firms in those fields in 1947 could sell virtually everything they could produce, but by 1954 shortages had abated and producers with less market advantages were apt to have trouble selling. Shortages disappeared in many durable materials as well, but in these fields the less well known firms were probably at little disadvantage in winning customers.

The 1947–54 period does not provide enough basis to reject any of these hypotheses. It is possible that all three tendencies were at work. The increase in concentration may have been partially a temporary phenomenon due to shortages or changing marketing requirements which need not be repeated, and partly a longer-run tendency due to unequal risks.

The information now available does not permit any very meaningful longer-term comparisons. Changes in industry definitions between 1935 and 1954 leave only three differentiated durables from our sample for which comparisons can be made: 'domestic laundry equipment' and 'boilershop products' where concentration increased sharply and 'tires and tubes' where it remained about the same. If industries of all sizes are considered, comparisons are possible for ninety-nine industries other than those with low coverage or specialization ratios or with 'not elsewhere classified' in their titles. Concentration increased in forty-six of these, decreased in forty-five, and did not change by more than one point in eight. Of the eleven consumer durables only 'motorcycles and bicycles' and 'statuary and other art goods' showed significant decreases, but only two of the nine consumer semi-durables showed increases. Increases and decreases were about equally matched in other industries, including the durable equipment field. The statistics available do not seem to warrant any elaborate analysis.

Other studies offer little help. Rosenbluth found concentration higher in consumer durables and non-durables and producer durables in 1948 in Canada than would have been predicted on the basis of his multiple regression study, but the difference between these and other industries was not significant. His comparison referred to concentration at a single date rather than changes over time (1957, pp. 49–51). Thorp and Crowder found little or no relationship between 1935–37 concentration changes and durability or type of ultimate user (or any other attribute for that matter). No statistical tests were offered and no attempt was made to investigate interaction between durability and type of user. Their sample consisted of 356 products which were often too narrowly defined to be meaningful.

(For example, it contained *eleven* classes of household or automobile radios, exclusive of parts) (Thorp and Crowder, 1941, pp. 335–7).

In general, the skimpy information for earlier years and for previous studies provides virtually no basis for either supporting or rejecting the hypothesis suggested at the start of this paper.[13] The experience of the 1947–54 period does seem to support it, but it is very far from proven. Much more exhaustive studies of individual differentiated durable goods industries as well as broad cross-section analyses for subsequent periods would seem to be worthwhile ventures. If the hypothesis presented here should be substantiated, one more 'dilemma for public policy' might be indicated. At least in the established consumer durable fields a general tendency for concentration to increase may be unavoidable unless we are willing to intervene to limit the severity of non-price competition in those industries.

13. Since this paper was completed, some of the 1958 concentration statistics have been published (US Senate, 1962). An analysis like that in Table 1 of this paper shows no overall tendency for concentration to increase more in the differentiated durable and semi-durable industries than in others in 1954–8, but the most highly differentiated of durables still show increases. No attempt has been made to compute values of P for the 1954–8 period.

At the same time, preliminary work on individual firm size data collected by the writer for six industries since the 1920s shows a positive relationship between $\sigma^2 {}_{(F_2 - F_1)}$ and C for most cases, suggesting that, if nothing else, increasing concentration is a price we may have to pay to attain high 'turnover rates' among firms.

References

ADELMAN, I., and PRESTON, L. (1960), 'A note on changes in industry structure', *Rev. Econ. Stats*, vol. 42, pp. 105–8.

ADELMAN, M. (1959), 'Differential rates and changes in concentration', *Rev. Econ. Stats*, vol. 41, pp. 68–9.

BAIN, J. S. (1956), *Barriers to New Competition*, Harvard University Press.

BLAIR, J. M. (1956), 'Statistical measures of concentration', *Bull. Oxford Inst. Stats*, vol. 18, pp. 351–72.

BLAIR, J. M. (1957), discussion with S. J. Prais, *Bull. Oxford Inst. Stats*, vol. 19, pp. 249–52.

BUREAU OF THE CENSUS (1958), *Census of Manufactures, 1954*, US Government Printing Office.

EVELY, R., and LITTLE, I. M. D. (1960), *Concentration in British Industry*, Cambridge University Press.

FTC (1950), *Report on Changes in Concentration in Manufacturing, 1935 to 1947 and 1950*.

HART, P. E. (1957), 'On measuring business concentration', *Bull. Oxford Inst. Stats*, vol. 19, pp. 225–480.

HART, P. E. (1961), 'Statistical measures of concentration v_1 Concentration ratios', *Rev. Econ. Stats*, vol. 43, pp. 85–7.

HART, P. E., and PRAIS, S. J. (1956), 'The analysis of business concentration: a statistical approach', *J. Roy. stat. Soc.*, vol. 119, pp. 150–81.

KALECKI, M. (1945), 'On the Gibrat distribution', *Econometrica*, vol. 13, pp. 161–70.

MANSFIELD, E. (1962), 'Entry, Gibrat's law, innovation and the growth of firms', *Amer. econ. Rev.*, vol. 52, pp. 1023–51.

NATIONAL RESOURCES COMMITTEE (1939), *Structure of the American Economy*.

PRAIS, S. J. (1957), 'Measuring business concentration – a rejoinder', *Bull. Oxford Inst. Stats*, vol. 19, pp. 249–51.

PRAIS, S. J. (1958), 'The statistical conditions for a change in business concentration' *Rev. Econ. Stats*, vol. 40, pp. 268–72.

PRAIS, S. J. (1961), 'A methodological afterthought on business concentration', *Rev. Econ. Stats*, vol. 43, p. 87.

ROSENBLUTH, G. (1957), *Concentration in Canadian Manufacturing Industries*, Princeton University Press.

SIMON, H. A., and BONINI, C. P. (1958), 'The size distribution of business firms', *Amer. econ. Rev.*, vol. 48, pp. 607–17.

STIGLER, G. (1958), 'The economies of scale', *J. Law Econ.*, vol. 1, pp. 54–71.

THORP, W., and CROWDER, W. F. (1941), *The structure of industry*, TNEC monograph 27.

US SENATE (1960), *Concentration in American Industry*, Subcommittee on Antitrust and Monopoly of the Committee on the Judiciary, 85th Congress, US Government Printing Office.

US SENATE (1962), *Concentration in Manufacturing – 1958*, Subcommittee on Antitrust and Monopoly of the Committee on the Judiciary, 87th Congress, US Government Printing Office.

15 F. M. Scherer

Stochastic Determinants of Market Structure

From F. M. Scherer, *Industrial Market Structure and Economic Performance*, Rand McNally, 1970, pp. 125–30.

Up to this point we have assumed that market structures are the more or less determinate result of tangible variables such as technology, the receptiveness of consumers to advertising, the size of the market, the effectiveness of managerial organization, merger decisions, government policies, etc. Another quite different view of the processes by which market structures emerge has been postulated by some economists. Let us begin by stating the hypothesis in its baldest, most radical form: the market structures observed at any moment in time are the result of pure historical chance.

This idea is best introduced by a concrete illustration. Suppose an industry comes into being with fifty member firms, each with first year sales of $100,000 and hence each with a 2 per cent starting share of the market. Now suppose the firms begin growing. Each is assumed to have the same average growth prospect as every other firm. But this average is subject to statistical variance; in any given year some firms will be lucky, growing more rapidly than the average, while others are unlucky, growing by less than the average. Let the probability distribution of growth rates confronting each firm be normal, with a mean of 6 per cent per annum and a standard deviation of 16 per cent. These parameters were chosen to reflect the average year-to-year growth actually experienced between 1954 and 1960 by 369 firms on *Fortune*'s list of the 500 largest industrial corporations for 1955. To repeat, each firm faces the same distribution of growth possibilities; its actual growth is determined by random sampling from the distribution of possibilities. What will the size distribution of firms look like a number of years hence?

By applying a bit of advanced probability theory it is possible to estimate the parameters of the resulting firm size distribution for any future moment in time. However, insight is enriched by employing an electronic computer to simulate the dynamic properties of the assumed growth process model. Each of fifty firms' growth in each year was determined through random sampling from a distribution of growth rates stored in the computer's memory with a mean of 6 per cent and standard deviation of 16 per cent. The growth history of each firm and the overall size distribution of the industry were then tabulated at twenty year intervals. The results of sixteen consecutive simulation runs are summarized in the form of four-firm concentration ratios in Table 1.

Contrary to what untutored intuition might advise, the firms do not long remain equal in size and market share, even though their growth prospects are identical *ex ante*. Patterns resembling the concentrated structures of much American manufacturing industry emerge within a few decades. After the growth process has run its course for a century, it is not uncommon to find a single industry leader controlling 25 or 35 per cent of the market while its former equals muddle along with 0·1 per cent. For the sixteen simulation runs at the 100 year mark, the range of leading firm market shares was 10 to 42 per cent, with an average of 21 per cent. The four-firm concentration ratios after a century of growth ranged from 33·5 per cent to 64·4 per cent, with a mean of 46·7 per cent.

The simulation displays a clear tendency for concentration to increase over time, first rapidly and then more gradually. This has interesting implications. Should similar growth processes operate in real-world manufacturing industries, as some economists have suggested (Hart and Prais, 1956, pp. 150–81; Simon and Bonini, 1958, pp. 607–17), we should expect aggregate concentration to be higher, the more mature a nation's industrial

Table 1 **Four-firm concentration ratios resulting from 16 simulation runs of a stochastic growth process model, with mean growth of 6 per cent per annum and a standard deviation of 16 per cent**

	Four-firm concentration ratio at year:							
	1	*20*	*40*	*60*	*80*	*100*	*120*	*140*
Run 1	8·0	19·5	29·3	36·3	40·7	44·9	38·8	41·3
Run 2	8·0	20·3	21·4	28·1	37·5	41·6	50·8	55·6
Run 3	8·0	18·8	28·9	44·6	43·1	47·1	56·5	45·0
Run 4	8·0	20·9	26·7	31·8	41·9	41·0	64·5	59·8
Run 5	8·0	23·5	33·2	43·8	60·5	60·5	71·9	63·6
Run 6	8·0	21·3	26·6	29·7	35·8	51·2	59·1	72·9
Run 7	8·0	21·1	31·4	29·0	42·8	52·8	50·3	53·1
Run 8	8·0	21·6	23·5	42·2	47·3	64·4	73·1	76·6
Run 9	8·0	18·4	29·3	38·0	45·3	42·5	43·9	52·4
Run 10	8·0	20·0	29·7	43·7	40·1	43·1	42·9	42·9
Run 11	8·0	23·9	29·1	29·5	43·2	50·1	57·1	71·7
Run 12	8·0	15·7	23·3	24·1	34·5	41·1	42·9	53·1
Run 13	8·0	23·8	31·3	44·8	43·5	42·8	57·3	65·2
Run 14	8·0	17·8	23·3	29·3	54·2	51·4	56·0	64·7
Run 15	8·0	21·8	18·3	23·9	31·9	33·5	43·9	65·7
Run 16	8·0	17·5	27·1	28·3	30·7	39·9	37·7	35·3
Average	8·0	20·4	27·0	33·8	42·1	46·7	52·9	57·4

sector is. We recall from chapter 3 (Scherer, 1970) that we in fact observed a positive association between aggregate concentration in five industrialized nations and the span of time elapsing since those nations entered Rostow's stage of technological maturity (cf. Scherer, 1970, p. 45). The correspondence of real-world structures to the behavior of the model could be sheer coincidence, but it might also reflect the conformity of actual growth processes to similar dynamic laws.

Why do concentrated firm size distributions arise from initial conditions which seemingly give each firm an equal chance? The answer, in a word, is luck. Some firms will inevitably enjoy a run of luck, experiencing several years of very rapid growth in close succession. Once the most fortunate firms climb well ahead of the pack, it is difficult for laggards to rally and rectify the imbalance, for by definition, each firm – large or small – has an equal chance of growing by a given percentage amount.[1] Furthermore, once a firm has, by virtue of early good luck, placed itself among the industry leaders, it can achieve additional market share gains if it should happen again to be luckier than average (as it will be in roughly half of all cases). In ten of the sixteen simulation runs underlying Table 1, the leading firm in year 140 occupied a position among the top four firms in year 60, and in four cases the year 140 leader was also first in year 60. In run 13, the leading firm held its leadership position at every single 20 year benchmark, and in run 5, the leader led at every 20 year point but one.

The simulation experiment reported here was designed to conform to the assumptions of Gibrat's law of proportionate growth (Gibrat, 1931, and Kalecki, 1945). Specifically, the population of firms was fixed, and the distribution of growth rates confronting each firm was the same, being independent of both firm size and the firm's past growth history.[2] Stochastic growth processes adhering to Gibrat's law generate a log normal size distribution of firms – that is, a distribution which is highly skewed when sales are plotted by the frequency of their actual values, one or a few firms realizing high sales while most make low sales, but which is normal and symmetric when the logarithms of firms' sales are plotted.[3] As we have seen in the preceding chapter [not reproduced here], the parameters of the

1. For an analogous illustration concerning runs in coin-flipping, see Feller (1957, pp. 83–5). See also the testimony of Weiss (1964, pp. 729–731).

2. In one sense Gibrat's assumptions were violated. A 'bankruptcy rule' was included causing a firm to drop out of the industry permanently if its sales dropped to $30,000 or less. There were only three bankruptcies in the 800 company histories simulated.

3. *Proof:* Let S_{oj} be the initial sales of the jth firm, and ε_i the random growth multiplier (in our numerical example, with mean of $1 \cdot 06$ and σ of $0 \cdot 16$) in the ith year. Then sales in year t are $S_{tj} = S_{oj}\, \varepsilon_1 \ldots \varepsilon_i \ldots \varepsilon_t$; that is, the cumulative product of initial sales times a string of random growth multipliers. Taking logarithms, we obtain: Log $S_{tj} = \log S_{oj} + \log \varepsilon_1 + \ldots + \log \varepsilon_i + \ldots + \log \varepsilon_t$. By the central limit theorem, the distribution of the sum of T random variables is asymptotically normal when $T \to \infty$.

log normal distribution have been proposed as indices of market concentration by some economists, and statistical studies reveal that a log normal distribution often (but not always) fits actual firm size data tolerably well.[4] However, the assumptions of Gibrat's law need not be satisfied rigidly to obtain results similar to those of Table 1. There is a whole family of stochastic growth processes which lead to the skewed firm size distributions typical of real-world industries.[5] All have the common feature of making a firm's size in, say, year $t+1$ proportional, subject to random variation, to its size in year t. Other dynamic processes lacking the proportionate growth property exist, but they typically fail to generate firm size distributions resembling those most frequently encountered in the real world. Reasoning backward from observation to hypothesis, Simon and Bonini argue that industry structures must in fact be determined by some such stochastic growth process, since actual size distributions 'show such a regular and docile conformity...that we would expect some mechanism to be at work to account for the observed regularity' (1958, p. 608).

We are all so thoroughly imbued in the belief that chance favors the well-prepared that it is difficult to accept a model which makes corporate growth the result of mere chance. Still it is not essential to interpret the stochastic growth models quite so literally. There are certainly aspects of business enterprise in which luck plays a significant role – e.g. in the hiring of key executives, in research and new product development decisions, in legal disputes involving critical patents, in the choice of an advertising campaign theme, or in a thousand and one other decisions among attractive but uncertain alternative courses of action. Given the operation of chance in these elemental decisions, high or low sales growth follows in a more traditionally deterministic manner.

One implication of this milder restatement is the possibility that growth rates for a given firm from year to year will not be independent, as assumed in the Gibrat model. For example, a lucky chief executive choice may affect growth favorably for a decade or more. Support for this assertion is derived from the study of 369 firms' growth on which the simulation model's parameters were based, for the standard deviation of cumulative growth over the full 1954–60 period was higher than it would have been

4. Cf. Hart and Prais (1956); Simon and Bonini (1958); and (for results suggesting that the lognormal distribution holds in roughly half the industries studied) Silberman (1967, pp. 807–31). For an alternative hypothesis attributing log normal firm size distributions to a particular type of oligopoly pricing, see Worcester (1967, chapters 5 and 6).

5. See especially Simon (1955, pp. 425–40). In fact, the distributions are sufficiently similar that it is difficult to find statistical tests which will tell which of several alternative stochastic processes generated the observed size distribution. See Quandt (1966, pp. 416–32).

had growth rates in each one-year interval been independent. Yet this is not a fatal objection. Ijiri and Simon have demonstrated in a simulation study that size distributions quite similar to those generated by Gibrat models can also be obtained when there is serial correlation in firms' year-to-year growth rates (1964; and Stein, 1963).

The assumptions of the Gibrat model may also be violated if growth rates, or the standard deviation of growth rates, are systematically related to firm size. Independence of size and growth rates implies that small firms operate at neither an advantage nor a disadvantage relative to large firms. If, on the other hand, substantial economies of scale exist, large firms would possess an advantage which might be exploited, *inter alia*, in the form of more rapid sales growth rates. Such a state of affairs, combined with a stochastic growth process, would lead to even more rapid concentration of output in the hands of the largest firms. Conversely, if small firms could grow more rapidly on the average, *ceteris paribus*, or if there were a continuous inflow of small new firms, the tendency toward increasing inequality of firm sizes would be moderated and under certain circumstances checked altogether. Several empirical investigations have been launched to determine whether firm growth rates do vary systematically with firm size. The conclusions have been predominantly negative: no significant correlation between growth rates and size could be found.[6]

There is less support for the Gibrat assumption that growth rate standard deviations are independent of firm size. With few exceptions, statistical studies have shown that the variability of growth rates for large firms is lower than for small firms; that is, large firms seem to enjoy more stable growth.[7] Still this qualification is compatible with the hypothesis that observed industry size distributions have been generated by some stochastic process.[8] Indeed, it strengthens the case. Chance will occasionally permit a small firm facing a highly variable distribution of growth rates to be propelled to large size, and such events increase concentration, *ceteris paribus*. But once a firm enters the large size bracket, the variance of its growth rate

6. For a survey of the literature, see Hymer and Pashigian (1962, pp. 565–6). See also Ferguson (1964, pp. 168–72); (for contrary results) Mansfield (1962) and Samuels (1965).

7. See the sources in note 6. In an analysis of cumulative growth for the years 1953 through 1961 covering 352 firms on *Fortune*'s 1955 list, the author found the standard deviation of growth rates for firms in the quartile of largest companies to be persistently lower than the standard deviation for firms in the smallest-firm quartile. There seemed to be some tendency for the disparity in standard deviations to level off and perhaps to decline over intervals exceeding seven years, which may explain why Hart and Prais found no correlation between size and variability of growth rates in their analysis spanning the exceptionally long 1885–1950 period. The question of very long-run relationships deserves further study.

8. Cf. Simon (1955; 1964, p. 81), and the testimony of Weiss (1964, pp. 736–9).

distribution diminishes, and so the chance that it will fall abruptly to a lower size level is much smaller. Thus, the statistical forces which might cause decreases in concentration, once it has developed, are blunted, while the forces which lead to increasing concentration remain intact. The conjunction of these phenomena may explain why market share turnover tends to be lower in concentrated industries than in atomistically structured industries (cf. Scherer, 1970, p. 66).

One final point implicit in the discussion thus far should be made explicit. The more variable firm growth rates are, the more rapidly concentrated industry structures will emerge, other things being equal. Two important implications follow.

First, despite its grounding in actual industry growth data, the simulation model of Table 1 probably overstates the length of time required for concentrated market structures to emerge as a result of random growth. The growth rate standard deviation of 16 per cent was based on a sample including only the largest firms. For smaller firms – e.g. companies of the size typical during an industry's infancy – variability of growth rates is likely to be much higher, implying more rapid convergence toward market concentration.

Second, the variability of growth rates is likely to differ from industry to industry, depending upon the nature of the product and the character of competition. We might expect variability to be especially high in industries characterized by a rapid pace of product design change due to technological or styling innovation and also in markets populated by fickle consumers who respond enthusiastically to clever advertising campaigns. The firm with a good design or promotional idea may leap ahead rapidly; the firm which misgauges market sentiments can suffer spectacular market share declines. The hypothesis that concentration should rise especially rapidly in differentiated durable goods industries because of the chance factors permeating design competition has been tested by Weiss (1963). He divided 87 four-digit industries with sales exceeding $500 million into several product characteristic classes. For the 1947–54 period, he found concentration rising significantly more rapidly on the average in the consumer durables, consumer semidurables, and durable equipment industries – lines which presumably experienced the most vigorous design change competition – than in four other product categories. However, this relationship failed to persist in the 1954–1958 period. New evidence reveals that after a hiatus in 1954–1958, concentration again rose more rapidly between 1958 and 1963 in the differentiated consumer goods industries, although the pattern in the consumer durables subset has not been analysed.[9]

9. See the testimony of Mueller (1967, p. 478) and Blair (1966).

Unfortunately, the waters are muddied by alternative hypotheses which could also explain concentration trends between 1947 and 1963. Notably, the above-average increase in differentiated consumer goods industry concentration may have been due to economies of scale in advertising and other aspects of sales promotion, instead of, or as well as, high growth rate variability due to chance elements in design and promotional rivalry. Further doubts are raised by Gort's finding that market shares tended to be more stable between 1947 and 1954 in industries with highly differentiated products than in industries with moderate or low degrees of differentiation.[10] At present, therefore, the implications of the stochastic growth process hypothesis in this area remain uncertain. What is needed is an attack on the problem which discriminates more effectively between those cases in which product differentiation solidifies existing market positions and those in which it works as a potent but unpredictable vehicle for upsetting the status quo.

To sum up, the random growth hypotheses have considerable appeal, both because chance clearly does play some role in company growth and because firm size distributions observed in the real world often correspond closely to those generated by stochastic process models. It would be unwise, however, to reject more conventional explanations of market structure out of hand. Economies of scale, government policies, and the like are surely influential, and not merely in a random way. Indeed, the fact that many industries remain atomistically structured despite the concentration-increasing forces associated with stochastic growth suggests that static and dynamic managerial diseconomies of large size and rapid growth must frequently retard the rise of firms to dominance. A sophisticated explanation of how industry structures came to be what they are must blend the conventional, more or less static, determinants with the kinds of dynamic considerations introduced by stochastic growth process models. This is where future research on the determinants of market structure is most urgently needed. And since we have gone about as far as we can go on the basis of present knowledge, it is also a suitable ending point for this chapter.

10. Gort (1963, pp. 58–9). See also Schneider (1966, pp. 58–63), who found no systematic relationship between leading firm market share stability and differentiation in eight industries.

References

BLAIR, J. (1966), Testimony in US Senate, Committee on the Judiciary, Subcommittee on Antitrust and Monopoly, Hearings, *Economic Concentration*, part 5, US Government Printing Office.
FELLER, W. (1957), *An Introduction to Probability Theory and Its Application*, 2nd edn, vol. 1, Wiley.

FERGUSON, C. E. (1964), *A Macroeconomic Theory of Workable Competition*, Duke University Press.

GIBRAT, R. (1931), *Les Inégalités Économiques*, Paris.

GORT, M. (1963), 'Analysis of stability and change in market shares', *J. pol. Econ.*, vol. 71, pp. 51–63.

HART, P. E., and PRAIS, S. J. (1956), 'The analysis of business concentration', *J. Roy. stat. Soc.*, vol. 119, pp. 150–81.

HYMER, S., and PASHIGIAN, P. (1962), 'Firm size and rate of growth', *J. pol. Econ.*, vol. 70, pp. 565–6.

IJIRI, Y., and SIMON, H. A. (1964), 'Business firm growth and size', *Amer. econ. Rev.*, vol. 54, pp. 77–89.

KALECKI, M. (1945), 'On the Gibrat distribution', *Econometrica*, vol. 13, pp. 161–70.

MANSFIELD, E. (1962), 'Entry, Gibrat's law, innovation and the growth of firms', *Amer. econ. Rev.*, vol. 52, pp. 1023–51.

MUELLER, W. (1967), Testimony in US Senate, Select Committee on Small Business, Hearings, *Status and Future of Small Business*.

QUANDT, R. E. (1966), 'On the size distribution of firms', *Amer. econ. Rev.*, vol. 56, pp. 416–32.

SAMUELS, J. M. (1965), 'Size and the growth of firms', *Rev. econ. Stud.*, vol. 32, pp. 105–12.

SCHERER, F. M. (1970), *Industrial Market Structure and Economic Performance*, Rand McNally.

SCHNEIDER, N. (1966), 'Product differentiation, oligopoly, and the stability of market shares', *W. econ. J.*, vol. 5, pp. 58–63.

SILBERMAN, I. H. (1967), 'On lognormality as a summary measure of concentration', *Amer. econ. Rev.*, vol. 57, pp. 807–31.

SIMON, H. A. (1955), 'On a class of skew distribution functions', *Biometrika*, vol. 42, pp. 425–440.

SIMON, H. A. (1964), Comment in *J. pol. Econ.*, vol. 72, pp. 81–2.

SIMON, H. A., and BONINI, C. P. (1958), 'The size distribution of business firms', *Amer. econ. Rev.*, vol. 48, pp. 607–17.

STEIN, J. L. (1963), 'Oligopoly in risk-bearing industries with free entry', *Economica*, vol. 30, pp. 159–64.

WEISS, L. W. (1963), 'Factors in changing concentration', *Rev. Econ. Stats*, vol. 45, pp. 70–77.

WEISS, L. W. (1964), Testimony in US Senate, Committee on the Judiciary, Subcommittee on Antitrust and Monopoly, Hearings, *Economic Concentration*, part 1, US Government Printing Office.

WORCESTER, D. A. Jr (1967), *Monopoly, Big Business, and Welfare in the Postwar United States*, University of Washington Press.

Part Four
Vertical Integration

The first four readings (Readings 16 to 19) are concerned, in the main, with the circumstances in which vertical integration is likely to be profitable; and their analyses have evident implications both for business policy as well as for public policy. Oi and Hurter (Reading 16) consider the rationale of decisions by manufacturers and traders to vertically integrate into road transport; their analysis has more general application. Bork (Reading 17) examines vertical integration as an instrument of monopoly, and dismisses a variety of arguments against the practice. The special case of bilateral monopoly is the subject of Machlup and Taber (Reading 18), while Vernon and Graham (Reading 19) demonstrate why a monopolist may find it profitable to engage in forward vertical integration even where the alternative is selling to a perfectly competitive customer industry. Adelman (Reading 20) sketches in a theory of changes in vertical integration over time, while Laffer (Reading 21) shows that there was no increase in vertical integration in United States industry over a period of four decades.

16 Walter Y. Oi and Arthur P. Hurter, Jr

A Theory of Vertical Integration in Road Transport Services

Walter Y. Oi and Arthur P. Hurter, Jr, *Economics of Private Truck Transportation*, William C. Brown Co., 1965, chapter 2, pp. 31–67.

One of the primary objectives of this study is to explain the emergence and pattern of use of proprietary motor transportation (PMT). Toward this end, the following sections develop a theory of private motor transportation in which PMT is viewed as the result of a rational decision based solely on economic cost and service considerations. It does not deny the possibility that the decision may have been influenced by other factors such as an ambitious traffic manager or a persuasive truck salesman. For the present study, however, these noneconomic factors will be ignored. If they are important, then the implications of our theory should be refuted by the available data. The discussion in this section is admittedly abstract and is intended to serve as a basis for the subsequent empirical sections. Portions of the analysis will be deferred to later sections to facilitate direct comparisons between the theory and evidence.

A firm's demand for transportation serves as a useful point of departure. In general, transportation demands cannot be adequately summarized by any single measure such as ton-miles; instead, one must consider various components of transportation. Conceptually, these components can be separated into two broad categories: (1) those related to the spatial movement of goods, and (2) those related to the quality of the transportation activity – the latter are commonly called the service features of transportation.

The components of the first category are largely quantifiable variables which can be described by the shipping documents of a firm. From such records it would be possible to construct summary statistics such as

(a) The total volume of shipments.
(b) The spatial distribution of consignees for outbound shipments and of suppliers for inbound shipments.
(c) The distance and weight profile of shipments,[1] and
(d) The regularity of shipments over time.

1. This simply refers to a frequency distribution of shipments, cross-classified by distance and weight.

On the other hand, the components of the second category defy explicit quantification; they are the intangible elements which make up the quality of service. Based on conversations with traffic managers, this latter category includes the following kinds of considerations:

(a) Speed or transit time of the movement.
(b) Reliability, meaning either waiting time or predictability.
(c) Damage to goods.
(d) Split deliveries and pickups.
(e) Night deliveries.

If all of the pertinent components of a firm's transportation requirements could be specified, then it would be theoretically possible to analyse how these requirements might vary as functions of rates, scale of output, or product prices.

The transportation requirements of a firm could be satisfied in various ways. Even if a firm relies entirely upon for-hire transportation, it must still choose among several competing carriers. Each carrier, in turn, offers a slightly different combination of rates and services. The most striking differences are those associated with various modes of transportation: rail, motor, water, or pipeline.

In addition to the for-hire carriers, each firm has the option of providing its own transportation by engaging in private carriage. This study is concerned mainly with the option of private motor transportation and will ignore other forms of proprietary transportation via water, rail, air, and pipeline.

Private motor transportation is clearly a form of vertical integration. It is manifest in the decision to produce one's own transportation services, rather than to purchase them from outside, for-hire suppliers. Vertical integration, after all, means an extension of a firm's activities into the production of some related good or service other than its primary product. The economic literature distinguishes two types of vertical integration: upstream and downstream, depending on whether the integration is away from or toward the ultimate consumer.[2] This dichotomy appears to break down in the case of trucking. PMT may simultaneously represent both an upstream and downstream integration. Private trucks may distribute final products to consignees and also transport raw materials to the factory. Despite this dual role of PMT, the explanations suggested by a theory of vertical integration warrant careful examination.

2. For example, the mining of bauxite by an aluminium plant exemplifies an upstream integration. On the other hand, if the aluminium plant extended its operations into the production of fabricated aluminium products, then it would be a downstream integration.

Reaction to noncompetitive prices

Vertical integration may be a reaction to noncompetitive prices. Suppose that the price of a particular kind of goods or service exceeds its marginal cost of production. In this case, it may prove profitable to integrate into the production of these goods if the *unit cost* of production to the firm is less than the price.

The condition that price is above seller's marginal cost is not sufficient to insure the profitability of vertical integration. On the one hand, the cost curve confronting any single firm may differ from that facing sellers of the goods. A firm thus may find that its unit cost curve still lies above the prevailing price. On the other hand, the same cost curve may apply for all firms but some firms may be precluded from operating at efficient rates of output. Consider a situation where there are economies of scale and barriers to entry in the sale of the goods to others. Any single firm may find that its requirements are not large enough to enjoy the economies of scale. This point can be demonstrated with reference to Figure 1. The total unit cost and marginal cost curves are designated by TUC and MC. To achieve the minimum unit cost of production, the firm must produce an output, OX_2. Suppose that the firm's typical requirement for X is given by OX_1. If the firm chose to produce this output, OX_1, itself, then the unit cost would be OC. Now if the price were OP, then vertical integration, meaning self-production, would be clearly irrational. The relevant comparison is between unit cost and price, since at an output, OX_1, it is possible that the

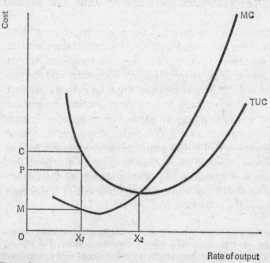

Figure 1

marginal cost, OM, is still below price. If there were no barriers to entry in the sale of X, then a firm could produce an efficient rate of output, OX_2, consume OX_1 units itself, and sell the remainder, X_1X_2, to other buyers at any price between OP and the minimum unit cost of production.[3]

Turn next to the implications of vertical integration with respect to the price and aggregate output of a good. Suppose that the price is set by a profit-maximizing monopolist or by a cartel which acts as though it were a monopoly. Let $X = F(P)$ denote the market demand curve for the good prior to any vertical integration. The elasticity of the market demand curve is defined as the relative change in sales in response to a given relative change in price.

$$E = \left(\frac{P}{X}\right)\left(\frac{dX}{dP}\right) = \left(\frac{P}{X}\right)F'(P). \qquad 1$$

The market demand, $X = F(P)$, is simply an aggregation of individual demands, $x_i = f_i(P)$. If there are N individual buyers then:

$$X = \sum_{i=1}^{N} x_i + \sum_{i=1}^{N} f_i(P) = F(P). \qquad 2$$

Let e_i denote the elasticity of demand for the ith individual. It follows that the elasticity of the market demand, E, is a weighted average of individual elasticities, e_i, where the weights represent the proportion of the total market demand taken by the ith buyer.

$$E = \sum_{i=1}^{N} \left(\frac{x_i}{X}\right) e_i. \qquad 3$$

The equilibrium price, P_o, is set to equate marginal cost to marginal revenue, yielding the following first order condition:

$$MC_o = P_o\left(1 + \frac{1}{E}\right) = P_o\left(1 + \frac{X}{P_o F'(P_o)}\right). \qquad 4$$

Suppose that H buyers now decide to produce goods themselves while the remaining $N-H$ buyers continue to purchase from the monopolist. The total market demand is now separated into two parts. Let $F_a(P)$ denote that part of the demand applicable to the H integrated buyers; $F_b(P)$ represents the demand of the remaining $N-H$ buyers.

3. One cannot simultaneously assume (1) identical cost curves for all producers of the goods (2) noncompetitive price for the goods, and (3) freedom of entry. The first and third assumptions imply a competitive price except for indivisibilities. The assumption of barriers to entry in the sale of the goods thus is essential to the argument.

$$X_a = \sum_{i=1}^{H} x_i = \sum_{i=1}^{H} f_i(P) = F_a(P). \qquad 5$$

$$X_b = \sum_{i=H+1}^{N} x_i = \sum_{i=H+1}^{N} f_i(P) = F_b(P).$$

$$X = X_a + X_b = F_a(P) + F_b(P) = F(P).$$

From equation 3, it follows that the elasticity of the total market demand E, is a weighted average of elasticities for the two parts.

$$E = \left(\frac{X_a}{X_a + X_b} \right) E_a + \left(\frac{X_b}{X_a + X_b} \right) E_b. \qquad 6$$

If vertical integration is profitable, then the H integrated buyers find that their unit cost of production is below the former price, P_O. Hence, their output and consumption of X will now be larger so long as $E_a < 0$.

The impact of vertical integration is to reduce the demand facing the monopolist via the withdrawal of the integrated buyers. Given the lower demand, $F_b(P)$, the monopolist will maximize profits by establishing a new price, P_1, where marginal cost equals marginal revenue.

$$MC_1 = P_1 \left(1 + \frac{1}{E_b} \right). \qquad 7$$

To examine the change in the equilibrium price, it is convenient to consider the ratio of price to marginal cost both before and after the withdrawal of the H integrated buyers.

$$\frac{P_O}{MC_O} = \frac{E}{E+1} \qquad 8a$$

$$\frac{P_1}{MC_1} = \frac{E_b}{E_b+1}. \qquad 8b$$

The behavior of the price to marginal cost ratio will depend, therefore, on the elasticities of demand for the two parts of the market, E_a and E_b. Thus, (P_1/MC_1) will be less than (P_O/MC_O), if E_b is algebraically less than E_a[4]. In the case of an upward sloping marginal cost curve, the new price P_1 will be less than P_O if the integrated buyers have a less elastic demand curve, meaning a larger algebraic value for E_a relative to E_b. If the converse holds, $E_b > E_a$, then one must know the elasticity of the marginal cost curve, the market share of the integrated buyers, and the magnitude of the difference in elasticities to conclude the direction of change in price.

4. If E_b is less than E_a, then from equation 6 it follows E_b is less than E. The three elasticities applicable to (1) the total market, E, (2) the integrated buyers, E_a, and (3) the nonintegrated buyers, E_b, are not mutually independent.

At least two arguments can be advanced to support the hypothesis that integrated buyers (those who engage in private carriage) have less elastic demands. It seems reasonable to suspect that buyers who choose to integrate into the production of goods are precisely those for whom there are few substitutes for the good. Moreover, some buyers may produce only a fraction of their requirements and continue to demand residual amounts from the monopolist. In this event, the total demand by an integrated buyer must be separated into two parts: that part which he produces himself enters into $F_a(P)$; the remainder constitutes part of the demand curve, $F_b(P)$. These residual purchases, it seems, would be most responsive to price changes. If these arguments are valid, then increased vertical integration should lead to a decline in the price of goods. If the noncompetitive price is set in some other fashion (say by regulation or cost-plus pricing), these implications do not apply.

The 'reaction to noncompetitive price' hypothesis offers an explanation for PMT. It is a widely accepted doctrine that transportation rates do not perfectly reflect costs of production. Furthermore, the discrepancies may go in either direction with some rates clearly above costs and others below. An admission of the presence of such discrepancies is manifest in numerous expressions of concern regarding the growth of PMT. It is alleged by the rail and motor common carriers that PMT takes away the 'cream traffic', leaving the 'undesirable traffic' to the common carriers. The implication of this allegation is that common carriers, perhaps through the regulatory practices of the Interstate Commerce Commission (ICC), exercise price discrimination in the establishment of freight rates. Shippers who bear the burden of high rates relative to costs therefore have an incentive to integrate into the production of their own transportation services.

The production of transportation services often involves joint costs which cannot be unambiguously allocated to specific activities.[5] Hence, it is difficult to determine whether any particular rate is above or below costs of production. In spite of this difficulty, one can discern certain broad tendencies which indicate systematic discrepancies between rates and costs:

5. The distinction between *joint costs* and *common costs* is clearly stated by Baumol *et al* (1962). Joint costs arise when two or more outputs are produced in unalterably fixed proportions. The term *common costs* applies to a situation in which a given bundle of productive inputs can produce two or more outputs in variable proportions.

Suppose, for example, that a driver's pay is $30.00 for a round trip between points A and B. What proportion of the $30.00 should be allocated to the trip from A to B as opposed to the return trip from B to A? In the ICC cost formula, the $30.00 would be apportioned to the two legs according to the average freight tonnages on the two legs. Thus, if the return trip generated no freight traffic the entire $30.00 would be assigned to the A to B leg. An alternative procedure might split the difference while another method could allocate the $30.00 according to the actual tonnages on each round trip.

1. *Value-of-service pricing and commodity differentials.* The concept of value-of-service pricing is predicated on the presumption that high-valued goods can bear a higher freight burden. Hence, freight rates on high-valued commodities are advanced to reflect the so-called value of the service. The economic rationale for this practice can be traced to a theory of price discrimination and the treatment of transportation demands as derived demands.[6] Where the freight cost accounts for a small proportion of the total cost, one would anticipate a smaller elasticity of demand (the responsiveness of the amounts shipped to changes in rates). Since carriers can separate markets according to commodity,[7] they can charge higher rates for those commodities with smaller elasticities of demand. Casual examination of freight rates reveals that value-of-service pricing exists, even though its quantitative importance has not been fully documented. Some commodity rate differentials may, however, reflect true cost differences. It would appear that the low-valued goods also happen to have lower costs; witness, for example, the movement of coal, wheat, and stone. These commodities move in large quantities and involve very low loading and unloading costs.

In summary, if the value-of-service component is important in transportation pricing, one should expect to observe the highest incidence of PMT for high-valued commodities. A corollary to this proposition is that rates below costs should tend to discourage PMT.

2. *Rate differentials by distance.* Freight rates understandably increase as a function of line-haul distance. Yet, insofar as the ratio of rate to cost varies with distance, there is a basis for PMT. In particular, one would expect PMT to concentrate in those mileage blocks where the ratios of rates to costs are highest.

Suppose, on the other hand, that the rate differentials due to distance are entirely attributable to the cost differentials experienced by common carriers. That is, the ratio of rate to common carrier cost is the same for all mileage blocks. Even in this case, PMT may still prove profitable for some shipments if private trucking costs differ from common carrier trucking costs. Hence, it is not surprising to find a concentration of private trucking in movements of similar distances.

3. *Rate differentials by weight.* For the purposes of quoting rates, common carriers currently identify only two weight categories: LCL *v* CL rates

6. A fuller development can be found in Oi and Hurter (1965), chapter 7. See also Meyer *et al.* (1959, pp. 172–88); and Pigou (1960, pp. 290–317).

7. The recent trends toward increased use of piggyback and containerization have operated to reduce the value-of-service component in pricing. The inability to identify the commodity content of the containers makes it difficult to separate markets. Also, increased intermodal competition has worked to reduce the extent of price discrimination.

for rail shipments, and LTL v TL rates for motor. The enormous costs of billing and documentation necessarily entail some simplification of tariffs which already threaten to become too cumbersome. Nevertheless, this simple dichotomy insures that rates will not perfectly reflect costs of production. Recognition of this point is evidenced by several requests before the Commission for volume rates on bases other than carload v less than carload. To the best of our knowledge, none of these requests have been accepted by the Commission. Whenever the quoted rates do not reflect true cost differentials, there will be an incentive for some shippers to turn to PMT.

4. *Regional differences in rates.* The posture assumed by the Commission on rate cases is not entirely consistent. It frowns on some forms of personal rate discrimination and, at the same time, sanctions other, equally blatant, forms of rate discrimination. Consider a hypothetical case where two shippers of iron rods wish to transport their products in truckload lots to a destination 200 miles away. If the origins and destinations were the same for both shippers, then the Commission would prohibit any rate differential. Now, suppose shipper A's goods are westbound out of Chicago, while shipper B's goods are eastbound. In this second case, it is likely that the rates will differ even though weight, distance, and commodity are identical. Finally, consider a third shipper C, whose product is iron ingots. Even if the cost of moving rods or ingots were the same, the Commission might well embrace different rates. The usual rationalization is that the value of the service differs. Commodity and place discrimination thus appear to be acceptable while personal discrimination (even if one shipper can provide a larger, steadier volume) is prohibited.

The paucity of published motor freight rates makes it difficult to determine the magnitude of regional rate differentials. For the rail sector, the waybill statistics show substantial variations in freight revenues. Unfortunately, the broad commodity groups preclude any separation of regional and commodity differences in rates.[8]

5. *Uniform rates over time.* Under certain conditions, costs may depend on the demands for transportation. Consider a situation in which demands fluctuate over time as they do in the seasonal movements of some commodities. Suppose that costs vary directly with demands, that is, costs are higher in periods of peak demands. If rates are not adjusted to reflect these variations in costs over time, there may be a basis for proprietary transportation.

Demands may also affect costs through their impact on the returns to the capital input which, for expository purposes, is assumed to be a truck.

8. Within each broad, commodity group there may be a wide variety of individual commodities, especially in the numerous 'n.o.s.' categories.

During any period, the return that accrues to a truck can be regarded as an economic rent that is determined entirely by demand. According to this interpretation, the rent is a residual return and, as such, has no effect on marginal costs. The rent, however, can be viewed also as a shadow price that serves to ration the available stock of trucks among competing uses. Put in this way, the rent represents the alternative cost of securing a truck for a particular use. In a period of peak demands, the alternative cost of the truck (or capital input) is indicated by a rise in the shadow price or rent.[9] However, the regulated, for-hire carriers are not allowed to vary rates in response to changes in these shadow prices. They must quote a uniform rate over time. Consequently, rates tend to be below alternative costs in periods of peak demands and above in periods of slack demands.

An individual shipper can take advantage of such a rate policy through partial integration into proprietary trucking. Suppose that a seller of fuel oil requires a fleet of five trucks to satisfy summer demands, but needs a fleet of ten trucks for his peak demands in the winter. The shipper in this case could procure a private fleet of five trucks which only partially satisfy his annual transportation requirements. The excess demand for trucks during the peak winter months would be diverted to the regulated, for-hire carriers. In this manner the private carrier can realize a saving during the summer months when rates exceed alternative costs. Notice, however, that the burden of fluctuating demands becomes even greater for the regulated carriers.

The pricing of transportation services is not the only consideration in the 'reaction to noncompetitive price' hypothesis. The possibility that private trucking costs could differ from common carrier costs was mentioned in the foregoing. To the extent that firms differ in their transportation require-ments, they will experience different private truck costs. A firm with several plants may be able to schedule a balanced flow of traffic. Through higher vehicle utilization rates, it therefore may achieve substantially lower costs than some other firm with a less fortuitous demand situation. The crucial variable is the ratio of the rate charged by for-hire carriers to private trucking cost.

Specificity of the transportation activity

Heretofore, transportation has been viewed as a general service that could be used by large numbers of shippers. In important instances, however, the transportation activity may be specific to a firm. Thus, a firm might employ

9. In the case of ocean tankers, there is a world charter market that serves to ration the stock of tankers among competing users. The owner of a tanker could, in principle, charter his ship, thereby treating the shadow price as a variable cost of production.

a type of transportation service that is geared to the firm's particular requirements and is not suited to any other firm. This specificity may take the form of specialized equipment, peculiar containerization of goods, or unique loading and unloading features. Where transportation is specific, a firm has an incentive to provide its own transportation rather than to rely on outside carriers.

Consider a case where the specificity arises out of the use of special equipment, which presumably reduces the cost of transporting this firm's products. Let C_s denote the transportation cost per ton with special equipment. If general-purpose equipment were used to satisfy this firm's requirements, it would involve higher costs, say a cost of K dollars per ton. The special equipment conceivably could be used to transport the products of other firms. Assume that the special equipment is inferior in this alternative use and results in an even higher cost of C_g dollars per ton for a comparable movement.[10] These assumptions could be summarized in tabular form as follows in Table 1:

Table 1

| | Transportation requirements of | |
	Firm A	Other firms
Special equipment	C_s	C_g
General-purpose equipment	K	K

It was assumed that $C_s < K < C_g$. The first column thus gives the cost per ton of satisfying firm A's requirements with two types of equipment. The second column tells us the cost per ton with the two equipment types to some other firm with comparable transportation requirements.

If all carriers – suppliers of transportation services – used general-purpose equipment, then even under competition the minimum rates to firm A would still mean a cost of K dollars per ton. One might argue that given the superiority of special equipment, some carrier would procure special equipment and quote a lower rate to firm A. This is, however, a very unlikely outcome.

Suppose that some carrier did purchase equipment that was specifically designed to A's requirements but inferior in alternative uses. So long as this carrier transports A's products, he can quote a rate as low as C_s dollars and still realize the same normal profits that he would have realized with general-purpose equipment and a rate of K dollars. If, however, he uses the

10. The distance of the movement and commodity characteristics are assumed to be the same. The cost differences thus are attributable to the use of two different types of equipment.

special equipment for general commodity traffic, he must meet the competition of other carriers and quote a rate of K dollars per ton. His cost in this alternative use is C_g dollars. In the alternative use, he therefore would lose (C_g-K) dollars per ton.

The specificity of special equipment to firm A places the carrier in an exploitable position. Since his special equipment is inferior in alternative uses, firm A can demand an even lower rate once the carrier has procured the equipment. Indeed, firm A could exact a rate as low as $C_s-(C_g-K)$ dollars per ton. At this rate, the carrier would incur the same loss as he would if he transferred his special equipment to general commodity traffic. The situation is completely analogous to one of bilateral monopoly. In the bargaining, the options available to firm A are:

1. To use other for-hire carriers at a rate of K dollars per ton, or
2. To engage in PMT at a cost of C_s dollars per ton.

A rational carrier would purchase such special equipment only if he could obtain a binding, long-term contract effective for the life of the equipment. Otherwise, he places himself in an impossible situation. The option of PMT sets an upper limit to the rate at C_s, while exploitation and inferiority of the equipment in alternative uses set a lower limit at $C_s-(C_g-K)$. A binding, long-term contract is, for all intents and purposes, equivalent to proprietary transportation. Although the carrier technically sells transportation services to A, he is legally bound to that firm's employ. This point is obvious when one considers the possibility that firm A could have established a subsidiary to perform its transportation activities.

The frequency of cases where transportation is truly specific to a *single* firm is probably quite small. This does not mean that it can be categorically dismissed. In recent years, applications before the Commission for specialized common carrier certificates have far out-numbered those for general-commodity certificates. This fact suggests that there are definite advantages to the use of specialized equipment. However, such specialized equipment is usually specific to an entire industry or group of shippers; e.g. padded vans for furniture shippers or heated tank-trucks for acids. Yet, for any particular geographic region, specificity to an industry may be the same as specificity to a single firm. Thus, in some territory there may be only one or two furniture shippers who do not generate enough traffic to warrant the establishment of a specialized carrier. These isolated firms, may, therefore, find it profitable to procure special equipment and provide their own transportation. We have also encountered a case where the sales activities of a firm have encouraged the purchase of custom-made trailers. Yet again, a large bulk-liquid shipper procured a fleet of odd-sized tank-trucks that had load capacities between the standard sizes. This practice was justified on the grounds that the odd-sized tanks were the usual size of orders. If this business had been directed to common carriers, it would have meant excess capacities on most shipments. Finally, delivery practices, packaging procedures, and mechanization of loading may all serve to make the transportation activity specific to a firm.

Managerial control and importance of transportation

The desire to achieve stability and reliability in the flow of some input is often cited as an important motive for vertical integration (see Neale, 1960). Steady flows of ore and coal thus are important to the efficient operation and survival of steel mills and may account for the integration by steel mills into the production of these raw materials. The formal economic justifications for this argument must ultimately rest on uncertainties regarding (1) availability of supplies and possible disruptions in supplies and (2) fluctuations in future input prices.

In the classical theory of the firm, it is assumed that price serves as a rationing device. Hence, any buyer can presumably procure any good at some price that is equal to, or only slightly above, the prevailing price. Although this assumption can, in principle, be accepted, the actual price mechanism during any short period may fail to function in the indicated manner. Indeed, casual observation suggests that non-price rationing is present in many markets, especially for short periods of one or two months. Queues, prior customer loyalty, purchases of related goods, or chance may allocate available supplies during periods of excess demand. The possibility of a disruption in the supply of an input to a firm therefore must be considered. Furthermore, the likelihood of a disruption in supply will vary over time and across inputs. Although a disruption in the supply of any input is potentially costly, the firm clearly cannot hedge against all contingencies. The rational firm will attempt to exercise control over certain inputs that are crucial to the viability of the firm.

The importance of an input to the viability of a firm will depend on two factors:

1. The degree of substitutability for the input.
2. The share of total costs attributable to the input.

If there are few good substitutes for the input,[11] then a disruption in that input's supply could seriously curtail output. In a sense, the input is essential in the production of the firm's product; attempts to use substitute inputs would lead to sharply advanced costs. On the other hand, if there

11. Conceptually, the degree of substitutability for an input could be measured by its partial elasticity of substitution with other inputs. If the input is truly essential in the production of the product, then the elasticity of substitution will be zero.

were good substitutes for some input A, then a firm could substitute other inputs whenever the supply of A is disrupted.

In addition, we argue that a firm will make greater efforts to exercise control over an input that accounts for a large proportion of total costs. This latter argument is related to the second justification regarding uncertainty of future input prices. An advance in prices may help to mend a temporary break in normal supply channels. The larger an input's share of total costs, the greater will be the advance in total costs due to any given percentage increase in that input's price. As long, therefore, as price advances act as a partial correction for breaks in input supplies, the firm will have an incentive to control those inputs that comprise the largest proportion of total cost.

A firm can exercise control over the supply of an input in at least three ways:

1. Futures markets and forward contracts.
2. Inventories.
3. Vertical integration.

A futures market is simply a collection of forward contracts where buyers and sellers agree to sales at some future dates. If a firm can negotiate a forward contract for delivery of an input at specified future dates, it assures itself of a supply of that input. The only risk is that the seller will renege on his contract. With the exception of mineral and agricultural staples, there are comparatively few organized futures markets. This avenue of control thus may be closed to the firm.

Inventories may represent speculative stocks or buffer stocks which are held to absorb random variations in demands and supplies. The costs of maintaining an inventory include

(a) The interest cost of capital invested in inventories.
(b) Storage and possible deterioration costs.
(c) Profit or loss on inventory values due to price changes.

These costs would appear to be sufficiently high to preclude the maintenance of extremely large inventories as hedges against possible disruptions in future supplies except for unusual situations. The anticipation of a strike in the spring of 1959 led, for instance, to sharp increases in steel demands for inventories. The use of inventories as hedges against breaks in supplies is, however, limited to material inputs where storage and deterioration costs are not prohibitive.

Vertical integration offers perhaps the most direct control over the supply of an input. By controlling the production of an input, a firm can channel this production to its own use, thereby assuring this source of supply for the input. The firm can, of course, integrate the production of several inputs that it regularly consumes in the course of producing its major product. The extension of the firm into other fields necessarily entails additional resources, especially managerial attention. Hence, one would expect that the firm is most likely to integrate the production of those inputs that are most crucial to the survival of the firm.

The second justification for the argument in favor of stable input flows rests on uncertainty regarding fluctuations in future input prices. Fluctuations in input prices are of concern only if the firm makes forward contracts for the sale of its products or if product prices for any reason are rigid relative to input prices. Under these circumstances, a firm may wish to hedge against input price variations. The options of futures markets and inventories are again available to the firm for this purpose. Furthermore, under special assumptions, vertical integration may also act as a hedge against fluctuations in future input prices.[12] Again, the hedge is of greater importance where the input comprises a larger proportion of total cost.

The importance of managerial control over certain inputs is, we believe, a significant factor in explaining proprietary transportation. Consider, for example, the case of proprietary transportation in ocean shipping. Ocean transportation of crude oil is an important input to the petroleum industry judged either by its share of total costs or the availability of close substitutes. Given the locations of producing wells and ultimate markets, ocean shipping via tankers is the only feasible means of transportation. Furthermore, the market for tankers' services is organized on a worldwide basis with regular quotations for both voyage and time charter rates. The functionings of this market seem to meet the competitive model. Nevertheless, each major oil company has a substantial investment in tankers.[13] The only tenable explanation is that these oil companies have entered the transportation business to assure themselves of a stable flow of tankers' services for at least a portion of their annual transportation requirements. It is interesting to note that most of the ore-carriers on the Great Lakes are operated by major steel companies. The United Fruit Company and Alcoa also happen to own two of the largest ocean fleets under United States control, largely under flags of convenience.

The preceding analysis suggests that the element of managerial control should encourage the use of PMT in industries where transportation

12. To the best of our knowledge, this point has not been developed in the literature. A formal analysis is therefore presented in the appendix.

13. The actual tanker tonnages that are owned outright by the oil companies are only a lower limit estimate of their private fleets. Many oil companies have signed twenty- and twenty-five-year-leases – the effective life of a tanker. These long-term leases are tied to particular ships that are committed to the lessee's service. They therefore should properly be viewed as part of the firm's private fleet.

accounts for a large proportion of total costs and where control over transportation is essential to the viability of firms in these industries. The dependence of an industry on transportation (the degree of substitutability) is an elusive concept defying explicit quantification. The costs of holding inventories, mobility of firms in an industry, and ties to raw material sources may provide rough evaluation in some cases. These probes would, it seems, meet with only limited success in any empirical investigation. On the other hand, the importance of transportation costs is an observable variable. For example, consider the ratio of transportation costs to the total delivered cost of a product. Other things equal, one would expect to find a higher incidence of PMT in industries with large ratios of transportation to total product costs.

Quality of transportation

The concept of 'service' simply refers to the quality of transportation. Under the mantle of 'service' are included such features as speed, damage to goods, night deliveries, flexibility of schedules, and split deliveries. These features, or attributes, are related to, but are not an essential part of, the spatial movement of goods. Taken together, they constitute the quality of the transportation activity.[14]

Although shippers generally express a preference for a higher quality of transportation, one usually cannot attach a monetary value to their preference. An improvement in the quality of goods surely enhances its value, yet product prices and values are constantly changing in response to shifts in demands and supplies as well as to changes in quality. The empirical separation of the quality component of price therefore poses some intractable problems. Similar measurement problems of evaluating quality changes in the case of durable goods have been discussed in the literature (US Congress, 1961, especially pp. 35 ff., and Burstein, 1961). A statistical approach is offered by the method of hedonic indexes (Griliches, 1961, pp. 173–97). It begins with the premise that all goods can be decomposed into components representing various attributes or features. A change in quality can be traced to variations in the way that these features are combined. For example, in the case of a refrigerator, one could identify such attributes as (1) cubic feet of space, (2) cubic feet of freezer capacity, (3) time requirement to freeze ice cubes, and (4) size of motor.[15]

14. This treatment of 'service' is analogous to that of quality for physical goods. An automobile thus is basically a four-wheeled vehicle with an internal combustion engine. The addition of such features as greater horse-power, cushioned seats, and automatic transmissions contributes to the quality of an auto but does not alter the basic product. In the case at hand, the only intrinsic difference is that transportation is itself a service and not tangible goods.

15. Dummy variables could be used to incorporate the effects of non-quantifiable

At any point in time, consumers are confronted by a large variety of refrigerators; each type will have slightly different attributes. The equilibrium price of each type of refrigerator will incorporate the values that consumers have placed on these attributes. Let A_{1i}, A_{2i},... A_{ki} denote the attributes of the ith type of refrigerator, whose price is given by P_i. In the hedonic index, the price, P_i, is expressed as a linear function of these attributes.

$$P_i = W_0 + W_1 A_{1i} + W_2 A_{2i} + ... + W_k A_{ki} + e_i \qquad 9$$

where e_i is a residual error term. Estimates of the parameters, W_0, W_1,...W_k, are obtained by a least squares regression based on data for $i = 1, 2,... N$ types of refrigerators. If the attributes, A_1,... A_k, do not enhance the quality of the product as revealed by the values that consumers place on the goods, then the slope parameters, W_1,... W_k, will not be significantly different from zero. A significant coefficient for some attribute means that consumers do respond to changes in that feature of the good. Thus, if W_1 is positive, an increase in the attribute, A_1, will increase the price people are willing to pay for the refrigerator. A change in quality is therefore described by changes in attributes. The slope parameters of equation 9 then may be applied to the changes in attributes, ΔA_1,... ΔA_k, to estimate the monetary values of the quality change. Essentially, the hedonic index simply imputes value to *ceteris paribus* changes in the various attributes. This value is based on the free market prices or values for variants of a generic product line.

Conceptually, a similar analysis could be undertaken to estimate the value of quality changes in transportation. The attributes might represent such things as speed, split deliveries, damage to goods, or flexibility of schedules. Unfortunately, the prices paid for different transportation services do not reflect free market prices. The regulated common carrier rates bear no necessary relationship to the values that shippers place on the quality of service offered by these carriers.[16]

If shippers can have superior service at lower costs from one mode of transportation, the problem of the choice of mode is uninteresting. Shippers always prefer lower costs, even with the 'same service'. If superior service necessitates higher transportation costs, then the question arises: 'Why do shippers demand superior service?' The answer lies in the integration of transportation with the other activities of the firm. Suppose that the profitability of the firm's other activities – those dealing with sales

variables such as exterior color or presence of an orange juice dispenser. The technique thus is not restricted to measurable attributes.

16. This approach might still be feasible in situations where unbridled competition prevails, provided, of course, that adequate data are available.

and production – is independent of the transportation activity. In this event, minimization of total transportation costs with respect to only the spatial movement of goods would lead to maximum profits for the firm. The 'service' features would be of no concern since, by assumption, transportation is neutral with respect to other activities.

In the typical situation, the various divisions of a firm complement one another in the production, sale, and distribution of the firm's products. Given these complementaries, suboptimization within divisions will, in general, fail to maximize total profits, that is, each division cannot act as though it were an autonomous entity. The integration of transportation with the firm's other divisions may therefore result in transportation costs that do not minimize the costs of simply moving goods through space. Higher transportation costs may be justified by lower costs in some other division or in greater sales.

The cost savings due to a higher quality of transportation can be traced to lower inventory costs or to the implicit value that shippers attach to predictable, stable flows of goods. Higher speeds and greater control of transportation may permit a firm to hold lower inventory levels. Damage to goods in transit leads not only to higher insurance costs but also to temporary disruptions in the supply of goods. The arguments developed on managerial control therefore again apply. Where large inventories and disruptions in supply are costly, one would expect shippers to place higher values on these service features.

Superior transportation service may also serve as a form of non-price competition in industries where price is not the major competitive weapon. It is sometimes argued that customers demand fast, reliable transportation, and firms must comply to retain their level of sales.[17] This argument assumes that customers prefer the superior transportation service to a reduction in delivered product prices. Where firms in an industry, formally or informally, agree to refrain from price-cutting, one observes the emergence of various forms of non-price competition such as advertising and customer service. Although it is difficult to assess the quantitative importance of this factor, the potential interaction between demand and the quality of transport services cannot be ignored.

Clearly, shippers differ in their evaluation of various attributes of transportation service. A shipper of high-valued, perishable goods may place a high premium on speed, while a shipper of canned goods may discount speed since it could increase his storage costs. The major modes of trans-

17. A traffic manager of a large private fleet frankly admitted to us that part of his private truck operation was uneconomical. He continues these uneconomical operations because the sales division feels that the superior service of private trucks is essential to retain customer loyalty.

portation – highway, rail, water, and air – reflect broad differences in these service characteristics. The systematic differences in rates across modes, coupled with their respective shares of traffic, offer some information on the way in which shippers value these service differentials. Thus, manufactures accounted for 88·8 per cent of truckload freight revenues by common motor carriers in 1959, while the corresponding percentage for carload rail freight revenues was only 50·0 per cent. Other examples of the preference for the generally faster speeds[18] and route flexibility of highway transportation can be found in various rate cases.[19]

By selecting a particular transportation mode, a shipper can obtain service features that differ substantially from those provided by competing modes. In addition, carriers using the same basic means of transportation may nevertheless supply varying combinations of these service features. The decision to enter PMT can thus be considered a choice of one particular form of highway transportation. It reflects a preference for one carrier – the shipper himself – to other motor carriers.

The element of 'service' looms large in the announced reasons for entry into PMT. A perusal of several shipper surveys reveals that the most important service features are flexibility of routes and schedules, split deliveries, speed, and, in some industries, damage to goods.[20] If these service features are truly important to shippers, then the crucial questions are: 'Can private carriers provide the requisite services more cheaply than for-hire carriers?' or 'Are the common carriers unwilling or unable to offer the requisite services?'

With respect to speed, the pertinent variable is clearly transit time. The time requirement for the line-haul will depend on distance and average highway speeds. For this portion of the trip, there is no reason to expect any systematic difference between private and common carrier trucks. The other component of transit time represents the time consumed in the pickup and delivery (P&D) of goods including loading times. In general,

18. A notable exception can be found in the transportation of fresh fruits and vegetables from California to points east of the Mississippi. There the rails achieve substantially greater speeds through the use of express freight trains.

19. The apparent importance of service is exemplified by the case of 'Fish from New Bedford, Massachusetts, to New York', 248 ICC 535 (1942). The only common carrier trucker was able to obtain as much of this traffic as he desired at a rate of 60 cents, even though the rail rate was 45 cents for carloads of 24,000 minimum weight. A reduction to 28 cents failed to divert traffic. Finally, the Commission allowed a rate of 20 cents at minimum weights of 20,000 pounds. The report failed to mention the necessity for such a large rate discrepancy. See Williams (1958, p. 39).

20. In the case of furniture, for example, shippers employ padded vans that greatly reduce breakage, tare weights, and packaging costs. Furthermore, these private shippers claim that specially trained drivers minimize damages during the loading and unloading of the goods. For a further discussion see Oi and Hurter (1965, chapter 6).

private trucks should experience less P&D time since they are less likely to require terminal trans-shipments. Common carriers often follow a practice of using smaller P&D trucks and then transferring goods to larger combination trucks for the line-haul. In addition, the simpler route structures applicable to private trucks tend to reduce scheduling delays.[21] Thus, any time savings enjoyed by private trucks must result from less P&D time and efficient scheduling. Hence, any time advantage for private trucks will become progressively less important as the distance of the line-haul is extended. Except for the shortest trips, the speed feature of private fleets would appear to be of only secondary importance.

The transportation requirements of many firms demand numerous pickups and deliveries of small shipments. This pattern applies to many food and beverage industries as well as the wholesale and retail trades. Multiple stops necessarily increase variable costs (mainly in drivers' wages) and reduce vehicle utilization rates. The higher costs are reflected in common carrier rates where surcharges are levied for additional deliveries or pickups. If these surcharges exceed the additional cost of multiple stops, then the emergence of PMT in this situation could be explained by the 'reaction to noncompetitive price' hypothesis. On the other hand, one might contend that private carriers can provide split deliveries at lower costs. The arguments to support this contention include

1. Lower variable cost, perhaps because of lower input prices via non-union drivers.
2. Route flexibility that permits a private carrier to operate on any route without regard to gateway cities or route certifications.
3. Synchronization of pickups and deliveries that could increase load factors.

With the possible exception of lower drivers' wages,[22] these arguments are, at best, tenuous. Surely it is more reasonable to suppose that the rate structure of the for-hire carriers offers the explanation for PMT in cases involving numerous deliveries and pickups.

A firm's demands for transportation obviously fluctuate over time with changes in the volume and spatial distribution of sales. These fluctuations necessarily entail appropriate short-run adjustments in the routing and scheduling of shipments. It is alleged that a private fleet can more readily

21. The value of a simplified route structure lies in efficient scheduling which, in turn, tends to increase equipment utilization. Continental Airlines, for instance, enjoys an equipment utilization rate that far exceeds that of any competing airline. The explanation apparently lies in Continental's extremely simple route structure serving only six major cities.

22. The large private fleets do employ union drivers. For these carriers such as Jewel Tea and Kraft Foods even this argument can therefore be dismissed.

accommodate these variations at lower costs than can a common carrier. One basis for this allegation is that the operations of a common carrier are circumscribed by the law. Each common carrier is certificated to carry certain commodities over specified routes. Thus, he is precluded from serving all points that pertain to a firm's transportation requirements. To satisfy its changing demands, the firm must make arrangements with several carriers. Even if one carrier accepts the responsibility for a single firm's transportation demands, he must still make arrangements for the requisite interline connections. To the extent that there are significant transaction costs of billing and documentation, the common carrier will incur higher costs. Furthermore, reliance on several imperfectly integrated carriers increases the likelihood of scheduling delays.[23] On the other hand, the flexibility of PMT may be limited by equipment shortages since private fleets are typically quite small. A lack of equipment in the right place at the right time therefore may preclude the use of private trucks to meet temporary demands. The common carrier has the advantage of greater equipment availability that permits him to meet peak demands. This advantage is often lost to the common carrier because comparatively few firms place complete reliance on their private fleets. The usual situation is one where a firm uses its private fleet to meet a base demand and employs common carriers for residual transportation demands. To sum up, private fleets could provide greater flexibility at lower costs for two reasons. First, the route restrictions imposed on common carriers circumscribe their operations. Second, the availability of common carriers for residual demands allows the firm greater latitude in the deployment of its private fleet.

In summary, the discussion in the preceding four sections offers several explanations for the emergence of private motor transportation. All of these reduce to lower cost and/or superior service. From the shipper's viewpoint, the pertinent comparison is that between rates charged by for-hire carriers and PMT costs. In addition to cost, shippers may turn to PMT to secure a quality of transportation that for-hire carriers are unwilling or unable to provide. Thus, PMT may be the only feasible method of obtaining a type of transportation that is specific to the firm. Vertical integration into PMT may also reflect a firm's desire to control the supply of transportation services.

Throughout, it was assumed that firms behave rationally in the conduct of their transportation activities. The validity of this assumption is seriously

23. Since a carrier often serves numerous shippers, his schedules will rarely be optimal for any particular shipper. Furthermore, different carriers will have different clients and their schedules may not be coordinated. The phenomenon of transfer delays is therefore a probable outcome.

challenged by responses that are recorded in various shipper surveys. For example, many shippers claim that they use PMT because it is cheaper, yet some of these same shippers are unwilling or unable to provide estimates of private truck costs. Haphazard management of large private fleets also contradicts the rationality assumption. This point is exemplified by a quotation from a recent article:

One major industry, for instance, had more money invested in trucks than in milk processing equipment; yet, the fleet was managed by a garage foreman who earned $500 a month – and whose full name was not known by a single company officer (*Dun's Review*, 1962, p. 97).

At first blush, it would seem that the utility of our theory is destroyed by these examples of irrational behavior. Yet, the same sort of attack – refutation by selected examples – could be lodged against most economic theories. In the classical theory of price, it thus is assumed that firms behave *as though* they maximized short-run profits. It is often possible to find examples where firms could have increased their profits by following some alternative course of action. Indeed, a survey of entrepreneurs might well reveal that short-run profit maximization is only one of several goals. The presence of exceptions and contradictory intentions does not mean that we must discard the theory. The critical test of a descriptive model is, after all, 'How well does the theory work in predicting observed behavior patterns?'[24]

Appendix
A note on vertical integration as a substitute for a future market[25]

The available theories of vertical integration provide no truly satisfying explanations for vertical integration in situations where both product and factor markets are competitively organized. Cases can be observed, however, in which vertical integration has occurred in precisely this type of situation. A plausible explanation is contained in the argument that firms may integrate the production of some crucial input to insure *stable* and *reliable* flows of that input. This argument presupposes an element of uncertainty but serves as a useful point of departure.

In our theory, vertical integration is regarded as a substitute for a futures market. A futures market, or for that matter any long-term contract, can

24. Further explorations into the relevance and usefulness of abstract economic theories are clearly beyond the scope of the present study. The interested reader is referred to: Friedman (1953, pp. 3–43); Robbins (1952).

25. When the heuristic argument was first set forth in an informal seminar, its theoretical validity was challenged by Professor M. L. Burstein. His questions led us to develop the formal theory that included an explicit statement of the requisite assumptions. We are deeply indebted to him, but any errors are, unfortunately, ours alone.

assure a stable input flow at some future date. An uncertain price in the future period can be replaced by a current futures (or contractual) price that can be known in advance. It will be demonstrated that vertical integration under certain conditions may fulfill the same function as a futures market. The analysis is greatly simplified if we begin with an overly restrictive set of assumptions. It hence will be assumed that:

1. The firm sells its product on forward contracts. The firm thus agrees to deliver output in some future period at a specified price P.
2. There is no production lag, that is, output during any period depends on flows of inputs in the same period. It is also assumed that the firm holds no inventories of final products or raw materials.
3. At least one of the inputs that enters the production function is a capital input.
4. There are no forward contracts or futures markets for capital inputs. All input prices are, moreover, assumed to be competitively determined in each period.

Consider a case in which the firm owns no resources but purchases resources or their services from outside suppliers – the ultimate owners. By assumption 1, the firm agrees to deliver a given output, X, in some future period at a specified price, P. The total revenue from the forward contract therefore is known in advance. The production function prescribes the flows of inputs that are required to produce X. The total cost of producing X can be written

$$C = AP_a + BP_b,$$

where the production function is assumed to involve only two inputs. Since there is no production lag (assumption 2), the input prices, P_a and P_b, must apply to the future period and can be regarded as random variables. Consequently, C will also be a random variable and so also will be the total profit, Y,

$$Y = PX - C = PX - (AP_a + BP_b) \qquad\qquad 1$$

The analysis can be simplified if the production function is assumed to be one with fixed technological coefficients.[26] We can always redefine the

26. This assumption is not required for the argument but facilitates the exposition. Suppose that the production function entails variable proportions. By assumption 4, competitive market forces determine input prices in each period. If a firm produces (or owns) an input, it still has the option of consuming or selling the input. The internal ration price of each input thus will be the equilibrium market price irrespective of the source of supply. Consequently, the optimal factor proportions will be the same to all firms – vertically integrated or otherwise.

units of measurement in such a way that the fixed ratios of output to inputs is unity in each case. The unit cost of production, denoted by c, is then simply the sum of input prices. The profit per unit of output, y, is given by

$$y = \frac{Y}{X} = P - c = P - (P_a + P_b).\qquad\qquad 2$$

The product price, P, is fixed in advance by the forward contract. In our analysis, P_a and P_b refer to input prices and are regarded as random variables. Hence, y is itself a random variable since it is a linear combination of random variables. The expected unit profit, $\bar{y}$, depends on the known product price and the expected input prices.
Thus,

$$\bar{y} = P - \bar{P}_a - \bar{P}_b,\qquad\qquad 3$$

where $\bar{P}_a$ and $\bar{P}_b$ denote the expected input prices in the future period corresponding to the date of the forward contract. Similarly, the variance of unit profits, σ_y^2, is a function of the variances and covariance of future input prices.

$$\sigma_y^2 = E[y - \bar{y}]^2 = \sigma_a^2 + \sigma_b^2 + 2\sigma_{ab},\qquad\qquad 4$$

where σ_a^2 and σ_b^2 represent the variances of future input prices and σ_{ab} denotes their covariance. The right-hand side is simply the variance of units costs since the product price, P, is assumed to be known and fixed.

According to assumption 4, input prices in each period are determined competitively. In the light of this assumption, the treatment of future input prices as random variables must presuppose stochastic market demand and supply functions for each input. Suppose that the market demand and supply functions for input A can be described by two linear stochastic equations.

$$a^d = M - NP_a + u,\quad \text{(demand function)}\qquad\qquad 5a$$

$$a^s = m + nP_a + v,\quad \text{(supply function)}\qquad\qquad 5b$$

where u and v are random disturbances with zero means and some covariance matrix whose elements are

$$E[u^2] = \sigma_u^2 \qquad E[uv] = \sigma_{uv} \qquad E[v^2] = \sigma_v^2.$$

If the market is cleared in each period (i.e. if $a^d = a^s$), solution for the equilibrium market price yields

$$P_a = \left(\frac{M - m}{N + n}\right) + \left(\frac{1}{N + n}\right)(u - v).\qquad\qquad 6$$

In this manner, the mean and variance of P_a can be traced back to the parameters of the market demand and supply functions and the covariance matrix of random disturbances, u and v. In particular, we have

$$\bar{P}_a = E[P_a] = \left(\frac{M-m}{N+n} \right), \qquad\qquad\qquad \textbf{7a}$$

$$\sigma_a^2 = E[P_a - \bar{P}_a]^2 = \left(\frac{1}{N+n} \right)^2 (\sigma_u^2 + \sigma_v^2 - 2\sigma_{uv}). \qquad \textbf{7b}$$

The random disturbances, u and v, can be interpreted as shifts in the market demand and supply curves – shifts that cannot be predicted at the time when the forward contract is made in the initial period. In an analogous manner, the price of input B could be traced to stochastic market demand and supply functions. A possible inter-dependence of input markets could be incorporated into the analysis by specifying more complicated demand and supply functions. This complication adds nothing to the argument and is ignored in the present analysis.

At this point, it is essential to define clearly the distinction between capital and variable inputs. A variable input is defined as one whose market supply curve is infinitely elastic. All other inputs will be called capital inputs. A competitive market supply curve is simply an aggregate of individual marginal cost curves. An infinitely elastic marginal cost curve implies that the supply price contains no element of economic rents. Put in another way, a rising marginal cost curve necessarily implies that some factor of production earns an economic rent.[27] The price of a variable input in some future period may still be treated as a random variable due to unpredictable shifts in the prices of the underlying factors used in its production. Cotton yarn, for example, could be a variable input for some firms. Even though the market supply curve of cotton yarn is infinitely elastic in each period, fluctuations in the price of raw cotton would result in shifts in the level of the supply curve for yarn.

Suppose that input B is a variable input. The counterparts to equations **5b** and **6** no longer apply since n approaches infinity. The supply price of a variable input is completely determined by the average and marginal costs of production in each period; the demand function determines only the equilibrium quantity of the input. The counterpart to equation **6** thus becomes

$$P_b = \bar{P}_b + w,$$

where w is some random disturbance applicable to the future period.

27. It is possible, in one case, to derive a rising marginal cost curve that includes no element of economic rents. A discriminating monopsonist could, in principle, eliminate all rents by paying the minimum supply price to each additional unit of the factor. We are indebted to W. F. Sharpe for pointing out this possible exception.

Vertical integration into the production of a variable input cannot provide a hedge against uncertainties in future input prices. Each producer of a variable input, including the integrated firm, finds that the equilibrium market price in each period is just equal to the marginal and average costs of production. Uncertainty about future input prices simply reflects the uncertainty in future marginal costs of production. A vertically integrated firm substitutes an uncertain future marginal cost of producing the input for an equally uncertain future input price. Hence, integration into the production of a variable input is neutral with respect to the variability of unit profits, $\sigma_y{}^2$.

An altogether different situation is posed by a capital input. In a pure case, the capital input might represent the services of a durable good. Suppose further that the short run supply curve of a pure capital input, say input A, is completely inelastic in any given period. A zero elasticity of supply implies that $n = 0$, and equation **5b** degenerates to

$$A^s = m+v.$$

When the forward contract is negotiated in the initial period, the position of the vertical short run supply in some future period may be regarded as a stochastic variable; hence, we may continue to include the random variable, v, in the supply equation. The equilibrium market price of a pure capital input, P_a, is a pure economic rent since the supply in each period is fixed. The economic rent or price, P_a, that accrues to the owner of input A at some future date may still be a random variable due to unpredictable shifts in demand (described by u), and random shifts in the future short run supply of A (indicated by v). If the underlying market demand and supply functions are described by equations **5a** and **5b**, we have

$$P_a = \left(\frac{M-m}{N} \right) + \left(\frac{1}{N} \right) (u-v).$$

The economic rent, P_a, applies to a flow of services that is generated by one unit of a durable capital good. Since P_a is determined by current market forces, it is a random variable. The present value of anticipated rents that would be earned by one unit of the capital good is also a random variable. If the probability of P_a implied by equation **6** is stable over time, the expected present value of one unit of the capital good is given by

$$\bar{R} = \left(\frac{\bar{P}_a}{r} \right) [1-(1+r)^{-T}], \qquad \text{8}$$

where r is the rate of interest per unit time period, and T denotes the life of the durable capital good. Let us suppose that in equilibrium the expected present value, $\bar{R}$, is equated to the initial cost of producing a unit of the capital good, C_k. Hence, the equilibrium condition may be written

$$C_k = \left(\frac{\bar{P}_a}{r}\right)[1-(1+r)^{-T}]. \qquad 9$$

In the context of our analysis, vertical integration into the production of a capital input is equivalent to the purchase of the durable capital good – the source of the services called input A. The vertically integrated firm has, in a sense, extended its productive activities to two markets: the market for product X and the market for input A. Since the firm can always sell input A to outside buyers, the equilibrium market price in each period, P_a, is obviously the appropriate internal ration price. The initial cost, C_k, can be transformed to a flow concept of cost corresponding to the amortization of C_k per unit time period. If the firm behaves in the same way as other owners of this capital good, we can assume that equation 9 applies. The amortization per unit time period becomes

$$\frac{rC_k}{[1-(1+r)^{-T}]}.$$

Where maintenance costs and salvage values are ignored and where the equipment has a fixed life, the quantity $\frac{rC_k}{[1-(1+r)^{-T}]}$ can be considered the current cost of the capital input. It follows then that vertical integration is neutral with respect to the expected unit profit, $\bar{y}$, from the forward sale of product X.

In a sense, the vertically integrated firm produces and then sells input A to itself. In any given period, the unit profit from this activity, y_a, is the difference between the market price, P_a, and the amortization of the initial cost of the capital good.

$$y_a = P_a - \left[\frac{rC_k}{1-(1+r)^{-T}}\right] \qquad 10$$

If the equilibrium condition, equation 9 holds, the term in brackets is simply the expected input price, $\bar{P}_a$. The expected profit from the subsidiary activity, $E[y_a]$, therefore is zero.

For a vertically integrated firm, the unit profit on the forward contract, denoted by y^*, combines the profits (or losses) from both activities.

$$y^* = y + y_a = [P - P_a - P_b] + \left[P_a - \frac{rC_k}{1-(1+r)^{-T}}\right] \qquad 11$$

or

$$y^* = P - \frac{rC_k}{1-(1+r)^{-T}} - P_b.$$

By recalling equation 9, y^* simplifies to

$$y^* = y + y_a = P - \bar{P}_a - P_b$$

where $\bar{P}_a$ is the amortization of C_k. The variance of y^* is given by

$$\sigma y^{*2} = E[y^* - \bar{y}]^2 = \sigma_b^2. \qquad\qquad 12$$

Through vertical integration of a capital input, an uncertain input price, P_a, is replaced by a fixed amortization of the durable capital good, $\bar{P}_a$. The variance of y^* is then entirely attributable to σ_b^2, the variance in the future price of the variable input, P_b. Notice that this result applies whether or not the equilibrium condition, equation 9, holds.

Although vertical integration is neutral with respect to the expected profit on the forward contract (i.e. $E[y] = E[y^*]$), it may reduce the variance in profits if σ_y^{*2} is less than σ_y^2. From equations 4 and 12 we may state the necessary and sufficient condition for a reduction in the variance of profits due to vertical integration as

$$\sigma_b^2 < \sigma_a^2 + \sigma_b^2 + 2\sigma_{ab}. \qquad\qquad 13$$

This inequality can be rewritten.

$$-\tfrac{1}{2} < \frac{\sigma_{ab}}{\sigma_a^2}. \qquad\qquad 14$$

To interpret this inequality, consider the regression of P_b on P_a, that is, the regression of the variable input's price on the capital input's price.

$$(P_b - \bar{P}_b) = \lambda(P_a - \bar{P}_a).$$

The least squares estimate for λ is simply $\left(\dfrac{\sigma_{ab}}{\sigma_a^2}\right)$ or the right-hand side of inequality 14.[28] The inequality is obviously satisfied if the two future prices, P_a and P_b, are positively correlated. A sufficient condition to insure the inequality is that the ratio of variances $\left(\dfrac{\sigma_b^2}{\sigma_a^2}\right)$ is less than one-fourth. This last condition is not wholly unreasonable. A capital input is more likely to exhibit a wider variance in price than a variable input. Hence, vertical integration of a capital input is likely to reduce the variance of unit profits.

[28] The covariance between input prices can be expressed as

$$\sigma_{ab} = r_{ab}\sigma_a\sigma_b.$$

Hence, the least squares estimate for λ reduces to

$$\lambda = r_{ab}\left(\frac{\sigma_b}{\sigma_a}\right).$$

Since $-1 < r_{ab} < +1$, it follows that $-\tfrac{1}{2} < \lambda$ if $\left(\dfrac{\sigma_b}{\sigma_a}\right) < \tfrac{1}{2}$.

In a sense, vertical integration provides a hedge against unpredictable fluctuations in the price of a capital input. A vertically integrated firm finds that a windfall in one activity is just offset by an equal loss in the other activity. Suppose, for example, that in the future period P_a happens to exceed the expected price, $\bar{P}_a$. In this event, the unit cost of producing X exceeds the expected cost. Consequently, the realized profit on the forward contract, y, will be below the expected profit, $\bar{y}$. If, however, the firm is vertically integrated, the firm in its role as an owner of input A realizes a profit in the sale to itself of input A; specifically, the profit is $y_a = P_a - \bar{P}_a$. Vertical integration can, therefore, provide a hedge by offsetting a loss on the forward sale of product X by an equal profit in the sale to itself of input A.

Up to now, the analysis has dealt with the two extremes – a variable input B with an infinitely elastic supply curve and a pure capital input A with a vertical short run supply curve. Integration of a variable input cannot reduce the variance in aggregate profits since changes in P_b reflect shifts in the supply curve for B due to changes in the prices of the underlying factors. The remaining intermediate case is one in which the supply curve for an input, say input q, has a positive slope. In this case, the production function for q requires some factor of production that earns an economic rent. It is possible, moreover, to determine the proportion of the market price, P_q, that is attributable to this economic rent. If the variance in future price, σ_q^2, is due primarily to random fluctuations in demand, P_q will be positively correlated with the proportion of P_q due to economic rents;[29] that is, a rise in P_q means an increase in the rents earned by the underlying factors of production. Under these circumstances, vertical

---

29. Let Q denote the equilibrium quantity of input q. The total revenue received by the sellers of q is simply QP_q. If we integrate the supply curve from 0 to Q, we obtain the total variable cost of producing Q. The ratio of total variable cost to total revenue is then the proportion of the market price attributable to factors that earn *no* economic rents; the remainder can be interpreted as the share due to rents. To illustrate, consider a linear supply curve,

$$P_q = a + \beta q.$$

The total variable cost, TVC, is

$$TVC = \int_0^Q (a + \beta q)dq = aQ + \frac{\beta Q^2}{2}$$

The total revenue, TR, is given by

$$TR = QP_q = aQ + \beta Q^2.$$

The proportion of the market price attributable to rents is defined as

$$1 - \frac{TVC}{TR} = \frac{\beta Q^2}{2[aQ + \beta Q^2]}.$$

integration of the intermediate capital input q tends to reduce the variance in aggregate profits in a fashion analogous to that examined for the case of a pure capital input.

To sum up, the analysis begins with a situation in which the firm sells its product on forward contracts so that total revenues are known in advance. The profit on each sale is, however, a random variable because future production costs are uncertain. It is also assumed that the firm wishes to minimize the variance of profits. A futures market (or forward contracts) for inputs offers one way in which the firm could hedge against uncertainties (fluctuations) in future input prices. Since these institutional arrangements are quite infrequent in most input markets, the firm must resort to alternative ways of achieving the same end. We have argued that vertical integration can serve as a substitute for a futures market so long as the pertinent input represents a capital input. A capital input was defined as one whose price during any period contains an element of economic rent. Through outright ownership, an uncertain future input price is replaced by a known input cost representing the amortization of the initial purchase price for some durable capital goods.

In our model, the gain from vertical integration is equivalent to a reduction in the variance of profits; integration is neutral with respect to the expected profit. The gains from integrating the production of any single input will be greater (meaning smaller variances in profits) if the following conditions prevail:

1. The price of the input during any period contains a large element of economic rent.
2. The variance in the future price of the input is large. Moreover, for any given relative variance, the higher the input's share of the total cost, the larger the absolute variance of future years.[30]

To the best of our knowledge, the available theories of vertical integration assume some element of imperfect competition. This type of theory was exemplified in our discussion when proprietary trucking was viewed as a reaction of noncompetitive freight rates. In this appendix, however, our theory is intended to explain the phenomenon of vertical integration in situations where both product and factor markets are competitively organized. Our model is predicated on very special assumptions which may

30. The relative variance can be described by the coefficient of variation – the ratio of the standard deviation, σ_a, to the expected price, $\bar{P}_a$. If the coefficient of variation is the same for all inputs, then the absolute variance, σ_a^2, will be proportional to the square of the expected price, $\bar{P}_a^2$. Under our assumption of fixed technological coefficients, the share of total costs attributable to input A is given by $[\bar{P}_a/(\bar{P}_a+\bar{P}_b)]$. Put in another way, if input A comprises a large share of total costs, any given relative variance in P_a will have a greater impact on the variance of total costs.

limit its application to actual situations. The two critical assumptions include a behavioral assumption (that firms wish to minimize the variance of profits) and an institutional assumption (that firms sell products on forward contracts). If product markets are *not* competitively organized, then the latter assumption could be replaced by an assumption about relative price variability. Specifically, it could be assumed that product prices fluctuate less than input prices and our analysis still applies. In the absence of a better theory, we are prepared to accept our explanation for vertical integration in situations approximating perfect competition.

References

BAUMOL, W. J. *et al.* (1962), 'The role of costs in the minimum pacing of railroad services', *J. Bus.*, vol. 35, pp. 357–66.

BURSTEIN, M. L. (1961), 'The measurement of quality changes in consumers' durables', *Manchester School*, vol. 29, pp. 267–79.

Dun's Review and Modern Industry (1962), Dun and Bradstreet Publications Corp, June.

FRIEDMAN, M. (1953), *Essays in Positive Economics*, University of Chicago Press.

GRILICHES, Z. (1961), 'Hedonic price indexes for automobiles: an econometric analysis of quality change', *Government Price Statistics*, *Hearings*, staff paper no. 3, US Government Printing Office.

MEYER, J. R. *et al* (1959), *The Economics of Competition in the Transportation Industries* Harvard University Press.

NEALE, A. D. (1960), *The Antitrust Laws of the United States of America*, Cambridge University Press.

OI, W. Y., and HURTER, A. P., Jr (1965), *Economics of Private Truck Transportation*, William C. Brown Co.

PIGOU, A. C. (1960), *The Economics of Welfare*, 4th edn, Macmillan.

ROBBINS, L. (1952), *An Essay on the Nature and Significance of Economic Science*, Macmillan.

US CONGRESS (1961), *Government Price Statistics*, *Hearings*, 24 January , US Government Printing Office.

WILLIAMS, E. W., Jr (1958), *The Regulation of Rail-Motor Rate Competition*, Harper & Row.

17 Robert H. Bork

Vertical Integration and Monopoly

Part II (pp. 194–201) of Robert H. Bork, 'Vertical integration and the Sherman Act: the legal history of an economic misconception', *University of Chicago Law Review*, vol. 22, 1954, pp. 157–201.

The utility of the vertical-integration concept for antitrust law seems a much easier subject than is the law that has been built around that concept. Yet there is hardly more agreement about the one than the other. It is the thesis here that the concept is almost entirely lacking in significance as an analytical tool for differentiating between competition and monopoly, and that, with one exception, its only proper use is as a term descriptive of corporate structure.

If it is accepted that the purpose of the antitrust law is the preservation of a competitive economy, an evaluation of the vertical-integration concept must run largely in terms of its value as a tool of economic analysis. The economics of the subject have been rather fully discussed by others,[1] so only a summary need be given here.

Monopoly power is usually defined as the ability to alter the market price for a product or service.[2] A firm effects the alteration of market price through changes in its own output that significantly change the total output of the industry. Thus monopoly power depends upon the percentage of the market occupied by the firm, and the ease of entry into that market. Vertical integration does not increase the percentage of the market controlled by a firm. It should be equally apparent that such integration does not impede entry into a market. Even though almost all of the myths concerning the ways in which vertical integration confers market power upon a firm, or facilitates the exploitation of such power, have been discredited, the theory that vertical integration prolongs monopoly by imposing greater capital requirements upon potential entrants is still confidently advanced in the literature (see *Yale Law Journal*, 1951, pp. 294 and 301–7; Kahn, 1953, pp. 28 and 43) as though it, too, had not been badly shaken. Of course, vertical integration could affect entry only if two levels or stages of

1. *University of Chicago Law Review* (1952, pp. 583, 611–16) contains much of the analysis adopted here. See also Adelman (1949); Hale (1949).

2. Courts often speak of monopoly as the power to exclude competition, actual or potential. Such exclusion, however, can be accomplished only through the mechanism of price changes (assuming the absence of 'natural' monopolies, patents, etc.); and so the two definitions come to much the same thing.

operation were monopolized by the integrated firm or cartel, so that entrants would have to come in on both levels at once. This would indeed require greater capital than would entrance upon one level. If there are greater-than-competitive profits being made in the industry, however, there seems no reason why the increased capital necessary for entry would not be forthcoming, unless there are impediments in the capital market that prevent capital from flowing to areas where it can most profitably be employed. Until such impediments have been shown to exist, the fact that increased capital is required for vertical integration must be assumed to have no adverse effect upon entry into monopolized markets. Therefore, since vertical integration does not increase the percentage of a market supplied by a firm and cannot be shown to impede entry into that market, such integration can be said to add nothing to monopoly power.

Nor does vertical integration affect a firm's pricing policy. If, for example, a firm operates at both the manufacturing and retail levels, it maximizes over-all profit by setting the output at each level as though the levels were independent. Where both levels are competitive, the firm maximizes by equating marginal cost and price at each level; each level makes the competitive return. Where the firm has a monopoly at the manufacturing level but is competitive in retailing, it will, of course, exact a monopoly profit at the first level. And the manufacturing level will sell to the retail level at the same price as it sells to outside retailers.[3] If the integrated firm has monopolies at both the manufacturing and retail levels, however, the levels will not maximize independently. It has already been explained that vertically integrated monopolies can take but one monopoly profit.[4] Therefore, if the manufacturing level charged a monopoly price,

3. The integrated firm would have no incentive to price its manufactured product lower to its own retailers than to outsiders. At best, if the marginal costs of retailing were constant, the result would be the same total profit as if the owned retailers had been charged the same as independent retailers. But if, as seems certain in a competitive market, the marginal costs of retailing were rising, the self-deception involved in selling more cheaply to the affiliated retailers would result in an increased output by those retailers, and the integrated firm would be paying more for the service of retailing than it would if it operated at a smaller scale on the retailing level.

4. . . . An interesting sidelight on vertically related monopolies is that it may be better from the consumers' point of view that such monopolies be integrated rather than in separate hands. Where the monopolies are integrated consumers will pay the monopoly price. But where the monopolies are in separate hands the higher monopolist may charge the full monopoly price to the lower who will in turn accept that price as a cost and further restrict output and raise price. The price as between the monopolists may be indeterminate, but the price to consumers will be higher than the single-monopoly price. Of course, the monopolists may negotiate and lower the price to consumers to the single-monopoly price in order to maximize the total profit to be split between themselves. Therefore, if both monopolies are legal, because of patent rights for example, vertical integration or collusion is to be desired rather than attacked. This analysis has interesting results for theories of countervailing power.

the retail level would not act independently and further restrict output, but would attempt to sell all of the manufacturing level's output at a competitive margin.

The above analysis supports the thesis that it is always horizontal market power, and not integration into other levels, which is important. This thesis has recently been attacked with the argument that, since the horizontal monopoly power may be impregnable (because it arises from a patent, natural monopoly in a basic supply, etc.), there may be no alternative but to dissolve the vertical integration which transmits the monopoly power from one level to another.[5] The answer to this argument is clear from what has gone before. Suppose a monopolist at one level does not integrate vertically. He will charge the monopoly price to his customers, and that toll will be passed on to the ultimate consumers. What has already been said shows that the gaining of a second monopoly vertically related to the first would not alter price, output, or the allocation of productive resources on the second level monopolized. Therefore, dissolving the vertical integration accomplishes precisely nothing.[6]

5. Kahn (1953, pp. 28 and 45). The author also states that 'integration that links areas in which competition is already seriously defective to other areas accomplishes by financial consolidation something very much like what is accomplished by the tie-ins prohibited by section 3 of the Clayton Act.' (p. 44). Insofar as this statement refers to vertical integration it is not completely accurate. A tie-in seems to be aimed at one of two things (1) price discrimination; (2) gaining a monopoly of a product that is complementary to another product of which a monopoly is already held. The tie-in may be used to accomplish price discrimination when the tied-in product is employed as a way of counting, and hence of charging for, the amount of use given the tying product. Thus, those who have the most use for a salt machine, for example, will pay the most for it through their purchase of salt tablets. (This explanation of the purpose of some tie-ins was suggested by Professor Director of the University of Chicago Law School.) In this respect a tie-in may be similar to some vertical integration, for the latter may occasionally be employed to effect a price discrimination. See text above. The use of a tie-in to gain a monopoly complementary to that already possessed is not, however, like vertical integration. The complementary integration of monopolies and their vertical integration have far different results; they should be kept analytically distinct. [The idea of a tie-in as a device for obtaining complementary monopolies is taken from Bowman and McGee (unpublished paper).] The writer has no idea which of these uses of the tie-in device is the more common.

6. This reasoning is applicable to proposals to increase competition in the oil industry by divesting major oil companies of their pipe lines. See Rostow (1948); Rostow and Sachs (1952, p. 856). The monopoly of the pipe-line companies would in no way be reduced by their separation from crude producing and refining facilities. Whatever the effect on nonintegrated crude producers, the price in final markets would be unchanged. Furthermore it is unlikely that such dissolution would affect nonintegrated firms at all. If the long-term costs of crude production are a function of scale, it would entail a loss for an integrated firm with a pipe-line monopoly to use that monopoly to gain control of crude production. If these costs are constant, it makes no difference to the pipe-line monopolist, or to the public, whether or not the monopoly is extended to crude. Neither

price discrimination

There is, however, one advantage a monopolist might not otherwise enjoy which he may obtain by vertical integration: the ability to discriminate in price between different classes of customers. A monopolist may have two classes of customers making different products, one of which is willing to pay more than the other, and yet, because of reselling between the classes, be unable to take advantage of the situation by discrimination. If, however, the monopolist should integrate with one of the classes, leakage would stop and discrimination become possible (see *University of Chicago Law Review*, 1952, p. 583, 613, note 184). It is not at all clear that this result is socially undesirable. One result of the discrimination is an increased profit for the monopolist. But the objection to monopoly is not that some people make too much money. It is that monopoly leads to a misallocation of society's resources through a restriction of output. In many cases, when a monopolist price-discriminates he tends to increase his output, and the resultant output is more like that dictated by competition than if he had not discriminated. In some cases this result may not occur, but on balance it seems more likely (see Samuelson, 1947). Therefore, if the horizontal monopoly is legal, there should be no objection to price discrimination, and hence none to vertical integration employed to effect discrimination. The real problem, once more, is horizontal, not vertical.

This brief statement makes clear the position from which the use of the vertical-integration concept is criticized. With this analysis in mind we turn to an examination of some of the more common judicial notions concerning vertical integration. (The italicized statements are abstracted from the cases.)

Vertical integration may be used to gain a monopoly at one level. This notion appears in the cases but the mechanism by which it operates is rarely mentioned. There is no such mechanism unless a monopoly at another level is already held. In that case the important issue is the first monopoly, not the vertical integration. In any event, the second monopoly adds no power the first did not confer.

Vertical integration makes possible, or lends itself to, the price 'squeeze' by which a monopolist at one level drives out competitors at another. The 'squeeze' does not automatically result from any internal efficiencies of integration, for the competitive unit does not maximize profit by reflecting

---

does it make any sense to say that the integrated firm practices price discrimination because its charge to itself is not a real charge whereas the charge to nonintegrated shippers is a real charge. That merely states that the pipe-line monopoly is charging a monopoly rate. The price discrimination has no effect that the presence of horizontal monopoly does not. That is, the firm would not think that its crude production units had lower shipping costs than competitive units and therefore increase output. That would result in an improper scale of operation. See the analysis in note 3 above.

cost savings in its selling price but by selling at the price established by its competitors.[7] Nor does vertical integration confer any unique ability to 'squeeze' as a monopolizing technique. A 'squeeze' is nothing more than a price-cutting campaign at one level. A nonintegrated firm can just as easily wage this sort of warfare by selling its goods at the cost of the raw materials as can the second level of a vertically integrated firm. The use of the term 'squeeze' serves only to make the practice seem peculiar to vertical integration and thus lend an undeserved sinister coloration to that form of organization.

The vertically integrated firm can monopolize one level by cutting prices there because it can offset its losses by advancing prices at another level. The theory of recoupment has been exploded many times. If both levels are competitive, prices can be advanced at neither; if either level is monopolistic, prices would already have been advanced there to make the maximum profit. In either case, recoupment of losses incurred in price-cutting is impossible. Leaving out the notion of recoupment, it is possible to say that predation in one market may be continued longer if money is being

7. *University of Chicago Law Review*, (1952, p. 583, 614 note 185), attempts an explanation of some 'squeezes' as follows. 'Suppose P is the sole producer of raw material X and has a subsidiary S which, together with firms T and U, has monopoly control of the manufacturing of the products into which X is manufactured. In setting its price to S, T and U, P will equalize marginal revenue with marginal cost and its price will include a monopoly profit for itself. Similarly, when deciding at what price S is to sell, P will want to equalize S's marginal revenue with its marginal cost. But the marginal cost of X as far as P and S are concerned will not be the price set for sales to the entire $S-T-U$ market since P is charging a monopoly price. Therefore, S's marginal cost will be less than that of T and U and S's sale price will be less than that at which T and U would normally expect to sell because of the lower cost figure used by S. Thus P's actions in setting prices as any monopolist normally would will have the effect of "squeezing" T and U even though P is not consciously attempting to drive T and U out of business, but only trying to maximize profits'. This reasoning appears fallacious. Assume first that P is unable for some reason to break down the monopolistic character of the market in which it sells. In this case, regardless of S's cost for X, S is not maximizing profits unless it sells at the price T and U are charging. S must here be viewed, for purposes of pricing policy, as an independent firm, and, as such, it will maximize by acting as a rational oligopolist. Since P cannot break down the oligopoly, it might as well enjoy the fruits of the oligopoly through the participation of S.

However, P would prefer that the $S-T-U$ market were competitive, for then no restriction in output would occur beyond that imposed by P, and P would reap the entire monopoly profit. This consideration is relevant in the case where it is possible to break down the monopolistic character of the market in which P sells. In this situation S would not engage in rational oligopoly behavior, but would increase its output and drive the selling prices of T and U ever lower until the processing of raw material X is competitive. This type of 'squeeze' should not be regarded as predatory.

Thus, in the first case no 'squeeze' will occur; in the second the 'squeeze' is not the unplanned result of P's maximization but a deliberate policy of reducing the profit margins of T and U.

made elsewhere. But this applies to horizontal and diversified, as well as to vertical, integration.

By eliminating profit at one level the vertically integrated firm can undersell competition at the next. This myth has been as thoroughly discredited as recoupment. The firm can do this only if it is willing to forgo the return on part of its invested capital. Any firm, integrated or not, may do the same thing.

A variation of the above, which appears in the District Court *A & P* opinion, is particularly interesting. *Profit is eliminated at the retail level, and, consequently, increased volume is achieved. The increased volume raises the profits of the manufacturing level. The firm, therefore, not only undersells its competitors at the retail level, but it sacrifices no profits in doing so.* This argument must assume that the manufacturing level had been operating at an inefficient scale so that the increase in volume made up for the loss of retail profits. Of course the firm could have made more money by allowing its manufacturing units to sell to outsiders, thus obtaining increased volume at that level without sacrificing any of its retail profits. When this is seen it becomes apparent that the mechanism described by the court is merely the sacrifice of profit in order to cut prices. Vertical integration is not relevant.

Money earned at one level gives a vertically integrated firm an advantage over its nonintegrated competitors at another level. This is especially true where the money is paid by the nonintegrated competitors. The advantage is said to be derived from the fact that the money paid in raises the costs of the competitors and lowers the costs of the integrated company. Of course, money received can never lower costs. The competitors' costs are not raised since they would have to pay for essential goods or services at that level in any event. Since output is determined by marginal cost and price (or marginal revenue where there is monopoly power), and since neither is altered by the situation described, the vertically integrated firm derives no competitive advantage.

One level of a vertically integrated firm may harm another of its own levels by charging it too high prices. The higher-than-market price to the second level would cause that level to decrease its output. So long as the market is competitive (or regulated) no one is damaged by this except the integrated firm which finds itself failing to maximize profits. If the market in which the second level sells is monopolistic, a restriction of output would occur anyway. The problem is then the monopoly and not the bookkeeping transactions between the two levels.

The discussion so far has shown that vertical integration is not a useful tool for economic analysis. Such integration confers no ability to alter market price, does not impede entry, and adds nothing unique to the ability to employ predatory tactics. On the contrary, vertical integration may lead to entirely beneficial results by enabling the firm so organized to bypass a monopoly at one level, or by enabling the achievement of internal efficiencies.

But it may still be urged that the concept is a useful one for the antitrust law because that law is not, and should not be, exclusively concerned with economic analysis. It has been argued that the antitrust law has always been concerned with 'unnatural' methods of growth. The concept of vertical integration by acquisition may be one way of talking about an 'unnatural' reaching-out for 'power'. Vertical acquisition creates 'size', and 'size' is said to be a sign of 'power'. This 'size' is apparently not relative size (percentage of market control), for vertical integration does not affect that. The 'size' referred to in this argument seems to be absolute size. If that is true, then the power it signifies must be something other than the power to affect price. Perhaps it is the sort of power that gains political favors. Power in this sense is an extremely amorphous concept, but it may nevertheless be something with which society should be concerned. However that may be, the law of vertical integration has not developed in that direction. The law's tests as to the legality of vertical integration are couched, however incorrectly, in economic terms, in terms of market power. Nor does the concept of vertical integration provide an appropriate way of talking about the 'power' created by 'size'. In the first place, many vertically integrated firms are of smaller absolute size than many firms not so integrated. In the second place, vertical integration creates no more absolute size than does any other form of integration, horizontal, diversified, or complementary. It has not been suggested that illegality should attach to the multiproduct firm with 10 per cent of three separate markets, even though it has great absolute size and, presumably, whatever 'power' goes with it.

A comparison of the law and the economics of vertical integration makes it clear that the two bear little resemblance. If the law in this area is to be concerned with the kind of competition with which economists are familiar, the concept of vertical integration will have to be abandoned as an analytical tool. The idea of horizontal integration is sufficient to the tasks of the Sherman Act, and presents, in the guise of market definition, problems enough for judicial ingenuity.

References

ADELMAN, M. A. (1949), 'Integration and antitrust policy', *Harvard law Rev.*, vol. 63.
BOWMAN, W., and McGEE, J. (unpublished paper), 'Product complementarity and the law of tie-in sales'.
HALE, G. E. (1949), 'Vertical integration; impact of the antitrust laws upon combinations of successive stages of production and distribution', *Columbia law Rev.*, vol. 49.

KAHN, A. E. (1953), 'Standards for antitrust policy', *Harvard law Rev.*, vol. 67.

ROSTOW, E. V. (1948), *A National Policy for the Oil Industry*, Yale University Press.

ROSTOW, E. V., and SACHS, A. S. (1952), 'Entry into the oil refining business: vertical integration re-examined', *Yale law J.*, vol. 61.

SAMUELSON, P. A. (1947), *Foundations of Economic Analysis*, Harvard University Press.

University of Chicago law Rev. (1952), 'Comment, vertical forestalling under the antitrust laws', vol. 19.

Yale law J. (1951), 'Comment, vertical integration in aluminium; a bar to "effective competition"', vol. 60.

18 Fritz Machlup and Martha Taber

Bilateral Monopoly and Vertical Integration

Fritz Machlup and Martha Taber, 'Bilateral monopoly, successive monopoly and vertical integration', *Economica*, vol. 27, 1960, pp. 101–19.

What are the effects of vertical integration upon output and prices? If an industry has been 'vertically fragmented', that is, if it has consisted of a number of separate firms each operating in only one of the successive stages of production, and if such firms are now combined by 'vertical merger', should one expect that, as a result of the integration, the total physical output of the industry will be increased and the price of the ultimate product reduced?

The affirmative answer to this question has been supported by many economists for a long time; but there have been others who denied the contention and again others who argued the opposite. The different answers were, of course, based on different sets of assumptions. The two major points of emphasis have been cost and market position. Some writers have believed that vertical integration would do little to alter market positions but might substantially alter *costs*. There is the possibility of economies of vertical integration, especially where technology is changing and productive establishments, hitherto spatially separated, are brought together; but there is also the possibility of diseconomies through a loss of specialization. Other writers have believed that vertical integration would do little to alter costs but might substantially alter *market positions*. There is the possibility that monopolistic positions are extended, strengthened or consolidated by the merger; but there is also the possibility that existing monopolistic restrictions are relaxed and monopoly prices reduced as a result of the merger.[1]

In this article we shall not concern ourselves with technology and production cost, but only with changing market structure and pricing practices.

---

1. For a discussion placing some emphasis on possible economies of vertical integration, see Adelman (1949, pp. 28 ff.). For a skeptical view on such economies, see Stigler (1951, pp. 189–90). On the probability of increased monopolistic power, see Edwards (1953, pp. 404–10). On the probability of a reduced degree of monopoly, see Spengler (1950, p. 347).

Vertical fragmentation and integration contrasted

The view that vertical combination or integration would most probably relax output restrictions and reduce prices to consumers has had a long history. In the fabric of this thought there are three main strands with subtle entanglements between them. They have in common the central conclusion that the existence of separate firms at different stages of an industry that contains monopoly elements may account for less-than-monopoly output and higher-than-monopoly prices.

1. In a vertically fragmented industry there may be monopolistic market positions in some of the stages of production. Possibly firms in these stages are few, perhaps as a consequence of previous horizontal merger; or geographic market structure has given each of the firms a partial monopoly; or practices have grown up that have eliminated vigorous competition. If such monopolistic conditions exist in two or more successive stages of the industry, problems of bilateral monopoly may arise. It has long been contended that, in bilateral monopoly, independent attempts by the monopolists to maximize their profits will lead to less production and higher prices than would result from a policy of joint profit maximization. Hence vertical integration, securing joint profit maximization in the integrated stages, would yield benefits to the consumers (and, on the usual assumption, bring the economy closer to the 'Pareto optimum').

2. Where no such conditions of bilateral monopoly have developed in a vertically fragmented industry, it is still very likely that monopolistic elements are prevalent in some of the successive stages. It is one of the characteristics of monopolistic pricing that the seller takes account of the elasticity of demand for his output. A monopolist's marginal revenue is lower than his selling price. The demand curve facing a seller at one stage of production (call him C) is derived from the demand curves facing the fabricators one stage later in the process (call them Ds). The sum of the marginal revenue-product curves of the D firms becomes the average revenue curve for C, whose marginal revenue curve will therefore be marginal to the aggregate marginal revenue-product curve of the Ds. The demand and marginal revenue curves which enter into C's calculations will, as a rule, be less elastic at equal quantities than those considered by the Ds. If C sets discriminatory prices for his intermediate product in an independent attempt to maximize his profits, the reduced elasticities of demand at given quantities will cause him to set higher prices and produce smaller output than would be the case if he combined with the D firms. An analogous argument holds for a monopsonistic buyer in any of the successive stages. Vertical integration between stages previously in the hands of independent successive monopolists or monopsonists would

avoid the cumulative downgrading of elasticities and would consequently secure larger outputs and lower prices to consumers.

3. When the conduct of firms, and especially their pricing practice, is based on the full-cost principle, vertical fragmentation of an industry may lead to a piling up of successive mark-ups. If each firm follows the practice of adding a fixed profit margin to its 'full cost', and if this full cost includes the profit margin of its suppliers, there must result a mark-up of mark-ups and an 'exaggerated' elevation of prices. Vertical integration would do away with intermediate mark-ups and would therefore, with given percentage mark-ups, reduce the ultimate prices to consumers; output would accordingly be increased.

These three strands of thought are often interwoven. Implicit in the case of bilateral monopoly are the problems of reduced elasticities of derived curves; and the cumulation of mark-ups will not exist unless the structure of the market is conducive to such pricing. But an analytical separation is possible and desirable, and the history of the analysis presents little difficulties on this score.

Bilateral monopoly: a review of the theories

The development of the theory of bilateral monopoly includes some of the greatest names in economics – which makes the temptation of a historical exposition irresistible.[2] A history of this theory has to start with two writers neither of whom used the words or had a clear notion of 'bilateral monopoly'. One was Augustin Cournot, who in 1838 analysed the case of two monopolists producing different commodities 'jointly consumed in the production of a composite commodity' (1907, p. 99); the other was Carl Menger, who in 1871 discussed the problem of 'isolated exchange' or barter between two individuals (pp. 175–81).

Cournot had no model of transactions between a sole seller and a sole buyer. But the case of complementary monopolists which he examined – in mathematical terms – has been generally considered analogous to the case of bilateral monopoly. Goods and services needed in successive stages of production are, of course, complementary; and this has led economists to assume, usually without discussion, that there is no significant difference between the complementary and the bilateral relationships. Marshall for example, mentions Cournot's illustration of the monopolists supplying the copper and zinc needed to make brass, and adds his own illustration of spinners and weavers supplying complementary services in the production

2. The historical survey which follows is regrettably incomplete because of its omission, for linguistic reasons of significant contributions in Italian literature, especially by Amoroso (1909, 1911, 1921), Fanno (1926), and Nardi (1934).

of cloth, without examining whether or not the more obviously vertical arrangement in his case makes any essential difference (1907, p. 495). Zeuthen was among the few economists who presented formal demonstration of the equivalence of the two cases. Indeed, he used the term 'bilateral monopoly' for both.[3]

A diagrammatic scheme of the two cases may be helpful:

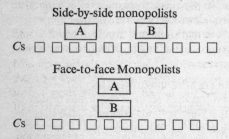

Now we can easily see a few differences in the two market structures: the side-by-side monopolists sell to a large group of competing buyers; on the other hand, one of the face-to-face monopolists sells to a monopsonist who is also a monopolist (or what has been called a monemporist (Nichol, 1943, p. 83; Weintraub, 1949, p. 260)). The most important difference, however, is in the extent to which the two monopolists will communicate with each other. The face-to-face monopolists necessarily deal with each other, negotiate and conclude contracts, settle prices and quantities. The side-by-side monopolists need not have any direct contacts with each other, and their 'getting together', if it occurs at all, will be fortuitous or deliberate rather than inevitable. These highly significant differences have recently received increasing attention.[4]

Cournot's particular assumptions permitted a determinate solution for both prices and quantities. Either of the complementary monopolists

3. 'The bilateral monopoly ... may concern two entrepreneurs supplying raw materials or services who are both sellers to a third, non-monopolistic party (the case of joint demand). It may, on the other hand, concern two monopolistic enterprises standing face to face as buyer and seller. In the main, however, the determination of price is the same in the two cases ...'. (Zeuthen, 1930, p. 89). See also (1930, p. 64), and (1933, pp. 1657 and 1661).

4. Another variant is the so-called 'mediate bilateral monopoly', where a monopolist sells to a mass of competitive buyers who are also competitive sellers to a monopsonistic buyer. Thus, the monopolist and the monopsonist face each other over a wall of competitive firms in the intermediate stage. They have no regular business dealings with each other, but are likely to entertain mutually conflicting conjectures and objectives. For a discussion see Stackelberg (1934, pp. 33, 41–2). Incidentally, Stackelberg finds that 'the position of this market relation is ... analogous to the case of complementary goods' (p. 42).

would take note of the price charged by the other, would assume that his own actions would not affect the other's price, and would then set his price in an attempt to maximize his own profit. His counterpart might now, however, find his own price inappropriate and, again assuming that his own action would not affect the other's price, would adjust his own price with a view to his own profit. A series of such moves would lead to a set of prices which would not induce either of the two complementary monopolists to make further changes. A determinate equilibrium is reached.[5]

Cournot's equilibrium quantity would be smaller than that which would maximize the joint profits of the two parties; and the sum of the two prices (and the price of the final product) would be higher than the price charged by a combined monopoly. The principle applies also when there are more than two complementary monopolists. Indeed, 'the more there are of articles thus related, the higher the price determined by the division of monopolies will be, than that which would result from the fusion or association of the monopolists' (1907, pp. 103–4). Their fusion or integration, consequently, would benefit the consumer.

Menger discussed 'isolated exchange' between two individuals trading their goods, each attempting to maximize 'subjective values'. Menger found that the 'price' would be indeterminate within certain limits, though he added that 'as a rule' the price would be equally far from the possible extremes if the two parties were equally strong and skilful bargainers (1871, pp. 178–9). His discussion was quite primitive, without the use of either calculus or geometry and without any mention of 'bilateral monopoly'.[6] But he proceeded immediately to the case in which one individual as the sole possessor of a good was trading it against another good possessed by several competing individuals; and he did speak of monopoly in this case (1871, pp. 181–6). The frame of reference was pure barter;

5. Readers who know Cournot's theory of duopoly may be struck by the difference in assumptions. In the case of duopolists – competing 'monopolists' – Cournot assumed that each in turn would adjust the *quantity* of his output, believing that his counterpart would not alter his quantity. In the case of complementary monopolists, Cournot assumed that each in turn would adjust the *price* of his product, believing that his counterpart would continue to sell at his former price. Edgeworth (1929, p. 122), explains this apparent contradiction, observing that Cournot's assumptions follow logically from the concepts of perfect substitutability and perfect complementarity. In a perfect market there can be only one price for perfect substitutes; hence competing monopolists can adjust only quantities. For perfect complements there can be only one quantity (in accordance with fixed coefficients of production); hence complementary monopolists can adjust only the price.

6. 'For bilateral monopoly we have a theoretical prototype, namely, the theory of isolated exchange', said Schumpeter (1954, p. 983), who cited Cesare Bonesana Marchese di Beccaria (1764) as one who anticipated Menger in showing the indeterminateness of the exchange.

production, division of labour, stages of production, money prices and money incomes were all outside Menger's model.[7]

Edgeworth presented a remarkable advance in the analysis of both pure barter and bilateral monopoly. He showed that 'contract without competition is indeterminate' (1881, p. 20); he delineated the range of indeterminateness by deriving 'contract curves' from the utility functions of the bargaining parties (pp. 20–50); and he discussed the place of intervention or 'arbitration' (pp. 51–6). Later (1897), Edgeworth criticized Cournot's theory of complementary monopolies as well as his theory of competing monopolies – now called duopoly – and concluded that there would not exist, as a rule, a determinate and stable equilibrium in such situation (1929, p. 126). He conceded that a stable equilibrium might be reached in bilateral monopoly 'on the extreme supposition that [one of the parties] is perfectly intelligent and foreseeing [while the other] cannot see beyond his nose' (p. 125).

Also for Pareto (1896 and 1909) the problems of isolated exchange and of bilateral monopoly were essentially the same. The solution for bilateral monopoly was indeterminate at least within 'pure economics'. Using 'pure' economic theory, '. . . we arrive at the conclusion that the problem is indeterminate because we do not know what use each of the two would make of his power'. A determinate solution requires additional assumptions 'of a more factual type'. Rejecting the models in which two monopolists alternatively establish their preferred prices, Pareto observed that really 'there is only one monopolist if the second accepts the price fixed by the first' (1896, p. 601).

The first four editions of Marshall's *Principles* made no reference to the problem. In the fifth edition Marshall (1907, p. 493) included a passage which was, in pleasant contrast to the writing of most of his predecessors and successors, set forth in simple English, without the 'aid' of mathematics. He evidently accepted Edgeworth's conclusions that there were no determinate solutions. Turning to Cournot's example of *A*, supplying copper, and *B*, supplying zinc, Marshall reiterated the view that

There would then be no means of determining beforehand what amount of brass would be produced, nor therefore the price at which it could be sold. Each would try to get the better of the other in bargaining; and though the issue of the contest would greatly affect the purchasers, they would not be able to influence it.

Under the conditions supposed, *A* could not count on reaping the whole, nor even any share at all of the benefit, from increased sales, that would be got by lowering the price of copper . . . For, if he reduced his price, *B* might raise the price of zinc; thus causing *A* to lose both on price and on amount sold. Each would . . . be tempted to bluff the other; and consumers might find that less brass

7. Menger, at the time, did not know Cournot's work. See Hayek (1934, p. 396).

was put on the market, and that therefore a higher price could be exacted for it, than if a single monopolist owned the whole supplies both of copper and of zinc; for he might see his way to gaining in the long run by a low price which stimulated consumption. But neither *A* nor *B* could reckon on the effects of his own action, unless the two came together and agreed on a common policy: that is unless they make a partial and perhaps temporary fusion of their monopolies. On this ground and because monopolies are likely to disturb allied industries it may reasonably be urged that the public interest generally requires that complementary monopolies should be held in a single hand (1907, p. 494).

Marshall added other examples of complementary or bilateral monopoly – a spinner and a weaver, a railway and a sea route. He also expressed an important qualification to the inference that fusion would serve the public interest, but with this we shall deal later.

Pigou re-emphasized the point that the results of bilateral monopoly 'without any agreement between the two monopolists' are 'different from those that emerge under a policy of agreements'. Without agreement, 'each monopolist takes account of the probable effect of his action upon the conduct of the other, and follows with a counteracting move every move of his opponents'. A continual chain of alterations of price and output would result. With agreement, however, there will be 'a less fluctuating condition of industry. . . . *Pro tanto* this consideration suggests that a policy of agreements among correlated monopolists is socially advantageous' (1908, p. 206). In his further analysis Pigou confined his attention to the case of bilateral monopoly without agreement or combination. In doing so he was probably influenced by his major interest in the theory of wage bargaining between monopolistic unions and monopolistic employers, where 'integration' is clearly not in the picture and 'combination' is rare (1908, p. 215; see also 1920 and 1905).

Bowley first took brief notice of the problem of bilateral monopoly in relation to bargaining between a worker and an employer. In his model, as in some of its predecessors, the employer fixes a wage rate and lets the labourer adjust the quantity of labour supplied. The process of moves and countermoves that follows will not lead to a determinate result except with 'collusion' between the two monopolists (1924, p. 62).

Wicksell (1925) objected: 'If the manufacturer can set the piece rate, then the worker . . . has no monopoly!' (1927, p. 276). For Wicksell the concept 'monopoly' evidently implied a certain behaviour pattern[8] and, if such a pattern is assumed to prevail, a determinate equilibrium position will be attained, contrary to the conclusions of Edgeworth and Bowley. Wicksell's exposition is enlivened by a picturesque illustration, drawn from

8. Stackelberg criticizes Wicksell for taking a definite behaviour pattern as part of the definition of monopoly (1934, p. 91).

a reference by Babbage (1832, pp. 199–201) to the only existing possessor of the skill of making dolls' eyes who sells to the only manufacturer of dolls (1927, p. 276). The Wicksellian equilibrium of the bilateral monopoly, as that of Cournot, involves injury to the independently acting monopolists as well as to the consumer, because profits as well as output will be lower than if the monopolists combined or merged (1927, p. 271).

Schumpeter (1927 and 1928) held that 'Wicksell was not quite fair to Bowley', but agreed – in contradiction to his own 1908 opinion (1908, p. 270) – that 'there will exist a determinate equilibrium position' if it is possible to accept Wicksell's assumptions: that both parties know the demand curves, that they pursue only their own individual interests but cannot (and do not try to) force the other 'to his knees', and that any deal is final for the whole period (1927, pp. 250–51; 1928, p. 371). In these circumstances 'the barter point between the parties is perfectly determined, and *not* only the range within which there will be barter. . . . Nor can it be held that the assumptions . . . are so very far from reality. They are, if anything, nearer to reality than the assumptions implied in the idea of theoretically perfect competition . . .' (1928, p. 371). Schumpeter maintained his position and restated it in his (posthumous) *History* (1954, pp. 983–5).

Incited by Wicksell's and Schumpeter's comments, Bowley elaborated his theory of bilateral monopoly. Reasoning in terms of a monopolistic supplier of ore who deals with a monopsonistic producer of steel, he presents case 1, in which the 'manufacturer [of steel] can dictate the price of the material, while the producer of the material decides the output'; case 2, in which 'the supplier of the material can dictate its price while the manufacturer decides the output'; and case 3, in which 'the manufacturer and supplier of material combine' (1928, pp. 653–4). Bowley shows that in cases 1 and 2 the party who establishes the price gains by far the largest share of the profit, while the one who adjusts the quantity receives a meagre monopoly profit; and that the profits of the two together will surely fall short of what could be obtained by combination. Not only would cases 1 and 2 yield indeterminate solutions, but they would be socially disadvantageous because of the lower output and higher price that would result.

If, in case 3, the 'manufacturer and supplier of material combine to maximize their joint gain', they will produce the simple-monopoly output, i.e. more than the output produced without collusion. The combined profit might be divided by agreeing on an ore price at the intersection of the 'manufacturer's demand curve and the supplier's offer curve'; but this would not be 'a position of stable equilibrium', because of the superior possibilities, for either party, of independent price dictation (1928, p. 656).

Zeuthen was most explicit in contending that, in any monopolistic market structure, several varieties of practices, procedures and attitudes are possible and will determine the outcome. There might be a determinate price and output,[9] an indeterminate jockeying for position, economic warfare or cooperation and agreement. 'The pure case in which two absolute monopolists are opposed, will in all probability seldom exist for very long without changing into a case of fighting or of cooperation' (1930, p. 71). Combination will be most likely when, as in bilateral monopoly, the two parties have to deal with each other directly. 'The direct negotiations between the parties in this case both as to price and sales' make an agreement the only alternative to complete withdrawal from the market (1930, p. 91). 'The express or tacit vertical agreement or combination will, in contra-distinction to the horizontal one, result in larger sales and lower prices, but in both cases the total profit will be increased' (pp. 69–70).

Schneider followed Wicksell, Schumpeter, and Zeuthen in arguing that a determinate and stable equilibrium can be attained in bilateral monopoly, provided the parties are peaceful profit maximizers rather than contenders for dominance resorting to bluff and economic warfare (1932, p. 72). Schneider differed from earlier writers when he rejected the supposed equivalence of bilateral monopoly with complementary monopoly on the one hand (p. 50), and with isolated exchange on the other (p. 80). He was particularly anxious to show the difference between the case of barter, where no third commodity is involved, and the case of bilateral monopolists, each of whom wants to maximize a third good, namely, money (pp. 78–82, 101–121). With all these deviations from widely accepted doctrine, Schneider still agreed that 'the price of the ultimate product which is set when the monopolistic suppliers of productive factors cooperate will be lower than the price when the monopolists act independently . . . and hence output of final products and input of factors will be greater, and total monopoly profits higher, under cooperation' (p. 54).

Stackelberg rejected the conclusions reached by Wicksell, Schumpeter, Zeuthen, and Schneider, concerning the possibility of a determinate equilibrium position under bilateral monopoly (1934, pp. 92–3). A fateful 'Gleichgewichtslosigkeit' – absence of equilibrium – was the main theme of his book. The same indeterminateness also characterizes 'bilateral oligopoly', which Stackelberg was probably the first to recognize explicitly under this name. Results were supposed to be more nearly determinate, though still unstable, in situations where a monopolist was selling to oligopsonists or where oligopolists were selling to a monopsonist (1934, pp. 27–9). Stackelberg mentioned the possibility, under bilateral monopoly, of options stipulating a 'fixed quantity or nothing', which might result in

9. 'Ma conclusion est donc en opposition avec la doctrine classique qui veut que le prix en cas de monopole bilatéral soit indéterminé' (1933, p. 1670).

normal-monopoly outputs being produced rather than the more restricted outputs characteristic of independent bilateral-monopoly pricing (pp. 26–7). This suggestion was not taken up for several years; most writers continued to hold the Edgeworth-Bowley position.[10]

A significant advance was Henderson's demonstration that contracts between two monopolists agreeing upon the volume at the simple-monopoly quantity were much more likely than mere price-quoting methods of bargaining (1940, pp. 241–3). To be sure, under the price-quoting method, one must expect 'that, except by accident, the output will be less than that which could maximize joint profits so that this form of negotiation will normally be less advantageous to the parties as well as to the final consumer than the alternative' (p. 242). He showed, however, that

... an agreement providing for definite deliveries at a given lump-sum price ... seems to be more likely ... [since] ... the parties taken together cannot lose and will probably gain by adopting this form of negotiation.

Now the amount ... is that which would be produced by a single combined monopolist, so that, in the case of a fixed contract, the joint profit will be maximized and the only uncertainty is with reference to the division of that profit between the producer and the monopsonist (1940, pp. 241–2).

Henderson agreed with most other writers that the division of the profits is indeterminate unless one can take account of bargaining power and bargaining skill. The division of profits or, what is the same thing, the price at which the intermediate product is transferred from the monopolist to the monopsonist does not influence the output produced or the price of the composite product to buyers at the next stage or to the ultimate consumer.

Nicholls (1941, p. 170) and Leontief (1946, p. 79) examined the possibilities of price-and-quantity agreements and found them probable in markets for industrial products, but improbable in agricultural and labour markets.

The new bilateral-monopoly solution for industrial products – where output is determinate and equal to the output under simple monopoly – was accepted and clarified by Fellner. He held that 'an all-or-none clause is implicit in the passing of a product from one firm to another in all cases except those in which a price is "quoted" regardless of the quantity that will be taken at that price' (1947, p. 525). Since the contract specifying

10. Hicks (1935, p. 16); Allen (1938, p. 381, problems 28 and 29), and Tintner (1939, p. 263) should be mentioned in this connection. A presentation of their views has been sacrificed to economy of space. A more complete review would also list the earlier re-statements of the problem by Leduc (1927, p. 256), Hicks (1930, p. 218), and Divisia (1934, p. 198).

a definite quantity yields the greatest profit it is the most likely outcome of bilateral monopoly in industrial product markets.[11]

In his survey of the literature, Haley (1952) reviewed the propositions advanced by Bowley, Tintner, Leontief and Fellner, and summarized the new solution (1952, pp. 23–4). Schneider's textbook contained a detailed exposition of the determinateness of the solution – depending on the conduct of each party (1949, p. 269). He spoke of price setters and price takers, quantity fixers and quantity adjusters, option proposers and option takers, where an option implies that both quantity and price are fixed.[12] Schneider concluded that the quantity transacted will be the same no matter which party proposes the option and which party takes it, with only the price (of the intermediate, not the ultimate product) differing. The quantity, moreover, will be the same as that which would secure the maximum profit to the two firms united in a merger (1949, pp. 275–6).

Bilateral monopoly: the present state of the theory

In summarizing the development of the theory of bilateral monopoly, three schools of thought can be distinguished. In the first it was concluded that both price and quantity would be determinate, but that the quantity would be lower than that fixed by an integrated monopolist, and the price to the consumer accordingly higher. In the second, it was held that both quantity and price were indeterminate within limits but, as before, the quantity would fall short of that under an integrated monopoly. The third school recognized that negotiations between separate monopolists would, in the case of intermediate products, necessarily be carried on in terms of both quantity and price, and that the quantity agreed upon between the parties would be the same as that produced by an integrated monopolist. The price to the consumer would consequently be determinate and no higher than it would be under integrated monopoly. Only the price for the intermediate product would be subject to bargaining. In other words, only the division of profits between the separate monopolists is in doubt, and

11. Fellner went much further when he asserted that bilateral monopoly will not induce any output restrictions whatsoever, but will produce the 'ideal competitive output', provided the two parties themselves are bordered and surrounded by perfectly competitive firms. He stated that not 'bilateral monopoly itself' but rather monopolistic positions in the preceding and subsequent stages will be responsible for output restrictions. Fellner's contention is correct only on the basis of such a wide definition of bilateral monopoly that it includes sellers and buyers who have no influence on the prices they receive or pay, respectively.

12. These concepts were first proposed by Frisch in an essay which touched only lightly on bilateral monopoly (1933, p. 243; 1951, p. 25). His suggestions concerning the distribution of 'action parameters' and the problem of negotiations proved eminently fruitful (1933, pp. 248, 253; 1951, pp. 28, 32).

fragmentation or integration makes no difference to the volume of output or to the price charged to consumers.

Why should it have taken economists so long to arrive at the third of these answers, and why have they been unable to agree on the comparative relevance of the various models? Why, after one hundred and twenty years' discussion, should the theory of bilateral monopoly still be 'on the agenda', as Zeuthen put it? (1955, p. 332). Why have economists most of the time assumed – following the second school of thought – that in a situation of bilateral monopoly one party would name a price only and wait for the other party to name the quantity?

We may guess that the writers who made this assumption carried over a technique that had proved useful in the analysis of unilateral monopoly, without due examination, to the case of bilateral monopoly. A monopolist selling to many buyers quotes a price and then lets buyers take the quantities they want. A monopsonist, buying from many sellers, names a price and then lets sellers deliver the quantities they choose. This technique is not appropriate when there is only one buyer and one seller, for the two must, of necessity, negotiate and contract for a definite quantity of the intermediate product at a price to which they can agree. Economists are sometimes victims of the habit of using tools that are ready in their kit, especially if these tools are 'elegant'. In this instance, the algebraic and geometric devices, involving offer curves and contract curves (in addition to indifference curves, outlay curves, and reaction curves), had done a neat job in the analysis of simple monopoly and duopoly. It was too tempting to apply them to the analysis of bilateral monopoly, too easy to overlook the fact that this application may imply assumptions concerning the behaviour of bilateral monopolists which are unsuitable in many situations.

The assumptions are not unsuitable in all cases that have been called 'bilateral monopoly'. There are situations in which prices are quoted by one party, or negotiated by the two parties, while the quantity is left open. Such arrangements are common in oligopoly situations, especially when one or both parties have incomplete control over quantity because they are merely agencies for a group of buyers or sellers rather than single firms.

The case of bilateral monopoly where one party is a collective monopoly or collective monopsony is immediately obvious. A trade union in its collective bargain with a monopsonist employer will normally set only the wage rate, while the quantity of labour offered and employed is left open. It was Leontief who was the first to show that the guaranteed annual wage was one way in which the price and quantity of labour could be fixed at the same time. But in this case, the quantity would be at a riskless level, well below the actually expected volume of employment (1946, p. 79). It was shown by Nicholls (1941, pp. 181–96) that an agricultural cooperative, such as a dairy farmers' cooperative, in its dealings with a monopsonist (or monemporist) distributor, will rarely be able to make price-and-quantity contracts. More often the quantity supplied by the milk producers will be left to them, and the quantity sold by the distributor in the fluid milk market will be decided by the final consumer. Only the discriminatory prices charged to fluid-milk consumers are decided upon in advance, and the lower prices for other milk products (cream, cheese, ice cream, etc.) are adjusted more flexibly (1941, pp. 181–96). Similarly a cartel of several producers will, as a rule, fix only the price, leaving quantity decisions to the members and the customers. This is even more true if the oligopoly is not organized but only incompletely coordinated, and it is most certainly true in the case of an uncoordinated oligopoly.[13] Even if we were to assume, for example, that automobile manufacturers were the only buyers of steel, the price leader in the steel oligopoly could not possibly establish the quantity for the industry as a whole. Thus the bilateral oligopoly of steel and automobile manufacturers is probably more adequately analysed by the model of the price-quoting type of bilateral monopoly than by the model featuring price-and-quantity contracts. For the case of bilateral oligopoly, consequently, the conclusion that vertical integration might lead to an increase in output could still be maintained.[14]

The one point on which nearly all economists of the twentieth century have agreed concerns the indeterminateness – in pure theory – of the division of profits between the two parties in a bilateral monopoly. Even those who concluded that the quantity was determinate and was equal to that produced by an integrated monopoly – and that the price to the next stage, or to the consumer, was determinate and equal to that charged by an integrated monopoly – agreed that the price of the intermediate product passing from the first to the second party in the bilateral monopoly was indeterminate and subject to 'bargaining skill'. Depending on the price of the intermediate product (or, alternatively, on the price charged for the service rendered by one of the parties) one party or the other might get the lion's share of the combined profits. There were intimations by some economists concerning a 'most reasonable' division of profits, but still the division was not determinate on the level of pure theory.[15] Whatever the

13. Price leadership is an example of an incompletely coordinated oligopoly, while guessing-game pricing would be an example of an uncoordinated oligopoly. For detailed explanations, see Machlup (1952, pp. 364–7, 491–511).

14. This seems to be the conclusion of Stigler (1951, p. 191), of Nicholls (1941, p. 177) and of Hoffman (1940, pp. 161–5).

15. In terms of the model used by Bowley for the ore monopolist facing the steel monopolist, the combined profit from ore and steel making might be divided by agreeing on an ore price at the level where the marginal cost of ore would equal the steel

division of the combined profit, it would not affect the quantity produced and the price charged to consumers. The division of profits between the two firms, if they remain independent, is, of course, subject to periodic negotiation, since all sales contracts are of limited duration. On the other hand, when the two firms merge, the division of the anticipated and capitalized profits is final. If cost and demand conditions remain unchanged, there is no reason to expect the outcome to be either more or less favourable to the consumer, one way or the other.

Successive monopolies: cumulative shrinkages of elasticities and cumulative mark-ups

The contention that vertical integration, on account of its implications concerning market position, will increase output need not be based on an assumption that there is a bilateral monopoly between any two stages of a non-integrated industry. To clarify, we resort again to schematic illustration.

A ■   (producer of copper)
B □ □ □ □ □ □ ■ □ □ □ □ □ (users of copper)
C □ □ □ □ ■ □ □ □ □ □ (users of brass)
D □ □ □ □ □ ■ □ □ □ □ □ (users of brass thermostats)

In stage A we may envisage a sole seller of a material, say copper, selling to a large number of buyers. One of these, B-7, happens to be the sole owner of zinc and is thus the only producer of brass. He has no monopsony power, since he competes with many other buyers of copper. As a monopolist in the sale of brass, he deals with a large number of buyers in stage C, the fabricators of brass. One of them, C-5, produces a patented brass thermostat for which there is no good substitute. He sells to many firms in stage D. One of them, D-6, uses this thermostat in the production of another patented product, perhaps a cooking device, which is significantly differentiated from other goods. We see here a sequence of monopolies, none of which has any monopsony power. We can conceive of an analogous pattern of successive monopsonists, none of them possessing any monopoly power. In either case the characteristics of bilateral monopoly are absent.

Many economists have argued that, in such a chain of monopolists or monopsonists, each of whom makes his policy independently, final output will be smaller and the final price higher than would be the case in a vertically integrated firm. The two methods of establishing this proposition

producer's marginal net revenue product of ore. See Bowley (1928, p. 656). See also Hicks (1935, p. 18). The same 'reasonable compromise price' was derived, perhaps independently, by Hawkins (1950, p. 190).

are so similar that the same authors can often be quoted on each: one method is based on the cumulative shrinkage of demand elasticities through repeated marginalization of revenue curves; the other method is based on a cumulation of price mark-ups by a succession of separate monopolists.

As Fellner puts the first argument, 'the seller of the raw material ... finds [his optimal output] by equating the marginal function corresponding to the demand curve of the buyer, that is, the function which is *marginal to the marginal value product function* of the raw material to the buyer ... with his own marginal cost function' (1947, pp. 505–6. Italics in the original).[16]

The cumulation of successive price mark-ups, which we have called the third strand in the texture of analysis, has been stressed both by writers expounding marginalist theories of the firm and by writers embracing full-cost theories of pricing. One of the marginalists, Zeuthen, discussed the case of

... five entrepreneurs all in a certain fixed proportion supplying monopolised raw-materials or services for the manufacture of the same article. The price ... will here be very much tightened up, and the quantity sold ... strongly reduced, since each entrepreneur will fix his monopoly price at the top of that of the others. The last monopolist ... adds the monopoly profit of the others ... to the common costs ... The five entrepreneurs may, however, combine, and thus ... take the greatest total monopoly profit [on a substantially increased output] (1930, p. 70).

In a later statement Zeuthen (1955) indicated that, even without complete combination, some of the same beneficial results may arise from the existence of financial liaisons, central organization, and tacit understandings (1955, pp. 332–3).

It is hardly necessary to search for statements of the theory of the cumulative mark-ups by successive monopolists in terms of the full-cost principle of pricing; the idea seems almost self-evident. It is interesting, however, to find a very early critic of this hypothesis. Macgregor (1906, pp. 97–8) pointed out that it would make no difference whether a mark-up is charged on the profit margin of the supplier of an intermediate product or on the interest on his capital, which evidently will reflect the capitalized profit. Thus, 'integration does not buy its material "at cost", if by this is meant "prime cost". When two capitals are joined, it still remains necessary to pay interest on both. The claim to buy at prime cost is purely a matter of book-keeping' (1906, pp. 97–8).

Lerner (1933–4) and McKenzie (1951), in discussing the measurement of social losses associated with monopoly, touched upon the cumulative effects of monopoly in the separate stages of non-integrated industry, though

16. Similar formulations appear in Bowley (1928, p. 654), Zeuthen (1930, pp. 66–9), Hicks (1935, pp. 17–18), Hoffman (1940, p. 165), Weintraub (1949, p. 308), and Hawkins (1950, pp. 183–4).

they did not expound in detail the reason for these cumulative effects. Lerner said:

The final degree of reduction of product will depend upon the degree of monopoly in all preceding stages. These have to be aggregated so as to give the tendency to divergence from the social optimum in the whole series of the production stages of the product. This phenomenon may be called the transitiveness of monopoly (1933–4, pp. 171–2).

McKenzie (1951, pp. 785–803) used this idea to demonstrate the inadequacy of Lerner's 'proportionality thesis' – the thesis that ideal output will exist if the degrees of monopoly in all industries are equal. If the ratios of prices to marginal costs are equal everywhere, but are greater than 1, ideal output will not be obtained. For the 'social loss will be greater, the larger the number of stages of production carried on by separate firms'.

While it is possible to conceive of successive monopolies none of which has any monopsony power (as in the hypothetical case of the brass thermostat discussed above) it is doubtful whether such situations are very common. If B is a pure competitor in buying his material, he must be one of a large number of relatively small buyers – though he is a monopolist in the sale of his fabricated product. Likewise C and D, monopolists at later stages of production, are very small buyers relative to the total output of what they buy, though large relative to the markets in which they sell. Would vertical integration seem very likely in such circumstances? A small fabricator could hardly acquire a large producer of his raw material, and the large supplier may have little interest in merging with a tiny customer. On the other hand, we may perhaps assume that successive *oligopolies* may involve output restrictions without the disproportionate sizes required for successive monopolies. In such cases, as Hoffman pointed out, merger may result in a relaxation of restrictions (1940, pp. 164–5).

Spengler, in presenting the case for vertical integration of successive monopolies, failed to take account of the disproportionate sizes of output which would be characteristic of such situations. He showed each of the representative firms in the three stages of production as producing an output precisely adjusted to that of its supplier and/or customer, yet drew the factor cost curves of firms B and C perfectly horizontal as if they were buying as pure competitors. Moreover, the demand curves visualized by his firms A and B were not derived from the demand for C's output, as they should have been. Thus his model does not fill the specifications either of successive monopoly or of bilateral monopoly. Despite these errors he arrives at the customary conclusion:

Vertical integration . . . has permitted our producer to evade imposts generated by horizontal integration and similar arrangements and thus reduce his selling prices below the level that would obtain in the absence of vertical integration. Vertical integration serves, therefore, to make price structures and factor allocation more ideal than they otherwise would be in an imperfectly competitive world (1950, p. 351).

The great qualification

Most of the economists mentioned in this paper have presented their case for the social blessings of vertical mergers between bilateral or successive monopolies without any fundamental qualifications. Yet it must be re-emphasized that joint profit maximization between monopolists, useful though it may be in mitigating the effects of horizontal combination, is not *the* ideal form of economic arrangement when there are possibilities of achieving greater degrees of competition in the several stages. It must further be re-emphasized that joint profit maximization itself can be achieved by other means than vertical merger; loose-knit agreements and, of course, direct and free negotiations of quantities and prices may do the job.

Where direct and free negotiation between bilateral monopolists yields price-quantity contracts, it is to be preferred over tighter combinations. Periodic re-negotiations of sales contracts do, to be sure, carry with them the danger of aggravated restrictions, but they leave the way open for new competition and new arrangements. Similarly, collusion or agreement between successive or bilateral monopolists may terminate; and this may again lead to independent profit maximization with its undisciplined restrictions, but on the other hand it may lead to undisciplined competition with all its advantages for the final consumer. Vertical merger has the great advantage that it commits once-separate firms permanently to a policy of joint profit maximization, but, on the other hand, it may well solidify and expand the monopoly position itself. The vertically integrated firm which has a monopoly in one stage of an industry may extend its monopoly power into other stages or subsidiary industries where competition might otherwise survive. A vertically integrated firm may be more able to discriminate between different purchasers and thus increase its profits, or strengthen its monopoly power, or both. Finally, it may, in periods of shortage, use its control of scarce material to eliminate or prevent the growth of independent fabricators.[17]

Thus, there is good sense in a policy of discouraging or restricting vertical merger. The most important advantage of a prohibition of certain kinds of vertical merger lies, it seems, in the temptation it creates for the monopolists or monopsonists on each separate stage to integrate forward or backward by establishing new facilities. Whereas vertical integration by merger may block the increase of competition in the industry, competition may

17. Some of these points were developed by Edwards (1953).

be effectively increased when firms extend their facilities to enter production at the stages of their erstwhile suppliers or customers.

Many economists, taking insufficient cognizance of these possibilities, have used the theoretical argument for vertical integration by merger as if it were a reliable guide to public policy. Not so Marshall. He combined practical sense with theoretical acumen and had the good judgement to ask whether there had not been some important possibilities locked up in the pound of *ceteris paribus*. Thus, after pointing to the '*prima facie* reasons for thinking that the public interest calls for . . . fusion' of complementary monopolies, he warns:

But there are other considerations of perhaps greater importance on the other side. For in real life there are scarcely any monopolies as absolute and permanent as that just discussed. On the contrary there is in the modern world an ever increasing tendency towards the substitution of new things and new methods for old, which are not being developed progressively in the interests of consumers; and the direct or indirect competition thus brought to bear is likely to weaken the position of one of the complementary monopolies more than the other. For instance, if there be only one factory for spinning and one for weaving in a small isolated country, it may be for the time to the public interest that the two should be in the same hands. But the monopoly so established will be much harder to shake than would either half of it separately. For a new venturer might push his way into the spinning business and compete with the old spinning mill for the custom of the old weaving sheds (1907, p. 494).

Making the same point with reference to complementary lines in the transportation industry, Marshall concluded:

Under some conditions it is more to the public interest that they should be in one hand; under others, and those perhaps the conditions that occur the more frequently, it is in the long run to the public interest that they should remain in different hands (1907, pp. 494–5).

References

ADELMAN, M. A. (1949), 'Integration and antitrust policy', *Harvard law Rev.*, vol. 63, pp. 27–77.

ALLEN, R. G. D. (1938), *Mathematical Analysis for Economists*, Macmillan.

AMOROSO, L. (1909), 'La teoria dell' equilibrio economico secondo il Prof. Vilfredo Pareto', *Giornale degli economisti*, series 2, vol. 39, pp. 353–67.

AMOROSO, L. (1911), 'La teoria matematica del monopolio trattata geometricamente', *Giornale degli economisti*, series 2, vol. 43, pp. 207–30.

AMOROSO, L. (1921), *Lezioni di Economia Matematica*, Bologna.

BABBAGE, C. (1832), *On the Economy of Machinery and Manufactures*, Charles Knight.

BOWLEY, A. L. (1924), *Mathematical Groundwork of Economics*, Oxford.

BOWLEY, A. L. (1928), 'Note on bilateral monopoly', *Econ. J.*, vol. 28, pp. 651–9.

COURNOT, A. A. (1838), *Recherches sur les principes mathématiques de la théorie des richesses*, Paris.

COURNOT, A. A. (1907), *Researches into the Mathematical Principles of the Theory of Wealth*, translated by N. T. Bacon, New York (translation of Cournot, 1838).

DIVISIA, F. (1934), 'A propos du duopole: fluidité d'un marché et élasticité d'une clientèle', abstract in *Econometrica*, vol. 2, pp. 198–9.

EDGEWORTH, F. Y. (1881), *Mathematical Psychics*, Macmillan.

EDGEWORTH, F. Y. (1897), 'Teoria pura del monopolio', *Giornale degli economisti*, vol. 15, pp. 13–31.

EDGEWORTH, F. Y. (1929), *Papers Relating to Political Economy*, vol. 1, Macmillan, pp. 111–42 (English translation of Edgeworth, 1897.)

EDWARDS, C. D. (1953), 'Vertical integration and the monopoly problem', *J. Marketing*, vol. 17, pp. 404–10.

FANNO, M. (1926), 'Contributo alla teoria economica del beni succedanei', *Annali di Economia*, vol. 2, pp. 329–469.

FELLNER, W. (1947), 'Prices and wages under bilateral monopoly', *Q.J. Econ*, vol. 61 pp. 503–9.

FRISCH, R. (1933), 'Monopole-polypole-la notion de force dans l'économie', in *Til H. Westergaard, Nationalekonomisk Tidsskrift*, supplement, pp. 241–59.

FRISCH, R. (1951), 'Monopoly-polypoly-the concept of force in the economy', *International Economic Papers*, no. 1, pp. 23–36, (English translation of Frisch, 1933).

HALEY, B. (1952), 'Value and distribution', in *Survey of Contemporary Economics*, Howard Ellis (ed.), vol. 1, Irwin, pp. 22–4.

HAWKINS, E. R. (1950), 'Vertical price relationships', in R. Cox and W. Alderson (eds.), *Theory in Marketing*, Chicago, pp. 179–91.

HAYEK A. VON (1934), 'Carl Menger', *Economica*, new series, vol. 1, pp. 393–420.

HENDERSON, A. M. (1940), 'A further note on the problem of bilateral monopoly', *J. polit. Econ.*, vol. 48, pp. 238–43.

HICKS, J. R. (1930), 'The indeterminateness of wages', *Econ. J.*, vol. 40, pp. 215–31.

HICKS, J. R. (1935), 'Annual survey of economic theory: the theory of monopoly', *Econometrica*, vol. 3, pp. 16–8.

HOFFMAN, A. C. (1940), *Large Scale Organization in the Food Industries*, US Temporary National Economic Committee, monograph no. 35, Washington.

LEDUC, G. (1927), *La théorie des prix de monopole*, Aix-en-Provence.

LERNER, A. (1933–4), 'Monopoly and the measurement of monopoly power', *Rev. econ. Stud.*, vol. 1, pp. 157–75.

LEONTIEF, W. (1946) 'Pure theory of the guaranteed annual wage contract', *J. polit. Econ.*, vol. 54, pp. 77–9.

MACGREGOR, D. H. (1906), *Industrial Combination*, Bell.

MACHLUP, F. (1952), *The Economics of Sellers' Competition, Model Analysis of Sellers' Conduct*, Blakiston.

MCKENZIE, L. W. (1951), 'Ideal output and the interdependence of firms', *Econ. J.*, vol. 61, pp. 785–803.

MARSHALL, A. (1907), *Principles of Economics*, 5th edn, Macmillan.

MENGER, C. (1871), *Grundsätze der Volkswirthschaftslehre*, Vienna.

NARDI, G. DI (1934), 'L'indeterminazione nel monopolio bilaterale', *Archivo Scientifico*.

NICHOL, A. J. (1943), Review of William H. Nicholls, 1941, *J. polit. Econ.*, vol. 51, pp. 82–4.

NICHOLLS, W. H. (1941), *Imperfect Competition Within Agricultural Industries*, Ames.

PARETO, V. (1896), *Cours d'économie politique*, Lausanne.

PARETO, V. (1909), *Manuel d'économie politique*, Paris. References in this paper are to second edition, 1927.

PIGOU, A. C. (1908), 'Equilibrium under bilateral monopoly', *Econ. J.*, vol. 18, pp. 205–20.

PIGOU, A. C. (1920), *Economics of Welfare*, Macmillan.

PIGOU, A. C. (1905), *Principles and Methods of Industrial Peace*, Macmillan.

SCHNEIDER, E. (1932), *Reine Theorie monopolistischer Wirtschaftsformen*, Tübingen.

SCHNEIDER, E. (1949), *Einführung in die Wirtschaftstheorie*, 2 Teil, Tübingen.

SCHUMPETER, J. A. (1908), *Das Wesen und Hauptinhalt der theoretischen Nationalökonomie*, Leipzig.

SCHUMPETER, J. A. (1927), 'Zur Einführung der folgenden Arbeit Knut Wicksells', *Archiv für Sozialwissenschaften und Sozialpolitik*, vol. 58, pp. 238–51.

SCHUMPETER, J. A. (1928), 'The instability of capitalism', *Econ. J.*, vol. 38, pp. 361–86.

SCHUMPETER, J. A. (1954), *History of Economic Analysis*, Oxford University Press.

SPENGLER, J. J. (1950), 'Vertical integration and antitrust policy', *J. polit. Econ.*, vol. 58, pp. 347–52.

STACKELBERG, H. VON (1934), *Marktform und Gleichgewicht*, Vienna and Berlin.

STIGLER, G. (1951), 'The division of labor is limited by the size of the market', *J. polit. Econ.*, vol. 59, pp. 185–93.

TINTNER, G. (1939), 'A note on the problem of bilateral monopoly', *J. polit. Econ.*, vol. 47, pp. 263–7.

WEINTRAUB, S. (1949), *Price Theory*, New York, Toronto, London.

WICKSELL, K. (1925), 'Matematisk nationalekonomi', *Ekonomisk Tidsskrift*, vol. 27 pp. 103–25.

WICKSELL, K. (1927), 'Mathematische Nationalökonomie', *Archiv fur Sozialwissenschaften und Sozialpolitik*, vol. 58, pp. 252–81.

ZEUTHEN, F. (1930), *Problems of Monopoly and Economic Warfare*, Routledge & Kegan Paul.

ZEUTHEN, F. (1933), 'Du monopole bilatéral', *Revue d'économie politique*, vol. 67, pp. 1651–70.

ZEUTHEN, F. (1955), 'La théorie du monopole bilatéral et multilatéral, toujours à l'ordre du jour', *Economie appliquée*, vol. 8, pp. 331–8.

19 John M. Vernon and Daniel A. Graham

Profitability of Monopolization by Vertical Integration

John M. Vernon and Daniel A. Graham, 'Profitability of monopolization by vertical integration', *Journal of Political Economy*, vol. 79, 1971, pp. 924–5.

It is generally accepted by economists concerned with merger policy that a monopolist does not have a profit incentive for integrating forward into a competitive industry unless there are cost savings to be gained.[1]

A representative statement of this proposition is as follows. A monopolist of input A, where input B and final product X are produced under purely competitive conditions, has no economic incentive to integrate forward into industry X (in the absence of cost savings of the type described above). The monopolist of A has the ability to extract all the potential profit from industry X by its choice of the price of input A. However, because the underlying theoretical model assumes fixed-proportions production in industry X, an important source of increased profit has been overlooked.

Assume that variable-proportions production exists in industry X. Now, the monopolist, by monopolistic pricing, imposes a deadweight loss on industry X by inducing a distortion in factor utilization. In principle, industry X could always benefit by paying the monopolist a lump sum equal to his profit on the condition that it be allowed to buy at marginal cost. Industry X could then use the inputs efficiently and thereby increase its profit. Hence, the vertical merger permits the integrated firm to achieve efficiency in factor utilization *and* capture the additional profit.

The point is shown graphically in Figure 1. Suppose that in premerger equilibrium the competitive industry produces output X^*. For simplicity, we represent the entire industry by isoquant X^*.

The ratio of the monopoly price of A to the price of B is given by the slope of PP^*. The ratio of the marginal cost of A to the price of B is given by MM^* (NN^* is parallel to MM^*). Measuring in units of B, the monopolist's premerger profit is PM. After merging and shifting production

1. This proposition is proved in Needham (1969) and Singer (1968), and its policy implications are discussed by Bork and Mueller in Weston and Peltzman (1969). Typical examples of the type of cost savings referred to are the elimination of sales promotion expenditures, inventory reduction, and reduced reheating in the successive stages of the steelmaking process.

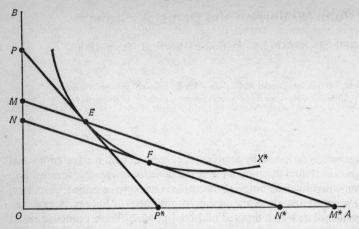

Figure 1

from point E to point F, the integrated firm could increase its profit by at least MN.[2] Clearly, the increment MN would not exist if the isoquant were of the fixed-proportions type.

2. Increment MN is the minimum increment to profit because we have assumed that the output X^* is unchanged after the merger. The profit-maximizing postmerger output will probably differ from X^*, and therefore the increment to profit may be still larger.

References

NEEDHAM, D. (1969), *Economic Analysis and Industrial Structure*, Holt, Rinehart & Winston.

SINGER, E. M. (1968), *Antitrust Economics*, Prentice-Hall.

WESTON, J. F., and PELTZMAN, S. (eds.) (1969), *Public Policy toward Mergers*, Goodyear.

20 M. A. Adelman

Vertical Integration and Market Growth

Sections 8 and 9 (pp. 318–21) of M. A. Adelman, 'Concept and statistical measurement of vertical integration', in National Bureau of Economic Research, *Business Concentration and Price Policy*, Princeton University Press, 1955, pp. 281–322.

Stigler has come nearer than anyone else to formulating a law of vertical integration (1951). Treating integration as the opposite of specialization, Stigler expects disintegration to be characteristic of an expanding industry, integration of a contracting one. As the industry (the market) expands, economies of scale become possible in the various processes and these tend to split off to be separately performed. Hence, in the absence of attempts at market control, there should be decreasing integration. . . .

Stigler doubts that we need a distinctive theory of vertical integration; this leads me to interpret the above situation as a pattern of industry development rather than a logical necessity. As a pattern, it is plausible and will doubtless be borne out in many instances. But in my opinion Stigler's analysis (correctly) contrasts a mature or large-scale industry with a small-scale industry, *not* an expanding industry with a contracting one. The distinction between process and result seems to be of crucial significance: I would guess that an expanding industry is more highly integrated than a relatively stable one. If we start with an industry in its earliest years, when it is an innovation, it is at first adapted to and fills a niche in the existing structure of markets and of factor supply. It is essentially a rearrangement of known and available resources. Few can discern its large possibilities for growth and for pushing the capacity of supplying industries and firms. The railroads were originally feeders to canals and turnpikes, and, later, pipe lines and trucks were considered as feeders to railroads; the automobile was a rich man's toy; wireless transmission of signals was intended for ship-to-shore telegraphy; and many other examples might be given.

As the firms and their industry grow, they do so under the forced draft of demand chronically in excess of supply at prevailing prices. This economic tension is transmitted to the factor markets as the firms bid not only for increasing amounts but for changing composition of factors. As larger quantities are needed, some factors become relatively scarce and substitution must be resorted to, often by painful trial and error. Economies of scale now appear, as Stigler rightly insists; my point is that they appear unforeseen and generally lagging behind a keenly felt need. A sluggish response will often force the growing firm to provide its own supplies and/or marketing outlets.

It may be regarded as axiomatic that integration takes place only in response to imperfections of competition in supplying or receiving markets. A firm does not normally integrate into a market where it can buy unlimited quantities at the going price and where the producers are receiving a normal (or subnormal) return. A firm does integrate into a broadening market whose service is scarce and expensive. The scarcity and the high price may be the result of monopoly control in the invidious sense, by a single seller or by a group whose several minds have but a single thought. But the scarcity may exist simply because of the time lag in supplying the new factor. A small, uncertain, and fluctuating supply is peculiarly subject to recurrent 'corners' and extortion. Also, there may be considerable monopoly profit. Even when this is not the case, if the factor is expensive or unsuitable, so that it takes additional costly processing before being ready for use or is uncertain in amount, the impact on the expanding firm is much the same. Thus the very expansion of demand which induces economies of scale in the associated markets also induces the firms in the growing industry to occupy the associated markets. Once established, the pattern perpetuates itself, unless the (private) diseconomies of integration are considerable.

An industry in rapid growth throws the process into boldest relief, but it is only the most extreme example of a more general problem. Given an expanding and changing economy, there must necessarily at any instant be a host of markets out of equilibrium into which it becomes profitable to integrate. This would explain the existence of vertical integration even in the absence of attempts to pre-empt an essential resource in order to prevent competitors from using it, or to insure the 'right' kind of price policy at later stages.

Given imperfect competition and no sharply defined loci of least-cost output, so that a firm may be well away from the optimum scale without ceasing to exist, then the half-forgotten history of an industry plus the power of inertia may largely explain its existing pattern of vertical integrtion. Chance alone may be no small part of the explanation. Imagine an industry comprising n stages with no economies or diseconomies of vertical integration. The joining of functions would then be purely random. There would be 2^{n-1} possible varieties or degrees of vertical integration; the 'average' firm would encompass $(n+1)/2$ stages, with $\sqrt{n-1}/2$ standard deviation.[1] Thus, with only a half dozen stages, one would find 32 possible patterns; the average number of stages encompassed would be $3\frac{1}{2}$, but this could be in any one of several patterns; furthermore, there would be

1. My thanks on this point are due to R. M. Solow.

one chance in three of any given firm encompassing less than $2\frac{1}{2}$ or more than $4\frac{1}{2}$ stages.

The foregoing sketch is not, I think, inconsistent with the evidence. The smallest firms appear to be specialists in a particular process. As the firm grows, it does not merely duplicate its activities; it takes over additional functions, performing some of the services it formerly purchased. Hence, both ratios would increase.[2] But for the firm which has grown into a large part of its available market, the trend to self-sufficiency may be reversed by the marketing necessity to carry a full line. Hence the firm purchases many finished or nearly finished goods to be marketed in conjunction with those it processes over a greater length of production line. This decreases the two ratios, but even with this reversal the large firm is more integrated than the small. A similar development takes place in the fully developed industry, where with the passage of time certain diseconomies of integration are slowly realized and certain functions are discontinued. For any growing industry or firm, the trend is to increasing integration, but this is counteracted both by the constant growth of new, less integrated industries and firms and by the reversal of the trend in highly mature industries.

Thus we have about four developmental patterns of vertical integration. For any given firm at any given time, they may be mutually exclusive but not over longer periods. Nor are they exhaustive. It would be most unfortunate if we looked for *the* typical pattern and tried to make of it a general theory of vertical integration. What we need is to increase our knowledge of various patterns and to multiply hypotheses while trying to practice some orderly housekeeping among them. The ratios proposed here, when used in conjunction with other evidence, may serve as useful tools in this task (cf. Balderston, 1953).

2. The two ratios referred to are the ratio of gross income (value added) to sales and the ratio of inventory to sales, which Adelman proposes as suitable measures of vertical integration (Ed.).

References

BALDERSTON, F. E. (1953), *Scale, Vertical Integration and Costs in Residential Construction Firms*, Princeton University Press.
STIGLER, G. J. (1951), 'The division of labor is limited by the extent of the market', *J. pol. Econ.*, vol. 59, pp. 185–93.

21 Arthur B. Laffer

Vertical Integration by Corporations, 1929–1965

Arthur B. Laffer, 'Vertical integration by corporations, 1929–1965', *Review of Economics and Statistics*, vol. 51, 1969, pp. 91–3.

When the surface of the economist is scratched we generally find a belief that vertical integration in the corporate sector has increased during the past few decades, if not longer. This proposition, however, has not been put to a rigorous empirical test for the entire corporate sector. According to Professor Bain, 'We must, in the present state of knowledge, confine ourselves to a few remarks based on miscellaneous scraps of evidence' (Bain, 1966, p. 357). In this note a measure of vertical integration in the corporate sector is developed. The measure is calculated for the year 1929 and for the period 1948 to 1965. The conclusion reached on the basis of this empirical evidence is that there has not been any discernible increase in the degree of vertical integration in the corporate sector. If anything, there might have been a slight decline.

The index we use is the ratio of corporate sales to gross corporate product standardized to abstract from the changes in output mix. A *rise* in this index implies a decline in corporate vertical integration and vice versa.[1] Because industry sales data are on a consolidated basis by corporation and most of the gross corporate product is on an establishment basis, this series reflects a preponderance of any general movements on the part of corporations to merge with suppliers or customers. If, for example, firm A has a gross corporate product of 500 and sales to firm B of 1000 (firm A's purchased material inputs are 500) and firm B has a gross corporate product of 500 and sales of 1500, then total corporate sales for both firms equal 2500 and total gross corporate product equals 1000. In this instance the ratio of sales to gross corporate product equals 2·5. If these two firms merge, total corporate sales will then be 1500 and gross corporate product will still be 1000. The new ratio of corporate sales to gross corporate product will be 1·5. Vertical integration has caused a decline in our ratio. As is readily apparent, neither pure horizontal integration nor a pure conglomerate movement will affect our ratio.[2]

1. Our index is in this form so that gross product weights instead of sales weights could be used.

2. It is necessary that at least one of the firms purchases from the other firm for their

There are natural differences among industries which preclude the meaningfulness of comparing the degree of vertical integration in one industry with that of any other industry. Thus a corporation in the service or mining industry will naturally have a much lower sales to gross corporate product ratio than a corporation in the retail or wholesale trade industry. If the proportional mix of total gross product is changing, we could very easily find a change in the aggregate sales to gross product ratio without any changes in this ratio for any specific industry. . . . In order to avoid the mix problem we calculate the aggregate ratio using the proportional mix of one base period.

More explicitly our methodology is as follows: For any year t, total corporate sales, S_t, is equal to the sum of total corporate sales for each industry, i. Thus,

$$S_t = \sum_{i=1}^{M} S_{i,t}$$

$i = 1, M$ where M is the number of separate industries. **1**

Likewise, total gross corporate product in any year t, GP_t, is equal to the sum of the gross corporate products for each industry i. Thus,

$$GP_t = \sum_{i=1}^{M} GP_{i,t}.$$ **2**

Naturally, for the entire corporate sector, the value of our ratio in any year t, R_t, is

$$R_t = S_t/GP_t = \sum_{i=1}^{M} S_{i,t} \left/ \sum_{i=1}^{M} GP_{i,t}. \right.$$ **3**

If $R_{i,t}$ is the individual industry's ratio in year t,

$$R_{i,t} = S_{i,t}/GP_{i,t},$$ **4**

then equation **3** can be written as follows:

$$R_t = \sum_{i=1}^{M} R_{i,t} \cdot GP_{i,t}/GP_t$$ **3′**

$GP_{i,t}/GP_t$ is nothing more than that proportion of total gross product accounted for by the gross product of the ith industry. For the purposes of this study, any change in R_t due to changes in $GP_{i,t}/GP_t$ are not changes in the degree of vertical integration. We, therefore, select a base year, b, and calculate the new standardized series R^*_t where

---

merger to affect our index. Pure horizontal integration – expansion in the same production stage – and a pure conglomerate movement – expansion in an unrelated field – do not imply any interfirm purchases and thus will not affect our index.

$$R^*_t = \sum_{i=1}^{M} R_{i,t} \cdot (GP_{i,b}/GP_b).$$

In equation **5** we have eliminated the effects of changes in the proportional mix of output and have captured all the effects of intra-industry changes in vertical integration.[3]

Results

In calculating the R^* series we used a ten-industry corporate classification. The industrial classes were (1) agriculture, forestry, and fisheries, (2) mining, (3) contract construction, (4) non-durable goods manufacturing, (5) durable goods manufacturing, (6) transportation, (7) communications, (8) electric, gas and sanitary services, (9) wholesale and retail trade, and (10) services.[4]

The base year selected for the proportional mix of gross product by industry was 1948.[5] In the table below we have listed for selected years industrial gross product proportions, GP_i/GP, and sales/gross product ratios, S_i/GP_i. The results of the calculations for the corporate aggregate are plotted in the graph below. [N.B. a rise in R^* implies a decline in vertical integration and vice versa.][6]

3. In any type of multiplicative discrete partition analysis as described above, there is an 'interaction' term which cannot be attributed solely to one of the multiplicative factors. In this case the 'interaction' term is

$$\sum_{i=1}^{M} \Delta R_i \cdot \Delta(GP_i/GP).$$

This term is extremely small in this instance of partition analysis and is therefore disregarded. Also, the standardization is only as complete as our industrial classification permits.

4. The corporate sales data by industry are from Table 6.19, pp. 142–5 of *The National Income and Product Accounts of the United States 1929–1965*. The gross corporate product data by industry are likewise from the US Department of Commerce, Office of Business Economics, but do not, as yet, appear in published form.

5. The selection of this base year as opposed to any other does not materially affect the conclusions.

6. The sales data for 1929 are from the source cited in footnote 4. The total gross corporate product figure for 1929 is calculated by multiplying the sum of 'income originating in corporate business' in 1929 (Table 1.13 on p. 22, *The National Income and Product Accounts of the United States 1929–1965*) and 'Corporate Capital Consumption Allowance' in 1929 (Table 6.18, p. 138), by the ratio of Gross Corporate Product in 1948 to the sum of the 'income originating in corporate business' in 1948 and 'Corporate Capital Consumption Allowances' in 1948. The percentage distribution of gross corporate product by industry in 1929 is calculated by assuming that the percentage of gross corporate product to gross product in each industry was the same in 1929 as it was in 1948. Combining these we obtained gross corporate product by industry for 1929.

Table 1 Gross product proportions and sales/gross product ratios for corporations by industry 1929, 1948, 1955, and 1965[a]

Industry	GP_i/GP				S_i/GP_i[b]			
	1929	1948	1955	1965	1929	1948	1955	1965
All industries	100·00	100·00	100·00	100·00	2·666	2·888	2·822	2·873
Agriculture	0·47	0·43	0·30	0·37	3·021	2·887	2·851	2·814
Mining	6·60	6·12	5·09	3·25	1·078	0·924	0·877	1·207
Contract construction	3·25	3·26	3·82	4·60	1·658	2·107	2·439	3·135
Non-durable manufacturing	22·19	24·27	21·80	20·51	3·459	3·446	3·338	3·363
Durable manufacturing	23·12	26·27	31·56	30·72	2·527	2·370	2·212	2·203
Transportation	14·33	10·06	8·26	6·74	1·300	1·353	1·381	1·566
Communication	3·07	2·78	3·32	4·01	1·269	1·223	1·369	1·420
Electricity	4·41	3·10	4·00	4·35	1·292	1·556	1·502	1·607
Trade	17·85	19·94	18·11	20·34	4·644	5·064	5·326	4·764
Services	4·71	3·77	3·74	5·11	1·353	1·696	1·752	1·876

[a] See footnotes 4 and 6 for sources.

[b] Any intertemporal comparison of the sales/corporate product ratio for a single industry is of tenuous value. The sales of a corporation are included solely in the industry in which the corporation does most of its business. In some instances the sales of a corporation may be included in one industry in one year and in another industry in the next year. Likewise, if a durable manufacturing firm buys a mining firm, smaller than itself, sales and gross product in the durable manufacturing industry will not change. Sales in the mining industry will fall and gross product in the mining industry will not change. Thus the sales/gross product ratio in durable manufacturing industry will not change, but this ratio in the mining industry will fall. This increase in vertical integration cannot be attributed solely to the mining industry as the sales/gross product ratio by industry would suggest. Neither of these problems exists in our R^* measure for the aggregate corporate sector.

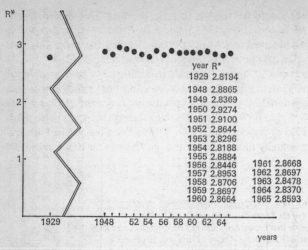

year	R*		
1929	2.8194		
1948	2.8865		
1949	2.8369		
1950	2.9274		
1951	2.9100		
1952	2.8644		
1953	2.8296		
1954	2.8188		
1955	2.8884		
1956	2.8446	1961	2.8668
1957	2.8953	1962	2.8697
1958	2.8706	1963	2.8478
1959	2.8697	1964	2.8370
1960	2.8664	1965	2.8593

Graph 1 The index of the degree of vertical integration over time, 1929–65

As is clear from the graph above, there is no discernible time trend in the degree of vertical integration.[7] With the exception of minor fluctuations, all the R^* points appear to lie on the same horizontal plane. Even cyclical movements are not readily visible. The recession years of 1949 and 1954 are minima, but the recession years of 1958 and 1961 are virtually indistinguishable from 1959, 1960 and 1962. The years 1956 and 1964 also are local minima.

One bias exists in the above calculations of R^*. If technological change, which results in relative price changes, is biased in favor of raw materials or finished goods, this may affect our index without necessarily implying any real change in the degree of vertical integration. As it turns out, prices of finished goods have risen much more sharply than prices of raw materials. During the period 1948 to 1955 raw material prices fell by 12·5 per cent, the prices of intermediate products and finished goods rose by 12·5 per cent and 7·6 per cent respectively (*Economic Report of the President, 1968*, Table B-49, p. 266). Thus with no change in the degree of vertical integration nominal sales of intermediate product producers and final

7. The absence of trend is amply indicated by the rank correlation coefficient of R^* with time of only −0·003. In order to have a statistically significant trend at the 5 per cent level of significance we would have to have a rank correlation coefficient greater than 0·4 or less than −0·4.

goods producers should fall relative to gross product. This should, *ceteris paribus*, bias R^* downward in 1955 relative to R^* in 1948. In fact, R^* in 1955 was almost identical to R^* in 1948, thus leaving the possibility that vertical integration may have actually declined over this period.

Similarly, between 1955 and 1965 raw material prices rose by only 2·3 per cent whereas intermediate product prices and final goods prices rose by 9·9 per cent and 12·0 per cent respectively (*Economic Report of the President, 1968*, Table B-49, p. 266). The bias during this period also tends to bias R^* in 1965 downward relative to R^* in 1955. Thus vertical integration may have actually declined even though there is no trend in our R^* series.

References

BAIN, J. S. (1966), *Industrial Organization*, Wiley.
Economic Report of the President, February, 1968.
The National Income and Product Accounts of the United States 1929–1965,
    US Department of Commerce, Office of Business Economics.

Part Five
Diversification

Weston (Reading 22) describes different types of diversified firms and ranges over several aspects of the economics of diversification, including those of special relevance for public policy. George (Reading 23) covers some of the same ground with a somewhat different emphasis. Berry (Reading 24) shows that simple statistics easily exaggerate the extent to which the largest firms in the United States are diversified. He also shows that, for an admittedly short period, new steps in diversification by these firms seldom went far from the diversifiers' established activities. Grabowski (Reading 25) studies the determinants of research and development (R & D) expenditures by firms in three industries. The study establishes the importance of the extent of product diversification as a determinant. It also examines the relation between size of firm and research and development expenditures and productivity.

22 J. Fred Weston

Conglomerate Firms

J. Fred Weston, 'The nature and significance of conglomerate firms', *St. John's Law Review*, vol. 44, 1970, special edition ('Conglomerate Mergers and Acquisitions: Opinion and Analysis'), pp. 66–80.

In order to gain an understanding of the significance of trends in conglomerate mergers, the nature and theory of conglomerates need to be clarified. The Federal Trade Commission has classified three types of conglomerate mergers. Product extension mergers involve firms which have some degree of functional relationship in either production or distribution. Market extension mergers involve firms which are in the same general product line, but sell in different geographic markets. The other category of conglomerates consists of essentially unrelated combinations.

The nature of conglomerate firms

The full significance of conglomerate mergers may be more completely conveyed by considering a broader spectrum of individual firm approaches to the market. Figure 1 illustrates such a spectrum in eight categories. Category 1 represents the prototype of the pure firm in economic theory. It consists of one product and one plant. Category 2 represents geographical diversification into multi-regional, national or international markets. The second type of diversification is suggested by category 3, which represents the multi-plant firm. The nature of the geographic diversification is, of course, influenced by the value versus transportation cost characteristics of the product. Different types of management control problems are likely to be posed if manufacturing operations are located in points geographically separated.

Still another type of diversification is indicated by category 4. This is the multi-product firm in which there is some relationship between research, manufacturing or marketing functions for two or more products.

While definitions are inherently arbitrary, misunderstanding might be reduced by adopting a more discriminating classification scheme in identifying conglomerates. The categories of the multi-regional marketing firm or the multi-plant manufacturing firm are not conglomerate, whether their geographic or market extension growth was achieved internally or by mergers. For category 4, the multi-product firm, the more appropriate term is 'concentric' rather than conglomerate. A common thread of

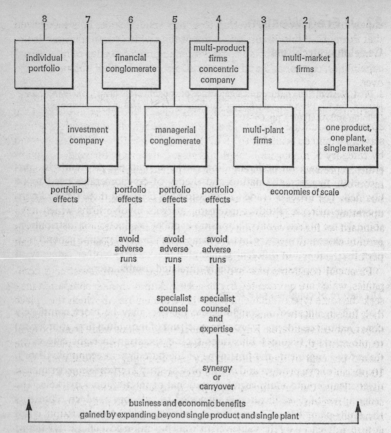

Figure 1 Eight categories of business firms

carryover in research, design, manufacturing or marketing activities is significant from a managerial standpoint. New management control problems are presented because of the different manufacturing costs, marketing effort and expense standards involved for planning and control of these different product activities. Nevertheless, a considerable potential carryover of specific management functional capabilities is offered. In fact, these carryovers must be exploited if the potentials of this kind of diversification, whether internal or external, are to be achieved.

Conglomerate corporations are represented by categories 5 and 6. These are companies whose diversification, either internal or external, involves products whose engineering, design, production and marketing functional capabilities requirements overlap to a very small degree. It is recognized that throughout this discussion we are dealing with a continuing spectrum. While category 4 represents a considerable amount of overlap of managerial capabilities, categories 5 and 6 represent a relatively small potential carry-over.

A number of different approaches could be taken to categories 5 and 6, the non-concentrically diversified companies – the conglomerates. One approach would be to provide a group of management specialists whose services would be available to all of the operating entities. This is suggested by category 5, managerial conglomerates. Category 6, financial conglomerates, represents a situation in which the parent supplies primarily financial resources. In turn, it applies a system of financial controls and reporting, but does not attempt to interact with the management decisions of the operating entity. A typical policy is that if performance does not satisfy the standard set for the operating company, the parent control group replaces executives with others whose experience and record indicate that they can perform the required managerial task.

Financial conglomerates are basically different from investment companies, which are represented in category 7. Although such companies may seek the same type of financial reporting from entities in which they place their investments or funds, they merely sell that investment if performance does not meet standards. Further technical distinctions result from the legal requirements that registered investment companies may not place more than 5 per cent of their funds in any one company nor hold more than 10 per cent of the voting shares of a company in which it makes its investment. Thus, the investment company does not exercise control in the sense of owning over 50 per cent of the shares of a company. On the other hand, considerable influence can be and is exercised when the holdings are as little as 10 per cent of the company's shares. But the predominant policy of investment companies, in the spirit of the Investment Company Act of 1940,[1] has been to avoid exercising influence over managements, using instead their buying and selling activities as a control on management performance.

The final category in the spectrum is the individual portfolio. Although the individual technically does not operate under the same constraints as investment companies, there is no fundamental difference in the position of the individual as compared with the investment company. On the other hand, the investment company's activities represent three differences. First, the investment company is generally able to assemble larger aggregates of funds than is the individual. Second, by combining funds from a large

1. Act of 22 August 1940 (chapter 686, §§ 1–53, 54 Stat. 789) (codified in scattered sections of 11, 15 USC).

number of different individuals, diversification is made possible for the individuals. Indeed, an individual might obtain a diversified portfolio by investing in a number of investment companies. Finally, the investment company provides professional management selection of securities and is compensated for expertise and specialization.

The foregoing taxonomy of eight categories of types of firms has three purposes. First, it illuminates the essential nature of the firm in economic theory. This is the characteristic of ultimate financial responsibility for the operations of the entity. A second purpose is to clarify the distinct differences between the categories in terms of financial responsibility and extension of managerial competence. For example, it is inaccurate and misleading to state, as has occurred in a number of discussions of 'conglomerates', that a multi-product firm is essentially no different from an investment company. Both of the preceding two purposes are related to the third: the framework provided by the foregoing category characterizations of types of approaches to business activity provides a basis for understanding their nature in a theoretical framework. This aspect shall now be pursued.

The theory of conglomerates

We shall now reverse the sequence in which the categories were discussed and start with the last two, 8 and 7. Category 8, the individual portfolio, achieves diversification consistent with the theory developed by Tobin (1958), Markowitz (1952, p. 77), Sharpe (1964) and others. If the investments combined in the portfolio are not all related by a perfect positive correlation, the portfolio will improve the return-risk trade-off. For a given return, risk will be reduced, or for a given risk, return can be increased.

Beneficial portfolio effects can be increased in either of two ways. One is to combine securities for which the correlation of returns is perfect but negative. Thus, if only two securities were in a portfolio, and if the correlation between their returns were negative 1, a portfolio of equal amounts of the two would eliminate any variation in their combined return.

Alternatively, even if the correlation between the two returns of the securities is not perfectly negative, variance can be reduced toward zero. Thus, if the correlation between the securities is not perfectly positive, some number of securities exist for some given pattern of correlations between +1 and −1 so that, in combination, risk is reduced essentially to zero. This provides a basis for a distinction between an investment company and the individual portfolio. Since investment companies can combine resources from an unlimited number of individuals, the power of investment companies to reduce variance is greater than that possessed by individual portfolios.

When we move to category 6, the non-concentric conglomerate exercising financial responsibility and controls, two additional elements are introduced. The risk reduction advantages of the portfolio can be retained. Utilizing the enhanced ability to raise funds which is conferred by its corporate form, the conglomerate firm can achieve both the diversification accomplishments of the investment company, i.e. the pure portfolio effect, and the augmented size of portfolio effect. By definition, category 6 assumes financial responsibility for the individual operating entities. Thus, the failure of an individual operating entity, because of gambler's ruin,[2] as its income or cash flow varies, can be avoided.

The second potential benefit from the pure financial conglomerate is that management's skill in formulating effective financial plans and controls, and the interactive effect of the implementation of financial planning and control principles, can improve the operations of the entity. Basically, what is involved here is a specialization and expertise in financial planning and control. Thus, inequality in competence on this one segment of management functions provides a theoretical basis for a rationale for financial conglomerates.

The managerial conglomerate, category 5, carries both of the attributes of the financial conglomerate further. By providing managerial counsel and interacting on managerial decisions, there is potential improvement of managerial performance. This is another pervasive element in a general theory of mergers. The existence of two firms with unequal management quality provides a sound economic basis for a merger. If, by combining the two firms, the superior management is spread over the two firms, true social gains have been achieved. Also, a business basis for a deal exists. If A is the firm with superior management and B is the firm with inferior management, the assets of firm B are worth more to firm A than they are to either the management or the present owners of firm B.

Another type of general theory for diversification, internal and external, is synergy. This aspect embraces a very wide range of elements which ultimately result in a $2+2 =$ more than 4 effect. Synergy results from complementary activities or from the carry-over of managerial capabilities. A few examples may be given to illustrate the point. One firm may have a strong research organization, while the other may excel in production and marketing; joining the two renders both firms more effective. Similarly, one firm may possess good product lines but lack the requisite marketing organization; the former's combination with the firm having the strong marketing organization of the type required benefits both firms. In the development of a product family, a firm may develop products that have

2. Gambler's ruin refers to the possibility that while the average return of the entity may be satisfactory, fluctuations in the average return may give rise to a series of losses or negative cash flows, causing bankruptcy for the operating entity.

consumer demand but require a variety of marketing channels. Again, appropriate merger combinations will achieve the requisite balance throughout the operation.

In the concentric firm, category 4, a high degree of carryover of functional management capabilities is achieved. Indeed, a fundamental characteristic of the concentric firm is that the nature of the interrelated activities is such that the cost of operations or quality of the product of a segment of the concentric firm, as a part of the concentric firm, is superior to what could possibly be achieved if that segment were operating independently, assuming equal quality of management under both situations.

For all three of the categories, the concentric firm, the managerial conglomerate, and the financial conglomerate, synergy of various forms and degrees may exist. While the greatest degree and types are likely to be found in the concentric firm, synergy is not necessarily absent in the other two categories.

While these principles of conglomerate mergers have both generality and plausibility, another basic question must be both posed and answered. Why did the wave of conglomerate mergers not occur decades earlier or later?

The timing of the increase in conglomerate mergers

A number of factors may be suggested as an explanation for the heightened activity in conglomerate mergers in recent years. The first involves the increased pace of technological change in our economy, and the maturation of several individual industries. For example, as a result of the impact of the automobile and airplane on the railroads, firms in the railway equipment industry were compelled to enter other industries in order to maintain growth. A similar set of forces operated on the textile industry with the development of synthetic fibers. The substitution of oil for coal had a similar impact on the coal industry.

Although its impact is admittedly less sweeping, a related factor which must be considered is the shortening of product life-cycles caused by the increased pace of technological change. This would be particularly true in the chemical industry, but it is also equally valid for individual product lines in a wide variety of industries.

A second pervasive factor is the general development of management technology. Improvements in generic management functions as well as the development of theory and decision models in the specific management function areas have had considerable impact. Where improvements have been achieved, the differences in quality of management have been sharpened. Another influence is that the ability to apply generic management capabilities and specific techniques such as financial planning, management, and control over a wide variety of industries has increased.

A number of changes which have encouraged conglomerate mergers have occurred in the equity markets. One aspect has been the generally rising equity prices since the mid-1950s. Another influence was the recognition of growth in earnings per share as an improvement factor in the valuation of securities. As a result of purely financial agreements in mergers and practices permitted by present accounting rules, earnings per share can be increased in a number of ways. If two companies with unequal price-earnings ratios merge on the basis of current market prices, the earnings-per-share of the higher price-earnings ratio company will increase. Similarly, a company which acquires for cash other companies having profitability will increase its earnings-per-share.[3] And finally, the acquisition of companies through debt instruments, both straight and convertible, and various other forms of senior securities such as preferred stock, also provides a basis for increasing earnings-per-share. Thus, the development and use of a variety of financial techniques have encouraged conglomerate mergers.

Another institutional influence in recent years has been the virtual prohibition of those horizontal and vertical mergers which involve firms of any substantial size. Thus, conglomerate mergers have increased because they have been less vulnerable to prohibition by regulatory agencies.

Any one of these explanations alone would be insufficient to explain the increased activity in conglomerate mergers; however, taken in combination, they provide a plausible framework for explaining the recent emergence of this phenomenon in the American economy. Additionally, it should be noted that these explanations suggest that the forces involved are not temporary. Consequently, since we may look to continued activity in the years to come, it becomes important to analyse the economic consequences of conglomerate mergers.

Analysis of antitrust aspects of conglomerate mergers

A number of objections to conglomerate mergers have been raised. These may be summarized into seven categories: conglomerate mergers

1. Extend monopoly power,
2. Encourage cross subsidization,
3. Increase 'deep pocket' advantages,
4. Increase entry barriers,
5. Result in increased, noneconomic reciprocity arrangements,
6. Increase macro-concentration, and
7. Increase the size of power groups.

3. For an explanation of the mechanics of these effects, see Weston and Brigham (1966, chapter 27).

Since little empirical analysis has been made of the above arguments, a conclusive evaluation will not be possible. Instead, each point will be analysed on the basis of its consistency with general economic concepts and prevailing principles and practices of business management.

Extended market power

The argument has been made that the objection is not to conglomerate diversification as such, but rather to conglomerate diversification achieved by the merger route (Heflebower, 1963). It is asserted that, unlike external expansion, diversification which is achieved internally must meet both business and market tests (cf. US Senate, 1965). This view is beguilingly attractive, but it ignores the significant potential economic benefits that are achieved through the forms of inter-firm combinations described in this paper. Furthermore, it misses the central, indeed critical, issue of market control. If the merger results in market control, then clearly public policy should raise barriers; but in the absence of market control, the resulting concentric or conglomerate firm is continuously confronted with the discipline of the marketplace.

Another related objection is that conglomerate mergers permit the extension of market power in one industry into other industries (cf. *Foremost Dairies*, 1962; Narver, 1967, chapter 7). This argument, upon analysis, generally turns out to depend upon one or more of the other specific objections. While the specification of what constitutes market power has not been formulated rigorously, the usual basis suggested is the combination of (1) a high (more than 10 per cent) share of the total market sales and (2) higher than average profits (cf. Shepherd, 1967). A full evaluation of this definition would require a separate paper. Suffice it to observe that high concentration may also be associated with the technological and managerial requirements or opportunities of the industry. In addition, high profits may reflect successful performance as well as market power in some sense. But the basic question is whether a strong and successful firm enjoys unfair advantages in unrelated industries (cf. Rill, 1967, pp. 1028 and 1055). The opposite conclusion seems more plausible, for conglomerate diversification by the acquisition of firms in other industries actually increases the vigor of potential competition. The threat of potential entry becomes pervasive because the range of potential entrants is increased. But the specifics of the market power argument usually constitute one or more of the following objections.

Cross-subsidization

The cross-subsidization criticism argues that in the large conglomerate, various types of predatory behavior can occur because activities that are less profitable can be subsidized by the profitable segments of activity. The effects are aggravated if the profitable segments exercise some elements of monopoly control over their markets (Blair, 1958, pp. 672, 673–4; Edwards, 1955; US Senate, 1966). However, this argument lacks plausibility on grounds of general economic theory. If some activities are unprofitable, it is better to dispose of them rather than to subsidize them. Overall performance of the conglomerate would be improved by discarding unprofitable segments of activity.[4] The argument that, as a form of predatory behavior, losses could be recouped after competition had been eliminated similarly fails to carry logic. Unless entry barriers are high, the attempt to raise prices and increase profits to recoup losses caused by earlier predatory pricing behavior will attract new competition.[5] And since conglomerate mergers reduce entry barriers, the increased crossing of industry boundaries by large firms seeking additional profit opportunities diminishes the feasibility of predatory pricing behavior.[6]

A related argument is that the entrance of large firms into a wide variety of industries, particularly those that have traditionally been the province of small firms, further restricts the potential area of operations for small firms. It is contended that this will lead to an undesirable restructuring of the American economy, in which only large diversified conglomerate firms could survive. This is a form of the 'deep pocket' theory next considered.

The 'deep pocket' theory

If the 'deep pocket' theory refers to helping operating units avoid gambler's ruin, it cannot be objected to on efficiency grounds, for it would be a social waste to permit bankruptcy and shifts of economic resources away from operations possessing long-run favorable productivity (cf. US Senate, 1965). However, the 'deep pocket' objection has also been defined as the ability of large firms to engage in heavy advertising and 'unnecessary model and style changes.' These are practices which smaller firms 'could not afford' or represent activities for which risks are so great that large aggregates of economic resources are required to 'play the game' (*Reynolds Metals Co.* v. *FTC*, 1962). However, this argument can also be extended to other, clearly socially desirable forms of competition, such as quality improvements and research and development expenditures. Product differentiation takes many forms, but all such efforts are profitable only if effective. If

4. The 'classic case' of predatory price discrimination turns out, on closer examination, not to be based on factual evidence (McGee, 1958, p. 137).

5. 'I am still waiting for the first verifiable example [of predatory pricing by a large firm]' (Adelman 1964).

6. 'To sum up, predatory pricing seems so improbable a consequence of conglomerate acquisitions that it deserves little weight in formulating antimerger rules based on prospective effects' (Turner, 1965, pp. 1313, 1346).

elasticities of demand response are not sufficiently high in relation to elasticities of cost outlays, the activity is unprofitable and, rationally, will not be pursued. To object to effective non-price competition is to deny consumer rationality or to object to the principle of competition generally. The objection, therefore, does not have a valid basis (cf. Andrews, 1964, pp. 123–7).

Effect on entry barriers

A variant of the foregoing is the objection that the preceding forms of activity increase entry barriers. Other things being equal, lower entry barriers are to be preferred to high entry barriers. Probably the most energizing of economic forces is entry or potential entry into a product market area.

Commentators generally have recognized five major forms of entry barriers (Bain, 1956; Mann, 1966, p. 296):

1. Control of scarce raw materials or control through patents.
2. Economies of scale.
3. Absolute cost advantages.
4. Product differentiation advantages.
5. Large capital requirements.

Analytically, these five barriers to entry should be regrouped into three. Large capital requirements represent a form of scale advantage. Product differentiation advantages represent either scale advantages or absolute cost advantages. Control over scarce materials represents truly a form of monopoly control. The same is true of patent protection; both are clearly within the province of public policy. But the trend toward conglomerate mergers is not likely to be significantly influenced by or to contribute greatly to entry barriers relating to control over scarce materials or patents. It is in the realm of increasing cost of entry requirements and product differentiation barriers to entry that conglomerate mergers are likely to have the greatest impact. However, there are, in fact, forms of cost advantages or scale economies, reflecting efficiency and providing economic justification for conglomerate mergers.

Reciprocity

A fifth concern with conglomerate mergers is the possibility of increased reciprocity, ... i.e. the practice of basing purchases upon the recognition of sales to the other party, rather than on the basis of prices and product quality. It is contended that the reciprocity would be 'spontaneous'; that a large conglomerate buys in large volume from many firms, and sellers will spontaneously recognize that the buyer may shift his purchases if reciprocal transactions are not made. Yet the evidence in the leading cases on reciprocity, an illegal practice, suggests that overt action is necessary if reciprocal transactions are to be achieved.[7] Indeed, in *United States* v. *General Dynamics Corp.* (1966) (hereinafter the *Liquid Carbonic* case), the efforts were not only overt, but strenuous; and even when vigorously pursued, the efforts to use reciprocity to increase sales yielded only small results. Reciprocity practices are increasingly viewed as a nuisance by business firms. With the broadened application in recent years of decentralized management responsibility and accountability, reciprocity increasingly conflicts with established management policies. Managers must be free to follow the most economic and efficient policies if they are to be fairly evaluated. If some managers were required to engage in transactions because it would help some other segment of the firm which was unable to meet market competition, the comparative performances by divisions and their managers would be distorted. Reciprocity is therefore unsound both from the standpoints of the firm and the economy.

But it may be argued that when all other factors are equal, 'spontaneous reciprocity' may influence buying decisions. If price, quality, service, financing, the relations with salesmen, dependability in delivery, etc., are all equivalent, recognition of sales to one firm rather than another may lead to purchases from the firm's customers. To have a basis for obtaining such business, the other firms would have to offer some superiority in price, quality or the other variables. If they failed to obtain the sales after offering a superior value, a basis for a charge of overt reciprocity behavior would have been established. In this connection, an excerpt contained in the court's decision in the *Liquid Carbonic* case is to the point. According to a Liquid Carbonic executive: 'All that is needed to place this program in dire jeopardy and bring strong corporate pressure for its demise is to have one irate letter written to federal authorities by a company resenting what was felt to be undue pressure.' Additionally, in view of the great suspicion of reciprocity potentials created by conglomerate firms, they are subject to pressure to avoid even the appearance of illegality. The corporate office of the conglomerate firm must promulgate clear criteria based upon competitive business and economic practices to guide its sales and purchasing departments. Thus, if reciprocity has been a practice in American industry, the widespread conglomerate development is likely to hasten its diminution rather than to increase it.

Macro-concentration measures

Great concern has been expressed over the Federal Trade Commission calculations which show that for the period 1948–57, the 200 largest manufacturing companies in the United States increased their share of

7. See e.g., *FTC* v. *Consolidated Foods Corp.*, (1965); *United States* v. *Ingersoll-Rand Co.*, (1963); *United States* v. *General Dynamics Corp.*, (1966).

total manufacturing assets from 48 per cent to 58·7 per cent. During the same period, the 100 largest firms increased their relative position from 40 per cent to 48 per cent.

Conglomerate mergers contributed to this increase in the market share of the largest firms. Table 1 shows the position of 60 conglomerates in

Table 1 60 Conglomerates' appearance in the Fortune 100 and 200 lists for 1961 and 1968

In top 100 – 1961	12
In top 100 – 1968	18
In top 100 – 1961 but not 1968	5
In top 100 – 1968 but not 1961	11
In top 100 – 1961 and 1968	7
In top 101–200 – 1961	15
In top 101–200 – 1968	16
In top 101–200 – 1961 but not 1968	10
In top 101–200 – 1968 but not 1961	11
In top 101–200 – 1961 and 1968	5
In top 200 – 1961	27
In top 200 – 1968	34
In top 200 – 1961 but not 1968	6
In top 200 – 1968 but not 1961	13
In top 200 – 1961 and 1968	21

Source: *Fortune Directory of the 500 largest US Industrial Corporations* (1969).

the largest 100 and 200 manufacturing companies between 1961 and 1968. A net increase of six conglomerates in the list of the top 100 occurred between 1961 and 1968; however, five that were in the top 100 in 1961 were no longer in that group in 1968. The number of conglomerates in the top 200 increased by a net seven during the interval, reflecting a gross increase of thirteen, offset by six eliminations. But the share of the top 100 and 200 firms, as measured, reflects some exaggerations. The identities of the largest firms do not remain constant over the time interval for which the statistics are calculated. Rather, the percentages are for whatever 200 or 100 firms happen to be the largest in a particular year. Thus, the statistics only measure the fact that the most successful companies are relatively more successful than the average for all manufacturing companies.

There may be another important exaggeration in these percentages. While the base is all assets in manufacturing, individual corporations are classified by their predominant activities. If its predominant activity is manufacturing, a firm is categorized as a manufacturing company, even though it may diversify into other industrial classifications. Similarly, if a corporation has diversified into foreign operations, its assets applicable to foreign sales should not be allocated to the domestic manufacturing operations. If nonmanufacturing assets and assets related to foreign operations are included in both the numerator and denominator of the share of the top 100 or 200 firms, an upward bias remains. Large firms may be expected to be more diversified than smaller firms, particularly in foreign operations.

Assume that the assets of large firms, as measured, are 50 per cent of total manufacturing assets, and that foreign operations account for 40 per cent of the firms' assets. Then 40 per cent of the 50 per cent is 20; the 50 per cent of the large firms less the 20 per cent devoted to foreign operation would be 30 per cent. The 100 per cent for the universe less the 20 per cent represented by foreign operations leaves 80 per cent. Thus, if foreign operations were eliminated, the concentration ratio would decrease from 50 per cent to $37\frac{1}{2}$ per cent, a decline of 25 per cent in the share of the largest firms.

The share of the largest firms is high because some industries are large in comparison with other manufacturing industries. Table 2 sets forth the facts. Of 155 three-digit industries, five representing 3·2 per cent account for 38 per cent of total manufacturing assets. Furthermore, forty-two of the largest 100 firms are in these five industries.

Table 2 **Relative importance of five three-digit industries and manufacturing concentration, 1968**

SIC	($ Billions) Total assets, end of 1968	Number of firms in largest 100
291 Petroleum refining	75·3	18
331 Primary iron and steel	26·8	6
371 Motor vehicles and equipment	35·9	3
372 Aircraft and parts	19·3	8
281 Basic chemicals	26·7	7
Sub-total	184·0	42
Total all manufacturing	485·9	
Per cent 5 industries to total value	37·9%	
(5/155) Number	3·2%	

Sources:
Columns 1 and 2:
US Bureau of the Budget (1967)
Column 3:
FTC–SEC (1968)
Column 4:
News Front (1969), pp. 56–72.

The basic force producing the largest market share of total manufacturing assets represented by the largest firms results from the concentration of total manufacturing assets in a few industries. Merger activity does not determine the relative share of individual industries in total manufacturing assets. The relation is established by basic economic characteristics of the industries. These are heavy industries which require large fixed investments. Economies of scale may also explain the preponderance of large firms. These 42 firms account for 29·3 per cent of total manufacturing assets. Thus, the main determinant of the high level of macro-economic concentration is the relative size of industries.

Trend to larger centers of power

A seventh concern in connection with conglomerate mergers is that the size of the firms involved is very large.[8] Large economic aggregates with potentially vast social and political power may result. Indeed, this has already occurred and we appear to be only at the beginning of the age of conglomerate mergers. Furthermore, if conglomerate mergers result in increased size of firms, the inhibitions against mergers by firms already large, but specializing in relatively narrow areas of activity, such as General Motors, General Electric Company, etc., will be diminished. If such firms engage in conglomerate mergers – and they may be so impelled to compete effectively for resources in the financial markets – the increased concentration of economic power may indeed have implications of very great concern for the aggregation of social and political power.[9]

Conclusions

A number of general principles in regard to diversification and mergers have been described. They may be summarized as follows:

1. Portfolio effects – reduction of risk.
2. Financial responsibility – avoidance of gambler's ruin.
3. Scale economies with utilization of generic management functions.
4. Cost advantages in effective utilization of specific management expertise.
5. Combining general management organizations of unequal quality.
6. A wide range of complementarities or synergies representing the achievement of a wide variety of 'carryover' economies.

Concern has been expressed about the trend toward conglomerate mergers. Perhaps the various criticisms are inapplicable to some degree to

8. Cf. Mueller (1969), and Blair (1969). See also US Senate (1964).
9. The nature of this power, how it is exercised, and in what spheres, has not been set forth. Careful, documented studies of presumed market power provide evidence of the strength of competitive forces. Cf. Adelman (1959).

concentric mergers, but they have been directed without distinction against firms which fall within the Federal Trade Commission's classification of conglomerates. This paper briefly examines seven criticisms:

1. Extension of market power.
2. Cross-subsidization.
3. Deep pocket advantages.
4. Increased entry barriers.
5. Reciprocity arrangements.
6. Increased macro-concentration.
7. Augmented power groups.

Each raises a broad set of issues not fully explored in this summary treatment. Each of the seven areas of concern needs much more careful study and analysis before a solid basis for public policy can be established. In sum, much more fundamental empirical research is required. This analysis seeks to provide a framework identifying some of the relevant hypotheses which, in turn, suggest the types of empirical tests required to evaluate alternative points of view.

The analysis does establish that there are substantial potential economic benefits from what has loosely been described as the recent conglomerate merger movement. However, it is clear that undesirable effects may also result. Thus, once again, more study and analysis is required before a firm basis for public policy can be established.

Finally, the foregoing analysis establishes that prohibitory policies by the antitrust authorities do not represent 'no loss' actions. One risks the loss of substantial economic benefits if sweeping prohibitions against 'conglomerate mergers' are put into effect. This risk is increased by the failure to recognize that the term 'conglomerate' has been inappropriately applied to a broad class of mergers that, more meaningfully, should be viewed as concentric. The importance of the distinction is that the probability of economic benefits from concentric mergers is very high and the applicability of the criticisms of conglomerate mergers is relatively low. Thus, net public benefits are likely to be achieved by concentric mergers. With regard to mergers which may appropriately be termed financial or managerial conglomerates, the conclusion is less certain, but no basis is provided for prematurely raising barriers against these types of mergers. The potential economic benefits are substantial. Undesirable consequences have not been demonstrated.

References

ADELMAN, M. A. (1959), *A & P, A Study in Price–Cost Behavior and Public Policy*, Harvard University Press.

ADELMAN, M. A. (1964), 'Market issues: an economist's view', in *The Impact of Antitrust on Economic Growth*, National Industrial Conference Board.

ANDREWS, P. (1964), *On Competition in Economic Theory*, Macmillan.

BAIN, J. S. (1956), *Barriers to New Competition*, Harvard University Press.

BLAIR, J. (1958), 'The conglomerate merger in economics and law', *Georgetown law J.*, vol. 46.

BLAIR, J. (1969), Paper in J. Weston and S. Peltzman (eds.), *Public Policy toward Mergers*, Goodyear.

EDWARDS, C. (1955), 'Conglomerate bigness as a source of market power', in *Business Concentration and Price Policy*, National Bureau of Economic Research, Princeton University Press.

FTC–SEC (1968), Quarterly Financial Report for Manufacturing Companies.

Federal Trade Commission v. *Consolidated Foods Corp.* (1965), 380 US 592.

Foremost Dairies Inc. (1962), 60 FTC, 944.

HEFLEBOWER, R. (1963), 'Corporate mergers: policy and economic analysis', *Q.J. Econ.*, vol. 77, p. 537.

MCGEE, J. (1958), 'Predatory price cutting: the Standard Oil (N.J.) case', *J. Law Econ.*, vol. 1.

MANN, H. (1966), 'Seller concentration, barriers to entry and rates of return in thirty industries, 1950–1960', *Rev. Econ. Stats*, vol. 48.

MARKOWITZ, H. (1952), 'Portfolio selection', *J. Finance*, vol. 7, pp. 77.

MUELLER, W. (1969), Paper in J. Weston and S. Peltzman (eds.), *Public Policy toward Mergers*, Goodyear.

NARVER, J. (1967), *Conglomerate Mergers and Market Competition*, California University Press.

NEWS FRONT (1969), June–July.

Reynolds Metals Co. v. *FTC* (1902), 309 F. 2d 223, (D.C. cir. 1962).

RILL, W. (1967), 'Conglomerate mergers: the problem of super concentration', *University of California law Rev.*, vol. 14.

SHARPE, W. (1964), 'Capital asset prices: a theory of market equilibrium under conditions of risk', *J. Finance*, vol. 19, p. 25.

SHEPHERD, W. (1967), 'On appraising evidence about market power', *Antitrust Bull.*, vol. 12, p. 65.

TOBIN, J. (1958), 'Liquidity preference as behavior toward risk', *Rev. econ. Stud.*, vol. 25, p. 65.

TURNER, D. (1965), 'Conglomerate mergers and section 7 of the Clayton Act', *Harvard law Rev.*, vol. 78.

US BUREAU OF THE BUDGET (1967), *Standard Industrial Classification Manual*.

US SENATE (1964), Hearings pursuant to S. Res. 262 before the Subcommittee on Antitrust and Monopoly of the Senate Committee on the Judiciary, 88th congress, 2nd session, part 1.

US SENATE (1965), Hearings pursuant to S. Res. 40 before the Subcommittee on Antitrust and Monopoly of the Senate Committee on the Judiciary, 89th congress, 1st session, part 2.

US SENATE (1966), Hearings pursuant to S. Res. 191 before the Subcommittee on Antitrust and Monopoly of the Senate Committee on the Judiciary, 89th congress, 2nd session, part 5.

United States v. *Ingersoll–Rand Co.* (1963), 320 F 2d 509, 3rd circular.
United States v. *General Dynamics Corp.* (1966), 258 F. Supp. 36 S.D.N.Y.
WESTON, J. and BRIGHAM, E. (1966), *Managerial Finance*, 2nd edn, Holt, Rinehart &
   Winston.

23 Kenneth D. George

Diversification and Aggregate Concentration

Section B (pp. 107–112), 'Aggregate concentration', of Kenneth D. George,
'Concentration and specialization in industry', *Journal of Industrial Economics*,
vol. 20, 1972, pp. 107–21.

One of the most striking features of the manufacturing sector of developed economies is the extent to which activity is concentrated in the hands of a relatively small number of firms. In Britain, the 100 largest companies held in 1965 approximately 60 per cent of net assets in the quoted public sector of manufacturing and distribution (Utton, 1970, p. 88). In the United States the share of manufacturing assets held by the 100 largest manufacturing companies in 1968 was 49 per cent, and for the 200 largest, 60 per cent.

Apart from the level of aggregate concentration there are two other important questions. First, what is the rate of turnover amongst the leading firms? Secondly, has there been any clear tendency for the aggregate level of concentration to increase over time?

Some evidence on turnover is to be found in a study by Collins and Preston, for the United States economy over the period 1909–58 (1961). They found that of the 100 largest firms (in terms of assets) in manufacturing, mining and distribution in 1909, 36 remained among the top 100 in 1958. The changes that have occurred are, of course, closely related to structural change in the economy. In particular, firms that were heavily engaged in food and clothing gave way to those in the newer industries such as automobiles and petroleum refining. It is difficult, however, to draw any clear-cut conclusions from such absolute measures of turnover. Indeed, whereas some are likely to be impressed by the fact that as many as thirty-six firms managed to keep in the top 100 over as long a period as fifty years, others might want to emphasize the fact that sixty-four firms failed to maintain their leading positions. There is no doubt at all, however, about one thing, and that is that over time the rate of turnover has declined. In the period 1909–19 the average number of exits from the top 100 firms in manufacturing, mining and distribution was 4·0 per annum; in the period 1919–29 it was 3·1; and in the periods 1935–48 and 1948–58 it was 1·5 and 1·6 per annum respectively. This trend towards the more entrenched position of the giant corporations is likely to have been due in large measure to the growing professionalization of management. The increasing importance of the divorce between ownership and control in the large corporation has been associated with the emergence of a management class whose main interest is to preserve the firm as an organization. In general, it has been in the interests of this class to avoid very risky projects, including too heavy a reliance on the production of a narrow range of commodities, and instead to seek greater security and status by emphasizing the growth of the organization, including growth by diversification.

As far as trends in aggregate concentration are concerned the evidence of the post-war years for the United States and Britain suggests that there has been some tendency for the degree of dominance of the largest manufacturing firms to increase. In the United States the 100 largest manufacturing firms accounted in 1947 for 23 per cent of value added; in 1958 the figure was 30 per cent and in 1966, 33 per cent (US Senate, 1963 and Bureau of the Census, 1966). In Britain the 100 largest companies in manufacturing and distribution increased their share of quoted public [company] sector net assets from 44 per cent in 1954 to 62 per cent in 1965. These trends have been due partly to the rapid expansion of industries in which large firms predominate, partly to increased merger activity within industries, and partly to the increasing importance of diversification in the growth of large companies (see Nelson, 1963; Gort, 1962). The third of these factors – the growing importance of diversification – deserves further comment. In particular it is worth looking at the significance of this development for resource allocation and for monopoly policy.

The factor that perhaps stands out more than any other is the way in which diversification has become more a 'strategy of development' than simply a response to adverse market conditions. Perhaps this is largely due to the greater professionalization of management which we have already noted, and in particular to the fact that management has become more long-sighted. Whatever the strength of this argument there is little doubt that diversification has been *facilitated* by developments in management techniques and especially as a result of the greater use of computers and the adoption of the decentralized or multi-divisional form of organization.

But what of the consequences of all this for the process of competition and for the performance of the competitive system?

On the one hand there are those who as yet see little need to be concerned about the large diversified company and indeed point to some actual or potential advantages. Thus, for instance, it is pointed out that even if the aggregate level of concentration were much higher than it is today this would be quite compatible with each large firm lacking significant monopoly power in individual markets. In this case large firms owe their size not to positions of dominance in one market but to the extensive diversification of their operations. Individual market shares, therefore, may be relatively low and competition between firms in each market, intensive.

Looking at the diversified firm in a more dynamic context it may be argued that it improves the performance of the economic system in two important although related ways. First, because it increases the degree of competitiveness by facilitating entry into industries where the barriers to entry are too high for the smaller, more specialized firm. Secondly, because there is some tendency for the direction of diversification to be towards industries characterized by above average profitability and growth rates (Gort, 1962). *Given* the fact that large companies finance a high proportion of their capital expenditure from retained profits, the diversified company may, therefore, facilitate more rapid resource reallocation and thus contribute towards a more adaptable economic system.

This advantage of flexibility in the allocation of investment funds may also be promoted by the internal organization of the large diversified firm, and especially by the division of function between different levels of management. Here the multi-divisional form of organization is of importance. In such an organization the formulation of investment plans will be made by branch or divisional managers who compete for the finance available to the firm. Top management, however, is responsible for allocating funds, and the fact that it has not been deeply involved in the formulation of plans means that it is not committed to them and, therefore, is free to accept, reject or modify them. By contrast, in more specialized firms where the division of labour in management is less and where top management is more closely involved in the formulation of plans, the degree of commitment to investment projects might be such as to lead to greater inflexibility.

All this is not to say, however, that there are no problems of coordination in the large firm. Clearly there are, and they frequently lead to substantial internal inefficiency. Problems of communication between different levels of management become more severe as the organization gets larger; vested interests within the firm may be powerful enough to succeed in delaying needed changes; the capacity of the top executive to coordinate effectively is limited, especially for firms operating in constantly changing environments. The decentralization of management, the development of more sophisticated accounting and budgetary techniques, and the use of computers have helped to reduce the problems but they have not eliminated them. Clearly, it is dangerous to generalize. There are examples of large diversified firms which seem to be very efficiently managed, but also several cases which could hardly be put forward as models of efficiency. My own view is that even in an age when it is fashionable to speak about management as a team effort, a great deal of the efficiency or inefficiency of very large companies depends on the presence or absence of the organizing genius of one or two people.

It remains to mention some other problems relating to the large diversified firm.

The most familiar is the danger of cross-subsidization. Thus, the large diversified firm can use its financial power to discipline specialist rivals who engage in price-cutting. The smaller producers recognizing the much greater financial strength of the new entrant may well be forced to modify their competitive policies for fear of retaliation from the large firm, and the latter may in effect become a price leader (Blair, 1958). Price-cutting subsidized by profits from other markets where the firm has monopoly power may also be carried further in an attempt to eliminate rivals from the market or to forestall the entry of new firms. There are clearly limitations to the profits which can be sacrificed in this way and whether such a strategy is worth while will depend on whether entry barriers can be raised sufficiently to ensure higher long-term profits. However, it must not be forgotten that the mere entry of a large diversified firm into an industry previously consisting of specialist producers only will change entry conditions for other specialized firms, making them more difficult than would otherwise be the case.

More important, however, is the use of excess profits in one market to engage in heavy advertising in another so as to extend a firm's sphere of monopoly influence. The danger is particularly great where marketing rather than production skill is the main basis of diversification. It is in the field of marketing that large firms have perhaps the main advantage over smaller ones – especially where such factors as brand names, national advertising and style changes are important. In this case a small number of diversified firms may well build up a position of dominance in several industries, using their monopoly position in one industry to finance heavy sales promotion expenditures in another. Furthermore, of course, once established in a dominant position the heavy marketing expenditures are themselves an entry barrier to new competition.

It has to be recognized of course that such developments, although leading to positions of greater dominance for large firms, could still be consistent with substantial competition *between* large firms themselves. Thus exploitation of a monopoly situation by one large firm carries with it the danger of attracting competition from another. It is highly unlikely however that large firms will achieve the same pattern of diversification. Rather, it is likely that in a number of cases the main activity of one firm will be a secondary activity of another and that, recognizing the dangers of spoiling one another's markets, firms will tend to develop 'spheres of influence'.[1] If mutual inter-penetration of markets does occur and profits are eroded then this may be followed either by restrictive trading agreements or by mergers or other (perhaps government sponsored) schemes designed to 'rationalize production'. There is certainly a danger that an increase in aggregate concentration resulting from the diversification activities of large firms will subsequently result in increased market dominance in the interests of a more rational industrial structure or of more 'orderly marketing'.

Finally, it must be recognized that even if, given the high proportion of finance which is generated internally by the large firm, the diversified form of organization facilitates more rapid resource allocation, there is the more fundamental question of whether high levels of self-finance should be accepted as inviolate, or whether firms should be forced to compete more for funds in the market. In this situation the allocation of resources would be subject to more stringent market tests and would be less influenced by forms of organization and types of management control.[2]

Where the balance of advantage and disadvantage lies in relation to the present positions of the large diversified company is difficult to determine. There is certainly need for much more research into many of the issues. In the meantime policy has to be formulated. My own view is that it would be better to err on the side of adopting a hard line rather than a soft line towards big business, and the area where this can most appropriately be done is in policy towards mergers. It would be silly to adopt any measures against diversification as such. The major cause for concern is the *way* in which expansion by diversification is achieved, and here there should be a very definite presumption in favour of internal growth and against mergers. This does not impose any undue burden on large as compared to small firms. Indeed the former have greater financial, managerial and marketing resources on which to base expansion. But when growth takes place in this way it is more likely to be grounded on efficiency factors and less likely to be based on financial and market power than is the case with expansion by merger.

1. On the spheres of influence hypothesis see Edwards (1955).
2. For a policy recommendation along these lines, see Meade (1968).

References

BLAIR, J. M. (1958), 'The conglomerate merger in economics and law', *Georgetown law J.*, vol. 46.

BUREAU OF THE CENSUS (1966), *Annual Survey of Manufactures*, US Government Printing Office.

COLLINS, N. R., and PRESTON, L. E. (1961), 'The size structure of the largest industrial firms', *Amer. econ. Rev.*, vol. 51, pp. 986–1011.

EDWARDS, C. (1955), 'Conglomerate bigness as a source of market power', in the National Bureau of Economic Research, *Business Concentration and Price Policy*, Princeton University Press.

GORT, M. (1962), *Diversification and Integration in American Industry*, Princeton University Press.

MEADE, J. E. (1968), Is the new industrial state inevitable?', *Econ. J.*, vol. 78, pp. 372–92.

NELSON, R. L. (1963), *Concentration in the Manufacturing Industries of the United States*, Yale University Press.

US SENATE (1963), *Concentration Ratios in Manufacturing Industry*, US Government Printing Office.

UTTON, M. A. (1970), *Industrial Concentration*, Penguin.

24 Charles H. Berry

Corporate Growth and Diversification

Charles H. Berry, 'Corporate growth and diversification', *Journal of Law and Economics*, vol. 14, 1971, pp. 371–83.

The rise to a position of dominance of the conglomerate merger is one of the more striking features of contemporary industrial organization (see FTC, 1968). The term conglomerate implies that the resulting firm is more broadly diversified than the merging partners, and there is at least the suggestion that these (conglomerate) firms are more broadly diversified than other manufacturing firms of comparable size. There is also a general presumption that industrial diversification by *all* large manufacturing firms has recently been on the increase.[1]

This paper is an attempt to document, and to report some preliminary analysis of, this aspect of changing industrial organization. Indices of diversification, as of 1960 and 1965, are developed for 460 of the nation's largest industrial corporations. These measures are in turn related to the growth of these corporations during the 1960–65 period. The paper is addressed, therefore, to essentially two questions: first, the degree to which increasing diversification – 'conglomerateness' – *has* been a feature generally characteristic of all large industrial corporations taken as a group, and second, whether such diversification, whatever its source, can be shown to be a factor significantly affecting, or affected by, the rate of growth of these large industrial concerns.[2]

The data

All findings reported are based on data for the 500 largest (in terms of sales) industrial corporations as identified by the 1961 Fortune Directory, less three corporations which reported no domestic manufacturing activity in 1960, 36 which merged (or liquidated) out of existence between 1960 and 1965, and the Hearst Corporation for which financial records are not

1. See for example, FTC (1969) and also Berry (1967).
2. Unfortunately, with the data employed here (or with other publicly available data), it is simply not possible to make the obviously desirable distinction between diversification resulting from merger and that resulting from purely internal corporate expansion. The focus of this paper is therefore *diversification*, not diversification by merger.

public.[3] The 460 corporations so defined accounted, in 1960, for total assets of $170 billion, about 61 per cent of all United States corporate industrial assets in that year. By 1965, those assets had increased to a little more than $250 billion, for an over-all five-year increment of roughly 47 per cent.

That growth reflected an increase both in the number of plant facilities and in the number of products reported by these corporations. The number of individual plants reported by the 460 increased from 10,147 in 1960 to 11,589 in 1965. On the average, a firm in this group produced in 3·8, 7·1 and 9·9 separate two-, three- and four-digit industries respectively in 1960. Those averages were 4·4, 8·7 and 13·9 in 1965. Table 1 shows the distribution of the companies by the number of separate industries in which each reported products in 1960 and 1965, and bears out in more detail the increas-

Table 1 460 Large industrial corporations, by number of two-, three-, and four-digit industries in which products were reported, 1960 and 1965

| Number of industries | Number of corporations | | | | | |
| | four-digit | | three-digit | | two-digit | |
	1960	1965	1960	1965	1960	1965
1–5	168	138	217	183	354	310
6–10	136	109	146	126	95	129
11–15	76	87	53	94	11	20
16–20	40	62	28	25	—	1
21–25	16	26	9	18	—	—
26–30	11	12	3	5	—	—
31–35	4	10	1	5	—	—
36–40	3	4	3	1	—	—
41–45	1	4	—	2	—	—
46–50	2	3	—	1	—	—
51–75	3	4	—	—	—	—
76 and over	—	1	—	—	—	—
Total	460	460	460	460	460	460

Source: *Fortune Plant and Product Directory*, 1961 and 1965–6.

ing diversification of large industrial corporations which has begun to be documented elsewhere (FTC, 1969, pp. 221–4). The average number of four-digit industries in which products were reported by these firms increased, according to these data, by an astonishing 40 per cent between 1960 and 1965.

3. Data for these corporations are drawn primarily from the 1961 and the 1966 editions of the *Fortune Plant and Product Directory*. This source, which is not to be confused with the annual *Fortune Directory of the 500 Largest US Industrial Corporations*, lists five-digit products by individual plants, and provides a crude measure of

An index of corporate diversification

The obvious problem is that diversification is to be gauged not only by the *number* of industries in which a firm is active, but also by the distribution of the firm's productive activity among those industries. A firm with 99 per cent of its output accounted for by a single five-digit product is scarcely diversified regardless of the number of four-digit industries represented by the remaining 1 per cent. A firm with its productive activity equally divided among four four-digit industries *is* likely to be 'diversified', even if no more than four five-digit products are involved.

The point is a familiar one, and in the past the most common remedy has been to judge the diversification of a firm either by the ratio of its output in its primary industry to its total output or, alternatively, by the number of industries necessary to account for some fraction – generally 50 per cent – of the firm's total production. Gort, for example, employs the former, and in addition introduces the total number of industries represented within the firm's total output (1962).

For the 460 Fortune corporations, a more complete index of diversification is here defined as:

$$D = 1 - \sum_{i=1}^{n} p_i^2,$$

where p_i is the ratio of the firm's output in the ith industry to the firm's total output in n industries. This index is an application of the Herfindahl Summary Index of Industrial Concentration, but applied to the distribution of a firm's industrial activity rather than to the distribution of an industry's sales among firms (Herfindahl, 1950).[4] This index of diversification takes the value 0 when a firm is active in a single industry, and approaches unity when the firm in question produces equally in a large number of different industries.

This index appears to approximate rather closely what is generally meant by diversification.[5] It has, in addition, the convenient property that when a firm is equally active in each of several industries, the index of diversification becomes $1 - 1/n$ where n is the number of industries in which the firm is active. For example, a firm producing equally in four industries will yield a diversification index of $1 - \frac{1}{4}$. A firm with a diversification index of $\frac{3}{4}$, which can be obtained in various ways, is, by this measure, diversified to a

---

employment for each plant. The 1961 edition covers the 500 largest industrial corporations as of 1960. The 1965–6 edition extends this coverage to the 1000 largest.

4. In this application, the Herfindahl index is subtracted from unity so that the resulting measure increases with increasing diversification.

5. For an interesting discussion of this question, and for the derivation of a closely similar measure, see Ash (1965).

degree equivalent to that of a firm producing equally in four industries. This property of the Herfindahl index has been discussed by Adelman (1969). A few illustrative values of the index are provided in Table 2.

Table 2 **Illustrated value of the Herfindahl-type index of diversification**

Percentage of firm's sales in industry					Index of diversification
1	2	3	4	5	
100	—	—	—	—	0
95	5	—	—	—	0·10
90	10	—	—	—	0·18
80	10	10	—	—	0·34
60	40	—	—	—	0·48
60	10	10	10	10	0·60
50	20	20	10	—	0·66
40	20	20	10	10	0·74
30	20	20	20	10	0·78
20	20	20	20	20	0·80

Diversification of the Fortune corporations

Table 3 contains the mean values (unweighted) of diversification at the two-, three- and four-digit levels of the 460 Fortune corporations in 1960 and 1965. The 1960 values shown approximately correspond to those which would have been obtained had each of these firms produced equally in 1·6, 2·2 and 2·7, two-, three- and four-digit industries respectively. This is very much less diversification – by about two-thirds – than naive extrapolation of the industry counts reported earlier would suggest. Not only that, but the change between 1960 and 1965 is slight – an increase of about 3 per cent at the four-digit level, and of 5 per cent in terms of two-digit diversification.[6] Given the initial level of diversification in 1960, that

Table 3 **Average two-, three-, and four-digit diversification, 460 large industrial corporations, 1960 and 1965**

Level of diversification	Diversification index	
	1960	1965
two-digit	0·361	0·379
three-digit	0·548	0·578
four-digit	0·627	0·645

Source: *Fortune Plant and Product Directory*, 1961 and 1965–6.

6. The ranking of these percentages can be misleading. Had a 'straight' Herfindahl index been employed (for example, $D = \sum p_i^2$), the ordering of these percentages at the two- and four-digit levels would be reversed. The percentages themselves, however, would remain small.

increase, at the four-digit level, would correspond to that which would have occurred with the addition by each firm of about 1/10th of a four-digit product had the production of each been equally divided among the four-digit industries represented.

There are two immediate conclusions. First, industry counts for these firms, as shown for example in Table 4 *very* markedly overstate the degree of industrial diversification of these corporations – or at least are highly susceptible to that interpretation. On the average, these corporations were active in 1960 in almost ten four-digit industries. Production among those industries was sufficiently unequal to make the resulting diversification equivalent, by the measure employed here, to equal production in fewer than three four-digit industries. The extent of this difference is indicated by Table 4 which compares the average number of industries in which these firms were on the average active with the 'Numbers Equivalent' implied by the average level of diversification of these firms.[7]

Table 4 **Average number of industries, and industry numbers–equivalent, 460 large industrial corporations, 1960 and 1965**

	Number of industries		Industry numbers-equivalent	
Industry level	1960	1965	1960	1965
four-digit	9·9	13·9	2·61	2·82
three-digit	7·1	8·7	2·21	2·36
two-digit	3·8	4·4	1·56	1·61

Source: *Fortune Plant and Product Directory*, 1961 and 1965–6.

Second, diversification by these firms *did* increase between 1960 and 1965, but not by as much as might have been expected. While the average number of four-digit industries in which production was reported by these firms rose by 40 per cent between 1960 and 1965, four-digit diversification by a measure weighting the relative importance of production within those industries increased by 1/10 as much.[8]

7. The 'Numbers Equivalent' is defined as the number of industries that would generate the same index of diversification were the production of the firm equally divided among those industries.

8. Even this is probably an over-statement of changing diversification. The underlying estimates of corporate diversification are, as noted, based on records of each five-digit product produced within each plant of each company in 1960 and 1965. Production by these plants at the two-, three- and four-digit levels was estimated by dropping terminal digits, and considering all products of the plant within the same industry category to be the same product. Indices of diversification for the company were prepared by assuming that the output of each multi-product plant was equally divided among the products reported. Each plant was weighted according to its estimated employment. This weighting of products equally within plants, and of plants equally within size categories, would tend to bias upwards the resulting estimates of corporate

Corporate growth and changing diversification

These averages, however, take no account of variance in the behavior of individual firms, and substantial decreases as well as increases occurred in this regard. As a whole, these corporations grew and diversified, but that does not necessarily indicate that increasing diversification has been a significant component of relative growth *within* this group of 460. Although what follows suggests that such a relationship is not strong, it also suggests that the relationship is not totally in accord with the proposition that increasing diversification is the new route to corporate bigness.

Table 5 contains regression results obtained when growth in the assets of these firms between 1960 and 1965 is regressed on independent variables which would be expected to be related to that growth. The regression models are of the usual additive form, unweighted, with intercepts. Corporate growth is defined as the percentage increase in total assets of each corporation between 1960 and 1965. Independent variables are defined as follows:

1. *Total assets, 1960.* Total corporate assets in 1960 as reported by the 1961 *Fortune Directory of the 500 Largest.* This variable is included to

Table 5 Regression coefficients and *t*-ratios, per cent increase in total assets on selected independent variables, 460 large industrial corporations, 1960–65

Independent variables	Regression coefficients and t-ratios[a]						
	1	2	3	4	5	6	7
Total assets, 1960[b]	−4·23 (−1·56)						
Log$_e$ total assets, 1960		−6·98 (−3·31)	−6·35 (−2·99)	−6·48 (−3·06)		−7·11 (−3·38)	−7·06 (−3·29)
Earnings, 1960	1·24 (2·48)	1·29 (2·61)	1·43 (2·88)	1·44 (2·89)	1·18 (2·38)	1·30 (2·63)	1·49 (2·97)
Projected growth	0·345 (2·86)	0·375 (3·31)			0·337 (2·79)	0·374 (3·12)	0·374 (3·07)
Per cent change, four-digit diversification	0·335 (4·00)	0·334 (4·02)	0·33 (3·98)	0·29 (4·56)	0·336 (4·01)	0·285 (4·59)	
Per cent change, two-digit diversification	−0·113 (−1·04)	−0·095 (−0·89)	−0·10 (−0·86)		−0·120 (−1·11)		0·192 (2·35)
R	0·29	0·32	0·28	0·28	0·28	0·31	0·26

Source: See text.

[a] *t*-Ratios are shown in parentheses. [b] Defined in dollars $\times 10^{-5}$.

---

diversification. If products and plants added between 1960 and 1965 tended to be relatively less important quantitatively than the corresponding average product or plant, change in diversification will also be biased upwards. No check on the quantitative importance of this is possible.

test for differential growth between the larger and smaller corporations in this sample. That test is appropriate for two reasons. On the one hand, much argument relating to recent increasing corporate concentration in industry generally asserts the advantage of the very large industrial corporation in the growth process, and a good deal of policy attention has been directed to this purely structural aspect of changing industrial organization (see for example Campbell and Shepherd, 1968; White House Task Force, 1969). On the other hand, it is not unreasonable to suppose the opposite – that a given percentage increase in total assets may, other things being equal, be more readily accomplished by the smaller firm. If for no other reason, the smaller firm is less likely to be constrained by the growth rates of its particular markets. In this context, the variable would make more sense were corporate size defined relative to the size of the relevant markets, but that simply is not attempted here.

2. *Earnings, 1960*. Net profit after tax as a percentage of total assets in 1960, again as reported by the 1961 *Fortune Directory*. This variable is a crude proxy for the availability of internal investment funds. Dividends paid are included on the grounds that the dividend payout ratio is determined internally by the firm. These total earnings are scaled by the same base (total assets) as the dependent variable. Note that the variable acts not as a rate of return – to which it is clearly related – but as a constraint on internal investment funds available to the firm.

3. *Projected Growth, 1960–65*. This variable is defined as $G = \sum_{i=1}^{n} w_i g_i$

where w_i is the proportion of the firm's output in the ith four-digit industry, and g_i is the 1958–63 percentage increase in the value of shipments of that industry. This variable corrects for differential growth among the various four-digit industries in which these firms are active. The earlier period of 1958–63 is selected on the grounds that corporate assets would tend to lag sales.

4. *Per cent change. Two-digit diversification*. Per cent change in the 'Herfindahl Index' of diversification at the two-digit level, 1960–65.[9]

5. *Per cent change. Four-digit diversification*. As in 4 above, but at the four-digit level.

In Table 5, coefficients on 1960 earnings and on changing four-digit

9. In these regressions, diversification at all levels is measured by a 'straight' Herfindahl index with a negative sign (for example, $D = -\sum p_i^2$). This modification was necessary to permit calculation of percentage change in the index, since many firms produce only within a single two-digit industry group.

diversification are consistently positive and significant.[10] If corporate size – total assets in 1960 – is entered in logarithms, the coefficient on that variable is also significant, though negative. Within this framework, and for this particular sample, there is no evidence that corporate size has been positively related to corporate growth. What evidence there is suggests the reverse.[11]

The coefficient on the projected growth variable is approximately 0·35, which is substantially and significantly below the coefficient of unity which would be consistent with growth by these corporations in exact proportion to the growth of their various industries. On the one hand, the significance of the coefficient does suggest that the 'accident' of initial industrial location *is* a factor explaining some of the relative growth by these firms. On the other, it suggests that such growth has been less rapid than that of the industries or markets in question. In part, this may be a consequence of the cyclical recovery during the time-period considered. In cyclically sensitive industries – steel for example – growth in sales between 1958 and 1963 probably represents more the elimination of excess capacity than the presence of an incentive for the creation of additional capacity.[12]

Interpretation of the coefficients on the measures of changing diversification is interesting, but, given the definition of those variables, not easy. When either variable – changing diversification at the two- or the four-digit level – is introduced independently of the other, the coefficient has the expected positive sign and is, by the usual tests, statistically significant. Corporate growth, within this group of 460, is positively associated with

10. Essentially similar results are obtained if changing diversification is measured at the three- rather than the four-digit level. The two measures are closely related. Slightly higher t-ratios are obtained with the latter.

11. The simple correlation between growth and size is also negative; $r = -0.12$ with size measured in logarithms.

12. There are other reasons as well. A plausible case can be made that independent variables relating to average *industry* earnings and changing diversification should be included in these regressions – in other words that the performance of a firm should be gauged in terms of its deviation from industry mean performance – and that in that event the coefficient on projected growth might be higher. Such industry measures are not available, and in the case of diversification are conceptually awkward. Firms, not industries, are diversified. Note, however, that the average growth of these corporations over the five years was about 47 per cent, whereas the mean projected growth rate is only 30 per cent. These corporations grew more rapidly than the industries in which they were initially present despite the relatively low value of the regression coefficient on projected growth.

In addition, Allen Zelenitz has pointed out to me that this regression coefficient is equivalent to the product of the inverse of the average initial capital-output ratio and the capital-output ratio implied by the five-year increments. Since the latter would be expected to be less than the former, the value of that regression coefficient may not be as surprising as it first appears.

increasing diversification regardless of the level at which that diversification is measured. However, when measures of changing diversification at the two- and the four-digit level are introduced simultaneously, that association is positive only at the four-digit level and it becomes negative, though not significant, at the two-digit level. If the signs of the coefficients on those variables are believed – collinearity between the variables does not bias the estimates – this result suggests a rather conventional model of corporate growth: that diversification leading to corporate growth has involved entry to four-digit industries related to – within the same two-digit industry group as – those four-digit industries within which the corporation in question has experienced past success. Put differently, the pattern of coefficients obtained is consistent with a world in which successful (profitable) corporations expand (diversify), but to product areas (industries) related to their areas of past success, and a world in which it is those corporations whose performance and potential growth have been unsatisfactory that are more likely to branch to new and unrelated areas of productive endeavor.[13]

Within this context, Table 6 contains similar results employing measures of entry and exit in lieu of the measures of changing diversification of Table 5. In these regressions, entry and exit are defined as simple product counts of the number of industries added or dropped at the SIC level indicated. For example, if a corporation reported in 1965 products in two four-digit industries in which that corporation had no products in 1960, four-digit entry for that corporation is two. 'Net entry' is defined as the difference between entry and exit, and is, therefore, the increase in the number of industries reported between 1960 and 1965.

In Table 6, four-digit entry variables have positive and significant coefficients. The coefficients on two-digit entry are, as in the case of changing diversification at this level, negative although again significance levels are marginal. Although these results are scarcely independent of those of Table 5, the somewhat higher level both of overall explanation and of the significance of the four-digit measures is consistent with the interpretation that growth by these corporations has been accompanied by expansion within established two-digit industry groups, and that the diversification which has accompanied that growth has been more horizontal than conglomerate.

These measures of the inter-industry activity of these firms are not, however, well suited to the purpose of making that distinction. It becomes ap-

13. Note that although the specification of the dependent variable in this regression model would appear to make it susceptible to negative heteroscedasticity with respect to the corporate size variable, this turns out not to be true to any substantial degree. The simple correlation between the absolute value of the residual and corporate assets *is* negative, but r^2 is 0·01 (0·04 with corporate assets in log form).

Table 6 Regression coefficients and *t*-ratios, per cent increase in total assets on selected independent variables, 460 large industrial corporations, 1960–65

Independent variables	Regression coefficients and t-ratios[a]				
	1	2	3	4	5
Log$_e$ Total assets, 1960	−10·09 (4·96)			−9·34 (−4·63)	−10·38 (−5·16)
Earnings, 1960	1·50 (3·21)	1·31 (2·74)	1·24 (2·61)	1·37 (2·94)	1·64 (3·55
Projected growth	0·235 (2·04)	0·203 (1·73)	0·232 (1·99)	0·275 (2·40)	0·215 (1·87)
Four-digit entry	4·61 (6·83)	4·17 (6·08)			4·19 (6·59)
Four-digit exit	−1·95 (−1·79)	−2·04 (−1·82)			
Four-digit net entry			3·83 (5·89)	4·22 (6·58)	
Second-digit entry	−4·05 (−1·70)	−3·82 (−1·56)			−3·21 −1·37)
Second-digit exit	0·559 (0·16)	−0·340 (−0·10)			
Second-digit net entry			−0·274 (−1·29)	−3·22 (−1·55)	
R	0·45	0·40	0·39	0·44	0·44

Source: See text.

[a] *t*-ratios are shown in parentheses.

parent here that more appropriate would be measures distinguishing for each firm that four-digit diversification (or entry) which is *within* two-digit industry groups from that which arises as a consequence of diversification *across* (or entry to) new two-digit categories.

In this regard, the entry variables employed above are somewhat superior. For example, for each two-digit industry that is entered, it necessarily follows that a four-digit industry has been entered. Hence, for a given corporation, the difference between four-digit entry and two-digit entry indicates the number of four-digit industries entered *within* two-digit industry groups in which the corporation was active in *either* the initial or the terminal year considered. If such four-digit entry within two-digit industry groups is written as $E_{4/2}$ (with two-digit entry as E_2) then regression (5) of Table 6 becomes

$$G = \ldots + 4\cdot19[E_{4/2} + E_2] - 3\cdot21\, E_2 \ldots \qquad 1$$

or

$$G = \ldots + 4 \cdot 19\, E_{4/2} + 0 \cdot 98\, E_2 \ldots \qquad 2$$

with the implication that growth-related entry has been almost exclusively four-digit entry *within* two-digit industry groups.

The disadvantage with this formulation is that four-digit entry within an *entered* two-digit industry group is thereby considered four-digit entry *unrelated* to two-digit entry, which is clearly not the case. The more appropriate measure would be the number of four-digit industries entered within two-digit industry groups within which the firm was active initially – in 1960 – and that measure cannot be derived from the preceding indices. In its absence, however, consider the following. The regression of four-digit entry on two-digit entry is, for these 460 firms

$$E_4 = 0 \cdot 929 + 2 \cdot 947\, E_2 + \mu \qquad 3$$

and regression (5) from Table 6 gives

$$G = \ldots 4 \cdot 19\, E_4 - 3 \cdot 21\, E_2 \ldots \qquad 4$$

If the predicted value of **3** above, $\hat{E}_4$, is taken as an estimate of that four-digit entry which results from entry at the two-digit level, it is then reasonable to examine

$$G = \ldots a_1 \hat{E}_4 + a_2\, [E_4 - \hat{E}_4] \ldots \qquad 5$$

where $\hat{E}_4$ and $[E_4 - \hat{E}_4]$ attempt to distinguish between inter- and intra-two-digit industry activity, both expressed in four-digit terms. The values of the regression coefficients of **3** and **4** give

$$a_1 = 4 \cdot 19 - 3 \cdot 21/2 \cdot 95 = 3 \cdot 10 \quad a_2 = 4 \cdot 19$$

or $\qquad\qquad\qquad\qquad\qquad\qquad\qquad\qquad\qquad\qquad\qquad\qquad$ 6

$$G = \ldots 3 \cdot 10\, \hat{E}_4 + 4 \cdot 19\, [E_4 - \hat{E}_4] \ldots$$

and the negative sign on the two-digit component is no longer present. The larger coefficient on the residuals, $[E_4 - \hat{E}_4]$, is consistent with the interpretation that entry within, rather than among, two-digit categories carries with it a greater impact on corporate growth, but this formulation suggests a positive contribution from the latter as well.

Similar manipulation of the coefficients of regression (2) of Table 5, given

$$\dot{D}_4 = 2 \cdot 407 + 0 \cdot 868\, \dot{D}_2 + e \qquad 7$$

yields

$$G = \ldots 0 \cdot 225\, \hat{\dot{D}}_4 + 0 \cdot 334\, [\dot{D}_4 - \dot{D}_4] \ldots \qquad 8$$

and essentially the same interpretation ($\dot{D}_2$ and $\dot{D}_4$ are per cent change in two- and four-digit diversification respectively). Here again the negative sign on the inter-two-digit variable is eliminated, although the coefficient on the intra-two-digit variable remains the larger of the two. Actual direct fitting of 6 and 8 results in coefficients that are statistically significant by the usual tests in all instances. The two coefficients themselves are statistically different from one another in the case of 8 but not of 6.

The across- or inter-two-digit variables, $\hat{E}_4$ and $\dot{D}_4$, are estimates based on the association between two- and four-digit activity for this group of firms as a whole. They identify only the relative intensity of two- as opposed to four-digit inter-industry activity by these corporations. Nevertheless, in each of the formulations, the results are indicative of corporate growth more responsive to (or more conducive to) inter-industry expansion within rather than among two-digit industries. A more positive result in this regard will require redefinition of the diversification and entry variables. Such redefinition is planned but not completed at the present time.

Some concluding remarks

These preliminary results are based on the record of growth and diversification by 460 corporations accounting for only a little less than two-thirds of all United States corporate industrial assets. For these firms, the degree both of diversification, and of recent change in diversification appears to be a good deal less than that which would at first glance be suggested by the number of industries in which these same firms have been active. On the average, the diversification of these firms is about equal to that which would be recorded by a firm with production equally divided among three four-digit industries, with that production in turn heavily concentrated within a single two-digit industry group. Given that these corporations are large corporations, apt frequently to be vertically integrated, and given also that the Standard Industrial Classification can place vertically related four-digit industries in different two-digit industry groups, the degree of diversification indicated by these firms is consistent with a relatively high prevalence of corporate specialization within the group as a whole.

Change in the *average* diversification of these firms is also small relative to the increased number of products shown by these firms over the five-year period. At the four-digit level, the average number of products rose by something like 40 per cent; the average index of four-digit diversification increased by less than 4 per cent. The implication is clear that those products added by these firms did not, in general, account for large proportions of the total productive activity of these firms.

On the other hand, from a structural standpoint, the addition of the new products may be the more significant development. The index of diversification defined earlier could, for example, register change simply as a consequence of unintended shifts in market shares within industries without any intent whatsoever on the part of the corporation involved to diversify. Entry, however, necessarily involves a commitment on the part of the corporation to expand or shift its activities to a new product or set of products. The significance of entry in this context is suggested by the earlier regression results which show a higher degree of association between corporate growth and the addition of new products than between corporate growth and change in the diversification index.

The most interesting aspect of those regression results related to the character of the relationship between corporate growth and entry or increasing diversification. The evidence, such as it is, appears to indicate consistently that the four-digit inter-industry activity which has been most conducive to corporate growth has been within rather than among two-digit industry groups. At least one possible interpretation of this finding is that diversification leading to relatively rapid rates of corporate growth (or accompanying it) has not in general been diversification to markets where the entering firms may be regarded as a new and potentially competitive force, but rather 'diversification' to markets related to – and potentially if not actively competitive with – those in which the entering firm will frequently be among those in possession of whatever market power already exists. That kind of diversification is only one small step removed from the consolidation of market power through horizontal acquisition. The issue which is raised by these regression results is far from idle in the context of an increasingly concentrated corporate industrial sector.[14] These results are preliminary. They are also highly suggestive.

14. This point is further developed in Berry (1970).

References

ADELMAN, M. A. (1969), 'Comment on the "H" concentration measure as a numbers-equivalent', *Rev. Econ. Stats*, vol. 51, p. 99.

ASH, R. (1965), *Information Theory*, Interscience.

BERRY, C. H. (1967), 'Corporate bigness and diversification in manufacturing', *Ohio State law J.*, vol. 28.

BERRY, C. H. (1970), 'Economic policy and the conglomerate merger', in 'Conglomerate mergers and acquisitions, opinion and analysis', *St. John's law Rev.*, vol. 44 (special edn).

CAMPBELL, J. S. and SHEPHERD, W. G. (1968), 'Leading firm conglomerate mergers', *Antitrust Bull.*, vol. 13, p. 1361.

FEDERAL TRADE COMMISSION (FTC) (1968), *Large Mergers in Manufacturing and Mining, 1948–67*, US Government Printing Office.

FTC (1969), *Economic Report on Corporate Mergers*, US Government Printing Office.

GORT, M. (1962), *Diversification and Integration in American Industry*, Princeton University Press.

HERFINDAHL, O. C. (1950), 'Concentration in the Steel Industry', unpublished Ph.D. dissertation, Columbia University.

White House Task Force on Antitrust Policy (1969) in Trade Reg. Rep. Supp. no. 415, III-1–III-13.

25 Henry G. Grabowski

The Determinants of R & D in Three Industries

Henry G. Grabowski, 'The determinants of industrial research and development: a study of the chemical, drug, and petroleum industries', *Journal of Political Economy*, vol. 76, 1968, pp. 292–306.

Economists have recently grown interested in doing research on research – or R & D, as it is called in industrial circles. Several studies have tested Schumpeter's hoary hypothesis that large firms are responsible for most industrial inventive activity.[1] Few of these studies, however, suggest why this hypothesis is apparently valid for some industries and not for others. And statistical studies going beyond this question, to try to relate R & D expenditures to firm profit expectations and the availability of funds as in other investment decisions, are rare (Mansfield, 1964; Mueller, 1967).

This paper reports the results of an empirical investigation into the determinants of research expenditures in three industries – drugs, chemicals, and petroleum refining. These industries have three advantages for such a study: (1) they are among the leaders in total R & D expenditures; (2) most activity is concentrated in an appreciable number of large or moderately large firms; and (3) government support of research work is relatively small, so that decisions are more closely analogous to ordinary investment decisions.[2] Data samples were constructed for the three industries by requesting total R & D expenditure figures, as defined by the NSF standards,[3] from firms in the 1960 *Fortune 500* listing. The response

1. Data collected by the National Science Foundation (NSF) definitely show that firms below certain threshold sizes perform very little organized R & D. For example, firms with 1000 employees or less in 1958 accounted for 60 per cent of total industrial employment but performed only 5 per cent of company-financed R & D (NSF, 1964, p. 6). However, the question which has been extensively investigated in recent studies is whether research intensity increases with size among firms clearly larger than the threshold levels. For a survey of these studies and an attempt to reconcile some conflicting results, see Markham (1965).

2. Of the six NSF industry classifications performing approximately $300 million or more of company-financed R & D in 1963, government-supported R & D was over 25 per cent of total expenditures except in chemicals and allied products and in petroleum refining. In these two industries it amounted to 21 per cent and 6 per cent, respectively.

3. The NSF definitions of R & D are given in the technical notes of all its published data reviews. These data have definite advantages over company published figures in that (1) they are based on a common externally devised definition; and (2) firms are

rate in each industry was almost exactly 70 per cent, with R & D data over the period 1959–62 provided by sixteen firms in chemicals, fifteen in petroleum refining, and ten in drugs.

Since the main variation in the data occurs over the cross-section of firms, rather than for each firm over time, the regression models will be primarily explaining interfirm differences in R & D. However, pooled cross-section time-series samples will be used in order to increase the number of available observations in each industry sample. For each equation estimated with these pooled samples, the hypothesis of time-invariant parameters was tested. Because this hypothesis cannot be rejected at the normal confidence intervals, data pooling may be advantageously employed in the present analysis of R & D determinants.

1 The characteristics of the model

When analysing the R & D behavior of a group of firms in which substantially different scales of operation exist, research intensity, rather than the absolute level of a firm's expenditures, is a more appropriate dependent variable. When absolute figures are used, heteroscedasticity is invariably present, and scale effects tend to dominate the regression equations. In order to avoid these problems, the procedure adopted in this paper is to measure R & D expenditures as well as size-correlated independent variables, relative to the total sales of the firm.[4] Although there are some good *a priori* reasons for choosing sales as the particular size deflator,[5] the results are substantially unaltered if either total assets or the number of employees is used instead.

The determinants of research intensity to be considered first relate to the returns from R & D activity. Since there is a considerable lag in the payoff to R & D, a firm's estimated set of returns from current projects will likely depend on its past results. While expectations based on past performance may not vary markedly from one budget period to the next for an individual firm, substantial variations should exist across firms due

assured of confidential treatment, thereby removing any incentives to inflate the figures artificially. While the NSF data are undoubtedly the best available statistics, it must be emphasized there are still many difficult conceptual problems in measuring inventive efforts by dollar outlays. See the discussions in Kuznets (1962) and Sanders (1962).

4. An alternative approach for dealing with heteroscedasticity is to estimate the equations using logarithmic transformations when the specifications of the models permit one to do so. Both procedures have been extensively used in dealing with samples that are cross-sectional in nature and span a large size spectrum. For a discussion of the problems associated with using the ratio approach, see Kuh and Meyer (1955).

5. This question has been analyzed by Scherer (1965b, pp. 256–61) in a commentary on some results of Hamberg (1964). Among the reasons for choosing sales are: (1) sales is a more neutral size measure, and (2) firms have emphasized the use of sales as a landmark for budget decisions in various interview studies.

to the cumulated effects of past differences in firm capacities and attitudes toward R & D. The first explanatory variable of research intensity is, therefore, an index of the research productivity of each firm over a prior period.

In order to construct such a proxy variable of research productivity, three possible measures of a firm's research output were considered: new-product sales, the number of patents granted to the firm, and the number of significant inventions made by the firm. Given the strong product orientation of industrial R & D, perhaps the best measure of the three from a conceptual standpoint is new-product sales. Unfortunately, new-product sales are not generally available, and furthermore, substantial differences in definitions and product classification among firms make the use of these numbers in a cross-section analysis quite hazardous. Of the two other measures of research output, patents is the more attractive, since all patented inventions must pass certain uniform criteria of the US Patent Office, and patent statistics are readily available.[6]

The measure of research outputs used in the model is, therefore, the number of patents granted to a firm in a specified prior period. To form the productivity variable, this output measure is divided by a research-input measure – specifically, the number of scientists and engineers employed by the firm over the approximate period when the patented inventions were conceived.[7] The first hypothesis put forth here is thus that firms with higher patented output per scientific worker in the past will, *ceteris paribus*, be more research-intensive than their rivals.[8] Of course, this variable at best measures only one aspect of the firm's returns from R & D – the technical quality of its research outputs. Another aspect, relating to the applicability of R & D to the firm's operations, will be considered below.

Before discussing the other explanatory variables, however, it should be mentioned that patents have been used elsewhere as a measure of inventive output, and their limitations in this regard have been extensively discussed

6. Attempts at constructing a series of significant inventions made by each firm were beset by serious methodological problems and therefore discarded. For some interesting attempts to measure inventive output in this manner, see Mansfield (1964, pp. 334–7).

7. Scherer (1965a, p. 1097) has estimated that over a period somewhat coincident with our sample the patent office took an average of three and one-half years to process a patent. Adding several more months as time necessary to draw up a patent application, the 'patent lag' is taken somewhat arbitrarily here to be four years in length.

8. This relationship is likely to operate in a forward as well as backward manner. That is, more research-intensive firms now should realize a higher level of patented outputs in the future. There is ample evidence that firm behavior often follows such recursive patterns. While firms may certainly radically change past modes of operation, R & D in particular is not an activity that lends itself to frequent and marked changes in emphasis.

(Kuznets, 1962; Sanders, 1962). One of the more serious problems incurred in using patent statistics is the possibility that the propensity to patent might be systematically correlated in a positive way with a firm's degree of research intensity. If this were so, a spurious positive relation between research intensity and patent output per worker would result. However, there are no strong *a priori* arguments why this will be the case, and some data are available to analyse this question for the firms under study. This problem will be taken up in the next section.

The second explanatory variable of research intensity in the present model is an index of each firm's output diversification. It has been postulated in the literature (see Nelson, 1959) that a firm's degree of diversification will positively influence its profit expectations from R & D. This hypothesis follows from the belief that a more diversified firm will be better able to exploit unexpected research outputs than one with a narrower base of operations. While the original formulation was meant to apply to scientific work at the research end of the spectrum rather than to development expenditures, this hypothesis also implies greater expenditures on total R & D unless these two component activities are complete substitutes, which is highly unlikely.

The index of diversification used in the present model is based on the number of separate five-digit SIC product classifications in which a firm produced during a middle year of the sample period.[9] This variable, like the index of past research productivity, is designed to capture interfirm differences in expected returns from R & D. It therefore varies only over the cross-section of firms and not over time. Over a four-year interval, the size of the firm's product mix does not change significantly, and the construction of the index as 'timeless' during this period is a satisfactory approximation.

Aside from expected returns, financial factors form another basic set of considerations relevant to industrial R & D expenditures. The relationships between financial variables and investment have been extensively explored

9. All the data on diversification come from the 1961 edition of the *Fortune Plant and Product Directory*. For the chemical and petroleum industries, an examination of the various product classes revealed that they are virtually all of sufficient technical character to have at least some potential relevance to the R & D activity. For these two industries, the index will therefore be the total number of separate SIC classifications encompassed by the firm's product mix. For the drug industry, however, product mixes of highly diversified drug firms indicate a tendency for them to expand into products only tangentially related to the manufacture of drugs proper (that is, adhesives, brushes, glass bottles, toilet preparations, plastic products, and so forth). These product lines offer little opportunity for the applicability of research outputs. It was therefore decided that a more appropriate index of diversification for the drug industry would be obtained by counting only the number of SIC classifications that are concerned directly with the manufacture of drugs proper.

in the literature on the determinants of fixed capital expenditures (for a bibliography, see Eisner and Strotz, 1963). There is considerable evidence from these studies that retained earnings and other internally generated funds have an especially significant effect on investment expenditures. This has been attributed to the general reluctance of firms to raise funds externally because of the added risks and transaction costs entailed in this type of financing. If this is so, it would seem applicable with some qualifications to investment in R & D.

In the short run, R & D expenditures can be expected to be much less sensitive to changes in cash flow, especially in the downturn. This is true because of the higher fixed cost component in R & D activity. Research workers whose salaries constitute a sizable percentage of total expenditures, are not perfectly elastic in supply and cannot be alternately fired and rehired in accordance with temporary changes in business conditions.[10] In the long run, however, a significant positive relationship between R & D and cash flow should be evident if firms behave as many previous investment studies suggest. Since the data samples investigated here are basically cross-sectional and span four years of reasonably stable growth for the firms involved, a long-run effect should be observed in the present case. The third explanatory variable in our model is, therefore, a measure of the firm's internally generated funds deflated by sales. The specific internal funds variable that will be used is the sum of the firm's after-tax profits plus depreciation and depletion charges, lagged one period.

The above three variables reflect some of the main technological, marketing, and financial factors that one would expect to influence the R & D expenditure decision. Some previous interview studies of R & D suggest some other relevant considerations (see NSF, 1956). One strong trend of thought running through these studies is that firm decisions on R & D are strongly influenced by the behavior of competitors, and, in particular, that a great deal of imitation exists among firms with respect to R & D allocations. Since most R & D is performed by firms operating in oligopolistic market structures and it is an activity presumably involving greater uncertainty than other undertakings, firms may imitate each other as a conservative strategy for minimizing risks. Because of the multitude of forms which such imitation may take, however, it is difficult to deal with this phenomenon in the framework of the present empirical analysis.

One particularly simple type of imitation discussed in these interview

10. That is, there will likely be significant downward rigidities in this relationship due to the technological necessity of maintaining a reasonably stable staff of researchers. Also, the increasing cost associated with rapid expansion will act to constrain this relationship in upturns in the short run as well. While material costs are more flexible, they account for a smaller percentage of total expenditures (for representative cost figures, see the NSF data reviews).

studies and frequently mentioned in the trade literature is the adherence by firms to a general industry R & D to sales ratio. If this kind of imitative behavior is present to any significant degree in the present industrial samples, it should be evident from the empirical analysis. Since research intensity as measured by the R & D to sales ratio is the dependent variable, imitation by firms of an 'industry' ratio would imply less variability in the dependent variable and cause the intercept of the regression equation to become statistically significant relative to the explanatory variables postulated above. The sign and statistical significance of the intercept term in the regression model therefore provide a first level test of this proposition. However, more subtle and complex forms of imitation are best analysed in a more disaggregative context than the data permit here.

The present discussion leaves us essentially with three explanatory variables of firm research intensity – a research-productivity variable consisting of the level of patented output realized by the firm relative to its input of scientific personnel over a prior period, an index of firm product diversification, and a variable dealing with the financial resources of the firm which is equal to the level of internally generated funds of the firm as a percentage of its total sales. The model may be expressed formally as

$$\frac{R_{i,t}}{S_{i,t}} = b_0 + b_1 P_t + b_2 D_i + b_3 \frac{I_{i,t-1}}{S_{i,t}}, \qquad \textbf{1}$$

where $R_{i,t}$ is the level of R & D expenditures of the ith firm in the tth period, $S_{i,t}$ is the level of sales of the ith firm in the tth period, $I_{i,t-1}$ is the sum of after-tax profits plus depreciation and depletion expenses of the ith firm in the $t-1$ period, P_i is the number of patents received per scientist and engineer employed by the ith firm in a prior four-year period (1955–9), and D_i is the index of diversification of the ith firm (the number of the separate five-digit SIC product classifications in which it produces).

The hypotheses discussed above suggest that coefficients b_1, b_2, and b_3 will all be positive. In addition, the intercept term, b_0, of this equation serves in a sense as a possible fourth explanatory variable since it shows the influence of sales on research expenditures and in particular provides a test of the proposition that firms adhere to an industry-wide R & D to sales ratio. The results of including some additional variables in equation **1** are also given in the section which follows.

2 The empirical results

Using the data samples described above, least-squares estimates of the coefficients of equation **1** were obtained. The results are presented in Table 1. All of the regression coefficients are of the postulated sign and are significant at the 1 per cent level except for the diversification variable

Table 1 **Estimation of regression equation** $R_{i,t}/S_{i,t} = b_0 + b_1 P_i + b_2 D_i$ $+ b_3(I_{i,t-1}/S_{i,t})$ **for the chemical, drug, and petroleum industries for the period 1959–62**

Industry	b_0	b_1	b_2	b_3	R^2	F	N
Chemicals	0·006	0·12*	0·019*	0·078*	0·63	29·76	60
	(0·004)	(0·02)	(0·004)	(0·023)			
Drugs	−0·03*	0·54*	0·41*	0·26*	0·86	73·71	40
	(0·01)	(0·12)	(0·07)	(0·05)			
Petroleum	0·002	0·016*	0·0049	0·020*	0·29	5·46	55
	(0·002)	(0·005)	(0·0071)	(0·006)			

* Significant at 0·01 level.

Note: Numbers below coefficient estimates are estimates of the standard errors; technological and diversification variables (P_i and D_i) have been multiplied by scale factors in order to present results more conveniently.

coefficient in the petroleum industry, which is positive but statistically insignificant. The over-all explanatory power of our model is quite good in the case of the chemical and drug industries, given the nature of the samples under study, ($R^2 = 0·63$ and $0·86$, respectively), but is low for the petroleum industry ($R^2 = 0·29$). An examination of the results in Table 1 also shows that the estimates of the intercept terms of equation **1** are such as to cast considerable doubt on the proposition that firms in this sample adhere to an industry-wide R & D to sales ratio. The only statistically significant intercept is negative (the drug industry), and the positive coefficients for the other two industries were negligible in value.[11]

The above regression results indicate that interfirm differences in technology, diversification, and the availability of funds are all important in explaining differences in research intensity with no single factor having a dominant influence. Table 1 also shows that the size of the regression coefficient associated with each of these variables increases with the research orientation of the industry involved – being the lowest in the petroleum industry and the highest in the drug industry in every case. Thus, as research looms more important as a comparative strategy to the firms of an industry, each of our independent variables exerts a correspondingly greater effect on the level of research that a firm performs.

The much poorer performance of the model in explaining research intensity in petroleum refining can be traced in part to certain structural

11. All of the results presented in Table 1 are substantially unchanged when the profit component of the available funds variable is measured by the firm's retained earnings rather than its total after-tax profits. The results on the significance of the variables are the same, and the fit of the regression becomes slightly better for chemicals ($R^2 = 0·67$) and slightly poorer for drugs ($R^2 = 0·80$).

factors that distinguish it from chemicals and drugs. Among these factors are:

1. R & D is much more process oriented in petroleum refining;[12]
2. the degree of integration within this industry is very uniform, and the amount of outward diversification is slight; and
3. R & D is more of a peripheral activity, consuming a portion of the budget which is at least an order of magnitude smaller than in the other two industries.

In an industry where research is process oriented, patents will likely be a poorer measure of technological output because firms will often wish to keep knowledge of such inventive activity concealed from their competitors. Furthermore, where R & D is a competitive strategy of lesser importance, as in petroleum refining, allocations to it tend to be more vulnerable to fluctuations in other uses of scarce funds. While there is no way to quantify the effects of the above three structural factors, together they probably explain a substantial part of the poorer performance of the model in this industry.

The positive relation observed between patented output per research input and the research intensity of a firm has been interpreted above as a measure of the effects of interfirm technology differences in research intensity. If it were true that more research-intensive firms have a greater propensity to patent than less intensive ones, this interpretation would be open to serious question. To investigate this latter possibility, data on the number of in-house patent attorneys for all the firms in our sample over the period 1955–59 were obtained. This is the most meaningful measure of patent activity available, although it is far from a complete index of it.[13]

Utilizing these data on patent attorneys, the correlation coefficient between a firm's research intensity and the number of in-house attorneys engaged per scientist and engineer was calculated for each of the three industry samples. Since the regression estimates have shown a significant relation between a firm's research intensity and the number of patents granted to it per research employee, one would also expect a significant relation between this variable and the number of in-house patent attorneys

12. The fifteenth annual McGraw-Hill *Survey of Business* for 1962 indicated that R & D planned by petroleum firms for that year was 42 per cent process oriented and only 6 per cent so in the chemical and allied products industries. In addition, the 1960 survey showed that new-product sales amounted to 16 per cent of total sales in the latter industry, while constituting only 2 per cent of total sales in the petroleum industry.

13. The crucial factor here is the relation of in-house patent attorneys to those hired from outside the firm. No statistics are available at present on the latter variable. The use of in-house attorneys by the firms in our sample was, however, quite extensive – almost all firms had at least one attorney, and most had several. In addition, the number of patent attorneys was well correlated with the number of patents ($r = 0.7$).

per research employee if this relation were merely the result of more research-intensive firms having a greater propensity to patent. The resulting correlation coefficient between these variables, however, is -0.2 in chemicals, 0.1 in drugs, and 0.3 in petroleum. These correlations, none of which is significantly positive at the 5 per cent level, do not support the hypothesis that more research-intensive firms tend to patent a greater proportion of patentable inventions. Although this is admittedly a rather slim reed of evidence, it is all that is currently available. However, since there is no strong *a priori* case for any kind of correlation, it may be tentatively accepted as support for the position that no systematic relations exist between these variables.

Finally, in order to investigate other possible factors affecting R & D which are omitted from the present model, a few variables that have been used with success in explaining investment in fixed capital were added to equation **1**.[14] In particular, the relevance of the traditional accelerator mechanism to R & D was investigated by including the first differences of sales in a given period (deflated by sales) as an additional explanatory variable of research intensity. While the normal rationale underlying the accelerator does not hold directly for R & D, a relation may still exist if expectations about future business conditions are strongly influenced by current changes in sales.[15] However, the results do not indicate that this effect is important for R & D expenditures in the present industrial samples. When the sales difference term is added to equation **1**, the estimate of the regression coefficient is quite insignificant and alternates in sign among the three industries. Specification of the accelerator with other time lags also yielded insignificant regression estimates. The fact that R & D is essentially an activity directed to the discovery and development of new products and processes with long periods until payoff may account for this apparent insensitivity to current sales changes.

3 Research intensity and firm size

All of the independent variables used in the above model – research productivity, the degree of internal liquidity, and diversification – have been cited in the literature as firm attributes positively associated with

14. In addition to the accelerator term discussed in the text, some variables relating to external conditions in financial markets and to the financial position of the firm (that is, the interest rate, the size of the firm's external debt, and the debt-equity ratio) were also included, but these all proved to be very insignificant.

15. There is some question as to the expected sign of this relationship. If firms undertake investments in R & D on the basis of optimistic expectations and vice versa, a positive sign would or could be anticipated. It has been postulated by Hall (1964, p. 9), however, that firms will turn to R & D as a principal strategy for reversing poor sales performance, and a negative sign would then be expected.

large size. It has been argued, therefore, that the large firms in a given industry will be more research-intensive than their smaller competitors, and vigorous government antitrust activity may have a harmful effect on technological progress. As noted above, there have been several recent investigations of this form of the Schumpeterian hypothesis, but the results have been quite mixed in nature. A study by Mansfield (1964, pp. 333–7), for example, found a significantly positive relation between research intensity and firm size in chemicals, whereas the drug and petroleum industries exhibited significantly negative ones. Since the variables supposedly underlying the Schumpeterian hypothesis yielded very good fits of research intensity in the chemical and drug industries – and yet these two industries apparently exhibit quite different structural relationships between research intensity and firm size – it is worth investigating the potential source of these differences.

First of all, in order to investigate the Schumpeterian hypothesis for the particular industrial samples under study, the following regression is estimated,

$$\frac{R_{i,\cdot}}{S_{i,t}} = \frac{a_0}{S_{i,t}} + a_1 + a_2 S_{i,t},$$
2

which in non-ratio form is the quadratic,

$$R_{i,t} = a_0 + a_1 S_{i,t} + a_2 S_{i,t}^2.$$
3

A quadratic estimated in the above fashion should indicate whether there is any tendency for research intensity to increase or diminish significantly as size increases through the behavior of the a_2 coefficient. The regression estimates of equation 2 for the chemical and drug industries are presented in the top of Table 2.[16] While a_1 is positive and statistically significant as expected in both cases, the estimate of a_2 is significantly positive for chemicals and significantly negative for drugs.[17] A plot of these estimated relations is given in Figure 1. It indicates that, for the drug industry, research intensity initially increases with firm size but is characterized by a decreasing relation for most of the relevant range. For the chemical industry, the

16. The petroleum industry could also be included here, but it is omitted because the independent variables of equation 1 explained only one-third of the total variance for that industry. If one repeats the procedures described in this section for it, however, the interpretation of the results are consistent with those presented for chemicals and drugs. For the details, see Grabowski (1967, pp. 75–83).

17. It may be noted that while the R^2's are quite modest for this regression equation, the standard errors of estimate indicate quite good fits to the data. This, of course, is because, in the ratio form of estimating equation 3 much of the explanatory power now comes from the intercept term a_1 which affects the goodness of fit of equation 2 but not the R^2; that is, the estimates of equation 2 explain a very large portion of the variation in absolute R & D expenditures (due to the high explanatory power of the a_1 term) but only a moderate amount of the variation in the research intensity of firms.

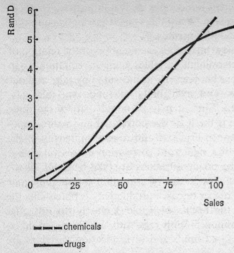

Figure 1 Estimated quadratic regression equation of R & D on sales for chemical and drug firms. The units of sales have been changed so that firms in the sample cannot be identified. The sales of the largest firms in each sample are represented in the new units by 100, and the smallest firms in each sample are between 1 and 10

estimated relation indicates that research intensity increases steadily throughout. Thus, the results of testing the Schumpeterian hypothesis on

Table 2a[a] **Estimation of regression equation $R_t/S_t = (1/S_t)(a_0 + a_1 S_t + a_2 S_t^2)$ for pooled time-series cross-sections of firms in the chemical and drug industries over the period 1959–62**

Industry	a_0	a_1	a_2	R^2	F
Chemicals	0·04	0·03*	$0·9 \times 10^{-5}$*	0·28	22·22
	(0·03)	(0·02)	$(0·2 \times 10^{-5})$		
Drugs	−6·21*	0·17*	$−0·4 \times 10^{-3}$*	0·40	19·35
	(1·29)	(0·02)	$(0·1 \times 10^{-3})$		

Table 2b[a] **Estimation of the regression equation $R_{i,t}/S_{i,t} = a_0/S_{i,t} + a_1 + a_2 S_{i,t} + a_3 (I_{i,t-1}/S_{i,t}) + a_4 D_i$ for same samples**

Industry	a_0	a_1	a_2	a_3	a_4	R^2	F
Chemicals	0·05	0·009	$0·006 \times 10^{-7}$	0·09*	0·020*	0·50	13·81
	(0·04)	(0·005)	$(0·28 \times 10^{-7})$	(0·03)	(0·006)		
Drugs	−2·18	0·01	$−0·14 \times 10^{-3}$	0·45*	0·44*	0·72	22·07
	(1·46)	(0·03)	$(0·09 \times 10^{-3})$	(0·13)	(0·10)		

[a] See footnotes to Table 1.

these samples show quite different behavior in the two industries. This is in essential agreement with Mansfield[18] and others investigating this question using different firm samples and time periods.[19]

Given these results, let us now turn to an examination of the relation of size to the three research determinant variables used in equation 1. In Table 3, the simple correlations between size as measured by sales and our technological, diversification, and availability of funds variables (P_i, D_i, $[I_{i,t-1}/S_{i,t}]$) are presented. First, it may be noted that, of the three variables, the patent variable is the least size-correlated and varies oppositely to the relationship between firm size and research intensity in the two industries. The absence of a significant correlation in this variable is particularly important for the policy questions at stake here. Of all the arguments put forth by the proponents of corporate bigness, the one maintaining large firms have higher research productivity is potentially the most significant. However, the results of Table 3 clearly do not offer any real support for this position.[20] With regard to the other two determinants, the internally generated funds and diversification variables are

Table 3 **Simple correlation of size and variables P_i, D_i, and $(I_{i,t-1}/S_{i,t})$ for the chemical and drug industries**

Industry	P_i	D_i	$(I_{i,t-1}/S_{i,t})$
Chemicals	−0·2	0·8**	0·5**
Drugs	0·3*	0·2	−0·4**

* Significant at ·05 level.
** Significant at ·01 level.

18. Mansfield's estimates (1964, pp. 333–4) were based on a logarithmic model (log R & D regressed on log sales) for pooled time-series cross-sectional data over the period 1945–59. For a review of other recent investigations of this question, see Markham (1965, pp. 328–32).

19. A qualification to the interpretation of the results obtained here and in the studies cited above arises from the fact that total firm sales is used as the independent variable rather than sales only in the particular three-digit industry for which the firm produces its principal products. Now, if it is the case that the nature of firm products in each of these industries varies significantly with size, then the above relationships may be due principally to this phenomenon rather than to any scale effects, such as those postulated above. As indicated earlier (see note 9 above), the large firms in the drug industry do tend to expand and diversify into non-pharmaceutical areas where the opportunities for R & D applications are low. It is therefore very desirable to estimate equation 2 using only pharmaceutical sales for each firm. Until the required data are available, however, the present approach must be used in such studies and, accordingly, is quite tentative in nature.

20. The empirical results here would also be open to question if the propensity to patent were significantly correlated with firm size. By similar procedures to those discussed in the previous section, this was not indicated to be the case. See also discussion of this issue in Scherer (1965a, p. 1110–13).

significantly positive in the chemical industry, which exhibited a positive structural relation with size. However, in drugs, where the relation was negative, the internally generated funds variable is significantly negatively correlated with size, and diversification exhibits a positive but insignificant correlation coefficient. Thus, the results suggest that the difference in the observed relation between research intensity and firm size in the two industries is due primarily to the flow of funds variable and, to a lesser extent, the diversification index.

In the current analysis, it has been assumed that the significant relation between research intensity and firm size follows from the size behavior of the underlying independent variables specified in the model. An alternative interpretation is that size is the relevant determinant variable and that the significance of these explanatory variables of the model is spurious, arising from their mutual correlation with size. In order to investigate this alternative hypothesis, a further regression equation was estimated. This involved adding the two significantly size-correlated variables, diversification and the measure of cash flow, to equation 2 and observing the behavior of the previously estimated coefficients between R & D and the size of the firm. As shown in the lower half of Table 2, when these two new variables are present, the a_1 and a_2 coefficients lose their statistical significance in both industries. On the other hand, the estimates associated with the two determinant variables, a_3 and a_4, are significant, as in Table 1. These results are thus consistent with the general interpretation of the regression estimates presented in this paper and not with the alternative hypothesis advanced above.

In summary, the analysis here indicates that there is no basis for the presumption that larger firms will necessarily possess the characteristics that promote a high degree of research intensity. Therefore, it is not surprising that tests of the Schumpeterian hypothesis have yielded such diverse results across industries. While it must be kept in mind that the results here only concern the firms in the *Fortune 500* listings, it is also true that this range of firms is most relevant from the standpoint of anti-trust policy.

4 Summary and conclusions

The main conclusion that emerges from the analysis is that interfirm differences in technology, product diversification, and availability of funds are all significant in explaining firm research intensity. The model presented here fits the two more research-oriented industries, chemicals and drugs, much better than petroleum refining. From a policy standpoint, these results indicate that the level of R & D expenditures will be sensitive to the broad class of government policy devices that affect the financial incentives confronting the firm. In particular, fiscal devices and other policy measures can be expected to influence the level of R & D expenditures through both profitability and flow of funds effects. Government policy actions directed toward stimulating growth should, therefore, be concerned with both of these effects if efficient programs are to be devised.

The major limitations of the present study arise from the substantial conceptual and empirical difficulties in measuring items such as R & D activity and its outputs. Considerable effort was therefore expended to obtain the best set of data that are currently available. While the results must be viewed as tentative, particularly because the total number of firms is small, they are nevertheless internally consistent and in general agreement with some of the past work in this area. They should, therefore, be of interest to economists and policy makers concerned with the economics of R & D.

References

EISNER, R., and STROTZ, R. H. (1963), 'Determinants of business investment', in Commission on Money and Credit, *Impacts of Monetary Policy*, Prentice-Hall.

GRABOWSKI, H. (1967), 'The determinants and effects of industrial research and development', Ph.D. dissertation, Princeton University.

HALL, M. (1964), 'The determinants of investment variation in research and development', *IEEE Transactions on Engineering Management*, EM-11, March, pp. 8–15.

HAMBERG, D. (1964), 'Size of firm, oligopoly and research', *Canadian J. Econ. polit. Sci.*, February, vol. 30, pp. 62–75.

KUH, E., and MEYER, J. R. (1955), 'Correlation and regression estimates when data are ratios', *Econometrica*, vol. 23, pp. 400–416.

KUZNETS, S. (1962), 'Inventive activity: problems of definition and measurement' in National Bureau of Economic Research, *The Rate and Direction of Inventive Activity*, Princeton University Press.

MANSFIELD, E. (1964), 'Industrial research expenditures: determinants, prospects and relation to firm size and inventive output', *J. polit. Econ.*, vol. 72, pp. 319–40.

MARKHAM, J. W. (1965), 'Market structure, business conduct and innovation', *Amer. econ. Rev.*, vol. 55, pp. 323–32.

MUELLER, D. C. (1967), 'The firm decision process: an econometric investigation', *Q.J. Econ.*, vol. 81, pp. 58–87.

NATIONAL SCIENCE FOUNDATION (1956), *Science and Engineering in American Industry*, National Science Foundation.

NATIONAL SCIENCE FOUNDATION (1964), *Research and Development in Industry 1961*, National Science Foundation.

NELSON, R. R. (1959), 'The simple economics of basic scientific research', *J. polit. Econ.*, vol. 67, pp. 297–306.

SANDERS, B. S. (1962), 'Some difficulties in measuring inventive activity', in National Bureau of Economic Research, *The Rate and Direction of Inventive Activity*, Princeton University Press.

SCHERER, F. M. (1965a), 'Firm size, market structure, opportunity and the output of patented inventions', *Amer. econ. Rev.*, vol. 55, pp. 1097–1125.

SCHERER, F. M. (1965b), 'Size of firm, oligopoly and research: a comment', *Canadian J. Econ. polit. Sci.*, vol. 31, pp. 256–66.

Further Reading

W. J. Adams, 'Firm size and research activity: France and the United States', *Quarterly Journal of Economics*, vol. 84, 1970, pp. 386–409.

B. T. Allen, 'Concentration and economic progress: note', *American Economic Review*, vol. 59, 1969, pp. 600–604.

Y. Brozen, 'Bain's concentration and rates of return revisited', *Journal of Law and Economics*, vol. 14, 1971, pp. 351–69.

N. R. Collins and L. E. Preston, 'Price-cost margins and industry structure', *Review of Economics and Statistics*, vol. 51, 1969, pp. 271–86.

W. S. Comanor, 'Market structure, product differentiation and industrial research', *Quarterly Journal of Economics*, vol. 81, 1969, pp. 639–57.

W. S. Comanor and T. A. Wilson, 'Advertising, market structure and performance', *Review of Economics and Statistics*, vol. 49, 1967, pp. 423–40.

L. Hall and L. Weiss, 'Firm size and profitability', *Review of Economics and Statistics*, vol. 49, 1967, pp. 319–31.

B. Imel and P. Helmberger, 'Estimation of structure–profit relationships with application to the food processing sector', *American Economic Review*, vol. 61, 1971, pp. 614–27.

R. W. Kilpatrick, 'Stigler on the relationship between industry profit rates and market concentration', *Journal of Political Economy*, vol. 76, 1968, pp. 479–88.

E. Mansfield, 'Size of firm, market structure and innovation', *Journal of Political Economy*, vol. 71, 1963, pp. 556–76.

E. Mansfield, 'Industrial research and development: characteristics, costs and diffusion of results', *American Economic Review*, vol. 59, 1969, supplement, pp. 65–71.

S. R. Reid, 'A reply to the Weston/Mansinghka criticisms dealing with conglomerate mergers', *Journal of Finance*, vol. 26, 1971, pp. 937–46.

F. M. Scherer, 'Firm size, market structure, opportunity and the output of patented inventions', *American Economic Review*, vol. 55, 1965, pp. 1097–1125.

F. M. Scherer, 'Market structure and the employment of scientists and engineers', *American Economic Review*, vol. 57, 1967, pp. 524–31.

F. M. Scherer, 'Market structure and stability of investment', *American Economic Review*, vol. 59, 1969, supplement, pp. 72–9.

D. Schwartzman, 'The effect of monopoly on price', *Journal of Political Economy*, vol. 67, 1959, pp. 352–62.

W. G. Shepherd, 'The elements of market structure', *Review of Economics and Statistics*, vol. 54, 1972, pp. 25–37.

L. G. Telser, 'Some determinants of the returns to manufacturing industries', in L. G. Telser, *Competition, Collusion, and Game Theory*, Macmillan, 1972, chapter 8.

L. W. Weiss, 'Concentration and labor earnings', *American Economic Review*, vol. 56, 1966, pp. 96–117.

L. W. Weiss, 'Business pricing policies and inflation reconsidered', *Journal of Political Economy*, vol. 74, 1966, pp. 177–87.

L. W. Weiss, 'Quantitative studies of industrial organization', in M. D. Intriligator (ed.), *Frontiers of Quantitative Economics*, North-Holland, 1971, chapter 9.

J. F. Weston and S. K. Mansinghka, 'Tests of the efficiency performance of conglomerate firms', *Journal of Finance*, vol. 26, 1971, pp. 919–36.

B. S. Yamey, 'Do monopoly and near-monopoly matter? a survey of empirical studies', in M. H. Peston and B. C. Corry (eds.), *Essays in Honour of Lord Robbins*, Weidenfeld, 1972.

Acknowledgements

For permission to reproduce the Readings in this volume
acknowledgement is made to the following:

1 University of Chicago Press
2 University of Chicago Press
3 *Economica*
4 *Review of Economics and Statistics*
5 *Review of Economics and Statistics*
6 *Review of Economics and Statistics*
7 American Economic Association
8 Richard D. Irwin Inc.
9 *Review of Economics and Statistics*
10 Basil Blackwell Publisher
11 *Journal of the American Statistical Association*
12 *Review of Economics and Statistics*
13 *Economica*
14 *Review of Economics and Statistics*
15 Rand McNally & Co
16 The Transportation Center at Northwestern University
17 Fred B. Rothman & Co
18 *Economica*
19 University of Chicago Press
20 National Bureau of Economic Research Inc.
21 *Review of Economics and Statistics*
22 *St John's Law Review*
23 Basil Blackwell Publisher
24 *Journal of Law and Economics*
25 University of Chicago Press

Author Index

Subject Index